KINGSHIP IN THE ENTHRONEMENT PSALMS

Biblical Hermeneutics Rediscovered

The Series as the name suggests will focus on Biblical Hermeneutics, i.e., literary works concerned with methods of interpreting the Old and New Testaments of Bible via different stream of topics like Literature & Poetry, Indigenous Philosophizing, Ethical response towards Ecology, Health & Healing, Science & Technology, Feminist Theology, Sociological approach towards Human Rights, Law & Politics, Arts, History of Ideas, Ancient Civilizations, Cultural Contiguity, Religious Cosmologies & Mysticism, Appraisal of various Theologians, World Peace & Harmony, Global Capitalism, Network Marketing, Cybertheology, Population & Demographics, Epigraphic Studies, Contextualized Education, and many others. We welcome a Mss. on any topic/s mentioned, whether they are original works, scholarly monographs, collections of conference papers, revised dissertations, or translations of historical documents. Through the Series we, the Publishers, are striving to put forward published works that may help Institutions, Academic Bodies, Researchers, Scholars and the World at large in furthering their respective knowledge and understanding on the concerned subject. We welcome your comments on our efforts and further suggestions on how we can enshrine new ray of analysing & explaining the written Texts through our upcoming books.

Biblical Hermeneutics Rediscovered - 17

KINGSHIP IN THE ENTHRONEMENT PSALMS

A Historical Literary Analysis of the Kingship Metaphor and Its Implications for Israel's Worship

Husazulu Chuzho

CWI

Christian World Imprints®

First Published in 2019 by

Christian World Imprints™
Christian Publishing & Books from India
H-12 Bali Nagar, **New Delhi-110015**
info@christianworldimprints.com
www.ChristianWorldImprints.com
Phone: +91 11 25465925

ISBN: 978-93-5148-290-1 (HB) ISBN: 978-93-5148-291-8 (PB)

Cataloging in Publication Data--DK
Courtesy: D.K. Agencies (P) Ltd. <docinfo@dkagencies.com>

Chuzho, Husazulu, 1979- **author.**
Kingship in the enthronement psalms : a historical literary analysis of the kingship metaphor and its implications for Israel's worship / Husazulu Chuzho.
pages cm. -- (Biblical hermeneutics rediscovered ; 17)
Includes bibliographical references.
ISBN 9789351482901 (HB)
ISBN 9789351482918 (PB)

1. Bible. Psalms--Criticism, interpretation, etc. 2. Bible. Psalms--Liturgical use. 3. Judaism--Liturgy. 4. God--Kingship--Biblical teaching. I. Title. II. Series: Biblical hermeneutics rediscovered ; 17.

LCC BS1430.6.G63C48 2019 | DDC 223.206 23

Printed in India.

Dedication

This book is dedicated to my inspiring Parents:
Mr. Ruyosayi Chuzho and *Mrs. Kahilu Chuzho*
For their endless Love, Support and Encouragement.

Contents

Foreword-I

Bringing out the theology of worship by focusing on the kingship metaphor that is used for Yahweh seems to me to be the first of its kind in the Old Testament Scholarship and especially in Indian sub-continent. Focusing implications of the metaphor for worship of One Sovereign God in pluralistic context with specific suggestions for use of music, gestures and postures was a much needed labor of love by Dr. Husazulu Chuzho.

Chuzho uses historical literary method in explicating the theology of the Enthronement Psalms 47, 93, and 95-100. She does this in way that avoids weaknesses of diachronic and synchronic methods but avails of their strengths. Thus, careful attention is paid to historical background and various contexts of the text including form critical and grammatical ones. In this way, she brings out the theology of worship which is anchored in exegetical depths of the text and applied to ecclesial doxology in its wider dimensions.

I have liked and been blessed to read the implications of not just theology of particularity, universality, sovereignty and majesty of Yahweh in worship but practical aspects of gestures, postures and music in worship. More specifically, in section 4.4, there is a good explication of clapping, shouting, kneeling and bowing in a way that motivates the readers to use these actions in worship. In 5.4, likewise, Chuzho brings out importance of glorifying God in worship, thanksgiving, listening and witnessing to God in worship. She illustrates how music saturated with the word of God can inspire both individual and collective aspects of worship. The very reading of this book proved to me to be both intellectually stimulating and spiritually enlightening.

I honestly believe that this book will be immensely useful to theological students in their exegetical and theological analyses of the Psalms. The text, its translation, exegesis and theology with its application to worship in Indian contemporary context are all found in this single book. It will also help both Pastors in Pulpit and People in pews for making their worship scripturally sound and holistically enlightening. If anyone wants to worship God in Spirit and Truth, will do well to buy and read a copy of this book. I thank and congratulate Ms Chuzho for this good and God-glorifying labor of love for God's people.

Rev. Dr. Eliya Mohol
Professor in Old Testament (Biblical Studies)
Monday, September 18, 2018
Pune, Maharastra: India

Foreword-II

The essence of worship is relationship, the relationship between the worshippers and the object of worship. It is the supreme expression of relationship between the creature and the creator. Worship, therefore is a spontaneous expression of presence of God the creator in every affairs of lives, thereby creating an atmosphere of harmony, solemnity and hope.

I personally came to know my acquaintance with Dr. Husazulu Chuzho when I joined the faculty of Discipleship Bible College (DBC) and serve as the principal of the college four years back. I came to know her more, especially through listening to her chapel devotional talks. A theological educator's life can best be known through one's sermon and interaction with the co-workers and student community in particular.

The core concern in this book is well thoughtfully, addressed the present life of the church in Nagaland in particular and India in general. Churches in Nagaland are considered as the biggest crowd in India. She enjoys about 88%-90% Christians, mostly Baptist denomination amidst popularity as Christian dominant state, church is quietly suffering from nominalism and materialism at the expense of healthy church. The need of the church in Nagaland is not numerical growth but the health of the church. Worship in only during the worship programs, there is a need for daily lives of each worshippers matters most. Worship is not just something to do with the programs and devoid of daily lives. This book, shall serve as diagnosing the sickness of the church and congregation and also a prescription for healing. The churches in Nagaland need to re-discover the Biblical meaning of worship as seen in relation to kingship metaphor presented in the enthronement psalms. Worship life of a believer rules out the compartmentalize understanding of life. Feeling of "Holiness" in the worship and worship life is missing, hence life do not change. There is a great hope for sickly church in Nagaland for better treatment by reading this book and restore the health of the church. This book by Dr. Husazulu Chuzho is indeed an eye opener for the contemporary Churches today for both far and near.

Once again I want to congratulate the author for her excellent contribution in the field of Old Testament Studies and making her research work available in a book form.

Rev. O. Alem
Principal of Discipleship Bible College
Dimapur, Nagaland

Acknowledgement

I thank God for his faithfulness, strength, and grace that sustained me throughout my research. Words are inadequate to express my gratitude to all those who have supported me for the success of this research.

My supervisor, Rev. Dr. Eliya Mohol, an exemplary teacher and scholar, for his guidance, and input of scholarship in to my research. I am grateful for his invaluable contribution to my scholarly pursuits, motivating me always with a smile. His trust and belief in me helped me to pursue and complete this work. His critique and prompt delivery of the corrected manuscripts enabled me to complete the task without delay.

Rev. Dr. John Samuel, Rev. Dr. Jagat Santra and Rev. Dr. Jangkholam Hoakip for reading through the first draft and offering their valuable comments and suggestions enabling me to develop a better perspective and to be more coherent. Patti Wiebe, Shekanah Mohol and Grace for their tireless efforts in diligently editing and proof-reading, and for the invaluable suggestions concerning the organisation of the material.

My loving parents Mr. Ruyosayi Chuzho and Mrs. Kahilu Chuzho, who made tremendous sacrifices. My brothers, sisters, in-laws and friends for their generous help. The board of governors of Discipleship Bible College, Dimapur for the privilege given to me to undertake Doctor of Theology studies under the SATHRI Senate of Serampore College (University) along with a partial scholarship. To different organisations for their financial support during my studies, like SATHRI (South Asia Theological Research Institute) and CBCNEL. I also express my thanks for the support of Rev. Dr. Paul Cho, my care group advisor, and my dear sister Duthilu Chuzho. The faculty and staff members, particularly the library staff, of Union Biblical Seminary, Pune, for their support and help throughout my residential period. The following libraries deserve a special mention: Union Biblical Seminary, Pune; United Theological College, Bangalore and Papal Seminary Jnana Deepa Vidyapeeth, Pune.

"PRAISE BE TO ALMIGHTY GOD."

List of Abbreviations

Biblical Books

Old Testament

Gen	Genesis
Ex	Exodus
Lev	Leviticus
Num	Numbers
Deut	Deuteronomy
Josh	Joshua
Judg	Judges
Ruth	Ruth
1 Sam	1 Samuel
2 Sam	2 Samuel
1 Kgs	1 Kings
2 Kgs	2 Kings
1 Chr	1 Chronicles
2 Chr	2 Chronicles
Ezra	Ezra
Neh	Nehemiah
Esth	Esther
Job	Job
Ps (s)	Psalms
Prov	Proverbs
Eccl	Ecclesiastes
Song	Song of Songs
Isa	Isaiah
Jer	Jeremiah
Lam	Lamentations
Ezek	Ezekiel

Dan	Daniel
Hos	Hosea
Joel	Joel
Amos	Amos
Obad	Obadiah
Jonah	Jonah
Mic	Micah
Nah	Nahum
Hab	Habakkuk
Zeph	Zephaniah
Hag	Haggai
Zech	Zechariah
Mal	Malachi

New Testament

Mt	Matthew
Mk	Mark
Lk	Luke
Jn	John
Acts	Acts
Rom	Romans
1 Cor	1 Corinthians
2 Cor	2 Corinthians
Gal	Galatians
Eph	Ephesians
Phil	Philippians
Col	Colossians
1 Thess	1 Thessalonians
2 Thess	2 Thessalonians
1 Tim	1 Timothy
2 Tim	2 Timothy
Titus	Titus
Philem	Philemon
Heb	Hebrews
Jas	James
1 Pet	1 Peter
2 Pet	2 Peter
1-2-3 Jn	1-2-3 John
Jude	Jude
Rev	Revelation

Journals, Series and References

ABD	*The Anchor Bible Dictionary*
AD	Anno Domini (After the Birth of Christ)
AIE	Ancient Israel Economy
AJT	*Asian Journal of Theology*
ANET	*Ancient Near Eastern Texts Relating to the Old Testament*
AWE	Ancient West Asia
BB	*Bible Bhashyam*
Bib	*Biblica*
B.C.E	Before Common Era
BDB	Brown, Driver, Briggs *Hebrew and English Lexicon of the Old Testament*
BibInt	*Biblical Interpretation*
BTF	*Bangalore Theological Forum*
Ca.	Circa (approximately)
CBQ	*Catholic Biblical Quarterly*
Cf	Confer (compare)
Chap.	Chapter
CTJ	*Calvin Theological Journal*
Ed(s)	editor (s) editors
EncJud	Encyclopaedia Judaica
EQ	*The Evangelical Quarterly*
et.al	*et alu* (and others)
HALOT	*The Hebrew and Aramaic Lexicon of the Old Testament*
HSS	Harvard Semitic Studies
HTR	*Harvard Theological Review*
IB	*The Interpreter's Bible*
ICC	*International Critical Commentary*
IDB	*Interpreters' Dictionary of the Bible*
IJBT	*Interpretation Journal of Bible and Theology*
Inc	Incorporated
ISPCK	Indian Society for Promoting Christian Knowledge
ITC	*International Theological Commentary*
JB	Jerusalem Bible
JBL	*Journal of Biblical Literature*
JNES	*Journal of Near Eastern Studies*
JNSL	*Journal of Northwest Semitic Languages*
JQR	*Jewish Quarterly Review*
JSOT	*Journal for the Study of the Old Testament*

JSOTS	*JSOT Supplement Series*
JSS	*Journal of Semitic Studies*
JTS	*Journal of Theological Studies*
NAC	*New American Commentary*
NICNT	*New International Commentary on New Testament*
NICOT	*New International Commentary on Old Testament*
NIV	New International Version
NJBC	*The New Jerome Biblical Commentary*
No.	Number
NT	New Testament
OM	Operation Mobilization Books
OT	Old Testament
OTL	*Old Testament Library*
PIW	*Psalms in Israel Worship*
Q	Qumran
SBT	*Studies in Biblical Theology*
SJT	*Scottish Journal of Theology*
SPCK	Society for Promoting Christian Knowledge
TDOT	Theological Dictionary of the Old Testament
TOTC	*Tyndale Old Testament Commentaries*
trans.	Translator, translated by
TRINJ	*Trinity Journal*
TynB	*Tyndale Bulletin*
TZ	*Thelogische Zeitschrift*
UBSJ	*Union Biblical Seminary Journal*
V, Vv.	Verse, Verses
vol.	Volume
VT	*Vetus Testamentum*
VTS	Suppliments to Testamentum
WBC	Word Biblical Commentary
ZAW	*Zeitschrift für die alttestamentliche Wissenschaft*

Ancient Texts and Versions

BHS	*Biblia Hebraica Stuttgartensia*
DSS	Dead Sea Scroll
LXX	Septuagint
Ms	Manuscript
Mss	Manuscripts
MT	Masoretic Text
SP	Samaritan Pentateuch
Syr	Syriac
Tg	Targum
Vg	Vulgate

Chapter 1

Introduction to the Research

1.1. Basic Background

The Kingship metaphor repeatedly occurs in the enthronement psalms in the context of worship.[1] This metaphor had a great deal of significance for Israel's worship. It still has much to contribute to our present day context. Yet, a little attention has been paid to it. This research fills the gap in bringing out the theology of kingship metaphor of Yahweh and its implications for Israel's worship and our context in India today.

1.2. An Elaboration

The kingship metaphor refers to the sovereignty of God and it is used in all the enthronement psalms, implying that the kingship of Yahweh is the dominant theme of these Psalms.[2] There are seven direct references. *First,* the phrase 'Yahweh reigns' יְהוָה מָלָךְ is mentioned four times in Psalms in 93:1, 96:10, 97:1 and in 99:1. *Secondly,* 'Yahweh is king' יְהוָה מֶלֶךְ is found in Ps 95:3.

---

1 I use the masculine term 'kingship' in relation to God but do not portray God as a man. King is a biblical term for God and is metaphorically used for God in the enthronement psalms. I do not intend to use kingship in terms of human gender. God is beyond human gender. I use the term king as a monarch who can be both male and female.

2 John H. Eaton, *Kingship and the Psalms* (Sheffield: JSOT Press, 1986), 105. Eugene H. Merrill, *Every Lasting Dominion: A Theology of the Old Testament* (Nashville: Broadman & Holman Publishers, 2006), 318. Erhard S. Gerstenberger, *Psalms Part 1 With an Introduction to Cultic Poetry* (Grand Rapids: Wm. B. Eerdmans Publishing Co, 1988), 198. Marvine E. Tate, "Psalms 51-100," in *Word Biblical Commentary,* vol. 20, edited by David A. Hubbard (Waco: Word Books, 1990), 149. Keith W. Whitelam, "King and Kingship," in *The Anchor Bible Dictionary,* vol. 4, edited by David Noel Frĝeedman (London: Doubleday, 1992), 43.

Thirdly, 'King Yahweh' מֶלֶךְ יְהוָה occurs once in Ps 98:6. *Fourthly,* 'a great king' מֶלֶךְ גָּדוֹל occurs once in Ps 47:3. *Fifthly*, 'Yahweh is great king' גָּדוֹל יְהוָה appears once in Ps 95:3. *Sixthly,* 'God reigns' מָלַךְ אֱלֹהִים occurs once in Ps 47:9. And *seventhly,* 'God is king' מֶלֶךְ אֱלֹהִים occurs once in Ps 47:8. Besides these direct references, there are other pointers to Yahweh's kingship: 'Yahweh's footstool' (Ps 99:5), 'your throne' (Ps 93:2), 'clothed in majesty' (Ps 93:1). The repeated occurrence of these aspects of this metaphor is striking and prompts us to ask why they have been used in the book of Psalms, particularly in the enthronement psalms, in the context of worship.

The repetition of a metaphor clearly shows its rhetorical or persuasive function. What does it persuade people to believe and to do? For example, Yahweh's sovereignty as represented by the metaphor would suggest that Yahweh ought to be worshipped by all. The metaphor's persuasion does not stop at its theology, *i.e.*, in persuading people to believe in a particular kind of God with a particular character but it goes on to encourage them to worship him. Therefore, it is necessary to look into this rhetorical purpose of the kingship metaphor.

I quote some of the earlier works that have dealt with similar themes connected to my work. This will show how far the previous writers have explored the subject while bringing out differences between my point of view and theirs. Hermann Gunkel and Sigmund Mowinckel, give more importance to translation of יהוה מלך. They, however, do not focus on repetition of the metaphor, thereby overlooking its rhetorical function and thus its theological implications for worship. Ollenburger brings out the theology of the metaphor but says little about how it is related to worship. He points out that rejoicing is a characteristic of the enthronement psalms. An exhortation to rejoice often follows an announcement of Yahweh's kingship (Pss 97:1, 6; 98:6).[3] I have found that Ollenburger explicates the theology of rejoicing but does not explicitly connect it with worship. Enthronement texts indicate that the presence of God brings deliverance. Hence, instances of joy and singing of new songs are associated with the presence of God in the temple. Thus, enthronement psalms encourage people to worship Yahweh by exhorting with shouts of joy. It is necessary to ask what relationship rejoicing has with worship.

In addition to 'rejoicing,' in the enthronement psalms, there are several phrases that relate the kingship of Yahweh with worship: 'clapping hands to God,' 'shouting to God' (Ps 47:1-2, 95:2, 98:4, 100:1), 'bowing down in worship,' 'kneeling before the Lord' (Ps 95:6), 'declaring God's glory,' 'revering Yahweh above all gods' (Ps 95:3-4), 'trembling before God'

3 Ben C. Ollenburger, *Zion the City of the Great King: A Theological Symbol of the Jerusalem Cult* (Sheffield: Sheffield Academic Press, 1987), 34. The psalmist here seems to argue for the worthiness of Yahweh, the king to receive the praises of the nations.

(Ps 96:9), and 'coming into God's presence with singing' (Ps 100:2).[4] All these phrases belong to the discourse of worship and demand that their usage and implication for Israel's worship be explored. Why have all these been used in Israel's worship? Do they point to the kingship metaphor of Yahweh for worship? If so, will this give insights into the particularity of Israel's worship of Yahweh? When God in the enthronement psalms invites the people of other nations to worship him, and thereby the enthronement psalms presuppose a religious pluralistic context, could we hold on a theology of particularity oriented worship in the ancient context in India today?

Another important issue that commentators observe is the universality of Yahweh's worship. Gesternberger talks about God of Israel becoming the king of the whole earth. Heaven and earth belong to God.[5] Whitelam points out that Yahweh is able to subdue all opposition and guarantee order, justice, peace, security and well-being, which are fundamental to Yahweh's kingship.[6] Ollenburger, in particular, highlights this universality of Yahweh's worship. The theophanic phenomenon that accompanies the announcement of Yahweh's rule causing the peoples to tremble and the earth to quake signifies that Yahweh is exercising the power of sovereignty over the gods.[7] Yahweh rules over the gods and peoples of the earth (Pss 95:2, 96:4, 97:9, 98:2-6). The enthronement texts (Pss 47, 93, 95, 96, 97, 98, 99 and 100) use the kingship metaphor of Yahweh as a theological theme in the context of worship.[8] The metaphor of kingship describes Yahweh as one who is for all the nations and encourages the nations to acknowledge and worship Yahweh alone. In other words, it evokes in them an attitude of worship, prompting them to worship. This universality of Yahweh's worship as depicted in the enthronement psalms, and its *missional implications*, calls for a specialized and elaborate treatment in a pluralistic context.

---

4 Robert L. Foster, "A Plea for New Songs: A Missional/Theological Reflection on Psalm 96," *Currents in Theology and Mission,* vol. 33, no. 4 (August, 2006): 287.

5 Erhard S. Gerstenberger, *Psalms Part 1: With an Introduction to Cultic Poetry* (Grand Rapids: Wm. B. Eerdmans Publishing Co., 1988), 198.

6 Keith W. Whitelam, "King and Kingship," in *The Anchor Bible Dictionary,* vol. 4, edited by David Noel Freedman (New York: Doubleday, 1992), 43.

7 Ollenburger, *Zion the City of the Great King*, 48-49.

8 Elmer A. Leslie, *The Psalms: Translated and Interpreted in the Light of Hebrew Life and Worship* (New York: Abingdon Press, 1949), 1-450. Sigmund Mowinckel, *The Psalms in Israel's Worship*, translated by D. R. Ap-Thomas (Oxford: Basil Blackwell, 1962), 1-335. John H. Eaton, *Kingship and the Psalms* (Sheffield: JSOT Press, 1986), 1-247. Hans-Joachim Kraus, *Theology of the Psalms*, translated by Keith Crim (Minneapolis: Augsburg Publishing House, 1986), 1-235. James Luther Mays, *The Lord Reigns: A Theological Handbook to the Psalms* (Louisville: Westminster John Knox Press, 1994). Bruce K. Waltke and James M. Houston, *The Psalms as Christian Worship: A Historical Commentary* (Grand Rapids: William B. Eerdmans Publishing Company, 2010), 1-626.

As it emerges from my own work, sovereignty is the denotation of kingship metaphor, and the metaphor is used to portray that Yahweh alone is worthy to be worshipped. Therefore, kingship metaphor was essential to portray the sovereignty of Yahweh particularly in the context of worship to let the people know that Yahweh is above all gods and therefore due worship belongs to him. The connotations of the metaphor are universality and holiness. They symbolized that Yahweh is to be worshipped by all the nations (Mal 1:11, Isa 56:7-8). Worshipping of God means pleasing him by imitating his attributes of love and mercy. Relationship with God is the essential principle in the understanding and worship of God.

Theological concerns pertaining to kingship of Yahweh focus on praising and exalting the faithfulness, goodness, and marvellous works of God. Yahweh is worthy to be praised (Isa 25:1, Pss 68:4-5, 71:8, 103:1, Heb 12:28), for Yahweh is good (Ps 100:5). Give thanks to the Lord, because he is good (Ps 136:1). Be holy as Yahweh is holy (Lev 20:26, 1 Peter 1:16). Worship the Lord in spirit and in truth (Jn 4:24). This talks about wholehearted worship. The Psalter in general and enthronement psalms in particular came into being over many centuries addressing the situations of the people.

Thus, theology expressed in the enthronement psalms impinges on our life. For instance, be holy because Yahweh is holy, also be good to others because Yahweh is good and merciful. All these above phrases explain the theology of worship and the practical aspect of theology in relation to the kingship metaphor of Yahweh. The theology drawn from kingship metaphor is still relevant for our present context, especially for worship. The kingship metaphor could be a key for developing the theology of worship. Thus, I expect this thesis to bring out the theological concerns pertaining to the kingship metaphor of Yahweh and its implications for Israel's worship as well as for today's worship. Therefore, there is a need to ask how God's sovereignty as represented by kingship metaphor would bear on the worship of the Indian churches today.

1.3. Significance of the Research

This research attempts to bring out the theological concerns pertaining to the kingship metaphor of Yahweh and its implications to worship for today. It will enable us to grasp who Yahweh is in the context of Israel's worship. The psalmists are good examples as worshippers of God. They acknowledge God as king in their lives, in creation and in history. The Psalter generally plays a vital role in the light of ancient Israelite worship. Despite different opinions about a number of themes related to the Book of Psalms, it is generally agreed that the psalms were used in Israel's worship. They opine that the songs and prayers were produced for use in the public worship of Israel.[9] Thus, psalms reflect patterns for worship that can be incorporated into congregational worship today.[10] The Psalter has been especially valued not just for *public worship*[11] but also for *private worship*[12] among Jews and Christians alike. Klaus Seybold remarks that the key phrase of יהוה מלך expounds the concept of the kingship of Yahweh for the benefit of a worshiping community.[13]

The Psalter can contribute greatly to the pattern and forms of worship today. Worship is at the heart of Christianity. However, when we evaluate present day worship, it seems that, in many churches, a common complaint is that the mood of worship is not lively. Probably, some churches have moved to in appropriate worship from true worship of God. This is why it is important to study the kingship metaphor of God, its significance and how it bears upon acceptable worship of God.

The kingship of God, particularly in the enthronement psalms, because it has great significance for the sovereignty of God in this multi-religious and multi-cultural context. The implications of the study of kingship metaphor are immense for Israelite worship as well as for enhancing the quality of contemporary in plurality of our context.

1.4. Definitions of the Terms

I have defined five terms which are necessary to understand how they are related and give insight to the thesis. They are: kingship, denotation and connotations, enthronement psalms, metaphor, and worship.

1.4.1. Kingship

מלוכה means 'kingship' refers variously to the rank, authority or office and dignity of the king.[14] It is also including the exercise of power over the subject

9 J. Clinton McCann, *A Theological Introductions to the Book of Psalms: The Psalms as Torah* (Nashville: Abingdon Press, 1993), 17.

10 Edward M. Curtis, "Ancient Psalms and Modern Worship," *Bibliotheca Sacra*no. 153 (July-Sept, 1997): 285.

11 Corporate worship is a term which signifies people coming together as a Church or one body and worshipping together under the kingship of Yahweh.

12 Private worship denotes the individual's act of worship. Private worship is an essential component of Christian spirituality. Jesus spent times in praying alone (Mt 6:6).

13 Klaus Seybold, *Introducing the Psalms,* translated by R. Graeme Dunphy (Edinburgh: T. & T. Clark, Ltd, 1990), 136.

14 Philip J. Nel, "מלך," in *New International Dictionary of Old Testament Theology & Exegesis,* vol. 2, edited by Willem A. VanGemeren (Grand Rapids: Zondervan, 1997), 956. Kingship stands for all kinds of monarchical rules. The king and kingship is not limited in the history of Israel but it is also found in Ancient West Asia. Kingship is a central symbol for the territory as well as symbolizing its prosperity and security.

of the state.[15] King and kingship have had a profound influence on Israelite history, in their religious and literary traditions.[16] According to 1 Kings 17:1, Yahweh had to contend with *Baal* for the kingship of Israel. L. Köhler maintains that, "God is the ruling Lord: that is the one fundamental statement in the theology of the Old Testament....Everything else derives from it. Everything else leans upon it. Everything else can be understood with reference to it and only it."[17] Kingship is a root metaphor for understanding Yahweh.[18] The Hebrew Bible mentions the kingship of God not only in Psalter but in other books as well (Ex 15:18, Deut 33:5 I Sam 12:12, 1 Chr 28:5). However, in Psalms, Yahweh is repeatedly proclaimed as king. For instance, Yahweh the great king over all the earth, subdues peoples under us, and nations under our feet (Ps 47:2-3). Yahweh is king, the Lord sits as king forever, (Ps 29:10), for just as "the world is firmly established...thy throne is established from of old" (Ps 93:2).

J. Gray and S. Mowinckel claim that the kingship of Yahweh is the central theme of the Old Testament. Yahweh's position as king acknowledged sovereignty over individual crises and the events that drive them, over national disasters, over the nations and their gods, and over the cosmos and its operation.[19] These events of deliverance, healing of individual and community express the fact that God reigns. It shows that king is a central metaphor for God in the psalms.[20]

---

15 Whitelam, "King and Kingship," 40. King is used to refer to someone who exercises authority over the territorial area and the state. In the Ancient West Asian, the role of king was attributed to the chief national god. During the OT time, this included El or Baal for Canaanites, Marduk for Babylon, Chemosh for Moab, Milcom for Ammon, Ashur for Assyria, Dragon for Philistia, Ra for Egypt, Qos for Edom and Hadad for Aram. John H. Walton, Victor H. Matthews & Mark W. Clavalas, *The IVP Bible Background Commentary: Old Testament* (**Downers Grove**: IVP Academic, 2000), 514-515. Anne Moore, *Moving Beyond Symbol and Myth: Understanding the Kingship of God of the Hebrew Bible Through Metaphor* (New York: Peter Lang Publishing, 2009), 10-15.

16 Whitelam, "King and Kingship," 40.

17 Köhler, *Old Testament Theology* (Philadelphia: Westminster, 1957), 30.

18 Kaufmann, *The Religion of Israel* (Chicago: University of Chicago Press, 1960), 60. Klaus Seybold, *Introducing the Psalms,* translated by R. Graeme Dunphy (Edinburgh: T & T Clark, Ltd, 1990), 102. Keith W. Whitelam, "King and Kingship," *The Anchor Bible Dictionary,* vol. 4, edited by David Noel Freedman (New York: Doubleday, 1992), 40-41. Jerald Praven, "A Search for a Theology of the Psalter," *ETJ,* vol. 2, no. 2 (May, 2013): 7-18. Philip J. Nel, "ךלמ," in *New International Dictionary of Old Testament Theology & Exegesis,* vol. 2, edited by Willem A. VanGemeren, (Grand Rapids: Zondervan, 1997), 956-957.

19 John H. Walton, Victor H. Matthews & Mark W. Clavalas, *Old Testament: The IVP Bible Background Commentary* (**Downers Grove**: IVP Academic, 2000), 515.

20 James Limburg, "The Book of Psalms," *The Anchor Bible Dictionary,* vol. 5, edited by David Noel Freedman (London: Doubleday, 1992), 530.

1.4.2. Denotation and Connotations

Though the words denotation and connotation have not been indicated in the title of my dissertation, I find it is necessary to define them because it is closely connected with the kingship metaphor of Yahweh. Also, the concept of kingship from these two words run through in the several portions of the research work. Before proceeding further, it is essential to clarify the meaning of denotation and connotation. *Denotation* refers to the literal meaning of a word. For instance, one of the denotative meanings of the word 'king' is a monarch, ruler, or emperor of a kingdom. It is also linked to sovereignty. *Connotation*, on the other hand, refers to the associations that are connected to a certain word or denotation. The connotative meanings of a word exist collectively with the denotative meanings.

Hence, the connotations for the word 'king' would include his role as a shepherd. Just as a shepherd protects, provides and leads the sheep so also the king should protect his people, provide for them and lead them. In order to protect his people, the king must have power and might. Hence, his role as shepherd is linked to his roles as protector, deliverer, powerful, mighty and guide. The king must judge people with justice and righteousness. He, therefore, must have holiness as part of his character so that he can fulfil these roles. Thus, connotations of the metaphor king include his descriptions as dominion, transcendence, powerful, mighty, highest, majesty, deliverance, protection, rejoicing, justice, holiness and shepherd. Mays and others suggest that Yahweh is called the shepherd of the people, who is also leading, protecting and guiding and revealing his divine nature to the people.[21]

Since Yahweh is the highest and one king above all, he must also be the king of all. So, universality is attached to his kingship. Thus, all these connotations emerge from the word 'king.' Ollenburger talks about Zion as a symbol and the symbol compromises not only a set of primarily denotations, but also a set of connotations.[22] He also asserts that Yahweh is depicted as king in connection to his power, and royal authority. The image of kingship of Yahweh bears the sense of honouring and respecting the highest Lord.[23] Mohol asserts that "the connotation and implication of the metaphor of Yahweh as

---

21 James Luther Mays, *Psalms : Interpretation: A Bible Commentary for Teaching and Preaching* (Louisville: Westminster John Knox Press, 1994), 116–117. See Marc Zvi Brettler, *God is King: Understanding an Israelite Metaphor* (Sheffield: Academic Press, 1989), 25–26. Martin Klingbell, *Yahweh Fighting From Heaven: God as Warrior and as God of Heaven in the Hebrew Psalter and Ancient Eastern Iconography* (Schweiz: Vanderhoeck und Ruprecht, 1999), 105. Eugene H. Merrill, *Everlasting Dominion: A Theology of Old Testament* (Nashville: Broadman & Holman Publishers, 2006), 570.

22 Ollenburger, *Zion the City of the Great King,* 22.

23 Ollenburger, *Zion the City of the Great King,* 23.

king is that to him belongs the prerogative of demanding exclusive allegiance from the Zion people."[24]

1.4.3. Enthronement Psalms

The term 'enthronement psalms' was coined by Sigmund Mowinckel in *The Psalms in Israel's Worship* (1962).[25] Generally, Psalms 47, 93, 95-100 are referred to as the enthronement psalms. All these psalms speak of Yahweh as king or use the language "the Lord [or God] reigns." Mowinckel theorizes that Israel celebrated a New Year festival in which the king was re-enthroned to commemorate the annual reenthronement of the Lord.[26] Mowinckel points out that the enthronement psalms are associated with the New Year festival and has in common the idea with the New Year festival in Babylon. He claims that the main points of the enthronement psalms are identified as the exhortation to praise, celebration, the mention of Yahweh's glorious presence and of the excellent deeds that Yahweh has just performed (Pss 97:1-5, 98:6-9).[27] He further says that the enthronement psalms declare Yahweh's arrival as the new king and victorious king.[28] Allan, Rosengren Petersen, and Mowinckel point out that the enthronement festival of Yahweh was celebrated yearly in Israel. Probably, this New Year festival celebration took place in the autumn.[29]

---

24 Eliya Mohol, "Metaphors of Zion Traditions and Their Relevance for Mission," *UBS Journal,* vol. 5, no. 1 (March, 2007): 88.

25 Mowinckel, *The Psalms in Israel's Worship*, 106-107. See *Psalmenstudien II: Das Thronbesteigungsfest Jahwas under der Ursprung der Eschatologie* (Kristiania, Oslo: SNVAO, 1922). Helmer Ringgren, "Enthronement Festival or Covenant Renewal?" 7 (1962): 45-48. Leo G. Perdue, "Yahweh Is King over All the Earth: An Exegesis of Psalm 47," *Restoration Quarterly* 17, no. 2 (1974): 85–98. John H. Eaton, *Kingship and the Psalms* (Sheffield: JSOT Press, 1986), Allan, Rosengren Petersen, *The Royal God: Enthronement Festivals in Ancient Israel and Ugarit* (Sheffield: Sheffield Academic Press, 1998), 15-33. James, Limburg. "Psalms," in *Word Biblical Commentary,* edited by Patrick D. Miller and David L. Bartlett (Louisville: Westminster John Knox Press, 2000), 156. Gerhard von Rad, *Old Testament Theology: The Old Testament Library,* vol. 1 (Louisville: Westminster John Knox Press, 1962), 363-364. J.J.M. Roberts, "The Enthronement of Yhwh and David: The Abiding Theological Significance of the Kingship Language of the Psalms," *Catholic Biblical Quarterly,* no. 64 (2002): 675–86. Daniel J. Estes, *Handbook on the Wisdom Books and Psalms* (Grand Rapids: Baker Academic, 2005), 185-186.

26 C. Hasssell Bullock, *Introduction to the Old Testament Poetics Books: The Wisdom and Songs of Israel* (Chicago: Moody Press, 1979), 142.

27 Sigmund Mowinckel, *The Psalms in Israel's Worship, Two Volumes in One,* translated by D. R. Ap-Thomas (Grand Rapids: William B. Eerdmans Publishing Company, 1962, revised 2004), 107-108.

28 Mowinckel, *The Psalms in Israel's Worship*, 113.

29 Allan, Rosengren Petersen, *The Royal God: Enthronement Festivals in Ancient Israel and Ugarit* (Sheffield: Sheffield Academic Press, 1998), 23.

Gunkel Hermann (1862-1932), applied the *Form Critical* study in the book of Psalms and he proposes that psalms originated in the cult of the sanctuary of Israel.[30] Sigmund Mowinckel (1884-1965) developed his approach in the study of psalms from the work of Gunkel. However, he differs from Gunkel's form critical approach to the psalms. He identifies that the psalms originated within the context of the New Year festival.[31]

Gunkel criticises Mowinckel's article written in *Psalmenstudien II* (1922). *First,* Gunkel finds that Mowinckel failed to recognise the *genres* and their *forms* which belong to different psalms and context. It shows that "Mowinckel jumps from one genre to another combining many psalms that belong to very different psalms."[32] Also, Gunkel is against Mowinckel's ideas of considering the festival of booths as a New Year festival and had the common features with the New Year celebrated in Babylon. *Secondly,* in Babylon there was a New Year festival and on that occasion, they enthroned Marduk again, addressing as king. But nowhere is reference of the New Year festival found in the enthronement psalms.[33] *Thirdly,* the New Year festival and the festival of booths are widely different. The festival of booths reflect on the gifts of the gathering received in the current year and express thanksgiving. On the other hand, the New Year festival looks to the future. Besides that, the New Year festival begins with a new time, whereas the festival of booths is recounted as the last of the pilgrimage festivals, signifying the conclusion of the entire series of festivals.[34]

Gunkel claims that these enthronement psalms are not only used as the royal address to Yahweh, but they imitate the motifs from royal poems and carry them over into a spiritual realm.[35] Similarly to Gunkel's view, Limburg points out that the psalms which speak of Yahweh having been manifested as

---

30 Hermann Gunkel, *Introduction to Psalms : The Genres of the Religious Lyric of Israel* (Macon, Georgia: Mercer University Press, 1998), 66-70. See Hermann Gunkel and Joachim Begrich *Einleitung in die Psalmen: die Gattungen der religiösenLyrik Israel* (Göttingen: Vandenhoeck & Ruprecht, 1933), 5-10.

31 Mowinckel, *The Psalms in Israel's Worship, Two Volumes in One,* 113-114.

32 Gunkel, *Introduction to Psalms : The Genres of the Religious Lyric of Israel*, 72.

33 Gunkel, *Introduction to Psalms : The Genres of the Religious Lyric of Israel*, 75.

34 Gunkel, *Introduction to Psalms : The Genres of the Religious Lyric of Israel*, 76. See, Allan, Rosengren Petersen, *The Royal God: Enthronement Festivals in Ancient Israel and Ugarit* (Sheffield: Sheffield Academic Press Ltd, 1998), 15-26. Nancy deClaisse-Walford, Rolf A. Jacobson, and Beth LaNeel Tanner, "The Book of Psalms," in *The New International Commentary on the Old Testament,* edited by Robert L. Hubbard (Grand Rapids, Michigan: Wm. B. Eerdmans Publishing Co, 2014), 14.

35 Gunkel Hermann. *Introduction to Psalms,* 66. These psalms glorify Yahweh as the king of the world (Pss 47:3, 8, 98:6, 99:4). Yahweh puts on majesty and power as royal garments (Ps 93:1). Yahweh also ascends along with shouting. Yahweh performs his deeds (Ps 98:1) and creates the new just order in Israel (Ps 99:4), 69.

king are called enthronement psalms. In other words, the hymns extolling the kingship of the Lord as well as describing the Lord as king are identified as the enthronement psalms.[36] There are different opinions with regard to the New Year festival in connection with the enthronement psalms.

For me, these ‘enthronement psalms’ focus on God’s eternal kingship and evoke praise to Yahweh as the sovereign Lord. Therefore, the motif of celebration in the enthronement psalms is all about the celebration of Yahweh’s kingship. As a result, the enthronement psalms portray the kingship of Yahweh. This concept is demonstrated substantially in the context of Israel’s worship. In my opinion, there may not be such New Year festival celebrated in connection with the kingship of Yahweh but that the enthronement psalms celebrate the kingship of Yahweh in *every time* of worship, both individual and corporate.

1.4.4. Metaphor

Metaphor is from the Greek word μεταφορα which means *transfer*, a figure of speech in which a word or phrase is used to describe something it does not literally denote.[37] Metaphor is a literary device which comprehends one object in the light of another.[38] It has a substantial impact on the poetic character of a literary work. It describes something in terms which is suggestive of something else and uses its accompanying range of associations. For instance, God is King (A is B) and hence God is (the associations of B are applied to A) royal and just.[39] “Metaphors are nouns that function in Israel in order to give access to the subject of verbs, who is endlessly elusive.”[40] It is an “unexpressed comparison; it does not use the word like or as.”[41]

Symbol is often used for all forms of figurative language and even metaphor is used for figurative language. Symbols and metaphors are sometimes regarded as synonymous. Although, metaphors are regarded as

---

36 Limburg, “The Book of Psalms,” 532.

37 Matthew S. McGlone, “What Is the Explanatory Value of a Conceptual Metaphor?” *Language Communication,* no. 27 (2007): 109.

38 Mohol, “Metaphors of Zion Traditions and their Relevance for Mission,” 85. For Ricouer, metaphors create surplus of meaning that cannot simply be reduced to some literal paraphrase. Metaphor may perhaps be used as an influential instrument for exploring the world as a microscope. Moreover by reworking the language, metaphors allow us to see things differently. See Kevin J. Vanhoozer, *Is there a Meaning in this Text? The Bible, the Reader, and the Morality of Literary Knowledge* (Michigan: Zondervan, 1998), 128-129.

39 Mohol, “Metaphors of Zion Tradition and their Relevance for Missions in India,” 85.

40 Brueggemann, *Theology of the Old Testament* (Minneapolis: Fortress Press, 2005), 230.

41 Henry A. Virkler, *Hermeneutics: Principles and Processes of Biblical Interpretation* (Grand Rapids: Baker Book House, 1981), 158.

sub-section of symbolism, metaphor is more specific than symbol.[42] Metaphor is related to a symbol in which the symbol has meaning within the cultural context.[43] Metaphors "serve to communicate, because they are an essential and creative part of the forming of meaning."[44] The truly creative power of metaphor lies in what may be called its richness and complexity.[45] Metaphors also talk about something in terms normally used to talk about something else.[46] There are three types of metaphors: (1) Metaphors functioning as the substitution. Thus, the metaphoric expression functions as the substitute for the literal term without losing the meaning. (2) Metaphoric functioning as comparison or similarity. In this case, an attempt is to describe why the substitution is involved. (3) Metaphors functioning as the source of interaction. This refers to the reciprocal semantic determination involving in the different lexical items in a metaphorical aspect.[47]Altogether, these three types of metaphors express the meaning and unique use of metaphors.

1.4.5. Worship

The word 'worship' is derived from the Anglo Saxon word *weorthscipe* 'worthship' which means 'to honour.'[48] There are different Hebrew words like עבד 'to serve' 'service 'which are translated as worship (1 King 12:4, Josh 22:27, Ex 12:25).[49] The verbal form of עבד which means 'to serve or to work' also refers 'to worship' (Pss 2:11, 97:7, 100:2). The noun form of עבד is 'slave or servant' and indicates 'worshipper' (Pss 27:9, 97:2, 116:16). Generally, עבד connotes loyalty and submission to Yahweh and implies homage to Yahweh.[50] The words כרע 'bowing' and ברך 'kneeling' are associated to acts of worship

42 Jan G. Van Der Watt, *Family of the King: Dynamics of Metaphors in the Gospel According to John* (Leiden: Koninklijke Brill NV, 2000), 1, 4.

43 Ollenburger, *Zion, the City of the Great King,* 19.

44 Watt, *Family of the King*, 5.

45 Shubert Spero, "Biblical Metaphor and the Dynamics of Jewish Demography: A Modern Midrash," *Jewish Bible Quarterly,* vol. 28, no. 4 (2000): 222.

46 J. M. Soskice, *Metaphor and Religious Language* (Oxford: Clarendon, 1985), 15, 49.

47 Watt, *Family of the King: Dynamics of Metaphors in the Gospel According to John*, 15-17.

48 E. F. Harrison, "Worship," *Evangelical Dictionary of Theology*, edited by Walter A. Elwell (Michigan: Baker Book House, 1984), 1192.

49 Husazulu Chuzho, "A Theological Appraisal of Worship of Yahweh Alone in Old Testament with Special Reference to the Book of Psalms," *BTC Journal,* no. V (2014): 2. The OT uses the word עבודה referring to the 'service' which means 'adoration or worship' of Yahweh.

50 Edward J. Bridge, "Loyalty, Dependency and Status with YHWH: The Use of עבד in Psalms," *Vetus Testam,* no. 59 (2009): 361–362.

(Ps 95:6). But the one used most is השתחוה which is a *hithpael of* שׁחה which means 'bow down or prostrate oneself' before God in worship.[51]

The word חוה is the root verb of השתחוה which appears frequently in the OT in general and in the enthronement psalms in particular. It means to bow, prostrate oneself, make obeisance and bend low. Bowing denotes an action performed to show respect to or submission before Yahweh in the cultic context of prayer or sacrifice.[52] Thus, the verb חוה is always directed towards a human or divine figure who is recognized as being in a position of honour or authority. The action may entail falling to one's knee as a sign of reverence.[53] For instance, Abraham bowed himself to the earth when he saw three men standing opposite to him (Gen 18:2). Also when Abigail saw David, she bowed herself to the ground (1 Sam 25:23). Even in the cultic realm חוה is described as homage and worship. For instance, before the host of heaven like sun, moon and stars (Deut 4:19, Jer 8:2), before the holy mountain (Ps 99:9), in the temple (2 Kg 5:18), before the angels of Yahweh (Num 22:31), before Yahweh (Gen 24:26, 48, 52).[54] But the Psalms explicitly express הוח as the act of homage paid to Yahweh the God (Pss 22:28, 29:2, 86:9, 95:6, 96:9, 97:7, 99:5,9).[55] The word השתחוה together with בוא 'come' עבד 'serve' or זבח 'sacrifice,' particularly in the Psalter, is related to the cult, referring to both prayer and worship of Yahweh the king.[56]

Even in the NT, different Greek words are translated as worship. The word προσεκύνειν, 'to worship,' is a verb present infinitive active from προσκυνέω which means 'worship, do obeisance to, prostrate oneself.' The word λατρεύω basically means 'to serve, to minister' (Heb 9:9, Rev 22:3).[57] The word πίπτω means 'fall down as a sign of devotion' (Mt 2:11; 18:26, 29; Rev 5:14). The

51 Francis Brown, S. R. Driver, and Charles A. Briggs, *Hebrew and English Lexicon of the Old Testament* (Oxford: Oxford University Press, First edition 1907, reprinted 1972), 1005.

52 H. D. Preuss, "השתחוה חוה," in *Theological Dictionary of the Old Testament,* vol. IV, edited by G. Johannes Botterweck and Helmer Ringgren, translated by David E Green (Grand Rapids, Michigan: William B. Eermans Publishing Company, 1980), 249.

53 Terence E. Fretheim, "חוה," in *New International Dictionary of the Old Testament Theology & Exegesis,* vol. 2, edited by Willem VanGemeren, (Carlisle, Cumbria: Paternoster Press, 1996), 43.

54 H. P. Stähli, "חוה," in *Theological Lexicon of the Old Testament,* vol. 1, edited by Ernst Jenni and Claus Westermann, translated by Mark E. Biddle (Peabody: Hendrickson Publishers, 1997), 398–399.

55 Stähli, "הוה," 399.

56 Preuss, "השתחוה חוה," 252. Ps 96:9 calls the nations to bow before Yahweh in worship. All nations shall come and bow down before Yahweh (Ps 86:9). Moreover, the psalmist affirms that the proud and the mighty shall bow to Yahweh (Ps 22). Additionally, even all the gods bow down before Yahweh (Ps 97:7). The host of heaven worships Yahweh (Neh 9:6), 253. Israel must not bow in worship before other gods (Ex 20:5).

57 Warren W. Wiersbe, *Real Worship* (Nashville: Thomas Nelson Publishers, 1990), 21.

most common word used is προσκυνέω (Mt 4:10; Jn 4:20, 12:20; Acts 24:11; 1 Cor 14:25; Heb 11:21; Rev 4:10; 14:7; 19:4). προσεκύνεω is used frequently with πιπτω 'fall down' (Mt 2:11, 4:9, 18:26, Acts 10:25, 1 Cor 14:25, Rev 4:10, 5:14, 7:11, 11:16, 19:4). This suggests that homage expressed by προσεκύνεω also occurs generally with prostration.[58] Therefore, προσεκύνεω denotes the picture of worship (Mt 2:2, 8:2, Jn 4:20-24, 1 Cor 14:25, Rev 15:4,). The use of προσεκύνεω in the NT is based on the OT. The exalted Christ appears next to God as the one worshipped (Rev 5:13).[59]

In the LXX προσκυνειν is the only rendering of השתחוה (Ps 97:7, 99:9). Προσκυνειν naturally suggests itself for השתחוה. Προσκυνειν indicates the element of נשׁק 'to kiss' including cultic kissing which is related to adoration and worship of the true God. Thus, προσκυνειν is practiced especially before the king or a superior.[60] Collins, and Schneider opine kissing expresses religious homage. The psalmist says נשׁק 'kiss' the son because the son deserves to be kissed (Ps 2:12). The word נשׁק kiss denotes homage and submission (Gen 41:40).[61] For instance, the Lord said to Elijah, "I will leave seven thousand in Israel, all the knees that have not bowed to Baal, and every mouth that has not kissed him" (1 King 19:18). Even in the NT καταφιλέω 'to kiss,' refers act of worship.[62] For instance, a woman presents herself at the 'feet of Jesus,' makes use of her hair to wipe the feet of Jesus and expresses her gratitude by kissing the feet of Jesus. Thus, kissing the feet is considered as an act of worship or giving reverence to Jesus (Lk 7:38).[63] In this text, the phrase 'kiss the feet' denotes a sign of special devotion to Jesus.[64] Thus, in this context the word 'kiss' is a metaphorical usage which conveys respect to the one who is on royal authority.

When NT uses προσκυνειν, the object is always something truly divine (Mt 18:26). Elsewhere the word always expresses true adoration (Mt 9:18,

58 J. M. Nützel, "Προσκυνεω," in *Exegetical Dictionary of the New Testament,* vol. 3, edited by Horst Balz and Gerhard Schneider (Grand Rapids, Michigan: William B. Eerdmans Publishing Company, reprinted 1994, 1982), 173-174.

59 Nützel, "Προσκυνεω," 175.

60 Heinrich Greeven Kiel, "Προσκυνεω," in *Theological Dictionary of the New Testament,* vol. vi, edited by Gerhard Friedrich, translated by Geoffrey W. Bromiley (Grand Rapids, Michigan: Wm. B. Eerdmans Publishing Co, June 1968), 760-761.

61 C. John Collins, "נשׁק," in *New International Dictionary of the Old Testament Theology & Exegesis,* vol. 3, edited by Willem A. VanGemeren (Grand Rapids: Zondervan, 1997), 197.

62 C. Schneider, "Καταφιλέω," in *Exegetical Dictionary of the New Testament,* vol. 2, edited by Horst Balz and Gerhard Schneider (Grand Rapids: William B. Eerdmans Publishing Company, 1991), 270.

63 John Nolland, "Luke 1-9," in *Word Biblical Commentary*, edited by David A. Hubbard and Glenn W. Barker; Dallas: Word Books, 1989), 354. Mt 26:49; Mk 14:45; Lk 7:38, 45; 15:20; Acts 20:37.

64 Schneider, "Καταφιλέω," 270.

Mt 14:33, 15:25, Mk 10:35). Also, in the conversation of Jesus with the Samaritan woman in Jn 4:20-24, Jesus speaks of προσκυνειν in spirit and in truth. Jesus says that the true place of worship is in the spirit and in truth. Therefore, the act of worship reflects a new dimension which is a worship in spirit and in truth.[65] Thus, the Greek word προσκυνεω in the NT refers back to OT Heb word השתחוה. Therefore, when all the words used for worship in both the OT and NT are considered, it is found that worship means to give homage to God. Thus, worship is an act of homage paid to Yahweh.

1.5. Scope and Limitation of the Research

This thesis does not intend to make a detailed study of the metaphor in all sections of the Hebrew Bible. As mentioned earlier, the study is based on enthronement psalms although it gives a survey of its usage in the Hebrew Bible as a point of groundwork. Therefore, I concentrate on the enthronement psalms (Pss 47, 93, 95-100). Emphasis has been given to the explication of the literary and theological meaning of the metaphor in its historical contexts. The research is limited to the Israelite worship with the theological implications for contemporary worship.

1.6. Survey of Previous Scholarship

A survey of the previous scholarship gives a broad view of how far scholars have explored the kingship metaphor in the context of worship. My intention is to fill the gap in the work of previous scholarship. Consequently, I find that highlighting previous scholarship gives useful insights into what has already been done in the study of Psalms generally, and enthronement psalms in particular.

Sigmund Mowinckel[66] talks about the psalms and cult, the cultic situation in the interpretation of enthronement psalms and the general pattern of ancient oriental cultic New Year festivals and its influence upon the Yahweh cult. In Psalms, we understand definite rituals acts, where the worshippers come into Yahweh's house with burnt offerings.[67] The psalms are considered to be a song sung to Yahweh, either in praise and thanksgiving, or prayers for help and deliverance. In this respect, we see the clear picture of cult.[68] The psalms present the actual songs and prayers that were produced for use in the public worship of Israel and especially of Judah before the destruction

65 Heinrich Greeven Kiel, "Προσκυνεω," in *Theological Dictionary of the New Testament,* vol. VI, edited by Gerhard Friedrich, translated by Geoffrey W. Bromiley (Grand Rapids: Wm. B. Eerdmans Publishing Co, 1968), 763.

66 Sigmund Mowinckel, *The Psalms in Israel's Worship*, trans. D.R. Ap-Thomas (Oxford: Basil Blackwell, 1962), 1-246.

67 Mowinckel, *The Psalms in Israel's Worship,* 2-6.

68 Mowinckel, *The Psalms in Israel's Worship*, 9.

of the Jerusalem temple in 587 B.C.E.[69] Enthronement psalms were meant to provide homage, where the authors called upon the congregation to worship to Yahweh, the king.[70] He consistently ascribes great significance of the use of psalms in Israel's worship. Thus, his idea of the New Year festival in Israel in which Yahweh was enthroned as king depended on his translation of the phrase יְהוָה מָלָךְ as Yahweh has become king. This phrase was a cultic shout uttered as part of the festival of Yahweh's enthronement.[71] He believes that it referred to something new and important that had just taken place, and therefore he translates יְהוָה מָלָךְ as "Yahweh has become king."[72]

The unique characteristic of the enthronement psalms is that they salute Yahweh as the king, who has just ascended to royal throne to wield the royal power.[73] This act of saluting would be significant in the context of worship. It also brings out, according to Mowinckel, the universality of Yahweh's worship. The enthronement psalms glorify Yahweh for all his mighty works and exalt Yahweh the king above all the kings. All peoples acclaim Yahweh; all other gods tremble before God and worship Yahweh the king of kings (95:3; 96:4, 97:7).[74] But I do not fully agree with Mowinckel when he says to salute Yahweh as the king who has 'just ascended to the royal throne.' The point is that Yahweh cannot sometimes be king and sometimes not be the king. Therefore, his translation seems theologically faulty. So, I will follow A. A. Anderson,[75] A. Johnson and Kraus in translating יְהוָה מָלָךְ as 'Yahweh reigns.'[76]

Hans-Joachim Kraus[77] observes that religion and worship in the whole of the ancient world reveal a similarity of ideas and expressions but the people of Israel were destined to be the bearers of the divine revelation. In its midst "the true religion was to be prepared and developed both in the inner consciousness and in the symbolism of worship."[78] In the first part of the book he sketches a history of worship which first covers the place of worship, then examines the various sacrificial customs, and finally deals with the festivals.[79] Kraus rejects

69 McCann, A *Theological Introductions to the Book of Psalms: The Psalms as Torah,* 17.

70 Mowinckel, *The Psalms in Israel's Worship,* 183.

71 Mowinckel, *The Psalms in Israel's Worship,* 100.

72 Whitelam, "King and Kingship," 47.

73 Mowinckel, *The Psalms in Israel's Worship,* 106.

74 Mowinckel, *The Psalms in Israel's Worship*, 107.

75 A. A. Anderson, *The Book of Psalms,* vol. 2 (London: NCB, 1972), 35-43.

76 Aubrey Johnson, *The Cultic Prophet and Israel's Psalmody* (Cardiff: Universality of Wales Press, 1979), 61-62.

77 Hans-Joachim Kraus, *Worship in Israel: A Cultic History of the Old Testament*, translated by Geoffrey Buswell (Oxford: Basil Blackwell, 1966), 1-246.

78 Kraus, *Worship in Israel: A Cultic History of the Old Testament,* 3.

79 Kraus, *Worship in Israel: A Cultic History of the Old Testament*, 5.

the translation 'Yahweh has become king' as well as the festival of Yahweh's enthronement proposed by Mowinckel. He uses 'Yahweh is king.' Babylonian worship could have influenced Israelite worship but it did not replace God and the faith of the worshipping community at Jerusalem, rather it gave a new vision of the "kingly majesty of Yahweh, supreme over all forces and powers."[80] Israelite worship talks about cultic life, yet the broader side is that Israelite worship claims 'Yahweh's universal kingship.' Yahweh is the creator of the nations.[81]

Harold Henry Rowley[82] traces the beginning of worship in the patriarchal age and the way in which Yahweh came to Israel. Rowley goes on to discuss worship during monarchy in the cult, temple, psalmody and relation of prophecy to liturgy. I.G. Matthews and R.H. Pfeiffers suggest that the patriarchs were animists. Nowhere are the patriarchs found worshipping the material objects. In the theophanies, the deity invariably appears in human form.[83] It is further remarkable that nowhere is it found that the patriarchs possessed or worshipped idols.[84]

In regard to psalmody, Rowley claims that there was a time when the Psalter was commonly referred to as the *hymn book of the second temple* and most of the individual psalms were believed to be composed during the post exilic period.[85] However, there is a great reluctance to speak of the Psalter as a hymn book since the Psalter was used to accompany rituals acts, shared with the priests in the official conduct of the worship of the temple.[86] Hence, he proposed that Israelites were worshipping Yahweh, the living God, along with the forms of rituals.

Leo G. Perdue[87] looks at how "Yahweh is king over all the earth in Psalm 47." He attempts a study of the major trends of cultic studies which specially deal with enthronement hymns and gives an exegesis on Psalm 47. All the enthronement psalms share the essential formal characteristic of the hymn. These psalms evoke praise of Yahweh as king and the cry of enthronement of Yahweh מלך.[88] Thus, Perdue affirms that the kingship of Yahweh is based

80 Kraus, *Worship in Israel: A Cultic History of the Old Testament*, 204-205.

81 Kraus, *Theology of the Psalms*, 106.

82 H. H. Rowley, *Worship in Ancient Israel: Its Forms and Meaning* (London: S.P.C.K, 1967), 1-324.

83 Rowley, *Worship in Ancient Israel: Its Forms and Meaning*, 16.

84 Rowley, *Worship in Ancient Israel: Its Forms and Meaning*, 19.

85 Rowley, *Worship in Ancient Israel: Its Forms and Meaning*, 176.

86 Rowley, *Worship in Ancient Israel: Its Forms and Meaning*, 177.

87 Leo G. Perdue, "Yahweh Is King over All the Earth: An Exegesis of Psalm 47," *Restoration Quarterly*, vol. 17, no. 2 (1974): 85-98.

88 Perdue, "Yahweh is king over all the Earth: An Exegesis of Psalm 47," 85.

upon the salvific acts Yahweh has performed on Israel's behalf, and Psalm 47 expresses in hymnic praise Yahweh's assumption of world rulership. This sovereignty is theologically based upon Yahweh's defeat of the nations.[89]

Daniel Jones Muthunayagom[90] has written a thesis with the title, "Kingship of God and Creation in the Old Testament" in 1982. He concentrated on the book of Psalms, and discussed the following areas: kingship of God and creation in the enthronement psalms, General hymns of praise and Lament psalms of the individual and of the community. He states that the kingship in relation to God as king was significant for Israelites to confess their faith in Yahweh. Yahweh the king of Israel and the king of universal is closely related to each worshipper. Therefore, the psalmist addresses Yahweh as 'My king.'[91] Again in 2009, he contributed an article in the *Bangalore Theological Forum* with the title, "The Image of God as King and the Nature of His Power in the Old Testament."[92] The study of the Ancient West Asian religions puts the concept of Yahweh into perspective, and the biblical literature suggests that the kingship of Yahweh is of central importance in developing a theology of kingship metaphor of Yahweh and its implications for worship. He also described the unending rule of Yahweh and his sovereign power as Creator. Thus, Yahweh uses his power to protect and liberate people from oppressive nature.[93]

John H. Eaton[94] deals with the royal idea expressed in the psalms and interprets the poetry and ritual mainly based on royal psalms, focusing on the king who "played an important part in the cultic action."[95] He affirms what Mowinckel argued that throughout the time of David's dynasty the autumn festival included a special celebration of Yahweh as king. According to Eaton, Gunkel's classification of the psalms had brought into prominence the hymns in which Yahweh is proclaimed and manifested as king in something like an act of enthronement.[96] Mowinckel saw that such texts had belonged to a regular ceremony of worship and testified Yahweh's superiority, over chaos

89 Perdue, "Yahweh is king over all the Earth: An Exegesis of Psalm 47," 98.

90 Daniel Jones Muthunayagom, "Kingship of God and Creation in the Old Testament" (M.Th. Thesis, United Theological College, Bangalore, 1982), 1-219.

91 Muthunayagom, "Kingship of God and Creation in the Old Testament," 1, 219.

92 Daniel Jones Muthunayagom, "The Image of God as King and the Nature of His Power in the Old Testament," *Bangalore Theological Forum*vol. XLI, no. 2 (December, 2009): 29-48.

93 Muthunayagom, "The Image of God as King and the Nature of His Power in the Old Testament," 34, 38.

94 Eaton, *Kingship and the Psalms* (Sheffield: JSOT Press, 1986), 1-247.

95 Eaton, *Kingship and the Psalms*, 101-103.

96 Eaton, *Kingship and the Psalms,* 105.

in creation and over enemies in history.[97] Even the nucleus of the relevant texts, which Mowinckel took to be Psalms 47, 93, 95-100, amply displays the themes of Yahweh's kingship. The kingship is part of a gospel of victory and a new era.[98]

Ben C. Ollenburger[99] focuses on the "great king in ancient Israel worship" with a theological symbol of the Jerusalem Cult based on the Psalter. The enthronement psalms present clear examples of the dominant conception of Yahweh as king in the cult tradition in ancient Israelite worship.[100] The characteristic expression of these psalms is יהוה מלך which occurs in Pss 47, 93:1, 96:10, 97:1 99:1. According to Ollenburger, the arguments for and against the celebration of Yahweh's kingship in an autumn festival is based largely on the translation of the phrase יהוה מלך in the enthronement psalms.[101] Enthronement psalms emphasize the kingship of Yahweh and are important for understanding the traditions of ancient worship cult in which Yahweh was revered as king.[102]

Ollenburger brings out two important ideas in relation to kingship and worship: 'rejoicing' and 'universality of worship.' 'Rejoicing' is a characteristic motif of these enthronement psalms. Often the announcement of Yahweh's kingship is followed by an exhortation to rejoice (Ps 93).[103] The theme of 'rejoicing' and of the 'new song' seems to be associated especially with the notion of Yahweh's kingship. In Psalm 96:10-13, the command to sing a new song is followed by a series of exhortations to praise grounded in Yahweh's greatness over and against the gods of the people. In Psalm 98, the command to sing a new song is followed by a description of Yahweh's faithfulness in securing victory on behalf of Israel. Then follows a command directed to all

---

97 Eaton, *Kingship and the Psalms*, 105.

98 Eaton, *Kingship and the Psalms*, 105-108.

99 Ben C. Ollenburger, *Zion the City of the Great King: A Theological Symbol of the Jerusalem Cult* (Sheffield: Sheffield Academic Press, 1987), 13-162.

100 Ollenburger, *Zion, the City of the Great King*, 24.

101 Ollenburger, *Zion, the City of the Great King*, 33.

102 Ollenburger, *Zion, the City of the Great King*, 24.

103 As in Psalm 96:10-13, the same progression is found in Psalm 93, the proclamation of יהוה מלך is a statement concerning the establishment of the earth and an allusion to Yahweh's demands, here in the form of a promise that Yahweh will judge the people fairly. There then follows an "exhortation to rejoice directed toward heaven and earth." This rejoicing is to occur because Yahweh is judge over all the earth and overall gods (Ps 47). There is thus a chiastic arrangement of the two themes, Yahweh's kingship and rejoicing, around the central section of the psalms. See Ben C. Ollenburger, *Zion the City of the Great King: A Theological Symbol of the Jerusalem Cult* (Sheffield: Sheffield Academic Press, 1987), 34.

the earth, exhorting its inhabitants to shout for joy הריען before Yahweh.[104] Thus, rejoicing is linked with universality.

Ollenburger affirms universality of Yahweh's kingship. He asserts that the enthronement psalms speak of Yahweh's accession as exhibiting Yahweh's rule over the gods and the population of the earth (Pss 95:2, 96.4, 97.9, 98. 2-6).[105] The announcement of the rule of Yahweh seated upon the cherubim is accompanied by typical theophanic phenomenon, the trembling of the people and quaking of the earth and shows execution of Yahweh's sovereignty over gods.[106] The sovereignty is also seen in Yahweh's founding of the world and the establishment of Yahweh's throne after Yahweh has subdued the chaos which threatens the established world order (Ps 93:3-4) in connection to Zion, the city of the great king.

Roberts[107] studies kingship language in the Psalter. Even in the early period, the metaphor of Yahweh as king was used in Israelite's attempt to make sense of the world of the gods that they encountered among their neighbors. That tradition consisted of three main points: (1) Yahweh is the great king, ruler over all the nations and gods; (2) Yahweh has chosen the Davidic house as human agents for the divine rule and has confirmed that choice with an eternal covenant (3) Yahweh has chosen Zion as royal city, and as the earthly point of God's universal rule.[108] In the Psalms, kingship of Yahweh is rooted in creation that is, in Yahweh's victory over the powers of chaos and in his establishment of a stable world order based on that mastery over chaos.[109] God's authority over the other nations arises out of the fact that God created the whole world. This is yet another enduring legacy of the worship of Yahweh as the great king.[110]

Jeremy J. Stewart[111] argues that AWA kingship had an insightful persuade on Israelite kingship.[112] It has its roots in the development of the position of the father, or elder of a clan or tribe. From this point the monarchies of the AWA can be categorized under three groups. In the Canaanite Uragitic documents, the former kings were recognized as demigods. The kings of Northern Syria

---

104 Ollenburger, *Zion, the City of the Great King*, 35.

105 Ollenburger, *Zion, the City of the Great King*, 45.

106 Ollenburger, *Zion, the City of the Great King*, 48-49.

107 J. J. M. Roberts, "The Enthronement of Yhwh and David: The Abiding Theological Significance of the Kingship Language of the Psalms," *The Catholic Biblical Quarterly,* no. 64 (2002): 675-686.

108 Roberts, *The Enthronement of Yhwh and David*, 676.

109 Roberts, *The Enthronement of Yhwh and David*, 679.

110 Roberts, *The Enthronement of Yhwh and David*, 682.

111 Jeremy J. Stewart, "King of Kings: The Enthronement of Yahweh," *Studia Antiqua,* vol. 2, no. 1 (2002): 101–27.

112 Stewart, "King of Kings: The Enthronement of Yahweh," 101.

were regarded merely as human beings. Transjordanian peoples follow a nationalistic form of kingship, in which a king led and was supported by the native military. Kingship in the regions of Mesopotamia and Egypt was regarded as a political order divinely ordained for the good of the empire.[113] In keeping with the notion that Israelite kingship was based on neighbouring models, some form of enthronement ceremony must have occurred to ensure Yahweh's throne. Mowinckel hypothesizes enthronement psalms (47, 93, and 95-100) to be related to those found in Canaan, Babylon, and Egypt.[114] They were compiled to be used in the temple of Jerusalem.יהוה מלך imply that the Lord will reign hereafter.

Walter Brueggemann[115] describes the leading motifs of ancient Israel's worship traditions in the Old Testament. The book is intended to be in the service of current theological and practical issues concerning the worship of the church in its ecumenical character.[116] Brueggemann argues that the study of the history of worship in ancient Israel is crucial because it stretches over long periods along with different contexts.[117] However, he sees one important theme in Israelite worship, 'covenant' that is actively marching on through the history of ancient Israelite worship. The other two prominent acts of public worship in Israel are the celebration of festivals and the offering of sacrifices. Thus, Brueggemann affirms that the "God who speaks in worship is the God who commands, guides and assures."[118] Israel's liturgical texts exercised great imagination in articulating Yahweh in a rich variety of metaphors and figures like king, warrior, judge, and bore witness to the wonder of the creator God who would judge the world with righteousness.[119] The psalms give evidence of Israel joyously entering in the presence of Yahweh and affirming the presence of God in Israel.[120]

Eliya Mohol[121] affirms that metaphors function within Zion tradition as a theological symbol of the Jerusalem cult tradition. The motif depicting Yahweh as triumphant king is central to Zion tradition.[122] The first reference to Yahweh

113 Stewart, "King of Kings: The Enthronement of Yahweh," 103.

114 Stewart, "King of Kings: The Enthronement of Yahweh," 113.

115 Walter Brueggemann, *Worship in Ancient Israel: An Essential Guide* (Nashville: Abingdon Press, 2005), 1-88.

116 Brueggemann, *Worship in Ancient Israel: An Essential Guide*, 1.

117 Brueggemann, *Worship in Ancient Israel: An Essential Guide*, 2.

118 Brueggemann, *Worship in Ancient Israel: An Essential Guide*, 26.

119 Brueggemann, *Worship in Ancient Israel: An Essential Guide,* 68-69.

120 Brueggemann, *Worship in Ancient Israel: An Essential Guide,* 73.

121 Eliya Mohol, "Metaphors of Zion Traditions and their Relevance for Mission," *UBS Journal* 5, no. 1 (March, 2007): 85-98.

122 Mohol, "Metaphors of Zion Tradition and their Relevance for Missions in India," 86.

as one who reigns evokes the exodus tradition (Ex 15:18) where it occurs in the context of Yahweh's promise to bring Israel into Zion, the mountain of God's inheritance. God ascends the mountain and enters the temple as the king of glory (Ps 24:8-10).[123] He claims that "Yahweh reigns and Yahweh is king of Zion are characteristic of the enthronement psalms."[124] Hence, the implication of the metaphor of Yahweh, as king, is that to God belongs the right of exclusive devotion from the Zion people.

Jan Muis[125] argues that "the king metaphor for God is an indispensable key metaphor in both the testaments."[126]A king metaphor is a metaphor with many implications; it can be used as a model which illuminates our understanding of God.[127] King has become a root metaphor in the canonical text of the Old Testament and Jesus' proclamation of the coming kingdom of God presupposes that God is king. God's kingship implies God's authority and power to fight the forces of evil, to liberate and to control the events of history. King is the only metaphor that can give expression to God's ultimate highness and authority.[128] In Psalms and Deutero-Isaiah, the theme of God's kingship is fully developed. It becomes a root metaphor, that is, a comprehensive model to understand God. It is remarkable that the metaphor of king did not disappear when Israel had no kings. During exile and after the return from exile, it became increasingly important to remind the people of the greatness of God.[129]

Bruce K. Waltke and James M. Houston[130] discuss the needs and ways to enrich the daily life of the contemporary Christian and to deepen the church's community worship in hearing God's voice both through an accredited exegesis of the psalms and through the believing response of the church.[131] "The psalms have occupied a unique role in both Israel and the Christian church, as the prayer book and hymnal of both their worshiping communities."[132] First, one of the major religious concerns of the second temple period was seeking how the Torah applied to the contemporary situation. Secondly, in this period of crisis, they used the psalms as resources for personal and corporate worship.[133]

---

123 Mohol, "Metaphors of Zion Tradition and their Relevance for Missions in India," 87-88.

124 Mohol, "Metaphors of Zion Tradition and their Relevance for Missions in India," 88.

125 Jan Muis, "God Our King," *HTS,* vol. 64, no. 1 (2008): 269-288.

126 Muis, "God Our King," 270.

127 Muis, "God Our King," 269-270.

128 Muis, "God Our King," 273.

129 Muis, "God Our King," 276.

130 Bruce K.Waltke and James M. Houston, *The Psalms as Christian Worship: A Historical Commentary* (Grand Rapids: William B. Eerdmans Publishing Company, 2010), 1-572.

131 Waltke & Houston, *The Psalms as Christian Worship: A Historical Commentary*, 2.

132 Waltke & Houston, *The Psalms as Christian Worship: A Historical Commentary*, 10.

133 Waltke & Houston, *The Psalms as Christian Worship: A Historical Commentary*, 24.

The psalms are referred to as hymnbook of the second temple. However, this does not mean that every psalm served a hymnic function in the second temple Judaism, rather there came a time when every psalm used in the temple service had to be from the Psalter.[134]

The focus of the previous scholarship is either on the entire Psalter or on a biblical point of view of looking into worship in Israel. Some have dealt with this from the cultic situation, while others have talked about the concept of Yahweh the king from general points of view. Even Christian worship was emphasized from a general perspective though based on the Psalter. Thus the conception of kingship metaphor in light of its historical background, of worship in enthronement psalms in particular, *has not been sufficiently explored*, though the theological importance of Yahweh, the king, has been pointed out. To my knowledge, a careful literary analysis of kingship metaphor in its historical literary context, in order to understand the implication of Israelite worship in the historical contexts, has not been explored so far.

Thus, I will focus on the theological implication of kingship metaphor in Israelite worship by exploring its historical literary context. In other words, the present study is an attempt to look at the kingship metaphor and interpret it in light of its historical background in Israel's worship, and to bring out its theological significance of worship by concentrating on the enthronement psalms.

1.7. Method of the Research

The method adopted in this study is the *historical-literary approach*. Historical-literary approach is employed by the commentators like Jonathan Gan.[135] He claims that traditional scholarship relies much on the historical-critical approach to biblical studies. But according to him these critical methods are insufficient in the study of the metaphor because metaphor is a literary device and needs support from other methods to give a broader aspect.[136]

The study of metaphor requires a method that is appropriate to the nature of the subject of study. In the study of metaphor, exegetical and literary skills are essential. The important aspects of the historical-literary method are historical criticism and literary-analytical exegesis. Exegesis covers three major areas. *First*, the historical context which involves more than historical timeline. It includes social, political, economic, and religious aspects of the text. *Secondly*, the literary context that involves source criticism, literary criticism, tradition

134 Waltke & Houston, *The Psalms as Christian Worship: A Historical Commentary*, 24.

135 Jonathan Gan, *The Metaphor of Shepherd in the Hebrew Bible: A Historical-Literary Reading* (Lanham: University Press of America, 2007).

136 Jonathan Gan, "The Metaphor of the Shepherds in Zachariah 11: 4-17" (M.Th. Thesis, University of South Africa, 2010). 2-3.

criticism and redaction criticism. *Thirdly,* the philological aspects of the text which means the study of language that includes grammatical principles, syntax, semantics and semiotics.[137] These contexts give a framework to direct the interpretive work which will cover the way for a comprehensive reading of the text.

Therefore, I use historical criticism and literary analysis in all the texts of the enthronement psalms. In analyzing the selected texts, literary devices such as the use of metaphor, figures of speech and literary approach will be used in order to discern the actuality of the particular text. Metaphor is a literary device utilized by authors to present ideas through this figure of speech and must be interpreted in its literary contexts.[138] Thus to undertake both historical and literary analyses, the approach employed must use tools from both literary criticism and historical criticism. Source, Form, Tradition History, and Redaction Criticism have been used for explicating the historical contexts of the metaphor and the literary critical and rhetorical criticism are employed to explicate the literary contexts. This approach is therefore called historical-literary approach. Previous approaches either focused on diachronic tools or synchronic tools. Those who followed the synchronic method disregarded the historical background, and those who followed the diachronic method did not consider the meaning of the individual passage in the light of the final form of the text. This historical-literary method does justice to both the historical background and final form of the text. This approach presupposes the literary nature of the Hebrew Bible in the perspective of historical progression. It requires literary competency in reading historical materials and relating them to their respective historical contexts.[139] This method aims to return religiosity to the Bible and explain literary skills from the meaning contained in the language. As a result, the metaphor derived from exegesis is understood in the context of its historical implication. Hence, this method fulfills the requirement for the study of metaphor.[140]

Historical-literary method uses Form Criticism but recognising the importance of this method in analysing the enthronement psalms, I have emphasized form criticism. In other words, though I have used historical-literary method as the primary method the significance of form criticism is taken into consideration in this research. For the past centuries traditional interpretation tool was very useful in the study of Psalms. However, by twentieth century a new way of approach in the study of Psalms was brought about. Hermann Gunkel revolutionized the study of the Psalms by introducing

137 Gan, *The Metaphor of Shepherd in the Hebrew Bible: A Historical-Literary Reading*, 24.

138 Gan, *The Metaphor of the Shepherds in Zachariah*, 3.

139 Gan, *The Metaphor of the Shepherd in Zachariah*, 3-4.

140 Gan, *The Metaphor of Shepherd in the Hebrew Bible,* 24-25.

the method called *Form Criticism* in the Old Testament Spectrum 1862-1932 with his work concentrating on the book of Genesis (1901)[141] and Psalm (1926-1928).[142]

Form Criticism is a method of analyzing and interpreting the literature of the Old Testament through a study of its literary types of genres. It means to identify the genres of literatures, structures, and settings in order to understand the oral stage of their development.[143] Hermann categorized psalms according to literary genres and he sought the original life setting that gave rise to each genre and therefore to each psalm within that genre. He remarked that those songs belonging together must naturally indicate common treasury of thoughts and moods.[144] Because each form can be linked to a particular kind of life setting that gave rise to it. Sigmund Mowinckel built upon the foundation of form criticism laid by Gunkel even though he stressed 'cult functional method.' Thus, form critical method is important in the study of Psalms and we cannot undermine the importance of form criticism.

I have also used insights from the work of Robert Alter. Robert Alter is a renowned literary expert. He published *The Art of Biblical Narrative* (1981) and it was a turning point of the literary approach to the Old Testament study, particularly in the study of Psalms.[145] Tremper Longman III claims that "the literary study of the Old Testament had been advocated by some before Robert Alter but Alter's study attracted the attention of the field in an unprecedented way and led to a renewed interest in the literary form of the biblical text."[146] Robert Alter an established literary critic with a specialty in comparative literature. The main purpose of writing on *The Art of Biblical Poetry* (1985) was to investigate the distinctive function of Hebrew poetry. He remarked that of all the books of the Bible in which poetry plays a role, Psalms is the one set of texts whose poetic status has been most strongly felt throughout the generations regardless of the vagaries of translation, typographical arrangement of verses, and notions about biblical literary form.[147] The literary approach advocated by

141 Hermann Gunkel, *Genesis*, trans. Mark E. Biddle (Macon: Mercer University Press, 1997).

142 Hermann Gunkel, *Die Psalmen Ubersetzt Erklart* (Göttingen: Vandenhoeck & Ruprecht, 1925).

143 Gene M. Tucker, *Form Criticism of the Old Testament* (Philadelphia: Fortress Press, 1982), 1.

144 Gunkel, *Introduction to Psalms: The Genres of the Religious Lyric of Israel*, 16.

145 Robert Alter, *The Art of Biblical Narrative* (New York: Basic Books, 1981), 1-5.

146 Tremper Longman III, "Literary Approaches to Old Testament Study," in *The Face of Old Testament Studies: A Survey of Contemporary Approaches*, edited by David W. Baker and Bill T. Arnold (Grand Rapids: Baker Books, 1999), 98.

147 Robert Alter, *The Art of Biblical Poetry* (New York: Basic Books, 1985) revised ed., 2011, 139.

Alter did not reject diachronic method totally but reordered priorities so that biblical texts were examined in their final context as a literary whole.[148]

1.8. Structure

After dealing with introductory issues in *Chapter 1,* I undertake the kingship of God metaphor in Ancient West Asian religions and in the poetic traditions of the Hebrew Bible in *Chapter 2.* Then in *Chapters 3 till to Chapter 10,* I look at the exegeses of the different enthronement psalms, bringing out the theological concerns pertaining to the kingship metaphor in the light of its denotation and connotations in each of the psalms as it impinges upon worship both in the Israelite contexts of Davidic monarchy and post-exilic period. After the thorough analyses of each of the enthronement psalms in the following Chapters, I proceed, drawing on the kingship metaphor of Yahweh and its implications for worship in a pluralistic context for India today in *Chapter 11.* Thus, followed by a concluding remark with the findings in *Chapter 12.*

148 Longman III, "Literary Approaches to Old Testament Study," 98.

Chapter 2

Understanding the Kingship Metaphor of God in Ancient West Asian Religions and in the Poetic Tradition of the Hebrew Bible

Introduction

The first chapter describes important aspects of the thesis like the significance, method of writing and purpose of the research. This second chapter studies the context of the Ancient West Asian religions in which the kingship metaphor was initially attributed to God. Analysing the kingship of God in Ancient West Asian religions helps in understanding the kingship metaphor of Yahweh better. It points out how the kingship metaphor of Yahweh differs from the Ancient West Asian religions and what the role and function of God as king are from historical literary point of view. The kingship metaphor was ascribed to the Canaanite city gods mainly in the myth linked to El and Baal. The metaphor of Yahweh as king was used by the people of Israel in order to make sense to the fellow Israelites regarding the nature of Yahweh in the larger realm of the gods that they usually faced among their neighbours.[1]

Using *form critical insights from* Hermann Gunkle and Sigmund Mowinckle, this chapter looks at the kingship of Gods.The points considered in this chapter are: *Firstly,* kingship metaphor of God in Ancient West Asian religions. *Secondly,* kingship of God and worship in the poetic traditions of the Hebrew Bible. *Thirdly,* a comparison with the ideology of kingship of God in West Asia, and poetic tradition in the Hebrew Bible where Yahweh

1 Daniel Jones Muthunayagom, "The Image of God as King and the Nature of His Power in the Old Testament," *Bangalore Theological Forum,* vol. XLI, no. 2 (December, 2009): 31.

is considered as the king who exercises supreme authority over the gods and nations.

2.1. The Concept of God as King in Mesopotamian Literature

The expression of kingship and lordship which dominates Mesopotamian literature suggests that the power and authority of the gods were vital factors in their opinion. In the early Mesopotamian tradition, the description of earthly found during the early period comprises the conceptual terms such as lord, one who exercises lordship and kingship, the leader of the military forces, shepherd of the land and as one who acts righteous in judgment. This idea and the power of kingship which the Mesopotamian kings enjoyed was lowered from heaven by the gods.[2]

2.1.1. The Kingship of Anu, Enlil and Enki

Anu, Enlil and Enki are the gods of the Mesopotamians. Anu is considered as the father of the gods whereas Enlil is the king of all lands. Anu is also addressed as the god of heaven, as the highest god and head of the pantheon of the gods. Anu is the father of Enlil. Enlil, lord of heaven and earth, is the determiner of destinies.[3] In the lamentation over the destruction of Ur, a similar relationship is found between Anu and Enlil. It is mentioned that Anu is above all; it is from him that the office of kingship comes, and he himself is king of the gods. Enki, whose name literally means the lord of the earth, is related to the earth, water, wisdom and craftsmanship, but his status as a god in his own realm is that of a king. Jacobsen posits that "Enki's office in the world state is that of a great nobleman of the realm . . . . A councillor. . . ."[4] But he is not a king, not a ruler in his own right. The position comes from Anu and Enlil he is their minister. But it is interesting to know that in the myth of Enki and Ninhursag, Enki is called the king by Isimud his messenger.

2.1.2. The Kingship of other Gods

In the Enuma Elish, Marduk is described in extraordinary terms, being far above the other gods at the time of his birth. He is given a throne, with whole authority, putting on him the most honoured position and kingship of the universe. After he is given a sceptre and a throne, he is asserted to be king and lord repeatedly. Hammurabi, in the prologue and epilogue to his law code, denotes Marduk as the highest one whose kingship was established in

2 Gary V. Smith, "The Concept of God/The Gods as King in the Ancient Near East and the Bible," *Trinity Journal,* no. 3 (1982): 19–20.

3 James B. Pritchard, ed., "Collections of Laws from Mesopotamia and Asia Minor," *Ancient Near Eastern Texts: Relating to the Old Testament,* Third Edition with Supplement, trans. S. N. Kramer (Princeton: Princeton University Press, 1969), 159.

4 Smith, "The Concept of God," 21.

Babylon.[5] Mesopotamian tradition holds that Marduk is the creator god and his enthronement was proclaimed at the Akitu New Year festival.[6] The lordship of Marduk was acknowledged by Nebuchadnezzar II who pointed out that he was called Marduk as lord and king. Nabonidus and Cyrus call Marduk "king of the gods and lord of lords."[7] Ancient near eastern texts mention how a psalm was composed to Marduk. It says Marduk returned to his temple, after a prolonged ceremony known as the Akitu, or New Year's Festival. All the main gods are summoned and asked to say to Marduk, "Be appeased."[8] Therefore, other gods exalted him as supreme god. This shows that other gods declare their submission to Marduk.

Henri Frankfort says, "Thou, O Marduk, art our champion; we gave thee kingship, power over all things. Take thy seat in the council; may thy word prevail, may thy weapon not yield, may it smite thy foes. Grant breath of life to lord (s) who put (their) trust in thee. But if a god embraces evil, shed his life."[9] Similarly to Henri Frankfort view we see in Ancient Near Eastern Texts, it says, before Marduk was simply our beloved son. Now he is your king, declare his title! A second speech they made, they all spoke. His name shall be Lugaldimmerankia, trust in him! When they had given the sovereignty to Marduk, they affirmed for him a formula of good fortune and success. Henceforth, thou wilt be the patron of our sanctuaries, whatever thou dost we will do.[10] According to one of the Ancient Near Eastern Texts,[11]

> He fixed its position with the gods its brothers.
> After Anu had decreed the fate of the bow,
> (And) had placed the lofty royal throne before the gods,
> Anu placed it in Assembly of the gods.
> When the great gods had assembled,
> They extolled the destiny of Marduk, they bowed down,
> They pronounced among themselves a curse,

---

5 Smith, "The Concept of God," 22.

6 Daniel Jones Muthunayagom, "Kingship of God and Creation in the Old Testament" (M.Th. Thesis, United Theological College, Bangalore, 1982), 46.

7 Smith, "The Concept of God," 22.

8 James B. Pritchard, ed., "Sumero-Akkadian Hymns and Prayers," *Ancient Near Eastern Texts: Relating to the Old Testament,* Third Edition with Supplement, trans. Ferris J. Stephens (Princeton: Princeton University Press, 1969), 389.

9 Henri Frankfort, *Kingship and the Gods: A Study of Ancient Near Eastern Religion as the Integration of Society & Nature* (Chicago: The University of Chicago Press, 1948), 236.

10 James B. Pritchard ed., "Akkadian Myths and Epics," in *Ancient Near Eastern Texts: Relating to the Old Testament*, Third Edition with Supplement, trans. A. K. Grayson, (Princeton: Princeton University Press, 1969), 502-503.

11 Pritchard, ed., "Akkadian Myths and Epics," in *Ancient Near Eastern Texts: Relating to the Old Testament*, 503.

Swearing by water and oil to place life in jeopardy.
When they had granted him the exercise of kingship of the gods,
When they had given him dominion over the gods of heaven and underworld,
Anshar pronounced supreme his name, Asarluhi (saying):
"Let us do obeisance at the mention of his name,
To his utterance let the gods gives heed,
Let his command be supreme above and below!"

Explanations of the gods in terms of kingship are found in ritual texts, hymns and prayers. Many praises are given to Ishtar, queen of women and the goddess of goddesses who wears the crown of dominion. The moon-god, Nanna or Sin, is called lord of the shining crown of dominion, hero of the gods, Father Nanna, who is extravagantly perfected in kingship. The New Year's festival at Babylon describes Bel as the excellent king, lord of the country which is equivalent to the title given to Marduk who is the great lord, the lord of the world, king of the gods.[12]

2.2. The Concept of God as King in Ugaritic Literature

The Semitic culture at Ugarit, the title king and its associated conceptual terms are found in the epic literature as well as in the writings of later Greek authors who explain their religion. The explanation of the Ugaritic earthly kings provides a standard for recognizing kingship terminology that was applied to their gods.[13]

2.2.1. El the King

In the Ugaritic epics, El is the king of the gods and maintains order in the cosmos. El exercises final authority in the universe and is the one to whom all the gods answer. According to Daniel Porter, the Ugaritic texts present El in a powerful position; however, while his decrees are final, he is sometimes not the supreme ruler one would expect the king of the gods to be.[14] The attributes and designates of El given by M. Pope, cited by Smith include: (a) father, with its more specific identification of father, father of mankind, father of the gods, and father of eternity which point to El's position in the family of the gods. All the other deities addressed him as father, (b) 'Bull' which symbolizes his

12 Smith, "The Concept of God," 22–23.

13 Smith, "The Concept of God," 23.

14 Daniel Porter, "God Among the God's: An Analysis of the Function of Yahweh in the Divine Council of Deuteronomy 32 and Psalm 82" (Master of Arts. Thesis, School of Religion, Lynchburg, Virginia, 2010), 1.

procreative powers, (c) wise, beneficent, holy, and kind, (d) creator of creatures and creator of earth, and (e) King.[15]

It is clear that from above description in the Ugaritic pantheon, El was king and father of the gods. His decree is wise and his wisdom eternal. He controls assemblies of the sons of El. El is portrayed in the highest place of authority in the assembly of the gods.[16] The name El means 'the strong one, or the leader.' Thus the Bull was an appropriate title given to El. And, therefore, El being the leader or strong one, has enough power to vanish all rivals.[17] Patrick D. Miller explains, the term bull, however, it has a twofold symbolism in the Ancient Near East. It is a symbol of fertility at times, but it is also a symbol of strength, might, and fighting prowess, both in the realm of the gods and in the realm of human. This latter symbolism, strength and belligerence, seems to be the primary characteristic of the bull imagery, though in many cases the imagery works a dual function, suggesting both fertility and might.[18]

All these indicated that the Canaanite high god El was regarded as the head of the pantheon and possessed the high authority of that position. In the light of being the head of the pantheon, El is addressed by every outstanding epithet as acknowledgement of his power and authority as king and creator.

2.2.2. Kingship of other Gods

The struggle for power and kingship of other gods is demonstrated in the Baal epic. Prince Yamm wants a house or palace like El and authority over Baal. At the same time, Baal also requests a house like the gods with a gorgeous throne. His intention in doing so is to declare his dominion over the earth and the gods, and be called Lord of the earth.[19] In another aspect Baal is the fertility god par excellence.[20] Even the name of Baal denotes his high position because Baal means owner, master, lord or husband. The most important use of the title refers to the great active god of the Canaanite pantheon, who controlled rain and fertility.[21]

There was a power struggle among the gods. "Baal's throne is built and Baal dwells in his house, Baal declares his dominion over the earth and the

15 Smith, "The Concept of God," 24.

16 Howard Elvin Hanson, "The Canaanite God El: His Role in Ugaritic Literature" (Master of Arts. Thesis, McMaster University, Ontario, 1970), 10–11.

17 Hanson, "The Canaanite God El: His Role in Ugaritic Literature," 54.

18 Patrick D. Miller, "El the Warrior," *Harvard Theological Review*no. 60 (1967): 418–419.

19 Smith, "The Concept of God," 26.

20 Miller, "El the Warrior," 419.

21 A.E. Cundall, "Baal," in *The Zondervan Pictorial Encyclopedia,* vol. I, edited by Merrill.C Tenney (Grand Rapids: Zondervan, 1976), 431–432.

gods, and is called Lord of the earth."[22] But soon Baal is chased from his throne of kingship, from the dais, the seat of his dominion and Puissant Baal is dead, the Prince, Lord of the earth is perished. Heiser describes the battle of Baal, and Yamm probably offers the strongest struggle among the gods. The specific context of this struggle is a banquet at El's abode, the traditional meeting place of El and his council. El is present at the feast with many flowers and among them Baal was standing beside El. Yamm sends messengers to El demanding that Baal has to be surrendered. El expresses a willingness to do so, and that angers Baal. Soon thereafter, the story describes Yamm and Baal in combat with each other. In this incident Baal was able to conquer and killed Yamm.[23] In this myth, the defeat of Yamm (sea) leads to Baal's declaration as king of the gods with the approval of El. In relation to this concept Smith states:

> EI suggests to Asherah, one of thy sons, I'll make king, to which Asherah first replies why, let's make Yadi Yalhan king, and secondly, let Ashtar the Tyrant be king. Ashtar does not fit on Baal's throne and thus his reign is ended. When Baal returns to life he is repeatedly called Lord of the Earth; and it is said of him, Baal mounts his throne of kingship, Dagon's son his seat of dominion. Other unspecified lesser gods are pictured as dwelling on thrones of princeship.[24]

The above discussion emphasizes high positions of El and Baal are in the Canaanite pantheon. Baal, though not as lofty as El, is by far the most significant deity in the Ugaritic texts. Several other gods were defeated by Baal; and, as a result Baal has become the most powerful god. However, the power of El and Baal cannot be compared to the sovereignty of Yahweh.

2.3. The Concept of God as King among the Hittites

The Hittite society was essentially feudal with the great king at the top. The king was the supreme commander of the army, supreme judicial authority, and chief priest.

2.3.1. The Kingship of Alalu, Anu and Kumarbi

According to ANE text, Alalus was king in heaven for nine years. In the ninth year, Anus gave battle to Alalus and he vanquished Alalus. Alalus fled before him and went down to the dark earth while Anus took his seat upon the throne

22 Smith, "The Concept of God," 27.

23 Michael S. Heiser, "The Baal Cycle as Backdrop to Daniel 7: A Paradigm for Jewish Binitarianism and the New Testament's High Christology," *ETS, Atlanta* (2003): 3.

24 Smith, "The Concept of God," 27.

and ruled as king in heaven for nine years.[25] In the ninth year, Anu gave battle to Kumarbis, and like Alalus even Kumarbis gave battle to Anu. When he could no longer endure Kumarbis' eyes, Anu struggled forth from the hands of Kumarbis. And, therefore, he fled like a bird and moved in the sky. However, Kumarbis rushed and apprehended him by his feet and pulled him down from the sky.[26]

Smith explains, "The cycle continued when Anu was defeated by Kumarbi, who in turn was defeated by Tesub, the storm-god. The king of Kummiya, appears to have taken Kumarbi's place for Tasmisus, the storm god's attendant, says that if Tesub moves from his place there will be no king in heaven."[27] The ANE text mentions that Anu plans to destroy Kumarbis with the help of the storm-god. And therefore the storm god might have overpowered Kumarbis and took over the kingship in heaven.[28] We can notice that the desire of each of the gods is to rule as king and struggle for authority is in terms of kingship.

2.3.2. The Kingship of the Sun and Storm Gods

The Hittite sun-goddess of Arinna is twice declared to be the one who controls kingship and queenship in the treaty between Suppiluliumas and Mattiwaza. In Pudu-hepa's prayer to the sun-goddess, she is entitled the queen of all the countries. Although, she was the supreme patroness of the Hittite state and monarchy, it was the sun-god who was the King of the gods. Thus, his name appears before the sun-goddess of Arinna on some Hittite treaties.[29] Smith mentions,

> Tesub, the Hurrian storm or weather-god is called king in the song of Ullikimus and is considered by some to be the supreme king... the real king and owner of the land of Hatti. In Mursilis' prayers, the storm-god is addressed as my lord and the king of heaven. In a treaty he is called the lord of heaven and earth. Among the other gods, Ea is once referred to as the king of wisdom; and Telepinus is told, there is no other deity more noble and mighty than thou...thou watchest over kingship in heaven and earth. In the oath formula which invokes the gods, one finds kingship terms used of. Ishara, queen of the oath, Hebat, queen of heaven and in other writings the Luwian god Santas is called king. These examples illustrate how

25 James B. Pritchard, ed., "Hittite, Myths, Epics, and Legends," in *Ancient Near Eastern Texts: Relating to Old Testament,* Third Edition with Supplement, trans. Goetze Albrechet (Princeton: Princeton University Press, 1969), 120.

26 Pritchard, "Hittite, Myths, Epics, and Legends," 120.

27 Smith, "The Concept of God," 28.

28 Pritchard, "Hittite, Myths, Epics, and Legends," 121.

29 Smith, "The Concept of God," 28.

> the Hittites used the kingship analogy to describe their chief gods. A great deal remains unknown about the relationships between the Hittite gods but the struggle for power and dominant position is consistently stated in kingship terminology.[30]

The above points indicate that among the Hittites there was the sun god and sun goddess whom they addressed as the king and the queen of the gods. There was also storm god, who was called the king of heaven. Thus, the Hittites used the kingship analogy to portray their chief gods.

2.4. The Concept of God as King in Egypt

A fundamental part of Egyptian thinking regarding their Pharaohs was that the king was divine. Titles such as 'King of Upper and Lower Egypt,' 'Lord of the Two Lands' and 'Son of Re' showed that the kings were identified as gods. Kingship in Egypt was the channel through which the powers of nature flowed into the body politic to bring human venture to fruition. Thus the maintenance of nature and civilization were dependent on the king.[31]

The king in Egypt was normally expected to maintain justice and order over the land, to serve as an intermediary with the gods, to be commander-in-chief of the army and the highest judicial official in the land. The Egyptians believed that the king and his authority were derived from and patterned after the gods. Thus the sun-god, Atum-Re, established order and justice, and the Pharaoh who was a model of the god-king-judge, Re, was the supreme judge in Egypt. The importance of the earthly king in Egypt echoes the importance of the kingship concepts among the gods.[32] Looking from this aspect, one can understand that the primary concept of Egyptian kingship viewed the king as having divine essence and being a god incarnate.[33]

2.4.1. The Kingship of Re

According to Egyptian tradition, 'Re' is the sun-god, the first king in Egypt. The kingship of Re, who is also known as Khepri, Atum and various dual names, goes back to the time of creation. The kingship of Re is frequently expressed in the formula king of the gods. As a result Amon-Re is called 'King of the Gods' in a Twentieth Dynasty legal document, in two texts which recount the Hyksos period, and by Thut-mose III who introduces himself as one who is 'Enduring in Kingship, like Re in heaven,' who serves 'Amon-Re, Lord of the Thrones of

30 Smith, "The Concept of God," 28-29.

31 Smith, "The Concept of God," 29. See H. Frankfort, *Kingship and the Gods* (Chicago: University of Chicago Press, 1948), 34.

32 Smith, "The Concept of God," 29-30.

33 Frankfort, *Kingship and the Gods: A Study of Ancient Near Eastern Religion as the Integration of Society & Nature*, 5.

the Two Lands.' The title 'Amon-Re, King of the Gods' is found in a document about a runaway slave, a list of the possessions which belonged to the temple of Amon, and in ritual texts.[34] According to ANE Texts,[35]

> The goodly beloved youth to whom the gods give praise
> Who illuminates the Two Lands
> And crosses the heavens in peace
> The king of upper and lower Egypt: Re, the triumphant Chief of the Two lands
> Great of strength, lord of reverence,
> The Chief one, who made the entire earth.
> More distinguished in nature than any (other) god,
> In whose beauty the gods rejoice.

Additionally in one of the hymn of Amon-Re says,

> "Amon-Re is the chief of all gods...Lord of the Thrones of the Two Lands…father of the gods, who made mankind and created the beasts…the king of Upper and Lower Egypt…beautiful of diadem, and lofty of White Crown…Lord of the Double Crown…lord of the gods…who gave commands, and the gods came into being...the chief of the Great Ennead…the sole king…maker of all mankind, Creator and maker of all that is…."[36]

Thus, as seen in the above discussion there are a number of hymns which describe Amon-Re as Lord of the Thrones of the Two Lands and King of the Gods.

2.4.2. The Kingship of other Gods in Egypt

Ptah is considered creator of the gods and of all creation. The god Seth was made the king of Upper Egypt and the god Horus the king of Lower Egypt, but Geb later gave Horus the kingship over all Egypt in order to end discord. Thus, Horus like the pharaoh stands as king of a united Egypt.[37] This myth continued through Egyptian history. With this idea, possibly all pharaohs were believed to be Horus. Subsequently, Ptah created the world by his word and took on the kingly title of 'Lord of the Two Lands.' On the other hand, the god Horus, the son of Osiris, appears as the king of Upper and Lower Egypt, thus setting

34 Smith, "The Concept of God," 30-31.

35 James B. Pritchard, ed., "Egyptian Hymns and Prayers," in *Ancient Near Eastern Texts: Relating to the Old Testament,* Third Edition with Supplement, trans. John A. Wilson (Princeton: Princeton University Press, 1969), 365.

36 Smith, "The Concept of God," 30-31.

37 Frankfort, *Kingship and the Gods: A Study of Ancient Near Eastern Religion as the Integration of Society & Nature*, 40.

forth the identification of the dead Pharaoh with Osiris and his successor with Horus. As a result, the position of Horus as the new king explains why the Egyptian Pharaohs Re were identified with Horus. The earthly king sits upon the throne of Horus who is called 'the good king of Egypt' and 'the ruler' in the contest of Horus and Seth. In celebration of the ascension of Mer-ne-Ptah to the throne, he is said to be 'great of kingship like Horus,' and at the ascension of Ramses IV, Horus is proclaimed to be 'upon the throne of his father Amon-Re.' In connection to this story, Pharaoh, then, is an incarnation of Horus, the Great(est) God, Lord of Heaven.[38]

"In Egypt, at the annual festival, the highest God Osiris was proclaimed king, being represented by the king and this was realistically set forth by the rite of his ascent upon his throne."[39] It is also said that the god Osiris was primarily associated with fertility and resurrection. Osiris was king after Geb his father, until he was assassinated and went to the world of the dead, and therefore he was addressed as the King of the Dead.[40] From there, the dead king Osiris, "is adored as the prototype and saviour of common dead."[41]

The fertility aspect of Osiris related his death and resurrection to the seasonal agriculture cycle, the seasonal rise and fall of the Nile and the daily rebirth of the sun.[42] Osiris is called King Wen-nofer and the dead King Unis is said to sit on the throne of Osiris. Though the popular Osiris cult challenged the solar cult of Re, the merger did not remove Re from his position as king of the living. As a result sometimes both Re and Osiris appear to be supreme kings, but the kingship of Osiris is exclusively in the land of the dead.[43]

The stories of Geb, Osiris and Horus indicate the centrality Egyptians assigned to the kingship of the gods. These gods are called kings, they sit on thrones, rule, judge and wear crowns and hold the sceptre of a king. As representatives of elements of the universe, they establish a relationship between nature and human, and in that Egyptians could consider such a bond through kingship.[44] The pharaoh is worthy of that adoration because "he is Re, by whose beams one sees, He is the one who illumines the two lands more than

38 Frankfort, *Kingship and the Gods: A Study of Ancient Near Eastern Religion as the Integration of Society & Nature*, 40.

39 Muthunayagom, "Kingship of God and Creation in the Old Testament," 46.

40 Smith, "The Concept of God," 31.

41 Frankfort, *Kingship and the Gods: A Study of Ancient Near Eastern Religion as the Integration of Society & Nature*, 197.

42 Frankfort, *Kingship and the Gods: A Study of Ancient Near Eastern Religion as the Integration of Society & Nature*, 181-182.

43 Smith, "The Concept of God," 32.

44 Frankfort, *Kingship and the Gods: A Study of Ancient Near Eastern Religion as the Integration of Society & Nature*, 182–183.

the sun disc."[45] This notion portrays that pharaoh is brighter than the sun and therefore deserves adoration.

2.5. The Kingship of God and Worship in the Poetic Traditions of the Hebrew Bible

The literary analyses of the Hebrew Bible point out that the kingship of Yahweh is a feature of Israelites' religion from early stages.[46] In the context of Israel's society, the kings of Israel ruled, shepherded and governed their people, sat upon a throne in a palace, judged important court cases, and were the commanders-in chief of the army similar to the kings in other neighbouring nations. But one important point is that the Israelites did not believe the human king to be mediator between God and humans, or the one who integrated and harmonized human with the natural world, as was the case in Egypt and Mesopotamia.[47]

Looking at the metaphor of kingship in Israel we can consider the following factors that draw the focus of attention to the unique character of Israel's true king called Yahweh. This uniqueness, however, does not deny totally certain conceptual or functional similarities with the Ancient West Asian ideas about the kingship of the gods. Moreover, Yahweh is above all the kings and gods because Yahweh is the eternal king. According to Smith, these three primary components which unite themselves in the Israelite metaphor of God as king are similar to those used in other religions: (a) "Yahweh (as other gods) is Lord and king of the world, (b) Yahweh (as other gods) is a mighty warrior who destroys his enemies, and (c) Yahweh (as other gods) is a judge over his kingdom."[48]

In this section I have discussed three areas: *First*, the kingship metaphor of Yahweh in Pentateuch. *Secondly*, the kingship metaphor of Yahweh in the prophetic books. *Thirdly*, the kingship metaphor of Yahweh in Psalms other than the Enthronement Psalms.

2.5.1. The Kingship Metaphor of Yahweh in Pentateuch

Yahweh, as king, is the sovereign ruler of all history and his decisive intervention as the Divine Warrior at the time of the exodus (Ex 15:3) revealed both his election of his people and his own redemptive power. Through his triumph over the Egyptians and their gods, his kingship over all the earth was

45 Frankfort, *Kingship and the Gods: A Study of Ancient Near Eastern Religion as the Integration of Society & Nature,* 431.

46 Patrick D. Miller, *The Religion of Ancient Israel* (Louisville: Westminster John Knox Press, 2000), 10.

47 Smith, "The Concept of God," 33.

48 Smith, "The Concept of God," 33.

recognized (Ex 15:18). Jacob Chinitz affirms that the king proclamation in Exodus 15 stands with full meaning and its significance at the close of the hymn of the sea. Through the mighty act of Yahweh the king, the Israelites learned that they have a king who alone is true God among all the gods of the peoples. Along with the children of Israel all the neighbours who had no such lords and leaders were gripped with fear when Yahweh acted mightily. So, Israel gave worship to Yahweh as being the one to whom alone kingship is due.[49] Because after Israel saw the miracles performed by Yahweh the king, they said to one another, come let us exalt and crown Yahweh, the king who disregards kings from their thrones, but he cannot be removed, for he is the king of kings. So he is in this world and he will be the Only One even in the coming world and above all for eternity. Chinitz points out, "His kingdom will be known in all the kingdoms, joins the others in seeing the kingdom in the future for Israel and for the entire world."[50]

The portrayal of Yahweh as king is addressed in the book of Exodus where it refers to Yahweh as the warrior who gave victory over the enemies. It says יְהוָה יִמְלֹךְ לְעֹלָם וָעֶד "Yahweh shall reign forever and ever" (Ex 15:18). "The metaphor was ascribed to the Canaanite city gods, especially in the myth related to El and Baal in and around the pre-Israelite Jerusalem. Even in the early period, the metaphor of Yahweh as king was used by Israelites in order to make sense to the fellow Israelites regarding the nature of Yahweh in the larger world of the gods that they encountered among their neighbours."[51] The exodus tradition itself revealed the kingship of Yahweh. The kingship of Yahweh carries with it the notion of being timeless, immutable and beyond human reach. Thus, Yahweh exercised his kingship over the king of Israel and all the neighbouring nations.

Smith and Stewart observed that Israel celebrated Yahweh's universal kingship from the very beginning of their history. For instance, in Exodus 15:1-18, the song of Moses and Miriam affirms Yahweh's triumph over all his enemies. As king, Yahweh functions as a divine warrior as it was revealed at the time of the exodus. At this point, Yahweh's victory over the Egyptians and their gods, and his kingship over all the earth, is established.[52] Yahweh the king "controls the natural elements, forcing the sea to withdraw and allow God's people through to safety."[53] Therefore, kingship is demonstrated when Yahweh

49 Jacob Chinitz, "The Three Tenses in the Kingdom of God: God of Israel or of the World," *Jewish Bible Quarterly,* vol. 38, no. 4 (2010): 256.

50 Chinitz, "The Three Tenses in the Kingdom of God: God of Israel or of the World," 257.

51 Muthunayagom, "The Image of God as King and the Nature of His Power in the Old Testament," 31.

52 Smith, "The Concept of God," 37.

53 Mary E. Mills, *Images of God in the Old Testament* (Collegeville: The Liturgical Press, 1998), 31.

asserts kingly power in history by throwing down the power of Egypt and their gods. The mighty deeds of Yahweh the king have a tremendous implication for the whole world. Dethroning or pulling down peoples' power reveals his supreme authority over them. Hence, it means that Yahweh exercises authority in due time.[54] "When Moses led the children of Israel out of Egypt, they left a world that revolved around divine kingship. With plagues and tumbling waters, Yahweh, the king of Israel, proved himself to be the king over all the other gods."[55]

The response of Yahweh, the enthroned king, came to his people in the form of a covenant. You have seen what I did unto the Egyptians, and how I bore you on eagles' wings, and brought you unto myself. Now, therefore, if you will obey my voice and keep my covenant, and then "you shall be to me a kingdom of priests and a holy nation. These are the words that you shall speak to the children of Israel" (Ex 19:4-6).[56] The above points point toward the recognition of Yahweh as king. Bellinger supports the view of Stewart and says Yahweh's kingship is rooted in acts of power and creation. He created and remained sovereign over all of creation and all within it. In addition, Yahweh the king creates, rules and also dwells with the community.[57]

Numbers 23:21, 24:3-9 also reflects the nature of Yahweh's kingship over his enemies. On the other hand, Yahweh's claim as king is associated with the concept of liberative action or providential and defensive actions towards his people. Because whenever an individual or the community faced the political threat of their enemies, death due to natural calamities or humiliation, they would seek Yahweh as their king with full hope that Yahweh would deliver them from any kind of threat.[58] The kingship metaphor of Yahweh is also revealed in the book of Deuteronomy. Selman comments that Yahweh was believed to be among the people and therefore Israel celebrated their conviction of his royal presence with a 'shout' which is connected to a regular homage among the chosen people of God (Deut 33:5).[59] These are the references pointing towards the kingship of Yahweh in the Pentateuch.

---

54 John Goldingay, "Psalms 90-150," in *Baker Commentary on the Old Testament Wisdom and Psalms*, edited by Tremper Longman III, vol. 3 (Grand Rapids: Academic Press, 2008), 71.

55 Jeremy J. Stewart, "King of Kings: The Enthronement of Yahweh," *Studia Antiqua,* vol. 2, no. 1 (2002): 108–109.

56 Stewart, "King of Kings: The Enthronement of Yahweh," 109.

57 W. H. Bellinger, *Psalms: Reading and Studying the Book of Praises* (Peabody: Hendrickson Publishers, Inc, 1990), 89-90.

58 Muthunayagom, "The Image of God as King and the Nature of His Power in the Old Testament," 32-33.

59 Martin J. Selman, "The Kingdom of God in the Old Testament," *Tyndale Bulletin,* vol. 40, no. 2 (1989): 181.

2.5.2. The Kingship Metaphor of Yahweh in Prophetic Books

The book of Isaiah highlights the kingship of Yahweh. During the 8th century, Isaiah the prophet saw a vision in the year that King Uzziah died which was around 740 BCE. The Israelites faced a difficult situation as Assyria threatened the Israelite state. But in this context, Isaiah had a message that the "Lord still had a word of new life to speak." Isaiah said, "I saw the Lord sitting on a throne, high and lofty and the hem of his robe filled the temple" (Isa 6:1). His response to this vision was terror: "Woe to me!' I cried. 'I am ruined! For I am a man of unclean lips, and I live among a people of unclean lips, and my eyes have seen the King, the Lord of hosts" (Isa 6:5). Thus, his vision indicates the sovereignty of Yahweh.[60] At the same time, Isaiah declares the coming of the king of kings around 733-732 BCE (Isa 9). He is called "Mighty God, Everlasting Father, Prince of Peace and his authority shall grow continually" (Isa 9:6-7). This Messiahship is linked with the perfect king. Isaiah 37:16 says, "God of Israel you alone of all the kingdoms of the earth." This indicates that Yahweh was not a localized deity like AWA gods but his authority stretched over all the kingdom of the earth.[61]

Concerning Yahweh, the prophet Isaiah declares, "The heaven(s) is my throne and the earth is my footstool" (Isa 66:1a).[62] Selman argues, "Yahweh's kingship is demonstrated in historical events, most notably the return from exile. Indeed, in Isaiah 40-55, the cry 'Yahweh reigns' sums up the prophetic call for God's people to return to their land, and especially to Zion itself."[63]

The prophet Ezekiel talks about the throne of Yahweh which denotes his kingship (Ezek 43:7). The image of God as a shepherd denoting his kingship is portrayed in Ezekiel 34.[64] Block and Brueggemann argued from a similar perspective regarding the kingship of Yahweh. Yahweh the king had the determination to rescue and set free the people from oppression and exploitation (Ezek 34:1-6, 45:8-9).[65] Brueggemann rightly points out that a human king cannot stop Yahweh from doing good. At the same time, though the Israelite king occupied the office of king, he was not king above Yahweh. That reveals that the king was not a free man. He was still under the mandate of Yahweh's will. This is because Yahweh is the king over all kings.[66] In support

60 J. A. Motyer, *The Prophecy of Isaiah* (Leicester: InterVarsity Press, 1993), 75-76.

61 Motyer, *The Prophecy of Isaiah*, 99.

62 Isaiah 10:12-15, 14:13-14, 37:23-24, 2:11, 5:15-16.

63 Selman, "The Kingdom of God in the Old Testament," 178.

64 Muthunayagom, "The Image of God as King and the Nature of His Power in the Old Testament," 32.

65 Daniel I. Block, *Beyond the River Chebar: Studies in Kingship and Eschatology in the Book of Ezekiel* (Cambridge: James Clarke & Co., 2014), 43.

66 Brueggemann, "First and Second Samuel," 109, 111.

of Block and Brueggeman's point, Wright claims that the nation of Israel is considered to be Yahweh's child (Ex 4:22, Hos 11:1, Jer 31:9). This shows that the nation of Israel is always under the authority of Yahweh.[67] Though monarchy was accepted in Israel, it did not replace the kingship of Yahweh, and this new institution was integrated into the already existing covenantal relationship between Yahweh and Israel.[68]

According to Jeremiah, the place of our sanctuary is a glorious throne, exalted from the beginning (Jer 17:12); Jerusalem shall be called the throne of the Lord or the city of the great king (Jer 3:17 cf 23:5). Also, the prophet Zachariah says, "*And the Lord will King over all the earth*" (Zech 14:9). Yahweh is a great king as he has achieved victories in history and they are known to all the nations. The world witnessed the mighty power and majesty of Yahweh who reigns over the world and no earthly power could overtake the rule of Yahweh.[69] Merrill comments that Yahweh rules in both heaven and on earth, and also watches everything, both righteous and unrighteous actions. One day, all the earth will come under the control of Yahweh and turn to him.[70] The nature of Yahweh's kingship is not just to rule over the chosen people, but over the whole world. God is the greatest ruler in history.[71]

Goldingay and Moore argue that Yahweh asserted kingly authority in Israel's history.[72] God is covenantal sovereign of Israel and also is ruler of the disadvantaged.[73] Yahweh was involved with Israel throughout its history and this relates to present worship in a number of ways. Unlike other gods, the sovereign God creates and also rules over all creatures. The idea of sovereignty is part of God's role as the divine king. Therefore, Yahweh's work and his reign are linked together.[74] As king, God is above all and no one is above God. No human king can be compared with Yahweh, the king and his power; we cannot command God, nor can we judge God.[75] These are some of references about kingship metaphor of Yahweh portrayed in the prophetic books of the Hebrew Bible.

---

67 Christopher J. H. Wright, *God's People in God's Land: Family, Land, and Property in the Old Testament* (Grand Rapids: William B. Eerdmans Publishing Company, 1990), 16.

68 R.P. Gordon, *1 & 2 Samuel* (Sheffield: Sheffield Academic Press, 1993), 46.

69 Sebastian Kizhakkeyil, *The Psalms: The Prayer Book of the Bible* (Ruhalaya, Ujjain: Ruhalaya Publications, 2005), 362-363.

70 Eugene H. Merrill, *Everlasting Dominion: A Theology of Old Testament* (Nashville: Broadman & Holman Publishers, 2006), 571, 575.

71 Merrill, *Everlasting Dominion: A Theology of the Old Testament*, 572.

72 Goldingay, *Psalms: Psalms 90-150*, 132.

73 Moore, *Moving Beyond Symbol and Myth*, 4.

74 Goldingay, *Psalms 1-41*, 70.

75 Jan Muis, "God Our King," *HTS*, vol. 64, no. 1 (2008): 284.

2.5.3. The Kingship Metaphor of Yahweh in Psalms

This study focuses on the enthronement psalms; however, in this particular portion, I would like to mention some of the other Psalms which also deal the kingship metaphor of God. Martin J. Selman affirms the wide dimensions of the kingship of God, his argument is that Yahweh established his throne in the heavens and he rules over the nations. There is no end for the kingship of Yahweh; his dominion is for all generations (Pss 45:6-7, 103:19, 146:10).[76] It is to be noted that the references to God's throne in the Psalms include both a heavenly throne (e.g. Pss. 2:4; 11:4) and an earthly throne in Zion (e.g. Pss 9:12, 22:4). There is perhaps a greater emphasis in the Psalms on the eternal kingship of Yahweh (e.g. Pss 9:8, 29:10; 93:2, cf I Chr 29:11-12, II Chr 9:8).[77]

Pleins suggests that creation and history are parallel to each other. "The God at work in the history of Israel's liberation is the God who is at work in creation. History, creation and salvation are one."[78] Yahweh's kingship is praised in both creation and in Yahweh's action in history.[79] Creation and redemption are the supreme manifestations of Yahweh's dominion and are linked with Yahweh's sovereignty over all. He alone is the sovereign of history. Yahweh's activity in creation and redeeming work magnifies his awesomeness.[80] The psalmist explains that by the word of the Lord the heavens were made (Ps 33:6, 9). This image of creation is consistent with the creation account in Genesis where the world is formed in response to God's repeated commands. The psalmist describes creation as the work of his fingers (Ps 8:3). He rules the raging of the sea (Ps 89:9).[81] All creatures, human beings and animals are radically dependent upon the creator God at every moment of their existence.

His works are wondrous and his qualities are incomparable (Pss 19, 104, 139, 147-148). Yahweh's unique creation itself is a work of wonder.[82] Yahweh the creator made summer and winter (Ps 74:12-17). He established the mountains and also controls the water of chaos (Ps 65, 104). At the same time, Yahweh controls the phenomena of day and night, of the heavenly bodies, the seasons and all creatures; nothing can compare with the power of God

---

76 Selman, "The Kingdom of God in the Old Testament," 174–175.

77 Selman, "The Kingdom of God in the Old Testament," 177.

78 J. David Pleins, *The Psalms: Songs of Tragedy, Hope, and Justice* (Maryknoll: Orbis Books, 1993), 134.

79 Westermann, *The Praise of God in the Psalms*, 127.

80 Anderson W. Bernhard, *Understanding the Old Testament* (New Jersey: Pearson Prentice Hall, 2007), 436.

81 Stacy R. Obenhaus, "The Creation Faith of the Psalmists," *Trinity Journal,* vol. 21, no. 2 (2000): 132.

82 Gerstenberger, *Psalms Part I With an Introduction to Cultic Poetry,* 16.

(Pss 50:1, 65:8-10, 74: 16:-17, 135: 7, 147:8-9). This shows that Yahweh has a relationship with all the creatures and apart from him, nothing came to exist.[83] Creation is not a theory, rather Yahweh's creation serves as an affirmation that the world is well-ordered and life-giving because the sovereign God has made it in such a way that the creatures continue to reveal his beauty and glory.[84] Without a doubt, the whole of creation is Yahweh's work and it proclaims the sovereignty of Yahweh.[85] The God who creates is the only God who exists. Yahweh is the sole creator who cares for all the creatures. Thus, Yahweh is worthy to receive all praises.[86]

The Psalmist says, "Yahweh is the king who set the earth on its foundations, so that it shall never be shaken" (Ps 104:5). The Psalms also affirm that God existed before creation, exists apart from it, and will continue to exist when creation passes away (Ps 90:2, 102:26-27).Yahweh was Israel's king in the past long before monarchy existed, and he will continue to be Israel's king as the kingship of Yahweh has no end.[87] Thus, Yahweh is the pre-existent God, the one who remains forever. Therefore, the people seek shelter in the eternal God.[88] Brettler asserts that God's eternal nature was understood within the framework of 'Yahweh is king.' You are the same, and your years never end (Ps 102:27). From everlasting to everlasting you are God (Ps 90:2). The psalmist declares, 'Your throne endures forever and ever' (Ps 45:6). Yahweh dynasty and his throne will last forever.

Smith[89] and Moore have made similar points about the eternity of the kingship metaphor. The eternity of Yahweh is connected with the motif of everlasting kingdom of God. Thus, Yahweh is worshipped as 'my God, my King' who stands for all generations (Pss 68:24; 84:3; 145:1).[90] Smith rightly points out two schools of thought: the *first*, Yahweh sits on the throne *rebuking the nation* for their wicked actions and *judging righteously* (Ps 9:5), and *secondly,* Yahweh judges the world with righteousness and equity by looking at the social life of the people (Ps 9:9). This concept further emphasizes that Yahweh is to rule over the earth and what is more, the achievement of justice and righteousness for people is to be the guarantee of Yahweh's actual presence

83 Obenhaus, "The Creation Faith of the Psalmists," 133-134.

84 Obenhaus, "The Creation Faith of the Psalmists," 137.

85 Theodore Mascarenhas, *The Missionary Function of Israel in Psalms 67, 96, and 117* (New York: University Press of America, 2005), 172, 178.

86 House, *Old Testament Theology*, 410-411.

87 Waltke and Houston, *The Psalms as Christian Worship,* 104.

88 Paul R. House, *Old Testament Theology* (Downers Grove: InterVarsity Press, 1998), 416-417.

89 Smith, "The Concept of God," 34.

90 Smith, "The Concept of God," 34.

as a king who has resolved to be a just king.[91] Yahweh acts against the nations who fail to judge people with justiceand righteousness. Thus, Yahweh, acting in the judicial assembly, has the decree of reality (cf. Ps 82).[92] Your royal sceptre is a sceptre of equity (Ps 45:6). This is how the psalmist presents the kingship metaphor of Yahweh in several places. There are several indications in the book of Psalms that speak of other gods as inferior (Ps 29).

Yahweh the king is worthy to be worshipped as the psalmist emphasized that the other gods proved to be powerless and were under subjugation to Yahweh the king. The worthiness of Yahweh's power is that all the worshippers of images lose confidence in their idols; they are defeated by the majesty of Yahweh and that prompts them to worship the divine king Yahweh.[93] For instance, the idols of the nations are silver and gold and the work of human hands. They have mouths but do not speak, eyes but do not see, ears but do not hear (Ps 135:15-16). According to Mays, Yahweh is worthy to be worshiped as he is the true king. He points out the following reasons. *First,* Yahweh is ruler of the gods. *Second,* Yahweh rules over the world, indeed the depths and heights of the earth; sea and dry land belong to the most high God. *Third*, Yahweh rules over all the nations and people. *Fourth*, Yahweh rules with integrity. Thus, righteousness and justice are part of the kingship of Yahweh.[94]

The concept of God as king is a fundamental basis of Israelite religious life which motivates them to adore Yahweh the king.[95] The declaration of the phrase "Yahweh is the king" is possibly a declaration of new governance and it is cause for great joy and jubilation among all the creatures.[96] Schaefer points out, "Yahweh's governance fans out to embrace the world."[97] Yahweh gives strength, blessing, and peace to all true worshipers (Ps 29:10-11).[98]

---

91 Smith, "The Concept of God," 35, 72.

92 Schroeder, *History, Justice, & the Agency of God,* 160.

93 Artur Weiser, *The Psalms: A Commentary*, edited by Peter Ackroyd (Philadelphia: Westminster Press, 1962), 634.

94 James Luther Mays, *The Lord Reigns: A Theological Handbook to the Psalms* (Louisville: Westminster John Knox Press, 1994), 14.

95 Aubrey Johnson, *Sacral Kingship in Ancient Israel* (Cardiff: University of Wales Press, 1967), 68.

96 Walter Brueggemann, *Theology of the Old Testament* (Minneapolis: Fortress Press, 2005), 239. The psalmist presented the greatest political rule of Yahweh the king. Yahweh as king in Israel, over all the nations and over all the gods and this ideology is parallel to political form of the supreme governance. Perhaps every people, nations and creatures comes under the control of Yahweh who has got the authority to control, rule and maintain. Indeed Yahweh is sovereign, all the other rulers dependent on Yahweh's authority. For the Lord your God is God of gods and Lord of lords (Deut 10:17), 239-240.

97 Konrad Schaefer, *Psalms; Studies in Hebrew Narrative & Poetry,* edited by David W. Cotter, (Collegeville: The Liturgical Press, 2001), 244.

98 Watts, "Psalms of Trust, Thanksgiving, and Praise," 403.

Moore affirms that the kingship metaphor of Yahweh is used "rhetorically to maintain Israel's allegiance over against rival religious claims. The function of the kingship metaphor of Yahweh is shaping in terms of advocating Israel's continued commitment to its covenant."[99]

The concept of Yahweh as king in the poetic traditions of the Hebrew Bible indicates that Yahweh is king over the nations and Israel in the realm of history. Yahweh is king over the gods in the realm of myth.[100] Along with his authority he cares for the people and nations whereas the other gods in Ancient West Asian religions probably reveal that their gods care for the land.[101] For Yahweh the king, people cast themselves down; bend the knee and honour God in praise, thanksgiving, and adoration.

2.6. A Comparison of the Kingship of Yahweh with the Kingship in West Asia

The intention here is to compare the kingship of Yahweh with the kings of Ancient West Asian religions while trying to determine the significance of the kingship of Yahweh in the context of Israel's worship. Yahweh, as the king, serves in ways similar to human kings. However the metaphor is used as a tool to show how Yahweh goes beyond how human kings serve.[102] In the biblical passages relating to the title of king ascribed to Yahweh, we discover that Yahweh the king uses his authority as king over the historical domain to depict kingship over Israel and the nations. He uses his authority as king of the mythological realm to show kingship over gods and also the universe.[103]

Indeed, the title of king was familiar to people in Ancient West Asia and the Hebrew Bible. The book of Psalms uses the metaphor to affirm that Yahweh is supreme and the only king to worship, praise and proclaim.[104] For instance, Yahweh is called as everlasting king; king over all the divine beings and king over all the earth. These terms are never applied to human kings. In fact, the superlative expression uses the metaphor of God as the king to turn God into overlord par excellence whose kingship goes beyond the human king.[105] The commentators like Beale, Menezes and Mays argue that there seems to be a

99 Moore, *Moving Beyond Symbol and Myth: Understanding the Kingship of God of the Hebrew Bible through Metaphor*, 253.

100 Muthunayagom, "Kingship of God and Creation in the Old Testament," 4.

101 Daniel I. Block, *The Gods of the Nations: A Study in Ancient Near Eastern National Theology* (Grand Rapids: Baker Books, 2000), 20.

102 Marc ZviBrettler, *God is King: Understanding an Israelite Metaphor* (Sheffield: Academic Press, 1989), 32.

103 Muthunayagom, "The Image of God as King and the Nature of His Power in the Old Testament," 32.

104 Mascarenhas, *The Missionary Function of Israel in Psalms 67, 96, and 117*, 187.

105 Brettler, *God Is King: Understanding an Israelite Metaphor*, 33.

sense of borrowing from the religious practices of neighbouring people, but, Israel has her own uniqueness regarding the religious practices and beliefs.[106]

The Israelites never adopted ideas from the neighbouring people without adapting them to Yahwism. Yahweh's kingship was established on its traditional, historical roots in the kingship traditions predominantly connected with the Ark in Shilo. In connection with this view, we may assume that Zion symbolizes security because Yahweh reigns in Zion as creator and protector.[107] For instance, Zion is considered to be the dwelling place of Yahweh. Beale suggests, "It is apparent that Israel intentionally alluded to facets of the pagan religion surrounding them (e.g., Egyptian, Canaanite and Babylonian) in order to affirm that what the pagans thought was true of their gods was true only of Israel's God."[108] For instance, we see there is a clear example of applying the sovereign attributes of the fertility god Baal to Yahweh in order to reveal that only Yahweh possesses such characteristics and no other gods. Muthunayagom following von Rad and suggests that the idea of Yahweh as king of the world portrays that the power and authority of a particular god in Ancient West Asia is limited when compared with the kingship of Yahweh.[109]

In Ancient West Asia, the king was considered as the son of God, having the authority of God himself. His word was as final as God's command. In Egypt, the Pharaoh was considered a physical son of the gods and was worshipped as god. His word was final. In Egyptian traditions, the Pharaoh could own the title of the son of God in the sense of an incarnate deity, begotten by the god Amon and born of the queen mother.[110] And, thus, the Egyptian Pharaoh was considered to be one of the gods.[111] In Mesopotamia too, the king was considered to be god's son, where the king of Babylon or Asshur (Assyria) was a servant or vassal of his gods.[112]

The idea that a god would become king is found in the Babylonian creation poem. When the gods, his father, saw the success of his utterance,

---

106 G. K. Beale, *The Temple and the Church's Mission: A Biblical Theology of the Dwelling Place of God, New Studies in Biblical Theology*, edited by D. A. Carson (Downers: InterVarsity Press, 2004).

107 Ollenburger, *Zion the City of the Great King*, 53.

108 Beale, *The Temple and the Church's Mission*, 29-30.

109 Muthunayagom, "The Image of God as King and the Nature of His Power in the Old Testament," 33.

110 Hans-Joachim Kraus, *Theology of the Psalms*, translated by Keith Crim (Minneapolis: Augsburg Publishing House, 1986), 113.

111 Harvey H. Guthrie, *Israel's Sacred Songs: A Study of Dominant Themes* (New York: The Seabury Press, 1978), 70.

112 Rui de Menezes, *The Legacy of Israel: Collected Essays*, vol. 3 (Mumbai: St Pauls, 2012), 45-46.

the people exalted and paid homage. Marduk is king for the Babylonian.[113] According to a mythical tradition we see among the west Asian religions, the supreme god was conceived as the king of all the other gods. For instance, in the Ugaritic literature, El is considered as the highest god as he bears the title of king. He is the king of the gods who leads over the assembly of gods. Also, in Enuma Elish, Marduk is considered as the supreme god after he won the battle with Tiamat and, therefore, the other gods honoured him with the honourable statement "you are the most honoured of the great gods."[114]

The kingship of Yahweh differs from the kingship of AWA because all the kings are under the rule of Yahweh the king who is in control, above and below. For Muthunayagom, "the rule of Yahweh as king and creator of the entire world and protector of human and earthly domain deabsolutizes or delegitimizies all other governance whether mythical or human which imagine that they are unfettered and absolute"[115]

Mays argues that it is probable that the psalmic language used for Yahweh is a kind of feature of Ancient West Asia. The use of the kingship metaphor is to express a coherent view of reality that arose with Ancient West Asian religions.[116] However, Menezes rightly said that while Baal became a king, Yahweh had always existed as the king and, therefore, Yahweh needs to take no attributes from another god or deity. The psalmist expresses, "For the Lord is a great king above all kings" (Ps 95:3). The ideologies and customs of the Near Eastern emperors and kings contributed much to Israel's concept of a king, but this is not the only source as Israel had her own.[117] In my opinion, the neighbouring religious practices cannot surpass the kingship of Yahweh. The reason is that there is no ending in the kingship of Yahweh.

The Ancient West Asian texts mention Marduk's kingship. The people exalted the destiny of Marduk, and even bowed down and worshipped him. In the light of these Ancient Near Asian parallels, the logic of Yahweh's acting as king in the poetical tradition of the Hebrew Bible becomes understandable. However, when we compare Marduk's kingship with Yahweh's kingship, we find they are not identical. Yahweh is above all human kings and authority. And therefore though Marduk is considered to be higher than the others he cannot be higher than Yahweh. Yahweh the king controls the destiny of all

113 Gunkel, *Introduction to Psalms: The Genres of the Religious Lyric of Israel*, 66.

114 Muthunayagom, "The Image of God as King and the Nature of His Power in the Old Testament," 33.

115 Muthunayagom, "The Image of God as King and the Nature of His Power in the Old Testament," 35.

116 Mays, *The Lord Reigns: A Theological Handbook to the Psalms*, 10.

117 Menezes, *The Legacy of Israel*, 45-46.

people. Other kings cannot overpower Yahweh's power and might.[118] The kingship displayed in the Hebrew Bible is that Yahweh the king is an effective ruler over all the kings. Therefore, Yahweh is exalted above all other celestial power and beings. The rule of Yahweh the king overshadows all other gods.[119]

Even though in Ancient West Asia it was a common notion that the king was the son of God, this cannot be compared with Yahweh the king.[120] Such mythological notions of the king's divine sonship are totally alien to Yahweh the king. The one enthroned was exalted and took part in Yahweh's glory (Ps 89:27, 110:1).[121] The king of Israel was adopted as a son by Yahweh on the coronation day. "You are my son, today I have begotten you" (Pss 2:7, 89:27-28).[122] Though we see adopted sonship in ancient west Asian notion of king as God. It is certain that there was no other deity as king before Yahweh the king.[123] Adjectives like powerful, awesome, and effective expound the verb of Yahweh's reign. It is forever and it is the unlimited power of Yahweh over the people.[124] The Israelites portray Yahweh as their king as he continues to support them in all life situations, providing their needs protecting them from all dangers of life. The kingship of Yahweh is not limited to the people of Israel and to the land he has given to them. His position had its origin before the existence of the people. As a result, if the people of Israel happen to be taken away from their land, he would still be their king. Truly, Yahweh is the king of Israel, his chosen nation, and also the supreme king over all the world.[125] The kingship of Yahweh is a divine kingship and last forever, this is how we see the difference between the kingship of Yahweh and Marduk.

In the light of the above discussion, we see how the kingship of Yahweh is different from all the ancient west Asian kingship of gods. In all these nations, the gods who are kings are also represented as the highest power with authority and dominion. However, when compared to other gods, the distinctive authority of Yahweh, the king, goes far beyond the dominion of Re who shared his power with the Pharaoh, or Anu or who was one of several gods who were called king.[126] Yahweh exercises his authority as king from the very beginning and will continue to do so forever. Yahweh is in control of all the power and other kings are subject to Yahweh. Nobody can measure

118 Mills, *Images of God in the Old Testament*, 31.

119 Pleins, *The Psalms: Songs of Tragedy, Hope, and Justice*, 130.

120 Kraus, *Theology of the Psalms*, 113.

121 Kraus, *Theology of the Psalms*, 113.

122 Menezes, *The Legacy of Israel: Collected Essays*, 46.

123 Goldingay, *Psalms: Psalms 90-150*, 67.

124 Mays, *The Lord Reigns: A Theological Handbook to the Psalms*, 15.

125 Block, *The Gods of the Nations: A Study in Ancient Near Eastern National Theology*, 9.

126 Smith, "The Concept of God/The Gods as King in the Ancient Near East and the Bible," 28.

the vastness of the kingship of Yahweh because it is beyond human reach and understanding.

Thus, Yahweh's kingship implies a kingship which is above everything else. There is a huge gap between the ideology of kingship of God in West Asia and from poetic traditions in Old Testament and enthronement psalms. I have proven that there is no end in the kingship of Yahweh. It reveals that due worship belongs to Yahweh the king. Thus, the everlasting kingship of Yahweh has an immense message for worship especially for a pluralistic religious context in India today.

Summary

The above discussion covered the concept of God's kingship in the following areas. *Firstly,* the concept of God as king in Mesopotamia. *Secondly,* the concept of God as king in Ugaritic Literature. *Thirdly,* the concept of God as king among the Hittites. *Fourthly,* the concept of God as king in Egypt. *Fifthly,* the kingship of God in the poetic traditions of the Hebrew Bible. Looking from all these aspects it shows the rich function of kingship of God in ancient west Asian religion. Probably the near eastern texts do talk about the concept of eternal kingship of other gods, however they gave priority of their relationship to the land rather than to the people. However, we can see differences between the kingship of Yahweh in the poetic tradition of the Hebrew Bible and the kingship concept in Ancient West Asian religions. The reason is that Yahweh is the king who holds the authority over all the kings. Thus, in my opinion the uniqueness of Yahweh's kingship lies in claim to absolute sovereignty. And also priority of his relationship to his people and not to his land or territory as against the ancient near eastern kings.

Chapter 3

Exegetical Study of Psalm 47 Yahweh, the Universal King

Introduction

In chapter 2, I have looked at the kingship metaphor of God in Ancient West Asian religions and in the poetic tradition of the Hebrew Bible as a whole. It provides the historical and literary background to the exegesis of the enthronement Psalms. I have put the enthronement psalms in order of their appearances in the book of Psalms. The enthronement psalms explicitly project the kingship metaphor in the light of Israel's worship. Therefore, enthronement psalms can be taken as a representative of the whole OT in the context of worship of Yahweh the king. In the Psalter, both the royal psalms and enthronement psalms talk about the kingship metaphor but I limit my study to the enthronement psalms. However, I use cross references from the royal psalms whenever they are relevant to the enthronement texts.

This chapter is an exegetical study of Psalm 47, applying *historical-literary critical tools* and *form criticism*. The aim is to bring out the implications of kingship metaphor for worship. Also, I have discussed the issue of the canonical distance of Psalm 47 from the rest of the enthronement psalms, because the enthronement psalms are found into two different sections of the Psalter. Psalm 47 is found in Book 2 and the rest of the enthronement psalms in Book 4. Thus, it is helpful to discuss the gap in the light of their divisions and then proceed to the text studies.

Hermann Gunkel categorized ten psalms by their subject matter of kingship as the royal psalms (2, 18, 20, 21, 45, 72, 101, 110, 132, 144:1-11).[1] Along with the ten Psalms Mowinckel includes more Psalms like 28, 44, 60, 66, 68, 80, 83, and 84 in his list of the royal psalms.[2] There is a disagreement with the exact number of the royal psalms among the psalms scholars. Eaton and Weiser agree with Gunkel's estimate of the number of the royal psalms.[3] The royal psalms play an essential role in the life of the people of Israel during the Davidic kingdom (1000-587 BCE).[4] After the fall of Jerusalem in 587 BCE they took on another significance projecting into the future a description of an ideal king to come.[5]

Why do the enthronement psalms occur into two separate books? Why is there a gap between Psalm 47 in Book 2 and Psalms 93, 95-100 in Book 4? *First, the Psalms with titles* could be related to the authorship. In the Psalter the heading of the Psalms indicat the author of a particular psalm.[6] Psalm 47 comes under the Korahite collection, and the following Psalms 42-49 are considered to be from the Korahite collection of the psalms. Psalm 47 is addressed as a *Psalm of the sons of Korah,* which denotes thatthe author of this Psalm could be one of the temple singers from the sons of Korah. The Korahites were Levites who were singers in the temple (I Chr 6:22).[7] The other enthronement psalms (93, 95-100) do not have any titles attached to them unlike Psalm 47.[8]

1 Hermann Gunkel, *Introduction to Psalms: The Genres of the Religious Lyric of Israel* (Macon, Georgia: Mercer University Press, 1998), 99. See Steven J. L. Croft, *The Identity of Individual Psalms* (Sheffield: Sheffield Academic Press, 1987), 80-81. John Day, *Psalms* (New York: T & T Clark International, 2003), 88-89. George P. Braulik, "Psalter and Messiah: Towards a Christological Understanding of the Psalms in the Old Testament and Church Fathers," in *Psalms and Liturgy*, edited by Dirk J. Human and Cas J. A. Vos (London: T & T Clark International, 2004), 14-22.

2 Sigmund Mowinckel, *The Psalms in Israel's Worship, Two Volumes in One*, trans. D.R. Ap-Thomas (Grand Rapids: William B. Eerdmans Publishing Company, 2004), 47.

3 John H. Eaton, *Kingship and the Psalms* (Sheffield: JSOT Press, 1986), 2. See Klaus Seybold, *Introducing the Psalms* (Edinburgh: T & T Clark, 1990), 115. See Artur Weiser, "The Psalms: A Commentary," in *The Old Testament Library*, edited by Peter Ackroyd (Philadelphia: Westminster John Knox Press, 1962), 63.

4 Delmar L. Jacobson, "The Royal Psalms and Jesus Messiah: Preparing to Preach on a Royal Psalm," *Word World* (1985): 193–194.

5 James Limburg, "The Book of Psalms," in *The Anchor Bible Dictionary*, vol. 5 edited by David Noel Freedman (London: Doubleday, 1992), 533.

6 John Eaton, *The Psalms: A Historical and Spiritual Commentary with an Introduction and New Translation* (London: Continuum International Publishing Group, 2005), 5.

7 Peter C. Craigie, "Psalms 1-50," in *Word Biblical Commentary*, edited by David A. Hubbard and Glenn W. Barker (Waco: Word Books, 1983), 28.

8 Sebastian Kizhakkeyil, *The Psalms: The Prayer Book of the Bible* (Ruhalaya, Ujjain: Ruhalaya Publications, 2005), 17.

This could be one of the canonical reasons that Psalm 47 is separated from the rest of the enthronement psalms in Book 4.

Secondly, the untitled Psalms found in Book 4 consist of 17 Psalms (Pss 90-106). The untitled psalms dominate this division and only three psalms have been attached with the titles: The name of Moses in Psalm 90 and David in Psalms 101, 103. All the psalms in Book 4 are put together under the common theme 'claiming or exalting the kingship of Yahweh' and are called the Mosaic Psalms.[9] In Psalm 90, the use of the old divine names El Shaddai and El Elyon refers to the God of Moses and Aaron. Also, these psalms mention the mighty works and eternal reign of Yahweh. The psalms encourage people to find refuge in Yahweh rather than in human rulers. This makes an appropriate link of these psalms with יהוה מלך psalms, which celebrate the kingship of Yahweh.[10] For Anderson, psalms of Yahweh's kingship are considered to be collections or additional psalms used by the choirs of the second temple.[11]

Finally, Psalm 47 comes under Elohistic Psalms. The Elohistic Psalms (Pss 42-83) consistently use אלהים as a prominent name for God. It shows "Elohistic Psalter as a separate component."[12] Seybold affirms that "the tetragrammaton YHWH was replaced fairly mechanically by the term Elohim. This is called elohistic redaction."[13] Anderson claims that "Elohistic Psalter at one time must have circulated as a separate hymnbook in which all these psalms show a decided preference to use the general name God 'Elohim' instead of the special divine name 'YHWH' usually translated the Lord."[14] Thus, אלהים was most commonly used in Book 2. Even Psalm 47 mentions אלהים eight times and יהוה only two times. This indicates that the compilers or authors preferred to use the name Elohim rather than Yahweh. The other enthronement psalms (93, 95-100) in book 4 mostly used יהוה for God, אלהים is only in a few places. In my view, the above points show why canonically Psalm 47 is separated from the rest of the enthronement psalms in Book 4 (Pss 93, 95-100).

Thus, Psalm 47 has historically and canonically a distinct context, but thematically it is connected to other enthronement psalms. Psalm 47 is classified as the first enthronement psalm. As seen in the above discussion, the enthronement psalms are found in books 2 and 4. Psalm 47 belongs to

---

9 Gerald H. Wilson, "Shaping the Psalter: A Consideration of Editorial Linkage in the Book of Psalms," in *The Shape and Shaping of the Psalter*, edited by J. Clinton McCann (Sheffield: Sheffield Academic Press, 1993), 75.

10 Wilson, "Shaping the Psalter," 75-76.

11 Bernhard W. Anderson, *Out of the Depths: The Psalms Speak for Us Today* (Louisville: Westminster John Knox Press, 2000), 12.

12 Hans-Joachim Kraus, "Psalms 1-59," in *A Continental Commentary,* trans. Hilton C. Oswald (Minneapolis: Fortress Press, 1993), 17.

13 Klaus Seybold, *Introducing the Psalms* (Edinburgh: T & T Clark, 1990), 20.

14 Anderson, *Out of the Depths: The Psalms Speak for Us Today*, 13.

Book 2 of the Psalter which consists of Psalms 42-72.[15] Enthronement psalms express the kingship metaphor of God particularly in the context of Israel's Worship.[16] Psalm 47 opens with a general summons to the jubilant praise of God.[17] Yahweh's kingship is based on Yahweh's divinity, for all the gods of the nations are nothing compared to the divine authority of God. The victory of Yahweh over the enemies would be seen as Yahweh's universal might. Psalm 47 highlights the kingship of Yahweh over all the kings and gods. The object of Yahweh's kingship is to call upon all nations and give them the privilege to come into the presence of the God Most High.

Thus, Psalm 47 carries various features of praise hymns which are set within the context of community worship. This section deals with *first,* the historical background of Psalm 47; *secondly,* the literary form and structure and *thirdly,* the textual comments in relation to the kingship metaphor and comments in relation to worship.

3.1. Historical Literary Analysis

Psalms have varied historical setting and as a result, it is not easy to put all the psalms under the same historical background. Therefore, it is important to study both the Davidic monarchical and the post-exilic settings as it helps us to understand the text. Hence, both the settings of Psalm 47 are discussed here.

3.1.1. Davidic Monarchical Setting

When we talk about setting, we find disagreement among biblical scholars; some support the monarchical setting while others, the post-exilic setting. Mowinckel, Perdue, Goldingay, Craigie, and Terrien support Psalm 47 in the Davidic monarchical setting. Psalm 47 is placed in a Davidic monarchical setting for several reasons. *First,* the enthronement psalms were in the cultic

---

15 Seybold, *Introducing the Psalms*, 18. Book I from Psalm 1-41 (41 Psalms) Book II 42-72 (31 Psalms) Book III 73-89 (17 Psalms) Book IV 90-106 (17 Psalms) Book V 107-150 (44 Psalms).

16 John Goldingay, *Songs from a Strange Land: Psalms 42-51* (Illinois: InterVarsity Press, 1978), 73-74. Traditionally, Psalm 47 has also been classified as an Enthronement Psalm (Psalms 47, 93, 96-99) or *Yahweh malak*-psalm (Anderson 1972: 360; Botha 1998: 24; Craigie 1983: 347; Gunkel 1986: 201; Hossfeld & Zenger 2005: 2; Kraus 1966: 348-349, 1988: 466; Muilenburg 1944: 235; Nel 1998: 72; Prinsloo 1996: 388; Sabourin 1969: 216; Schaper 1994: 256). Although, these psalms share the prominent theme of praising the Lord as King, the historical setting in which this *might* have taken place is unclear. The great separation between Psalm 47 in Book 2 of the Psalter and the rest of the Enthronement Psalms in Book 4 of the Psalter serves as ample reason to read it as an independent pericope. Peter C. Craigie, "*Psalms 1-50,*" in *Word Biblical Commentary,* vol. 19, edited by David A. Hubbard, (Waco: Word Books, 1983), 347.

17 Elmer A. Leslie, *The Psalms: Translated and Interpreted in the Light of Hebrew Life and Worship* (New York: Abingdon Press, 1949), 65.

context in connection with the festival in ancient Israel that gives the idea that the setting of Psalm 47 is in the early period of the monarchy.[18] *Secondly,* during King Saul's time, the Ark of the Covenant was captured by the Philistines (1 Sam 5-7). When David brought the ark back to Jerusalem, the entire house of Israel shouted to the Lord with great joy (2 Sam 6:15).[19]

Though the ark is not specifically mentioned in Psalm 47, the reference to God's throne is mentioned. Perdue suggests that throne in these case refers to the ark (Ps 47:9). The ark was regarded as the throne of Yahweh during the monarchical period. Thus, Psalm 47 describes the history of how David brought back the ark to Jerusalem and this is why Psalm 47 is found in the monarchical setting.[20] *Thirdly,* Psalm 47 is probably in the pre-exilic period because there was no ark in post exilic period.[21] *Fourthly,* Psalm 47 is in the pre-exilic period as Psalms 1-72 concentrated on the earliest period of the formation of the nation and the monarchical period.[22] Thus, like the other Korahite psalms, Psalm 47 was possibly used in the sanctuary in the monarchical setting.[23]

From these points, it seems clear that the early period of monarchy is the likeliest setting of Psalm 47. As the ark is used as a symbol of Yahweh's presence in the early period of Israel's history.

3.1.2. Post-Exilic Setting

Gunkel and Kraus support the post-exilic period. *First,* the historical interpretation of this Psalm regards it as a victory song in respect to a recent triumph (e.g. the defeat of Sennacherib cf.2 Kings 19:35) and this could be

18 Mowinckel, *The Psalms in Israel's Worship*, 106. The enthronement psalms are meant to be the song of praise which welcomes Yahweh on his epiphany. For Mowinckel, most of the psalms had their setting in the worship of Israel. He put all the enthronement psalms into cultic setting by reflecting the New Year festival. 106-110. Like Gunkel, Sigmund Mowinckel proposed a classification of literary genres, highly in their cultic context. The difference in these two prominent psalms scholars is that Mowinckel deeply favoured a pre-exilic origin (nine through sixth century BCE) for many hymns and prayers. See Samuel Terrien, *The Psalms: Strophic Structure and Theological Commentary* (Grand Rapids: William B. Eerdmans Publishing Company, 2003), 2. Bruce K. Waltke and James M. Houston, *The Psalms as Christian Worship: A Historical Commentary* (Grand Rapids: William B. Eerdmans Publishing Company, 2010), 76.

19 Goldingay, *Songs from a Strange Land: Psalms 42-51*, 74.

20 Leo G. Perdue, "Yahweh Is King over All the Earth' An Exegesis of Psalm 47," *Restoration Quarterly* 17, no. 2 (1974): 94-95.

21 John Day, *Psalms* (New York: T & T Clark International, 2003), 16.

22 George, A. F. Knight, *Psalms: The Daily Study Bible Series*, edited by John C. L. Gibson (Edinburgh: Saint Andrew Press, 1983), 2.

23 Samuel Terrien, "*The Psalms: Strophic Structure and Theological Commentary: Psalms 1-72*," in *Eerdmans Critical Commentary*, vol. I, edited by David Noel Freedman (Grand Rapids, Michigan: William B. Eerdmans Publishing Company, 2003), 379.

a major reason for it being in the post-exilic setting. *Secondly*, Gunkel gives special focus to literary features in the study of Psalter in relation to their life situation (*Sitz im Leben*), especially in the early post-exilic era. With the same focus, he looks at enthronement psalms according to their literary types and situation.[24] He rightly states that "One understands these psalms when one recognizes the form of the enthronement songs and their eschatological content."[25] This possibly situates Psalm 47 in post exilic period. *Thirdly*, the enthronement psalms is in the post-exilic setting because of its dependence on Deutero-Isaiah.[26]

Regarding the setting, above two different hypotheses have been proposed. Psalm 47 however, may have been composed during the pre-exilic but used extensively during the post-exilic period in worship liturgy. So, it is possible that the psalm may also have post-exilic redactional setting. Therefore, it is better to take the Psalm as originating in the pre-exilic setting, but having post-exilic redactions.

3.2. Literary Analysis of the Text

This section looks into translation, critical notes, form and structure, repetition which occur in Psalm 47. This helps the reader to understand how the literary usage was involved in a particular text. The same pattern follows with the rest of all the enthronement psalms.

---

24 Gunkel, *Introduction to Psalms: The Genres of the Religious Lyric of Israel*, 66-70. In his view, the various psalm types had their origin in the cult and were very much associated with certain cultic situations in biblical history. He distinguished six major types of psalms, namely hymns of praise, enthronement psalms, laments of the community, royal psalms, and laments of the individual and individual songs of thanksgiving. A. A. Anderson, "The Book of Psalms : Psalms 1-72," in *New Century Bible Commentary*, vol. 1 (Grand Rapids: William B. Eerdmans Publishing Company, 1985), 29. Samuel L. Terrien, "The Psalms: Strophic Structure and Theological Commentary: Psalms 1-72," in *Eerdmans Critical Commentary*, edited by David Noel Freedman, vol. 1 (Grand Rapids: William B. Eerdmans Publishing Company, 2003), 12.

25 Gunkel, *Introduction to Psalms: The Genres of the Religious Lyric of Israel*, 68-69.

26 Kraus, *Psalms 1-59*, 467. See John H. Eaton, *Kingship and the Psalms* (Sheffield: JSOT Press, 1986), 110. Kraus considers the following points: (1) It could be that in pre –Israelite Jerusalem, an enthronement festival of the royal divinity was celebrated. This festival and its traditions might have had some effect on the worship of Israel. (2) It could be that in the course of the cultic history of Jerusalem, Assyrians or Babylonians influences brought the idea and use of an enthronement of the divinity to Jerusalem. (3) It seems Psalm 47 has symbolic illustration that was taken from the model of an enthronement of an earthly king. (4) There might be possible dependence of Psalm 47 on Deutero-Isaiah (Isa 52:7), 467.

3.2.1. Translation

1 למנצח לבני־קרח מזמור :	1. For the music director, A Psalms of the sons of Korah.
2 כל־העמים תקעו־כף הריעו לאלהים בקול רנה :	2. All you *peoples*,[27] clap your hands, raise a shout to *God*[28] with the voice of joy.
3 כי־יהוה עליון נורא מלך גדול על־כל־הארץ :	3. For the Lord most high is to be *feared*,[29] A great king over all the *earth*.[30]
4 ידבר עמים תחתינו ולאמים תחת רגלינו :	4. He subdued people under us, And nations under our feet.
5 יבחר־לנו את־נחלתנו את גאון יעקב אשר־אהב סלה :	5. He chose our *inheritance for us*,[31] the highness of Jacob whom he loved. *Selah*[32] (Pause)
6 עלה אלהים בתרועה יהוה בקול שופר :	6. God has ascended with a shout, The Lord with the sound of a horn.

27 V. 2a. Dahood (Psalm 1, 283-84) translates העמים 'you strong ones' but in context this is probably unlikely, for עמים 'peoples' is a main subject running throughout the psalm (Ps 47:4, 10). See Peter C. Craigie, "*Psalms* 1-50," in *Word Biblical Commentary* (Waco: Word Books, 1983), 347.

28 V. 2b. לאלהים 'to God' is absent in a few manuscripts. Dahood translates 'you gods,' interpreting it as the vocative *lamedh* (Psalm 1) but in this context, this interpretation is most unlikely. See Peter C. Craigie, "*Psalms* 1-50," in *Word Biblical Commentary* (Waco: Word Books, 1983), 347.

29 V. 3 a. נורא to fear a few manuscripts and the Syriac version of the Old Testament add נו. See Karl Elliger and Wilhelm Rudolph, eds., *Biblia Hebraica Stuttgartensia* (Stuttgart: Biblia Hebraica Stuttgartensia, 1997), 1129.

30 V. 3c. few manuscripts of Old Testament have אלהים 'God.' See Karl Elliger and Wilhelm Rudolph, eds., *Biblia Hebraica Stuttgartensia* (Stuttgart: Biblia Hebraica Stuttgartensia, 1997), 1129.

31 V. 5a. נחלה Septuagint, Syriac version of the Old Testament have suffix 3rd person singular translated as 'his inheritance.' Alternatively, it is translated as 'his inheritance' in the (G) Greek Old Testament and in the (S) Syriac Old Testament. See Peter C. Craigie, "*Psalms* 1-50," in *Word Biblical Commentary* (Waco: Word Books, 1983), 347.

32 V. 5b. סלה 'pause' this is absent in the Syriac Version of the Old Testament. The meaning of Selah is uncertain. Therefore, many suggestions have been made as to what it could mean, based on the renderings of the ancient versions. Septuagint, Symmachus and Theodotion interpret the word διάψαλμα means 'pause'. See Norman H. Snaith, "Selah," *Vetus Testam.* 2, no. I. January (1952): 54. Anderson argues that the Vulgate omits the word completely and Aquila has the word forever. See A. A. Anderson, "The Book of Psalms: Psalms 1-72," in *New Century Bible Commentary*, vol. 1 (London: William B. Eerdmans Publishing Company, 1985), 48. Thus, in agreement with LXX we can take it to indicate a pause in the singing of the psalm, perhaps an instrumental interlude.

7 זמרו אלהים זמרו זמרו למלכנו זמרו :	7. Sing praises to *God*,[33] *sing praises*,[34] sing praises to our king, *sing praises*.[35]
8 כי מלך כל־הארץ אלהים זמרו משכיל :	8. For God is the *king*[36] of all the earth; sing praises with a wisdom psalm.
9 מלך אלהים על־גוים אלהים ישב על־כסא קדשו :	9. God reigns *over the nations*,[37] *God*[38] sits on his holy throne.
נדיבי עמים נאספו עם אלהי אברהם כי לאלהים מגני 10 ארץ מאד נעלה :	10. The nobles of the nations assembled, as the *people of God*[39] of Abraham; For the *rulers* of the earth belong to God, he is highly exalted.

3.2.2. Text Critical Notes

First, the text mentions כל־העמים 'all people,' (Ps 47:1). Anderson rightly points out this phrase as 'all people' with a rhetorical expression. It could mean Israel who was called to be a representative of all the nations.[40] According to C.A. Briggs and E.G. Briggs, כל־העמים 'all people' which indicates Israel is calling upon the foreign people to unite with them in celebrating the triumph of Yahweh by worshipping and honouring Yahweh.[41] Oesterley stresses the eschatological perspectives, and refers to it as an invitation to all the nations to praise God. Dahood considers העמים 'for strong ones,' referring to the heathen

---

33 V. 7a.'Lord,' few manuscripts have לא Septuagint the Geek version of the Old Testament read as ונהלאל. See Karl Elliger and Wilhelm Rudolph, eds., *Biblia Hebraica Stuttgartensia* (Stuttgart: Biblia Hebraica Stuttgartensia, 1997), 1129.

34 V. 7b. זמרו *Piel* imperative masculine plural 'to make music,' however Syriac Version of the Old Testament has in splendor. See Karl Elliger and Wilhelm Rudolph, eds., *Biblia Hebraica Stuttgartensia* (Stuttgart: Biblia Hebraica Stuttgartensia, 1997), 1129.

35 V. 7c. זמרו *Piel* imperative masculine plural, 'to make music,' is missing in several manuscripts and Syriac Version of the Old Testament.

36 V. 8a. מלך noun common masculine, 'king,' many manuscripts added, על over, besides, on, upon. See Karl Elliger and Wilhelm Rudolph, eds., *Biblia Hebraica Stuttgartensia* (Stuttgart: Biblia Hebraica Stuttgartensia, 1997), 1129.

37 V. 9a. על־גוים preposition, noun common masculine plural absolute, 'upon the nations,' several manuscripts and Septuagint added לכ 'all, every.' See Karl Elliger and Wilhelm Rudolph, eds., *Biblia Hebraica Stuttgartensia* (Stuttgart: Biblia Hebraica Stuttgartensia, 1997), 1129.

38 V. 9b. אלהים noun common masculine plural absolute, 'God,' is absent in one manuscript perhaps deleted. See Karl Elliger and Wilhelm Rudolph, eds., *Biblia Hebraica Stuttgartensia* (Stuttgart: Biblia Hebraica Stuttgartensia, 1997), 1129.

39 V. 10a. Reading עם עם as implied by Septuagint and Syriac have μετα and assuming that MT represents a haplography. See Karl Elliger and Wilhelm Rudolph, eds., *Biblia Hebraica Stuttgartensia* (Stuttgart: Biblia Hebraica Stuttgartensia, 1997), 1129.

40 Anderson, *The Book of Psalms: Psalms 1-72*, 361.

41 Augustus Briggs, *The Book of Psalms*, 398.

gods,' it could mean all the gods will come and worship Yahweh, the living God. However, Craigie notes כל־העמים is one of the important points that run through this psalm; for example, verse 4 is the parallel to and synonymous with verse 9, 'all people are called to worship by giving praises.' Though we see different usages of *all people* in this translation, possibly most of the exegetes take the traditional interpretation as people.[42]

Secondly, דבר 'speak' (Ps 47:4). The word דבר in *qal* and *piel* perfect form is translated as 'to speak' and *niphal* is 'to speak with.' For *hiphil* the perfect form is to 'lead.' In the text דבר is in the *hiphil* imperfect 3rd person masculine singular jussive in form, and it is translated as 'subdues.' Krausand others translated דבר as *subdues* peoples under us (Ps 47:4).[43] Therefore, following Kraus, I have translated דבר not as 'to speak' but as 'subdues,' since it is also *hiphil* imperfect.

Thirdly, use of סלה *'pause'* סלה occurs in the middle and end of the division of strophe or change of mood. The term סלה is unique to Psalter literature. סלה is used probably 71 times in the Psalter while three times in the book of Habakkuk. Altogether Selah occurs 74 times in Hebrew Bible and a single appearance is found in Psalms 47:5, in the enthronement psalms.[44] Though סלה occurs only once, it has immense significance especially in the context of worship. There are several meanings given to the term Selah.[45] They are:

1. Selah is taken as a *pause.* Under the meaning of pause we can see the following interpretations about the meaning of Selah: (a) Selah can mean silence. The LXX uses *διάψαλμα* which indicates silence.[46] The Hebrew

42 Prasad, "Psalms 47: A Case Study in Poetic Techniques in the Psalm," 8.

43 Kraus, *Psalms 1-59*, 465. See Leo G. Perdue, " Yahweh Is King over All the Earth: An Exegesis of Psalm 47," *Restoration Quarterly,* vol. 17, no. 2 (1974): 91. Peter C. Craigie, "Psalms 1-50," in *Word Biblical Commentary*, edited by David A. Hubbard and Glenn W. Barker (Waco: Word Books, 1983), 346. Artur Weiser, "The Psalms: A Commentary," in *The Old Testament Library*, edited by Peter Ackroyd (Philadelphia: Westminster John Knox Press, 1962), 374. A. Philip Brown II and Bryan. W Smith, eds., *A Reader's Hebrew Bible* (Zondervan, 2008), 1147.

44 The word Selah is inserted in the following Psalms and in the book of Habakkuk. They are: 3, 4, 7, 20, 21, 24, 32, 39, 44, 46, 47, 48, 49, 50, 52, 54, 55, 57, 59, 60, 61, 62, 66, 67, 68, 75, 76, 77, 81, 82, 83, 84, 85, 87, 88, 89, 140, and 143. The use of Selah in the book of Habakkuk denotes that the poem of Habakkuk was incorporated into the worship of Israel.

45 Anderson, *The Book of Psalms: Psalms 1-72*, 49. O. Palmer Robertson, *The Books of Nahum, Habakkuk, and Zephaniah*: *The International Commentary on the Old Testament,* vol. 28, edited by R. K. Harrison, (Grand Rapids: William B. Eerdmans Publishing Company, 1991), 213. Richard J. Clifford, *Psalms 1-72: Abingdon Old Testament Commentaries* (Nashville: Abingdon Press, 2002), 227.

46 Ernest C. Lucas, *Exploring the Old Testament: A Guide to the Psalms & Wisdom Literature*, vol. 3 (Downers Grove: InterVarsity Press, 2003), 43. Norman H. Snaith, "Selah," *Vetus Testamentum,* vol. 2, no. I (January, 1952): 43-56.A. A. Anderson, "The Book of Psalms:

text reads הגיון סלה, in Greek it is translated διαψαλατος and accordingly, it understands the Hebrew as a construct connection הגיון which means either *thinking or silence*.[47] The root word סלל also instructs worshippers to think and pray at the end of each section. (b) Selah can mean interlude. The Greek word *διάψαλμα* also emphasizes musical interlude.[48] It is intended to signal that the song should be interrupted by an instrumental *ritornellos*.[49] Thus, Selah refers an interlude. (c) Selah can mean sign to repeat. As Selah means *da capo*[50] and it is a sign to repeat in chanting the hymn. *A Reader's Hebrew Bible* puts it in this way סב למעלה השר. *da capo,* 'change in reading,' for the purpose of repeating.[51] Snaith suggests that the choir is to repeat after which the people are to say "Amen" or to say "Praise the Lord."[52] Therefore, Selah indicates a sign to repeat.

2. Selah means *lifting up* the voice. *A Reader's Hebrew Bible,* John Philip and Goldingaysupport Selah as 'lifting up.' *A Reader's Hebrew Bible interprets* סלה as "raising the voice to a higher pitch." It signals change of voice while singing.[53] Philip claims that it is a kind of crescendo mark in music because Selah has got something to do with music.[54] Goldingay translates the word סלה 'to lift up' which means lifting up the voice in worship (Ps 47:5).[55]

3. Selah refers to *kneeling and bowing*. Selah refers to the worshippers who "fell prostrate in respectful homage and submission to God" (cf. Mowinckel, *PIW,* 211).[56] It is an obeisance as a sign of reverence with affirmations of faith in God by the worshippers.[57] According to a tradition maintained in the Mishnah

Psalms 1-72," in *New Century Bible Commentary*, vol. 1 (London: William B. Eerdmans Publishing Company, 1985), 48.

47 Kraus, *Psalms 1-59,* 28-29.

48 *Ritornello* is an Italian word. This is a short instrumental refrain or interlude in a vocal.

49 John Samuel Raj, "Cosmic Judge or Overseer of the Word-Order? The Role of Yahweh Portrayed in Psalm 7," *Bangalore Theological Forum,* vol. XXXIV, no. 2 (2002): 11.

50 *Da capo* is a musical term in Italian. It is a composer command to repeat the previous part of music.

51 A. Philip Brown II and Bryan W. Smith, eds., *A Reader's Hebrew Bible* (Zondervan, 2008), 1147.

52 Snaith, "Selah," 55.

53 Brown II and Bryan. W. Smith, eds., *A Reader's Hebrew Bible*, 1147. See Charles A. Briggs, "An Inductive Study of Selah," *Jewish Biblical Literature* 18 (1899): 142.

54 John Philips, *Exploring Psalms: An Expository Commentary*, vol. 2 (Grand Rapids: Kregel Publications., 2002), 30. A. A. Anderson, "The Book of Psalms: Psalms 1-72," in *New Century Bible Commentary*, vol. 1 (London: William B. Eerdmans Publishing Company, 1985), 49.

55 Goldingay, *Psalms 42-89*, 74.

56 Anderson, *The Book of Psalms: Psalms 1-72*, 49.

57 Eaton, *The Psalms,* 13.

(*Tamia* vii, 3), the daily psalm of the Second Temple was sung in three parts, and the conclusion of each part had a pause during which two priests blew their trumpets, and the worshippers prostrated themselves in submission to God. Based on this tradition, a search throughout the Psalter reveals that this could refers to Selah.[58]

4. The word Selah refers to a concluding expression *forever, always*.[59] The Palestinian tradition supports the idea that Selah would indicate the place where the blessing of God for ever, or the benediction, should be connected with the recitation of the psalms.[60] Hence, Selah means a sign of forever or always.

As seen above the word Selah usually occurs at a place where a very significant statement has been made, making a good place for a break to reflect, meditation or pause. Selah help the worshipers to ponder in the word of God and it is also a time to re-evaluate their relationship with Yahweh the king. Thus, Selah plays an essential part in worship.

Fourthly, זמרו 'to make music' (Ps 47:7, 8). This word occurs in verse 7c. זמרו *piel* imperative masculine plural, 'to make music,' is missing in several manuscripts and Syriac version of the Old Testament. According to *BDB* (2167) זמר means 'make music in praise of God' or make music. Briggs points out that the 'repeated emphasis on instrumental accompaniment.'[61] This is how we see the variations of the word זמר. Kraus argues that this imperative call is repeated five times in verses 7 and 8 probably for the sake of special emphasis. It most likely addresses the temple singers and musicians. The Hebrew word זמר 'to sing praises' is connected with מזמר 'Psalm.'[62] Eaton claims the renewed call to praise has an ecstatic quality, as the same verb זמר to sing praises or to make music of psalmody is repeated five times just in verses 7 and 8.[63] זמר, "which puts the emphasis on the music: It covers both singing and playing."[64]

The word for psalm מזמר comes from this root word which means a religious song. I assume that repeated uses of זמר inmusic is one of the poetical expressions of the psalmist in the Psalter.[65] I have used 'sing praises' in my translation because this זמר is in *piel* imperfect form that is suitable to the

58 Norman H. Snaith, "Selah," *Vetus Testamentum,* no. 2 (January, 1952): 43.

59 John Samuel, Raj, "Cosmic Judge or Overseer of the Word-Order? The Role of Yahweh Portrayed in Psalm 7." *Bangalore Theological Forum,* vol. XXXIV, no. 2 (2002): 11.

60 Briggs, "An Inductive Study of Selah," 141-142.

61 Augustus Briggs, *A Critical and Exegetical Commentary on the Book of Psalms,* 399.

62 A. A. Anderson, "The Book of Psalms: Psalms 1-72," in *New Century Bible Commentary,* vol. 1 (London: William B. Eerdmans Publishing Company, 1985), 363-364.

63 Eaton, *The Psalms,* 193.

64 Goldingay, *Songs from a Strange Land: Psalms 42-51*, 73.

65 Goldingay, *Songs from a Strange Land: Psalms 42-51*, 73.

text and its context, where people are making music or giving praises to God. Why is *piel* suitable for the worship context? *Piel* is in active form and it usually expresses intensity or repetition. *Piel* imperfect expresses the idea of possibility; it is also used to express continuity.

Fifthly, עם אלהי means 'people of God.' This phrase is found in Psalm 47 verse 10. [a-a] עם אלהי 'people of God,' it has been proposed עם אלהי 'people with the God.' There are more textual problems with the phrase עם אלהי אברהם 'people of the God of Abraham.' This is how the MT reads, which parallels the first part thereby indicating that all the nations are now regarded as the people of the covenant cf. Gen 12:1-4. Whereas LXX and Syriac read עִם for עַם thus, changing the translation to "with the God of Abraham." *BHS* conflates the two readings, arguing one should read, עִם עַם "The princes of the peoples are gathered together with the people of the God Abraham. Perhaps this suggestion is preferable, pointing to a cultic assembly of all nations together with Israel to demonstrate their acceptance of Yahweh's rule."[66] Nations coming together to worship Yahweh symbolizes the fulfillment of God promise to Abraham (Gen 12:1-4).

Finally, the word אסף means 'assemble.' This word appears in verse 10. אסף 'assemble,' in *niphal* form whereas *qal* and *piel* means 'to gather,' for *pual* 'to be together.' In the text it is in *niphal* form, נאספו verb *niphal* perfect 3rd person common plural, and it is translated as 'assemble.' I assume that the word assemble gives sense to the text and context as well because assemble talks about all the members together. It means that even though people live in different places, they are all one under the kingship of Yahweh. They all come as one body and worship the true God.

3.2.3. Form of the Psalm

The psalm as a whole belongs to the form of songs of praise or hymn. The psalm glorifies Yahweh's majesty.[67] For Gerstenberger, the psalm falls in two parts, each of them contains all the essentials of a Hebrew song of praise.[68] The hymnic beginning in verse 1 talks about imperative calls for exultation. It is followed by the word כי 'for' (Ps 47:2, 8) characteristic of songs of praise in which the reasons for the glorification of Yahweh kingship are expressed.[69]

Terrien rightly points out that with regard to the form of Psalm 47, it is considered a hymn of praise. It comprises two strophes that face each other

---

66 Perdue, "Yahweh is King over All the Earth, An Exegesis of Psalm 47," 97.

67 Kraus, *Psalms 1-59*, 466.

68 Erhard S. Gerstenberger, *Psalms, Part I, with An Introduction to Cultic Poetry: The Forms of the Old Testament Literature*, Vol. XIV (Grand Rapids: William B. Eerdmans Publishing Company, 1988), 196.

69 Kraus, *Psalms 1-59*, 466.

in parallel symmetry with the proclamation of divine kingship over the whole earth.[70]

3.2.4. Structure of the Psalm

Ollenburger notes that the psalm structure indicates liturgical character and is divided into two parts verses 2-6 and verses 7-10.[71] According to the literary structure of Psalm 47, there are two divisions, both begin with a call to praise verses 1 and 6. Anderson claims that there are two main sections, verses 2-5 and verses 7-10.[72] Even Craigie talks about two visibly structured literary units in Psalm 47, however it is not the same. For Craigie, it is a hymn having two parallel visible structures and each section repeats the call to praise:[73]

A. Call to praise (v 2)
B. And praise of God's victories (vv 3-6).
A. Call to praise (v 7)
B. And praise of God's kingship (vv 8-10).

The word כי 'for' introduces the "substance of praise and concluding declaration of praise providing a structure for the psalm as a whole." Both the sections of praise are parallel in the use of מלך 'king' and כל הארצ 'the whole earth.'[74]

3.2.5. Repetitions

When we talk about repetition in the context of worship, it means not just simply repetition but repetition with a purpose. There are several repetitions of words and phrases in Psalm 47. The overall unity of themes in the psalm is emphasized by the repeated usage of the following words; עם 'people' in verses 2, 4, 10, מלך 'king' in verses 3, 7, 8 and ארץ 'earth' verses 3, 8, 10, כל 'all' repeated in verses 2, 8. All these words add to the portrayal of the metaphor of the kingship of Yahweh.[75] These words impact not only Israel as a nation but also other peoples or nations so that they too will worship Yahweh. Repetitions qualify the explicit reference for worship of Yahweh the

---

70 Samuel L. Terrien, "The Psalms: Strophic Structure and Theological Commentary: Psalms 1-72," in *Eerdmans Critical Commentary,* vol. 1, edited by David Noel Freedman (Grand Rapids: Eerdmans Publishing Company, 2003), 377.

71 Ben C. Ollenburger, *Zion the City of the Great King: A Theological Symbol of the Jerusalem Cult* (Sheffield: Sheffield Academic Press, 1987), 45.

72 Anderson, *The Book of Psalms: New Century Bible Commentary*, 360.

73 Craigie, *Psalms 1-50*, 347.

74 Craigie, *Psalms 1-50,* 347.

75 Craigie, *Psalms 1-50*, 347.

great king.[76] The word זמר 'sing' occurs 4 times in verse 7 and once in verse 8. This word communicates that the context of worship always involves praising and shouting to God. In other words, in the act of worship both Israel and her people are to sing praises about the ultimate sovereignty of God.[77]

The repeated word כי 'for' is found in verses 2 and 8. This may be very insignificant but in the context of worship it carries meaning. In ritual performances, this might have been repeated as a sign of responding to Yahweh.[78] From verses 8-9, we see the phrases of repetition in the form of parallelism, king of all the earth, reigns over the nations, enthroned on his holy throne. All these rhetorical expressions persuade people to believe in and worship God. The opening verse exhorts the people to worship Yahweh and ends with people again which is parallel with the opening verse.[79] It shows that Yahweh is the great king who ascended the throne so that everyone will see the glory of God and worship God whole-heartedly.[80]

3.3. Comments in Relation to the Kingship Metaphor

This section is not a commentary of the text but is an explanation of the important key words and phrases which are related to kingship metaphor of Yahweh and its implication for worship. *Firstly,* the verb form מָלַךְ means 'reigns.' The verb *qal* is perfect 3rd person masculine singular. Rogerson claims that, God reigns, that is 'actively exercises his kingly power.' Those who give the psalm a dramatic setting prefer to mention 'God has become king' (Mowinckel) or 'God has ascended his throne as king.'[81] I assume that it is more or less the permanent kingship of God, therefore I would prefer to say God, who sits on his holy throne, is king all the time.

Secondly, 'sing praises to our king' (Ps 47:7). Prasad points out that there is a debate over the phrase 'sing praises to our king' as to whom it is addressed. Dahood, Roberts and Watson suggest that pagan gods were called upon to praise God. But this view does not hold justice to the text as most of the translations (like *RSV, NAB*, and *NRSV*) support and take it as 'to God.'[82] Sing

76 John Goldingay, "Psalms 42-89," in *Baker Commentary on the Old Testament Wisdom and Psalms*, vol. 2, edited by Tremper Longman III (Grand Rapids: Baker Academic, 2007), 77, 79.

77 Craigie, *Psalms 1-50*, 348.

78 Gerstenberger, *Psalms Part I, With An Introduction to Cultic Poetry,* 196.

79 Goldingay, *Psalms 42-89*, 80-81.

80 Jacob Prasad, "Psalms 47: A Case Study in Poetic Techniques in the Psalm," *Bible Bhashyam,* vol. XXIX, no. 1 (March, 2003): 23.

81 J. W. Rogerson, *Psalm 1-50* (London: Cambridge University Press, 1977), 223.

82 Prasad, "Psalms 47: A Case Study in Poetic Techniques in the Psalm," 12. The commands in both sections mention to shout, or sing, and it is based on the kingship of Yahweh. The two characters of Yahweh the great king, in Psalm 47 are mentioned here. The first section

praises to our king is associated to the kingship metaphor of Yahweh because he is the greatest King among all the kings. Therefore, due praises belongs to him. Thus, the Psalm clearly presents the kingship of Yahweh over the nations.

Thirdly, יהוה עליון 'the Lord of Most High' (Ps 47:3-5). The word ןוילע 'Most High' is the poetic name of Yahweh, as, Most High is exalted in majesty over all the earth.[83] Poetic parallelism sets the expression 'great king' in parallel with Yahweh ןוילע. The transcendence of יהוה עליון 'the Most High God' knows no geographical limitations, he is worthy to be worshipped by all humankind with awe, gratitude and humble recognition (cf. Deut 7:23).[84]

Fourthly, מגני 'shields' (Ps 47:10) is noun common both plural construct. The commentators like Arthur G. Clarke[85] and Elmer A. Leslie[86] have translated מגני as princes, protectors of the people. Eaton translate מגני as 'shields.'[87] Anderson suggests the shields seems to be another expression for 'the princes of the peoples.' Our shield is parallel to thine anointed and the same word is identical with our king, therefore this can be consider the 'rulers' of the earth.[88] According to Craigie מגני 'shields' סגני 'rulers' is read with *BHS*, as implied by the context.[89] I also support Craigie's view taking as *rulers,* not as shields, because it gives a better argument to my work, as I study the kingship metaphor in the enthronement psalms.

The above terms relate to the kingship metaphor of Yahweh because it reflected the power and authority of Yahweh above all. Thus, these terms help us to understand better in relation to the kingship of Yahweh.

---

affirms the identity of Yahweh as *Elyon,* the great king. The second section is based on the status of God as king of the whole world. See Ben C. Ollenburger, *Zion the City of the Great King: A Theological Symbol of the Jerusalem Cult* (Sheffield: Sheffield Academic Press, 1987), 45.

83 Augustus Briggs, *The Book of Psalms*, 398. He is awe-inspiring, to be revered and regarded as majestic. Yahweh is a great king not only of Israel but of all nations, universally (95:3, 97:7, 98:6, and 99:4). Yahweh is greatly exalted, as the great king, victorious over the enemies. The triumphant nature of the living God is seen at the entrance of holy sanctuary and throne. 399-400. See (Gen 14:18-20, Deut 32:8, Num 24:16, 2 Sam 22:14, Hos 11:7, Lam 3:35, Isa 14:14, Dan 4:17, Pss 9:2, 18:13, 21:7, 46:4, 47:2-3, 50:14, 57:2, 73:11,77:10,78:35, 83:18, 91:1).

84 Terrien, *The Psalms: Strophic Structure and Theological Commentary*, 377.

85 Arthur G. Clarke, *Analytical Studies in the Psalms* (Grand Rapids: Kregel Publications, 1979), 132.

86 Leslie, *The Psalms: Translated and Interpreted in the Light of Hebrew Life and Worship*, 67.

87

88 Anderson, "The Book of Psalms: Psalms 1-72," 366.

89 Craigie, "Psalms 1-50," 347.

3.4. Comments in Relation to Worship

I have found three major points in this Psalm in relation to worship. *First, universal worship.* The whole of history points to the sovereignty of God that embraces the whole world. By this very thought, the psalm links together the beginning and the end of history in that it follows the concept at the beginning of the *heilsgeschichte* in Israel and looks to the completion of the *heilsgeschichte* in Yahweh's enthronement as king of the whole world.[90] Weiserand Mark D. Futato hold the view that the context of Psalm 47 demonstrates that "the nations are no longer fighting against the Lord but are worshipping him throughout the earth."[91] This refers to the theocentric and universal worship of Yahweh. Weiser holds that the psalm exclusively focuses on God who is the only one worthy to be worshipped and who is highly exalted and sits enthroned for ever as the Lord of the whole world.[92]

The text uses the phrase אלחים עם אברהם 'as the people of the God of Abraham.' The MT עם 'people' parallels the first stichos, thereby indicating that all the nations are now regarded as the people of covenant (Gen 12:1-3). However, the LXX and Syriac read עִם for עָם thus changing the translation to 'with the God of Abraham.'[93]

Let us now look at the context of עם אלחי אברהם 'as the people of the God of Abraham' (Ps 47:10). Muilenburg and Perdue support the cultic context and claim that all the nations will join in the worship of Yahweh and "the nations will receive the divine blessing through their relation to Israel" (Ps 102:23).[94] According to Perdue, this is more appropriate to the cultic context where all the nations come together with Israel to worship Yahweh. Together with Israel, they show their acceptance of Yahweh's kingship and worship his sovereignty.[95] Thus, the words 'all you people' portray Israel calling upon the foreigners to unite with them in celebrating the triumph of Yahweh.[96]

---

90 Weiser, "The Psalms: A Commentary," 377.

91 Mark D. Futato, *Interpreting the Psalms: An Exegetical Handbook* (Grand Rapids: Kregel Academic & Professional, 2007), 106.

92 Weiser, *The Psalms,* 378-379.

93 Elliger and Rudolph, *Biblia Hebraica Stuttgartensia*, 1129.

94 James Muilenburg, "Abraham and the Nations: Blessing and World History," *Interpretation* 19, no. 4 (1965): 396. See Peter C. Craigie, "Psalms 1-50," in *Word Biblical Commentary*, edited by David A. Hubbard and Glenn W. Barker (Waco: Word Books, 1983), 350. John Goldingay, "Psalms 42-89," in *Baker Commentary on the Old Testament Wisdom and Psalms*, edited by Tremper Longman III, vol. 2 (Grand Rapids: Baker Academic, 2007), 80. John Goldingay, *Old Testament Theology: Israel's Faith*, vol. 2 (Illinois: InterVarsity Press, 2006), 832.

95 Perdue, "Yahweh Is King over All the Earth, An Exegesis of Psalm 47," 97.

96 Charles Augustus Briggs and Emilie Grace Briggs, "A Critical and Exegetical Commentary on the Book of Psalms," in *The International Critical Commentary,* vol. 1 (Edinburgh:

Now, let us look at the two main views of the translation for the phrase עם אלהי אברהם. (1), I deal with the view of the scholars who favoured the translation 'with the people of the God of Abraham.' Kraus and Anderson support the translation 'with the people of the God of Abraham.' They adopt the translation of 'with the people of the God of Abraham' because it is a sign for a realization of the universal rule of Yahweh.[97] Other nations gather together 'with the people of the God of Abraham' to give reverence to Yahweh. This reveals that the kingship tradition has reference to the Abrahamic promise (Gen 12:1-3, 22:8). Here the word 'with' refers to 'coming together' and worshipping Yahweh who is the God of Abraham. This reference to Abraham also suggests that he is 'the father of all the faithful' and the blessing of Abraham has a universal aspect.[98] Nations coming together to worship Yahweh symbolizes that they become one great people of God, the people of the God of Abraham. Therefore, the promise of Abraham has found its fulfilment.[99]

(2), I deal with the view of the scholars like Muilenburg and Wilcock who supported the translation 'as the people of the God of Abraham.'Muilenburg and Wilcock opt for the translation עם אלהי אברהם 'as the people of the God of Abraham.' Israel rejoices because her God has become king over all the earth and that the representatives of the peoples gather together 'as the people of Abraham's God.' This shows the nations become one in the oneness of the God of Abraham.[100] The nobles of the nations assemble 'as the people of the God of Abraham.'[101] God is seated on his holy throne. Therefore, the nobles of the nations assemble 'as the people of the God of Abraham (Ps 47:9-10).'[102]

T & T Clark Ltd, 1906), 398.

97 Hans-Joachim Kraus, "Psalms 1-59," in *A Continental Commentary*, translated by Hilton C. Oswald (Minneapolis: Fortress Press, 1993), 470. Hamilton, Victor P, "The Book of Genesis Chapters 1-17" in *NICOT,* edited by R. K. Harrison (Grand Rapids: William B. Eerdmans Publishing Company, 1991), 372. Theodore Mascarenhas, *The Missionary Function of Israel in Psalms 67, 96, and 117* (New York: University Press of America, 2005), 19. Christopher J.H. Wright, *The Mission of God: Unlocking the Bible's Grand Narrative* (Illinois: InterVarsity Press, 2006), 478-483.

98 Anderson, "The Book of Psalms: Psalms 1-72," 66.

99 Weiser, "The Psalms: A Commentary," 378. See Christopher J. H. Wright, *Knowing Jesus through the Old Testament* (Chennai: UESI Publication Trust, 2001), 83-85.

100 Muilenburg, "Abraham and the Nations: Blessing and World History," 395.

101 Michael Wilcock, "The Message of Psalms 1-72," in *The Bible Speaks Today*, edited by Alec Motyer (England: InterVarsity Press, 2009), 172.William R. Taylor, "The Book of Psalms," in *The Interpreter's Bible,* vol. IV, edited by George Arthur Buttrick (New York: Abingdon Press, 1955), 247. J. W. Rogerson, *Psalm 1-50* (London: Cambridge University Press, 1977), 223. Artur Weiser, "The Psalms: A Commentary," in *The Old Testament Library*, edited by Peter Ackroyd (Philadelphia: Westminster Press, 1962), 375.

102 Geoffrey W. Grogan, *Psalms: The Two Horizons Old Testament Commentary Psalms* (Grand Rapids: Wm. B. Eerdmans Publishing Co, 2008), 271.

The scholars who opt for 'as' affirm that the nations are treated as equal to the people of the God of Abraham as they worship together with the same God. This is linked with the Genesis account which mentions the blessing of all nations through Abraham.

There is also a section of scholars who support both the translations. For instance, Gerstenberger claims foreigners gather together, "as the people of the God of Abraham or together with the people of the God of Abraham." The ideas of 'with' or 'as' both stand for a worldwide aspect to celebrate the kingship of Yahweh.[103]

As Gerstenberger supports both the words 'with' and 'as', as per my opinion the translations of the phrase עם אלהי אברהם 'as' or 'with' 'the people of the God of Abraham' have the significance of Yahweh's universal reign. Therefore, whichever way the phrase is translated, it is a fulfilment of Yahweh's promise to Abraham. However, I support Muilenburg and Wilcock's translation 'as the people of the God of Abraham' because in God through Jesus Christ there is no distinction between Jews and Gentles which means all are one in Christ. It is said, "For all of you are one in Christ Jesus" (Gal 3:20, 28, Eph 2:11:22, Rom 12:3, 1 Cor 12:27). All nations will become his chosen ones along with Israel by worshipping the same God. I want to argue that the text indicates all the nations are now the people of the covenant. Thus, nations gathered together 'as the people of the God of Abraham' implies equality for all the peoples when it comes to worship of Yahweh the king.

Secondly, the psalm suggests *singing and praising in the worship of Yahweh.* Singing and praising has a *doxological* claim. The Psalmist calls for a shout to God, a shout of joy and singing praises to God. All these components signify joy and happiness in the presence of God. Eaton states, "This is a hymn, surely a high moment of worship, the excitement in the praise runs high."[104] Psalm 47 contains the standard call of the peoples to join in the worship of God. The cultic acts expressed here are clapping hands, giving praise and shouting to the living God. God is portrayed as the great king who performs great deeds beyond human understanding and, therefore, all peoples must praise God with a song of joy.[105] Making noises and clapping hands are considered to be an expression of the inner feeling of a person in the presence of God. Therefore, Psalm 47 urges all people to shout to God with resounding voices and give homage because Yahweh alone is worthy to receive all our praises and adoration.[106] We can rightly conclude that Psalm 47 portrays that

103 Gerstenberger, *Psalms Part I, with An Introduction to Cultic Poetry: The Forms of the Old Testament Literature*, 198.

104 Eaton, *The Psalms*, 45.

105 Prasad, "Psalms 47: A Case Study in Poetic Techniques in the Psalm," 23.

106 Goldingay, *Psalms 42-89*, 61, 77.

worship components have vital implications because theologically they are considered to be a confession of faith through outward expressions.

Thirdly, the psalm clearly mentions being *united in one by worshiping one true God.* Rogerson, Anderson, and Menezes comment that the nations stand together before God. "The outworking of the process of election in history may look like unfair favoritism but its culmination is the day when the princes of the nations stand before God together with the elect" (Ps 47:10).[107] Psalm 47:9-10 refers to an assembly of the nations and it clearly focuses on the concept of oneness in the kingdom of God. The calls all nations together with the people of the God of Abraham to worship. Therefore, for the psalmist, the kingship metaphor has reference to the Abrahamic promise in Gen 12:1-3, 22:18). All the families of the earth must worship God and "pay tribute of glory and power."[108] "The Psalmist shares his experiences of salvation with his fellow human beings in the congregation in order that they too may praise and worship Yahweh.[109] We can see a parallel concept in other Psalm (cf. Ps 22:24 where it is indicated that Yahweh does not despise any one, all humans can share his salvation.

The nations have assembled together by their own free will to worship their common divine king. They have all become one people belonging to God. The psalm is in line with the eschatological understanding of the NT since both the Testaments hold the view that there will be "one flock and one shepherd."[110] Thus, now the blessing of Abraham has found its fulfilment. The faith in which he confronted God is now the spirit in which all families will be united as one and participate in worshipping the Lord as they stand before him.[111] We can also see the point that the nations were able to share in Israel's privileged relationship with Yahweh. The nations acknowledge the sovereignty of Yahweh in the world.[112] The central theme of this particular point is that it is the mighty works of Yahweh which unite the people to one true God.

Inviting all people implies that the grace of Yahweh is for all people and in response to that, all nations are called to worship Yahweh faithfully and sincerely (cf. Jer 10:7, 10; Mal 11). Worshipping God is not limited to a particular nation, but includes all the nations. Thus, the motif of universal worship and also singing, praising in the worship have contributed the vast implications in relation to worship.

---

107 Rogerson, *Psalm 1-50*, 223.

108 Menezes, "Theology of Israel's Hymns," 44.

109 Kondasingu Jesurathnam, *Dalit Liberative Hermeneutics: Indian Christian Dalit Interpretation of Psalm 22* (Delhi: ISPCK, 2010), 53.

110 Weiser, *The Psalms: A Commentary*, 378.

111 Weiser, *The Psalms: A Commentary*, 378.

112 Goldingay, *Psalms 42-89*, 81.

3.5. Theological Concerns Pertaining to the Kingship Metaphor of God

This section deals with the theological themes which emerge from the kingship metaphor in the exegetical study of Psalm 47. The theological concerns relating to the kingship metaphor of Yahweh is discussed from the perspective of denotation and connotations.

3.5.1. Kingship and Sovereignty

Sovereignty is a denotation of the kingship of Yahweh and it refers to the rule of God. The psalmist uses תחת, which means 'subjugate' or putting 'underneath', in the context of other nations (Ps 47:4). The metaphor of 'under our feet' most probably arises from the practice and artistic symbolism of victory and it is linked with the kingship metaphor.[113] Here, the victory of Yahweh over the enemies is seen as a demonstration of Yahweh's worldwide might and proves the legitimacy of his claim to be king of all the earth. Not only did Yahweh defeat other nations, he also defeated their gods and so revealed his sovereignty over all the world.[114] The sovereignty of Yahweh always means unlimited power of justice and peace of God over the world.[115]

When the psalmist says 'he subjugates… nations under our feet,' the context of the text indicates that the word 'subjugate' does not carry a negative connotation, but has a theological conviction about God's dealings with Israel and the nations under his kingship. It points to the justice of Yahweh whose universal reign would one day be acknowledged by all. Therefore, the word 'subjugate' means the just rule of God that will be exercised over all the nations.[116] All the benefits from God gratefully received in Israel's history would also eventually be a matter of gratitude for the rest of the nations. The only appropriate response to blessings and benefits received at God's hands was worship and obedience. All nations need to come within the sphere of God's blessing.[117] The fact that Yahweh will reign in justice will cause the nations to worship and bring their praise to him.[118]

113 Craigie, *Psalms 1-50*, 349. See Leo G. Perdue, "Yahweh is King over All the Earth: An Exegesis of Psalm 47," *Restoration Quarterly* 17, no. 2 (1974): 94. James Luther Mays, *The Lord Reigns: A Theological Handbook to the Psalms* (Louisville: Westminster John Knox Press, 1994), 14-15.

114 Perdue, "Yahweh is King over All the Earth: An Exegesis of Psalm 47," 94.

115 Mays, *The Lord Reigns: A Theological Handbook to the Psalms*, 14-15.

116 Christopher J. H. Wright, *The Mission of God: Unlocking the Bible's Grand Narrative* (Illinois: InterVarsity Press, 2006), 474-475.

117 Wright, *The Mission of God*, 478.

118 Wright, *The Mission of God*, 480.

Yahweh possesses the power to overcome all the forces which are against the kingship of God. As a result, the theological significance in the idea of dominion brought out in the enthronement psalms is that Yahweh is above all nations and gods and is capable of bringing them under his kingship. Yahweh exercises his dominion with justice rather than exploitation.Yahweh's dominion over the people and nature implies the fact that he created them and he is definitely Lord. Thus, the psalmist demonstrates Yahweh's kingship as solidly rooted in creation.[119] God proves the infinite greatness of his might and the pre-eminence of his kingship even over the gods in that he is the creator of the whole universe.[120] Yahweh is sovereign over people and everything that he has made. All this causes people to worship him. Therefore, Yahweh deserves to be exalted above all kings and gods.

The denotation of sovereignty denotes the distinctive power of Yahweh. This power is used positively for establishing justice and peace among the nations. Yahweh is enthroned and seated on high as King of kings. Therefore, he deserves to be worshipped.

3.5.2. Kingship and Universality

Universality is a connotative meaning of Yahweh's kingship. Yahweh is the king, above all the kings; therefore he deserves to be revered. The metaphor of the kingship of Yahweh explicitly depicts universal worship.

The exegetical studies explicitly demonstrate that Yahweh is the king of Israel and king of all the nations. As shown in exegesis, we see that מלך גדול על־כל־הארץ 'great king over all the earth' (Ps 47:3). כי מלך כל־הארץ אלהים 'for God is the king over all the earth' (Ps 47:8) מלך אלהים על־גוים 'Yahweh reigns over all the earth' (Ps 47:9). These phrases point to the universal and immediate ground of the kingship of Yahweh in relation to all his vassals, both in Israel and to all the people.[121] The declaration that 'Yahweh is the king over the whole world' contains the idea of Yahweh's special relationship with the nation of Israel and to other nations.[122] This special relationship represents his particularity while his relationship the other nations shows universality of his plans. Yahweh's kingship knows no limitations because he is the king of the universe worthy to be worshipped by all humankind with awe, gratitude, and humble recognition (cf. Deut 7:23).[123] Psalm 47 particularly recognizes the universal implications of universal kingdom that all peoples shall assemble

---

119 Shawn W. Flynn, *YHWH is King: The Development of Divine Kingship in Ancient Israel* (Leiden: Koninklijke Brill NV, 2014), 40.

120 Weiser, *The Psalms: A Commentary*, 626.

121 Craigie, *Psalms 1-50*, 349.

122 Moore, *Moving Beyond Symbol and Myth,* 238.

123 Terrien, *The Psalms: Strophic Structure and Theological Commentary*, 377.

"as the people of the God of Abraham" (Ps 47: 9).[124] The power of the heavens and the earth belong to Yahweh who rules over them and is highly exalted and enthroned forever as the God of the whole world.[125] As a result, he is not only king over the chosen nation, but he is the king over all nations.

In this paragraph I deal with the phrases that are significant to the idea of universal worship. There are translation variations for "people of the God of Abraham." For example, "The people are gathered unto the people of the God of Abraham" (Ps 47:9 *KJV*). Most of the versions translate this as "the people of the God of Abraham" (*RSV, NIV* and *NAS*)." Various interpretations are also followed among scholars in regard to this phrase. Craigie[126] and Kraus[127] translate it as "with the people of the God of Abraham," while Weiser[128] Eaton[129] and Terrien[130] translate it as "the people of the God of Abraham." Eaton interprets it as "all peoples will become the people of the God of Abraham, and their shields (rulers) will belong to God in loyalty and service."[131]

Leslie translates as "along with the people of the God of Abraham." He interprets it as the nations of the earth, the pagan people, recognize the supremacy of Israel's God. So they gather with the God of Abraham. In the psalmist's thought, however, they remain as vassals of Israel. In order to take part in the blessings of Israel, they join themselves to Abraham's God.[132] Some ancient versions (LXX, Syr) and also modern commentators read "with the people of Abraham" instead of the MT "[as] the people of the God of Abraham."[133]

I am not fully convinced by Leslie's comment because I support the translation "as the people of the God of Abraham" which gives inclusive and equal standing with Israel. Looking at translation variations and interpretation of "as" or "into," the people of the God of Abraham, it broadens the horizon in such a way that even foreign people are gathered as the people of the God of Abraham. It presents a feeling of oneness with all the peoples which brings about true universal worship of Yahweh. The idea of Yahweh as the creator of the world and the king above all gods leads to the belief that God is not only the God of Israel, but of the entire world. Also, it means that not just Israel

124 Watts, "Psalms of Trust, Thanksgiving, and Praise," 403.

125 Goldingay, *Songs from a Strange Land: Psalms 42-51*, 80.

126 Craigie, *Psalms 1-50*, 346.

127 Kraus, *Psalms 1-59*, 346.

128 Weiser, *The Psalms: A Commentary*, 374.

129 Eaton, *The Psalms,* 192.

130 Terrien, *The Psalms: Strophic Structure and Theological Commentary: Psalms 1-72*, 376.

131 Eaton, *The Psalms,* 194.

132 Leslie, *The Psalms*, 67.

133 Terrien, *The Psalms: Strophic Structure and Theological Commentary: Psalms 1-72*, 78.

should pay homage to God but all the families of all people are encouraged to do so before Yahweh.[134]

Universalism in the kingship of Yahweh always involves both vertical and horizontal aspects. On the horizontal axis in Psalm 47, Israel exhorts the nations to praise Yahweh. The reference to Jacob conveys the tradition of how Israel gained its territory and Abraham father of all nations (Ps 47:5, 10, Gen 12). As king of all the earth and nations, God is depicted as the universal sovereign. On the vertical axis, God is symbolized as ruling from heaven over all the earth.[135] Briggs affirms that worshipping God is not limited to a particular nation but includes all nations. Even if the nations have their own gods, the God of Israel is the king over them all (95:3).[136]

My view is that by faith, all nations will become the children of Abraham. The God of Abraham has universal significance and this idea is parallel to Genesis 12:2-3. Here, the Lord made a commitment to bless Abraham so that he will be a blessing to the people and nations. This is how the call of Abraham is very significant in the concept of universalism. We also see a parallel concept from the prophet Isaiah's oracles where it talks about the worship that God demands. 'I am coming to gather all nations and tongues and they shall come and shall see my glory' (Isa 66:18-20). The prophet declares that all nations will come and worship the king of kings.The kingship of Yahweh is acknowledged and celebrated in the worship of Israel. The object of Yahweh's kingship, achieved through the aspect of its *universality* is to call upon all the nations and give them the privilege to come into his presence. All nations are welcome to come into his presence to worship and rejoice. Thus, universality is a connotation of the kingship of Yahweh who is in control of everything both above and below.

3.5.3. Kingship and Pause

As shown in my exegetical study סלה *'pause'* is associated with the connotation of Yahweh's kingship as worshippers pause in the presence of Yahweh (Ps 47:5). In my exegetical study, I translate סלה as *pause* following Eaton's translation. The theology of pause and kingship are closely linked. People exalt Yahweh as the King of kings and pause in reverence. Therefore, סלה is referred to as a liturgical use of the Psalter.[137] As a result, the worshippers acknowledge God's sovereignty and the congregation is asked to think or

134 Tate, *Psalms 51-100*, 149.

135 Jo-Marí Schäder, "Psalm 47-How Universal Is Its Universalism? An Intra-Inter-and Extratextual Analysis of the Poem" Magister Artium in Ancient Languages and-Cultural Studies in the Faculty of Humanities (Thesis, University of Pretoria, 2008), 67.

136 Augustus Briggs, *A Critical and Exegetical Commentary on the Book of Psalms*, 294.

137 Raj, "Cosmic Judge or Overseer of the Word-Order?" 11.

reflect upon what has been already said or sung. Briggs clearly notices that there is an absence of Selah in the major portion of kingship Psalms 93-100 though these psalms are intrinsically suited for public worship. He points out that Selah was already in certain psalms before the Hebrew Psalter was finally arranged in its present form, and for that the editors made no additions to its use of Selah.[138] However, the mention of Selah even one single time in the kingship psalms has implications for worship. Pausing is considered one of the vital components in worship, where worshippers can communicate with God while pausing.

There are cross references regarding pausing in the presence of God. For instance, "Be still before the Lord" (Ps 37:7[a]). For God alone my soul waits in silence, for my hope is from him" (Pss 62:5). Both the psalms talk about דמם which means quiet or pause. דמם shows two connotations. The first is to be silent, and this is for a variety of reasons. For instance, it is a time of seeking help from God (Ex 15: 16, 1 Sam 2:9, Ps 31:17). But there is also the silence of trust. In doing this, a worshipper meditates on and testifies the kingship of Yahweh.[139] The psalmist reminds the people to pause and reflect on the majesty and faithfulness of Yahweh. Therefore, pausing is a tool for stimulating the mind of worshippers. One must pause in the presence of the Lord, meditating on who Yahweh is and embracing the awesomeness of God. The main intention of pause is to encourage thoughtful reflection on the meaning of the song and word of God.[140]

Selah can be considered as lifting up of the voice and it is parallel to the function of concentration. The purpose of lifting up is not that music has to be louder. To me, *to lift up* means the hearts of worshippers are to be lifted up in worship and praise to God for the truths that connect our life to God. In this, the worshippers are focusing on the majesty of Yahweh by fully submitting themselves to God. Eaton points out that when Selah occurs, this might have been the time for a general submission with an affirmation from the worshippers.[141] The psalmists affirm that the act of pausing is an essential element in Israel's worship. Hence, even for today's worship, pausing can be a time where worshipers can reflect from the word of God, sing songs and respond to God whole-heartedly. Besides, the congregation can also pause for a moment in meditation with a spirit of humility before Yahweh, the king.

---

138 Briggs, "An Inductive Study of Selah," 133.

139 John N. Oswalt, "דמם," in *New International Dictionary of Old Testament Theology & Exegesis,* vol. I. edited by Willem VanGemeren (Grand Rapids: Zondervan, 1997), 972-973.

140 Donald P. Hustad, "The Psalms as Worship Expression: Personal and Congregational," *Review & Expositor,* vol. 81, no. 3 (Sum, 1984): 407.

141 Eaton, *The Psalms,* 13.

Thus, worshippers can concentrate by lifting up their hearts and pausing before the sovereignty of God.

Summary

In the analysis of Psalm 47, we see the following dimensions of worship. *First,* the text emphasizes the kingship metaphor of Yahweh with its implications for worship like *universal worship, singing and praising in the worship of Yahweh.* The supreme description of Yahweh as king is essential from the perspective of Israel's history. Israel was usually under the authority of foreign kings - Assyrian, Babylonians, Persian or Greek. Now the psalmist declares that Yahweh is the King of kings, who is the God over all gods. *Secondly,* we have discovered that singing and praising is a vital part of Israel's worship. People worship the Lord with songs of praise for what he has done for them throughout their journey in their struggles as well as in their happy moments. *Thirdly,* the psalms invite all nations into the worship of Yahweh. Therefore, worshipping the true God brings nations and God's people together (Ps 47:10). Thus, Psalm 47 portrays the divinity of Yahweh, the universal king, to be worshipped by all.

Chapter 4

Exegetical Study of Psalm 93
Yahweh the Creator King

Introduction

Like Psalms 96, 97, 99, Psalm 93 has a vital reference to the kingship: יְהוָה מָלָךְ 'Yahweh reigns' (93:1). It brings out alongside Yahweh's kingship, relevant parallel themes like majesty, eternity, greatness and supremacy of Yahweh over all. Therefore, Psalm 93 presents the powerfulness of Yahweh over all the rebellious nature of creation. It also presents reliability and holiness of Yahweh. Thus, it projects Yahweh as incomparable, creator king, deserving worship and adoration by all.

Here I focus on: *First,* the historical setting of Psalm 93, how and in which historical period it could have been composed or redacted. *Secondly,* the literary function which helps in understanding the text and linking the kingship metaphor of Yahweh with worship. *Thirdly,* a fuller comprehension of the text with exegetical studies. *Fourthly* comments in relation to the metaphor king. *Finally,* comments in relation to worship.

4.1. Historical Analysis

This section explores both the Davidic monarchical and the post-exilic settings. Also, look at how Psalm 93 emerged and redacted.

4.1.1. Davidic Monarchical Setting

Eaton, Hans-Joachim Kraus and Artur Weiser, place Psalm 93 in the Davidic monarchical setting. *First,* looking at the text, it is widely acknowledged that this is an ancient psalm dating from the early monarchy, as both style and content indicate.[1] This early setting is to be found in the context of the autumn festival. *Secondly*, along with Mowinckel and Weiser, Tate claims that from the historical perspective, the evidence for the date of the content of Psalm 93 points toward the conclusion of an early pre-exilic date.[2]

Thirdly, in Psalm 93:5 we see the word תודע which refers to God's law, and the cultic expression of God's law are from older traditions that refer to the fall festival of Israel or the feast of tabernacles, 'thus allowing us to place' Psalm 93 in Davidic Monarchical setting (cf. Deut 31:10).[3]

Thus, following Eaton, Mowinckel and Weiser setting it is plausible to put the date of Psalm 93 in the Davidic monarchical setting.

4.1.2. Post-Exilic Setting

Several commentators like Gerstenberger, Anderson,Westermann and John Philips place Psalm 93 in a post-exilic setting. *First,* Psalm 93 would have a late origin because there is no superscription in the Psalm. *Secondly,* in addition, its loyalty to *Torah* and the temple suggests a post-exilic setting. The use of this psalm in the synagogues worship services also points in this direction.[4] *Thirdly*, the Mishnah suggests that Psalm 93 was sung on the sixth day of the week in expectationof the time 'that shall be Sabbath and rest in the life everlasting.' Thus, this hymn may have been used at a later period to commemorate the return from Babylonian exile.[5] *Fourthly,* according to Westermann, the declarative style of the psalm of praises is transformed into an eschatological style which reflects a post-exilic setting.[6] *Fifthly,* the psalm

1 John Eaton, *The Psalms: A Historical and Spiritual Commentary with an Introduction and New Translation* (London: Continuum International Publishing Group, 2005), 331. See Hans-Joachim Kraus, "Psalms 60-150," in *A Continental Commentary*, translated by Hilton C. Oswald (Minneapolis: Fortress Press, 1993), 233. Artur Weiser, "The Psalms: A Commentary," in *The Old Testament Library*, vol. 20 edited by Peter Ackroyd (Philadelphia: Westminster John Knox Press, 1962), 617. Marvine E. Tate, "Psalms 51-150," in *Word Biblical Commentary*, edited by David A. Hubbard (Dallas: Word Books, 1990), 233.

2 Marvine E. Tate, "Psalms 51-150," in *Word Biblical Commentary*, edited by David A. Hubbard (Dallas: Word Books, 1990), 478-479.

3 Hans-Joachim Kraus, "Psalms 60-150," in *A Continental Commentary*, translated by Hilton C. Oswald (Minneapolis: Fortress Press, 1993), 233.

4 Erhard S. Gerstenberger, *Psalms, Part 2 and Lamentations: The Forms of the Old Testament Literature*, vol. XV (Grand Rapids: William B. Eerdmans Publishing Company, 2001), 176. A.A. Anderson, "The Book of Psalms: Psalms 73-150," in *New Century Bible Commentary*, vol. 2 (London: William B. Eerdmans Publishing Company, 1989). Claus Westermann, *The Praise of God in the Psalms*, translated by Keith R. Crim (Virginia: John Knox Press, 1965), 151. John Philips, *Exploring Psalms : An Expository Commentary*, vol. 2 (Grand Rapids: Kregel Publications, 2002), 54-46.

5 Anderson, "The Book of Psalms: Psalms 73-150," 665.

6 Claus Westermann, *The Praise of God in the Psalms*, translated by Keith R. Crim (Virginia: John Knox Press, 1965), 151. However, there is no lack of defenders for the post-exilic

reflects the excitement of the Jews who came back to reclaim the promised land in the name of God and they praised Yahweh out of joy and happiness by declaring his supremancy through the singing of the hymn.[7]

Through an analysis of both the settings, I suppose that the Psalm 93 more likely reflects a post-exilic setting, because the psalm indicates eschatological motif. The post-exilic writings especially the apocalyptic sections emphasize eschatological motif (cf. Ezekiel 40-48; Daniel; Isaiah 56-66; Malachi). Probably eschatological motif is the work of the post-exilic redactor. Thus this eschatological motif is seemly visible in this Psalm 93 though we have different views.

4.2. Literary Analysis of the Text

A literary analysis focuses on the following aspects: translation, text critical notes, form, structure and repetitions. All these characteristics contribute toward a profound understanding of the text.

4.2.1. Translation

1 יהוה מלך גאות לבש לבש יהוה עז התאזר אף־תכון תבל בל־תמוט ׃	1. The Lord reigns, he is robed with majesty, the Lord robed, majesty he has *girded*[8] himself with strength, also he has established the world that cannot be shaken.

period. We can also see who is in support of the post-exilic period and the early days of restoration after returning from Babylon like Kirpatrick. Buttenwieser put this hymn in the context of deuteron-Isaiah. See Marvine E. Tate, "*Psalms 51-100*, " in *Word Biblical Commentary* (Dallas: Word Books, 1990), 478.

7 John Philips, *Exploring Psalms: An Expository Commentary*, vol. 2 (Grand Rapids: Kregel Publications., 2002), 46. For Warrent W. Wiersbe, "Psalm 93 was perhaps written by one of the Levites who returned to Judah with the Jewish remnant after the Babylonian captivity." Around 539 BCE the Medes and Persians defeated Babylon and it seems the next year Cyrus, the new king, gave permission to the Jews to go back to their own nation. However, it was a tough time for them to begin normal life. In that situation the people needed encouragement and support to continue the work. There was no one who could encourage them and there was only discouragement. They found that only Yahweh was their supporter and encouragement. Therefore, this short hymn magnifies the Lord by presenting three divine assurances: (1) God reigns supremely (2) God is Greater than our Circumstances (3) God always keeps his word. See Warrent W. Wiersbe, *Be Exultant: Psalms 90-150* (Lincoln: Victor Books, 2004), 30.

8 V.1b התאזר had girded, this translation put before *copula*. For Anderson, this concept might have developed from a military expression. See Anderson, *The Book of Psalms: Psalms 73-150),* 667. For you have girded me with strength for the battle (2 Sam 22:40).

2 נכון כסאך מאז מעולם אתה :	2. *Your*[9] throne is established from long ago, you are from eternity.
3 נשאו נהרות יהוה נשאו נהרות קולם ישאו נהרות דכים :	3. *Floods*[10] have lifted up, Lord; the floods have lifted up their voice, *the floods lift up their pounding.*[11]
4 מקלות מים רבים אדירים משברי־ים אדיר במרום יהוה :	4. More majestic than mighty of waters, more majestic than the waves of the sea, the Lord is majestic on high.
5 עדתיך נאמנו מאד לביתך נאוה־קדש יהוה לארך ימים :	5. Your decrees are very reliable; holiness adorns your house, Yahweh for long days.

4.2.2. Text Critical Notes

First, Title of Psalm 93. There is no title in M.T but LXX has *εις τημεραν τοῦ προσαββατν ὅτε κατώκισται ἡ γῆ αἰνς ὡδας τῶ Δανιδ* which means, "for the day before the Sabbath, when the land was inhabited: a praise song for David." Here, the filling of the land may refer to creation, and thus to Sabbath, or to the arrival from the exile.[12] Muthunayagom suggests that the LXX title might have been used at a later period to commemorate the return from the Babylonian exile.[13] In my opinion, Psalm 93 might have developed during David's time that could be a reason why it was attributed to David as the title 'a praise song of David' suggests. However, this Psalm might have been used extensively in post-exilic period.

Secondly, the word תכון 'he had established' the world (Ps 93:1). Anderson argues this expression may refer to the creation of the world. Yahweh is the creator of all the created things.[14] Eaton affirms that through Yahweh an order of life is established, chaotic forces are subdued, the earth is made firm in all

9 V.2a Targum inserted אל masculine common singular. It means that Yahweh is understood, but not added to the text. See Karl Elliger and Wilhelm Rudolph, eds., *Biblia Hebraica Stuttgartensia* (Stuttgart: Biblia Hebraica Stuttgartensia, 1997), 1175.

10 V. 3. נהרות 'rivers or floods, it is in noun common masculine plural absolute. Therefore, I have translated it as 'floods.' These are rivers out of control, destructive, divesting. See Arthur G. Clarke, A*nalytical Studies in the Psalms* (Grand Rapids: Kregel Publications, 1979), Arthur G. Clarke, *Analytical Studies in the Psalms* (Grand Rapids: Kregel Publications, 1979), 237.

11 V. 3 a-a. This is absent in Septuagint, the form of the word is a probable conjecture. Thus this is considered as incomplete information. See Elliger and Rudolph, *Biblia Hebraica Stuttgartensia.*

12 Tate, *Psalms 51-100*, 472.

13 Daniel Jones Muthunayagom, "Kingship of God and Creation in the Old Testament" (M.Th. Thesis, United Theological College, Bangalore, 1982), 97.

14 A.A. Anderson,"The Book of Psalms : Psalms 1-72," in *New Century Bible Commentary*, vol. 1 (Grand Rapids: William B. Eerdmans Publishing Company, 1985), 201.

the conditions for life.[15] Thus, the psalmist expresses that Yahweh deserves all adoration from the universe.

Thirdly, the word עולם 'long duration' or 'forever' (Ps 93:2). עולם differs from context to context. The meaning of the nominative of עולם does not seem to mean eternity in the philosophical sense of the word, neither unbounded time nor timeless eternal (Ex 21:6). The Hebrew term for time עולם is closely linked to the occurrences of events. Thus, עולם is usually used to describe events extended into the distant past or future. For instance, such distant time is evidently relative, it can be a time in one's own life or a life span (Ps 77:5).[16]

However, the meaning of the nominative of עולם in relation to the kingship of Yahweh has the idea of eternity. The psalmist says, "From everlasting to everlasting you are God."[17] Tomasino and Kraus suggest that in Psalm 93:2 the nominative עולם refers to the idea of eternity for it says אתה עולם 'you are from eternity' which refers to God. Here, God is described as from all eternity which means more than merely the distant past. He is an everlasting God.[18]

Fourthly, אדיר מים 'water, majestic' (Ps 93: 4). This supposes that מים waters is assumed to be repeated before אדיר מים 'majesty' synonymous with "breakers of the sea."[19] Similarly, A.A. Anderson argues that the מים waters probably refer back to the foods in verse 3, and portraying the majesty and glorious is Yahweh who is in absolute control of the great waters or flood thought they seems to be strong before the great king of Yahweh they are limited.[20] Anderson rightly points out that from a human perspective there is disorder in the world that this challenges the sovereignty of God. However, Yahweh is enthroned triumphantly over the powers that threaten his power as God and he stands beyond history and beyond the cosmos.[21]

Fifthly, the noun בית 'house or dwelling place.' For Eaton, בית implies "the house of the Lord and is his heavenly abode, but also its earthly manifestation

---

15 Eaton, *The Psalms,* 332.

16 Anthony Tomasino, "עולם," in *New International Dictionary of Old Testament Theology & Exegesis,* vol. 3, edited by Willem A. VanGemeren (Grand Rapids: Zondervan, 1997), 346.

17 Tomasino, "עולם," 346, (Gen 21:33, Isa 60:19-20, 1 Chron 16:34, 36, 2 Chron 20:21, Ezra 3:11, Pss 61:4, 89:2, 100:5, 106:1, 107:1, 110:4, 118:1, Jer 33:11).

18 Tomasino, "עולם," 347. See Artur Weiser, "The Psalms: A Commentary," in *The Old Testament Library*, edited by Peter Ackroyd (Philadelphia: Westminster John Knox Press, 1962), 619. John Goldingay, "Psalms 90-150," in *Baker Commentary on the Old Testament Wisdom and Psalms*, vol. 3, edited by Tremper Longman III (Grand Rapids: Academic Press, 2008), 68-69.

19 Tate, *Psalms 51-100*, 473.

20 Anderson, "The Book of Psalms: Psalms 73-150," 669.

21 Benhard W. Anderson, *Out of the Depths: The Psalms Speak for Us Today* (Philadelphia: Westminster John Knox Press, 1983), 178.

in Zion."[22] The beauty and holiness of Yahweh makes the house or temple a source of blessing for the people.[23]

Finally, נוח in Qumran 4QPsb and assumes that it is נוח in the sense of an abode for shepherds and flocks. The scholars like Howard[24] and Tate[25] suggest that נוה קדשך your holy habitation in Ex 15:13 is relevant, and translates Ps 95:5 as your decrees are affirmed, mighty one, in your house, your holy habitation for length of days.

The above points affirm that the power of God is exhibited in the highest form in this Psalm. They also emphasize that the whole world is under the everlasting authority of Yahweh.

4.2.3. Form of the Psalm

Psalm 93 is a hymn, or a praise psalm, that celebrates Yahweh's kingship and victory over primordial forces. The form came under hymns because it expresses praise of Yahweh for his deeds and supernatural qualities. This psalm is usually treated with (Pss 47, 96-99) as a subgroup of hymns that proclaim the kingship metaphor of Yahweh.[26] Westermann argues that psalm 93 is not descriptive praise.[27] Dahood says the psalm refers to Yahweh's victory over the forces of chaos.[28] Kraus notes that Psalm 93 belongs to the category of praise hymn.[29]

For Muthunayagom "This psalms is a hymn or descriptive psalm of praise celebrates the majesty and the royal power of Yahweh as king and creator."[30] For me this psalm comes under a hymn based on the theme of the kingship of Yahweh which generates adoration and praise.

4.2.4. Structure of the Psalm

Psalm 93 is concise and shows strong metrical relationships through its repetitions. It begins with the 4+4 meter where we see the declaration יהוה מלך with two accents producing the effect that two-plus meters joined to each other establish the picture of the verse. As we see in verse 1b, the three-member verse structure begins which is to be read in the 3+3+3 meter.[31] And

22 Eaton, *The Psalms,* 332.

23 Tate, *Psalms 51-100*, 480.

24 David M. Howard, *The Structure of Psalms 93-100* (Winona Lake: Eisenbrauns, 1997), 48.

25 Tate, *Word Biblical Commentary: Psalms 51-100*, 474.

26 Tate, *Psalms 51-100*, 474.

27 Westermann, *The Praise of God in the Psalms*, 150.

28 Mitchell Dahood, *Psalms 51-100: The Anchor Bible* (New York: Doubleday, 1968), 328.

29 Kraus, *Psalms 60-150*, 232.

30 Muthunayagom, "Kingship of God and Creation in the Old Testament," 95.

31 Kraus, *Psalms 60-150,* 232.

this structure is unique to Psalm 93. When we observe the structure of this particular enthronement psalm, it seems it is a combination of proclamation in verse 1 and direct addresses Yahweh in verses 2 and 3. Howard treats verse 1c in relation to verse 2a, b as a unit, noting a 3+3+3 pattern in the remainder of the poem. But, Tate prefers to read verses 1-2 as a unit.[32]

Tate and Firth say the structure of Psalm 93 is fairly simple and brings out the following visible structures: 1. Operating a paired set of statements of Yahweh as king in (Ps 93:1-2). 2. Two paired statements about waters affirm Yahweh is mighty on high in (Ps 93: 3-4). 3. An association of Yahweh's reign and authority over the chaos of the waters of creation imply Yahweh's decrees and holiness in the temple (93:5).[33] Gerstenberger has put the parallel structure in the following ways:[34]

1. Hymnic affirmation v.1
2. Adoration of community v.2
3. Creation Hymn v.3-4
4. Adoration of Communication v.5

This is the visible form and structure particularly in Psalm 93. Thus, through the form and structure, the message for Israel's worship is revealed.

4.2.5. Repetition

Though Psalm 93 is brief, we can see the richness of repetition and the meaning behind the use of repetition. Why the worshippers repeatedly express some words and phrases is because of the *joyful mood* in worship! The idea of Yahweh לבש 'putting on or being robed' (Ps 93:1), is parallel to being cloth (Ps 104: 1-2, Isa 51: 9, 59:17). This figurative language was very exciting and it also resulted in excessive repetition.[35] The word כון 'establish' is found in both verse 1 and verse 2 which are poetically together. The kingship of Yahweh was established from the very beginning, the earth has been made firm in all aspects so that Yahweh's throne has been established in the beginning and for eternity. Therefore, the singer praises the creator whose "sovereignty was destined from eternity, from the unimaginable and ultimate beginning."[36]

32 Tate, *Psalms 51-100,* 474.

33 David G. Firth, "The Teaching of the Psalms," in *Interpreting the Psalms: Issues and Approaches*, edited by Philip S. Johnston and David G. Firth (England: InterVarsity Press, 2005), 170.

34 Erhard S. Gerstenberger *Psalms, Part 2 and Lamentations: The Forms of the Old Testament Literature*, vol. XV (Grand Rapids: William B. Eerdmans Publishing Company, 2001), 171.

35 Gerstenberger, *Psalms, Part 2 and Lamentations,* 174.

36 Eaton, *The Psalms,* 332.

In verse 3, we see the word נהר rivers or floods, it appears three times and the figurative language here indicates that the kingship and power of Yahweh is contrasted with the power of the chaotic waters. The flood waters of chaos are overwhelming and irresistible, but Yahweh's power is more powerful than all the threats of chaos.[37]

The word נשא 'to lift' is repeated three times. This reflects the reliability of Yahweh's sovereignty as having been established from ages past and affirms that the rebellious waters are no longer a danger. Yahweh's instituted throne prevents all the chaotic forces from lifting their voices in opposition to him.[38] The word אדיר 'majesty' repeated twice in verse 4, once אדירים in adjective masculine plural absolute, and once in אדיר adjective masculine singular absolute. For Eaton, this continues to reflect the Lord's victory over the chaos of the waters and waves of the sea. It is Yahweh who is high above them and in whom the true mighty power belongs to him alone.[39] All these repeated words in this psalm are used to exalt the sovereignty of Yahweh over the chaotic forces. Thus, the psalmist worship Yahweh, the creator, for his reliability with a song of praises.

4.3. Comments in Relation to the Kingship Metaphor

First, יְהוָה מָלָךְ 'Yahweh reigns' (Ps 93:1). There are various translations of the phrase יְהוָה מָלָךְ 'Yahweh reigns,' Mowinckel translates יְהוָה מָלָךְ as 'Yahweh has become king' as cultic affirmation of the celebration of Yahweh's kingship (S. Mowinckel *Psalmenstudien*, II, 1921, 6-8). The major argument centres on the phrase 'has become king.'[40] Kraus[41] and Goldingay[42] translate Yahweh is king whereas Dahood, יְהוָה מָלָךְ is translated as 'Yahweh reigns.' Placing

37 Walter Brueggemann, *The Message of the Psalms: A Theological Commentary* (Minneapolis: Augsburg Publishing House, 1984), 146.

38 Tate, *Psalms 51-100*, 480.

39 Eaton, *The Psalms,* 332.

40 Tate, *Psalms 51-100*, 472. See John Day, *God's Conflict with the Dragon and the Sea: Echoes of a Canaanite Myth in the Old Testament* (Cambridge: Cambridge University, 1985), 35-36.

41 Kraus, *Psalms 60-150*, 233.Sigmund Mowinckel, *The Psalms in Israel's Worship, Two Volumes in One*, trans. D.R. Ap-Thomas (Grand Rapids: William B. Eerdmans Publishing Company, 2004), 107.

42 John Goldingay, "Psalms: Psalms 90-150," in *Baker Commentary on the Old Testament Wisdom and Psalms*,vol. 3, edited by Tremper Longman III (Grand Rapids: Baker Academic, 2008), 66. Richard J. Clifford, *Psalms 1-72: Abingdon Old Testament Commentaries* (Nashville: Abingdon Press, 2002), 25. See Samuel L. Terrien, "The Psalms: Strophic Structure and Theological Commentary: Psalms 73-150," in *Eerdmans Critical Commentary,* edited by David Noel Freedman, vol. 2 (Grand Rapids: William B. Eerdmans Publishing Company, 2003), 657.

Yahweh before the verb indicates the emphasis that the psalmist stresses on the fact that no other 'deity exercises kingship,' except Yahweh.[43]

Kraus observes word order of יְהוָה מָלָךְ in the text (Ps 93:1). He claims that the verbal statement of מלך יהוה refers to a lively and exciting incident to the conclusion of the act of enthronement (I King 1:11, Ps 47:8, Isa 52:7). Therefore, the statement of a stipulation יְהוָה מָלָךְ on the other hand, describes an unchangeable state of being (cf. 1 Kings 1:18, Pss 93:1, 96:10, 97:1, 99:1). One may object to this syntactical explanation; the word order יְהוָה מָלָךְ as a statement of the condition may not be contrasted with the verbal statement מלך יהוה that putting יהוה in the first position merely has the force of a special emphasis "Yahweh has become king."[44] We cannot support fully יְהוָה מָלָךְ which is of a higher degree than מלך יהוה. We can see that the unchanging, eternal state of Yahweh's kingship is stressed. When we see the translation of "Yahweh has become king," there is a tendency to think that "for a time he actually loses" his loyal rule. This view is inconsistent with OT faith in God.[45] Thus, Kraus rightly supports the translation of 'Yahweh reigns.' I agree with Kraus translation of יְהוָה מָלָךְ as Yahweh is king.

Secondly, the verb לבשׁ means 'to put on or being robed' in majesty which is a metaphorical account of Yahweh's mighty nature. The idea of Yahweh לבשׁ 'putting on or robed' power or majesty like cloth parallel from (Ps 104: 1-2, Isa 51: 9, 59:17). A.A. Anderson argues this expression may refer to the creation of the world. Yahweh is the "creator and all the created things and beings in God's universe."[46] John Eaton affirms that through Yahweh an order of life is established, chaotic forces have been subdued, the earth has been made firm in all the conditions for life.[47] Thus, Psalmist expressed that Yahweh deserves all adoration from the universe, Yahweh made all things possible.

The commentators like A. A. Anderson, A. Weiser and D. J. Muthunayagom argued that Yahweh is robed in majesty neither denotes to the act of the enthronement nor to the contemplation of a historical happening at which Yahweh has assumed of his kingly power. It does not refer to the end time when his kingdom would be established over the entire world. It does refer to the fact that it is Yahweh who exercises his kingship since from the beginning. This is a cultic acclamation of the worshipper's fidelity to Yahweh's kingship and power over the chaotic forces.[48] Ollenburger rightly

43 Mitchell. Dahood, *Psalms 51-100: The Anchor Bible* (New York: Doubleday, 1968), 340.

44 Kraus, *Psalms 60-150*, 233.

45 Kraus, *Psalms 60-150,* 233.

46 Anderson, *The Book of Psalms: Psalms 1-72*, 201.

47 Eaton, *The Psalms: A Historical and Spiritual Commentary with an Introduction and New Translation*, 332.

48 Muthunayagom, "Kingship of God and Creation in the Old Testament," 97–98.

points out that Yahweh's heavenly power is demonstrated in the form of earthly sovereignty which is referring to the idea that Yahweh is robed to majesty, and "centred in the temple which unites heaven and earth."[49] Looking from the form critical study, the psalmist used this idea to put Yahweh the king on the highest place and, therefore, deserved to be worshipped among all kings and gods.

Thirdly, the psalmist mentions כסא 'throne' (Ps 93:2). Throne is an interesting word which reflects the kingship metaphor of God. For Perdue, כסא best refers to the 'ark of God' which is indicated in Jer 3:16 and Ps 99:1. God's ascension to the throne initiates his reign as king and judge.[50] Craigie claims that Yahweh sits on the throne and this is a poetical parallelism with God's reign.[51] The text clearly mentions that Yahweh has conquered the force which threatens the earth and now sits on the holy כסא 'throne.'[52] According to Muthunayagom "the throne of Yahweh is a symbol of Yahweh's victory over the chaotic powers in the beginning itself as well as a symbol of his continuing presence in the world."[53] To me the כסא refers to Yahweh's greatness, who seated on the highest place as the king who is highly exalted upon all the kings of the earth. Thus this word denotes Yahweh is the king whose kingship last forever.

Fourthly, the noun עדות 'testimony or decrees.' This עדות implies that "Yahweh's guidance for human conduct has proved true and reliable as stable

---

49 Ben C. Ollenburger, *Zion the City of the Great King: A Theological Symbol of the Jerusalem Cult* (Sheffield: Sheffield Academic Press, 1987), 34.

50 Perdue, "Yahweh Is King over All the Earth, An Exegesis of Psalm 47," 97. For Kraus, the ark of Yahweh is at the characteristic places in the OT called the throne of Yahweh (Jer 3:16, 17: 12, I Sam 4:4). Therefore in connection with throne and ark we should pay attention to other texts of the OT that reveal a cultic installation of the ark in the temple or worship place and moreover pay attention to the entrance of the king's sanctuary; not a human king but Yahweh the king. See Hans-Joachim Kraus, "Psalms 1-59," in *A Continental Commentary*, translated by Hilton C. Oswald (Minneapolis: Fortress Press, 1993), Hans-Joachim Kraus, *Psalms 1-59*, trans. Hilton C. Oswald, A Continental Commentary (Minneapolis: Fortress Press, 1993), 87.

51 Craigie, Psalms 1-50, 350. See Erhard S. Gerstenberger, Psalms, Part I, with an Introduction to Cultic Poetry: The Forms of the Old Testament Literature, vol. XIV (Grand Rapids: William B. Eerdmans Publishing Company, 1988). John Eaton, Psalms of the Way and the Kingdom: A Conference with the Commentators (Sheffield: Sheffield Academic Press, 1995), 84. V. Steven Parrish, A Story of the Psalms: Conversation, Canon, and Congregation (Collegeville: Liturgical Press, 2003), 86.

52 Tate, *Psalms 51-100*, 479. Throne refers to the ceremonial seat of a king and in a broader sense, it symbolizes kingship as a whole. See A. A. Anderson, "*The Book of Psalms: 73-150,*" *in New Century Bible Commentary*, vol. II (London: William B. Eerdmans Publishing Company, 1989), 667. Anderson W. Bernhard, *Understanding the Old Testament* (New Jersey: Pearson Prentice Hall, 2007).

53 Muthunayagom, "Kingship of God and Creation in the Old Testament," 100.

as the throne of God."[54] In other words, the Lord's testimonies will remain in force forever. Additionally, the term עדות is associated with covenant stipulations where an agreement took place between Yahweh and Israel.[55] Goldingay claims that Yahweh does not act violently to subdue the forcefulness of the waves. God simply issues a decree. This is how we see the qualities of Yahweh that distinguishes him from human and earthly nature and forces. The holiness of Yahweh cannot be compared with any person.[56] Yahweh's reign is extended and it will always undergird the world's security. It is futuristic in declaring that the kingship of Yahweh, implemented at creation, will continue even in the future.[57]

God's law עדות appears as an extremely reliable element in worship. עדות certainly does not refer to prophecies but it is to be understood rather in the sense of Ps 19:7 and Ps 119 as it talks about the perfectness of God's law. In the context of worship, God's law has its firm place from of old.[58]

Fifthly, there are no gods who can compare to the mightiness of God. He is the Almighty God who does mighty things through which he reveals his kingship to the world. The text points out the strength of Yahweh from the word אזר which means 'to gird,' and this is used metaphorically for the strength of Yahweh.[59] In Psalm 93:1, the language used belongs to the realm of kingship. The image of royal mantle and adornment of the divine ruler, poetic inspiration and reverent awe unite.[60] The phrase 'Yahweh is on high' affirms the mighty strength of Yahweh (Ps 93:4). Yahweh has the power to put away rivers' waters which threaten his kingship because he is above all the powers and forces. Yahweh is on high, the sea breakers can reflect the majesty of Yahweh.[61] The psalmist explicitly presents Yahweh as one who belts himself with strength and is also exalted to be victorious over his enemies.

---

54 Tate, *Psalms 51-100*, 480.

55 Eugene H. Merrill, *Everlasting Dominion: A Theology of Old Testament* (Nashville: Broadman & Holman Publishers, 2006), 319. He goes on to say that in the context of the Lord's work of creation, those stipulations could be understood as the creation mandate of Gen 1:26-28, where the only decrees are found in the creation account. The command is founded on the Lord's sovereign claim to authority where Yahweh the king triumphs over human and the chaotic waters.

56 Goldingay, *Psalms 42-89*, 70-71.

57 Goldingay, *Psalms 42-89*, 71.

58 Kraus, *Psalms 60-150*, 236.

59 Anderson, *The Book of Psalms : Psalms 73-150*, 667.

60 Artur Weiser, *The Psalms: A Commentary*, *The Old Testament Library,* edited by Peter Ackroyd (Philadelphia: Westminster John Knox Press, 1962), 619.

61 Goldingay, *Psalms: Psalms 90-150*, 70.

4.4. Comments in Relation to Worship

The exegesis of Psalm 93 bring out the following essential points and relation to worship. *First,* the psalmist *stresses raising in worship.* Watts points out that although the Lord's sovereignty is threatened by the power of raging seas (Ps 93: 3), God's throne is secure and permanent (Ps 2). The worshippers praise the sovereignty of God.[62] Eaton notes that worship, praise and obeisance exalt the supremacy of the Lord as creator and ruler.[63] The metaphor of Yahweh's kingship is associated with Yahweh's power as creator and defender, this supreme nature of Yahweh is grounded in the creation of the world.[64] "Yahweh's kingship is based on the idea of creation because Yahweh has established the world and it cannot be shaken."[65]

The sovereign perfection of Yahweh is raised above all the violent powers of chaos. Besides that the mythical descriptions of the struggles with chaos are fully thrown off.[66] Because "Yahweh is the God who was, who is and who is to come, and before whose reality the barriers of time fade away so that what happened long ago and what will come to pass in the future both simultaneously call for a decision" to adore Yahweh the king with all praises.[67] The eyes of faith exalt Yahweh and focus on his reality. The kingship of God is revealed and is praised in the form of an account of the way in which God performs.[68] There can be no other God. Yahweh is the Lord who reigns above all and deserves all our praises.

Secondly, the psalm expresses *exalting of the holy God in worship*. The house of the Lord is holy because Yahweh dwells there (cf. Deut 12:5, 14:23, I King 11:36), and that holiness demands that all who enter into the houses of the Lord should maintain holiness and participate in the worship of Yahweh.[69] נאוה־קדש יהוה *holiness of Yahweh beautifies* which means holiness beautifies the temple of God (Ps 93:5b). Holiness portrays the divine nature of God. Thus, "the scene of the prostration is characterized by holiness."[70] The word holiness is the spiritual quality which the temple must have in order to be an abode worthy of Yahweh and effective for the purpose of worshiping the יהוה

62 John D.W. Watts, "Psalms of Trust, Thanksgiving, and Praise," *Review Exposition,* vol. 3, no. 81 (Sum, 1984): 403.

63 Eaton, *The Psalms*, 331.

64 Ollenburger, *Zion the City of the Great King*, 54.

65 Weiser, *The Psalms: A Commentary*, 618.

66 Kraus, *Psalms 60-150*, 235.

67 Weiser, *The Psalms,* 618. God revealed himself at work in the light of that revelation. The glory of God is praised in the form of an account of the way in which God performed. 619.

68 Weiser, *The Psalms: A Commentary,* 618-619.

69 Anderson, *The Book of Psalms: Psalms 73-150*, 669.

70 Kraus, *Psalms 60-150*, 236.

קדש 'holy God.' Psalms 93 portrays that the presence of Yahweh is to be set apart in the temple for the full effective order as of old.[71] The holiness of God is in the temple. Worshippers are expected to exalt the holiness of Yahweh.[72]

As in Psalm 19, the hymn of creation is made specific in verse 5. The eternal king, who is Lord of all the earth, has revealed an עדות 'decree' which is extremely trustworthy. In this עדות the God who is enthroned on high from primeval times comes to humankind and reveals himself. In the temple, the Lord of the earth and the king is the *dues praesens* who is honoured and worshipped in holiness.[73]

The threatening sea and uncontrollable power of the floods, as well as the sky god are some of the motifs that are common in Ancient West Asian mythology, however, these threatening forces are shown to be subject to Yahweh's reign.[74] As the text reflects "Your decrees are very reliable; holiness adorns your house, Yahweh, for endless days" (Ps 93:5). That shows that the worshippers of Yahweh are to exalt the greatness and holy nature of Yahweh. Thus, the worshippers exalt God's holiness.

Thirdly, the psalm talks about the *eternity* is the context of worship. The reign of Yahweh has no end. The chaotic waters cannot take away the eternal power of God. The psalmist affirms that Yahweh is praised objectively because he is the eternal God and the kingdom of God will never vanish.[75] This psalm confidently affirms Yahweh's eternity by adapting the kingship metaphor of Yahweh. The psalmist declares that Yahweh is eternally enthroned. This gives the faithful reason to have confidence to worship and exalt God, to face the reality of the situations and ask God to help them.[76] Even the royal psalms mentions that the throne is considered to be the central key in describing the kingship metaphor of Yahweh, that the throne of Yahweh is eternal so that the reign of Yahweh has no end. The psalmist says that an eternal throne is a symbol of Yahweh's kingship and worshippers praise him (Ps 45).[77]

---

71 Mowinckel, *The Psalms in Israel's Worship*, 126.

72 Weiser, *The Psalms*, 621.

73 Kraus, *Psalms 60-150,* 236. It seems that the waters of chaos revolted against the creator God in all possible ways. Here, the conceptions of the ancient myth concerning the battle against dragons and chaos come through. In Psalm 93:3b, the hymn continues to the present time and sees destructive, rebellious forces still at work (cf. Ps 46:2). See Hans-Joachim Kraus, *Psalms 60-150: A Continental Commentary*, translated by Hilton C. Oswald (Minneapolis: Fortress Press, 1993), 235.

74 Firth, "The Teaching of the Psalms," *Interpreting the Psalms: Issues and Approaches*, 170.

75 Gerstenberger, *Psalms, Part 2 and Lamentations,* 175.

76 David M. Howard, "A Contextual Reading of Psalm 90-94," *The Shape and Shaping of the Psalter*, edited by J. Clinton McCann (Sheffield: JSOT Press, 1993), 114.

77 John H. Eaton, *Kingship and the Psalms* (Sheffield: JSOT Press, 1986), 118–119.

Psalm 93 talks about the eternity of Yahweh and demonstrates the super nature of the majesty which the world could see as the endless kingdom of Yahweh. The sovereign power of the creator and Lord of the world is unchangeable and eternal. All the powers of chaos fade away before the eternal God. Therefore, the true worshipper must give due praises to the eternal God and worship him. In my opinion, praising God had associations for Israel's worship and has implications for present day worship.

4.5. Theological Concerns Pertaining to the Kingship Metaphor of God

Psalm 93 mentions some theological concerns which are connected to the kingship of God. I have discussed a few points in the light of Yahweh's kingship metaphor in relating to connotations.

4.5.1. Kingship and Majesty

Majestyis a recurring connotation in Psalm 93 which is emphasized through the words *robed in majesty*. A royal robe refers to the status of God as king. Yahweh robed himself with majesty, glory and splendour through which his kingship is reflected to the nations. The text rightly points out that Yahweh's kingship is evident in the firm formation of the world. This is indicated through parallelism and chaism. Moore[78] rightly put it in the following ways,

A. "Yahweh reigns,
B. he is robed in majesty,
A. robed is Yahweh,
B. he had girded with strength.
A. he had established the world that cannot be shaken" (Ps 93:1).

The centre of the chaism focuses on Yahweh's majesty and strength and their connection to the establishment of the world which affirms Yahweh's kingship.[79] Yahweh's supreme majesty has established his reign and the stability of the world is the reality of Yahweh robed in majesty.[80] The psalmist affirms that from the beginning to the end, Yahweh robes himself with supremacy and

78 Anne Moore, *Moving Beyond Symbol and Myth: Understanding the Kingship of God of the Hebrew Bible through Metaphor* (New York: Peter Lang Publishing, 2009), 244.

79 Moore, *Moving Beyond Symbol and Myth*, 245.

80 James Luther Mays, *The Lord Reigns: A Theological Handbook to the Psalms* (Louisville: Westminster John Knox Press, 1994), 15.

glory.[81] Yahweh reigns in majesty and power.[82] Israel calls her God the king and the master. For Israel, God is the great king and master of all the created universe (Ps 29:10). The majesty of God is revealed through the mighty deeds of Yahweh in the life of the people and no one can perform in the way Yahweh has done. Therefore, in Israel's worship, people give praise to God for his acts of wonders.[83]

The declaration of the mighty works of God obtains the meaning of glory, majesty, and greatness. Several references describe a God who is clothed with majesty (Ps 104:1, Job 40:10). The word הדר 'splendour' plays a special role in Israel's praise as an expression of God's royalty.[84] The association of God's splendour with his activity in history is broadened to include Yahweh's glory which is revealed in the creation account (Ps 104: 1). Even when Israel speaks of God's majesty as steadfast (Ps 96:6), it means that which takes place through God's power (Isa 35: 2, 63:1). The splendour of God's majesty is the experience of the people even in Yahweh's judgment. Israel recognizes God's splendour in creation and consequently it gives praise to the creator (Ps 8:6).[85]

The declaration of God's highness and majesty is an expression of royalty. In all the expression of majesty implies the experience of astonishment and joy. The significance of the term lies in its theological usage. God's הוד 'majesty' has been revealed to Israel in the deeds of the Lord of history and of creation. Israel manifests Yahweh and acknowledges his majesty with the expression of his הוד.[86] Israel can speak of Yahweh's sovereignty all over the world through the praises of his majesty (Ps 96:6, 1 Chron 16:27, 29:11). Combinations with similar terms illuminate the connotation of the term in reference to God's grandeur and majesty. The word הוד is parallel with glory, radiance and strength. The pair הוד־והדר 'splendour and majesty' describe Yahweh's royal radiance (Pss 96:6 104:1, 112:3, 145:5).[87]

In summary, the connotation of majesty, which is highly expressive of Yahweh who reigns in majesty and power.

---

81 John Eaton, *Psalms of the Way and the Kingdom: A Conference with the Commentators* (Sheffield: Sheffield Academic Press, 1995), 110.

82 Dennis Sylva, "The Rising נהרות of Psalm 93: Chaotic Order," *Journal for the Study of Old Testament,* vol. 36, no. 4 (2012): 481.

83 Pezhumkattil, "Israel's Faith Reflected in the Psalms," 158-159.

84 G. Wehmeier, "הדר," in *Theological Lexicon of the Old Testament,* vol. I, edited by Ernst Jenni and Claus Westermann, translated by Mark E. Biddle (Peabody: Hendrickson Publishers, Inc, 1997), 353.

85 Wehmeier, "הדר," 354-355.

86 D. Vetter, "הדר," in *Theological Lexicon of the Old Testament,* vol. I, edited by Ernst Jenni and Claus Westermann, translated by Mark E (Peabody: Hendrickson Publishers, Inc, 1997), 354-355.

87 Vetter, "הדר," 356.

4.5.2. Kingship and Eternity

Human kingship changes from time to time but the kingship of Yahweh is eternal. Therefore, eternity is linked with the kingship metaphor of Yahweh who continues to reign. The psalmist says, "Yahweh is the king who set the earth on its foundations, so that it shall never be shaken" (Ps 104:5). In ancient Israel that God is eternal was understood within the framework of the metaphor God as king.[88]

The psalms also affirm that God existed before creation, exists apart from it, and will continue to exist when creation passes away (Pss 90:2,102:26-27). Yahweh was Israel's king in the past long before monarchy existed, and he will continue to be Israel's king as the kingship of Yahweh has no end.[89] Thus, Yahweh is the pre-existent God, the one who remains forever. Therefore, the people seek shelter in the eternal God.[90] Brettler asserts that God's eternal nature was understood within the framework of 'Yahweh is king.' You are the same, and your years never end (Ps 102:27). From everlasting to everlasting you are God (Ps 90:2). You are from everlasting; my holy God you never die (Hab 1:12). God's eternal nature is connected to Yahweh's kingship. This suggests that the Israelites understood God's eternal life primarily as an implied kingship.[91] The psalmist declares that "Your throne endures forever and ever" (Ps 45:6). Yahweh's dynasty and his throne will last forever.

The verbal declaration יהוה מלך 'Yahweh reigns' describes the unchangeable status of Yahweh being king.[92] As shown in the textual study the eternal being of God and his power will last forever. עולם varies with the context, for instance, it can also denote a human life time. According to Psalm 93:2 gives a reference to creation. Ever since then, Yahweh has been there exercising power in the world. In such a context, עולם denotes eternity.[93] The biblical text associates God's eternity with the root מלך 'to reign' (Ps 93:1, 2). In ancient Israel, God's eternal nature was understood within the framework of the metaphor, God is king.[94]

The theological theme of this psalm is 'everlasting kingship of Yahweh' or the never-ending dominating power of Yahweh. עדות 'Yahweh's decrees' includes not only the mighty deeds of Yahweh but also Yahweh's promises

88 Moore, *Moving Beyond Symbol and Myth*, 62.

89 Waltke and Houston, *The Psalms as Christian Worship,* 104.

90 Paul R. House, *Old Testament Theology* (Downers Grove: InterVarsity Press, 1998), 416-417.

91 Marc Zvi Brettler, *God Is King: Understanding an Israelite Metaphor* (Sheffield: Academic Press, 1989), 52-53. See Psalms 72:8, 89: 29-37, 72:5, 47:2, 93:1, 96:10, 97:1, 98:6, 99:1, 4.

92 Kraus, *Psalms 60-150*, 233-234.

93 Goldingay, *Psalms: Psalms 90-150*, 69.

94 Moore, *Moving Beyond Symbol and Myth*, 62.

and commands which is linked with the everlasting kingship of Yahweh.[95] The poet sets the beginning of the Lord's reign in eternity past and amazingly declares that it was present even before creation and that it will last forever.[96] Eternity is one of the characteristics constantly linked with Yahweh's kingship and rests on the everlasting nature of the divine sovereign.[97]

The text mentions אתה עולם which means eternity, 'You are from eternity.' Theologically, it affirms that Yahweh exists from eternity (Ps 93:2b). It is also considered as a declaration of the psalmist's faith that Yahweh is the king, both now and forever. Additionally, in this phrase, the psalmist describes the permanent kingship of Yahweh who exercises the power of timeless truth, as the ever-present king of eternity.[98] By the royal power of Yahweh, the world was brought into order and under his kingship, the world will be in the knowledge of God. It is stated that the rule of Yahweh is unchanging.[99] Eternity expresses that God's victory over his enemy is eternal, which is from everlasting to everlasting.

Therefore, Yahweh's eternal kingship it denotes the unending power of Yahweh. Yahweh will continue to bethe *everlasting* king and therefore, his kingship is eternal, which cannot be shaken by human rule. That is the reason why the kingship of Yahweh is not just powerful for a moment or the time being, but it is everlasting. In other words, the rule of Yahweh's government lasts forever and continues to exercise divine power over the universe.

4.5.3. Kingship and Warfare

Warrior is a connotation of Yahweh's kingship metaphor. The warrior is not just a title for Yahweh. It symbolizes that Yahweh the king, is a fighter who fights on behalf of the oppressed, defending them and exercising justice. The text portrays the element of oppositions like the force of floods, mighty waters and the waves of the sea who oppose the power of God (Ps 93:3). However, Yahweh asserts kingly authority over them; they cannot overtake the King who is a divine warrior. For instance, "Thus far shall you come, and no farther, and here shall your proud waves be stopped" (Job 38:11).[100]

There are evil forces in the world but the divine warrior will not be defeated. Yahweh stood for the right, therefore, warrior, also means the reverse

---

95 Anderson, *The Book of Psalms: Psalms 73-150*, 666, 669.

96 Merrill, *Everlasting Dominion: A Theology of the Old Testament*, 319.

97 Moore, *Moving Beyond Symbol and Myth*, 245.

98 Eaton, *Psalms of the Way and the Kingdom: A Conference with the Commentators*, 104.

99 Eaton, *Psalms of the Way and the Kingdom: A Conference with the Commentators,* 110.

100 Goldingay, *Psalms: Psalms 90-150*, 72.

of Yahweh the lover or redeemer or protector.[101] The divine victory over flood and sea voices the fact that God defeats and triumphs over all powers, and here the text points out that it is especially in the context of historical enemies who try to exercise power above Yahweh. This shows that Yahweh is more powerful than all opposing forces (Ps 93:3-4).[102]

God is seated as the supreme God, the master of all deities, and he is the commander of the divine army (Pss 82:1, 89: 6-7). The text points out קדשו ימינו וזרוע 'His right hand and his holy arm.'[103] This indicates God's mighty action as the divine warrior (Isa 52:10). The right hand and holy arms of God are the metaphors for God's divine military power and strength. The psalmist says, "If the Lord is not on our side in the attack of the enemies they might have swallowed us alive" (Ps 124:2-3). The nations have witnessed Yahweh who executes the role of a great warrior and performs marvellous deeds.[104]

The connotation of *warrior* is connected with the kingship metaphor. It illustrates the divine power of Yahweh who stands along with the righteous and saves them in their struggles. Yahweh rules over rebellious nature and has victory over all oppositions, who controls everything, no power can overtake the sovereignty of God. Therefore, Yahweh comes with might as a warrior to save his people through divine, military action.

Summary

To summarise the praise of Yahweh's majesty (Ps 93:1-2) is followed by a description of Yahweh's victory over hostile forces (Ps 93:3-4) and finally by the remembrance of the law and of the temple (Ps 93:5).[105] The following points emerge from above analysis. *First,* Psalm 93 expresses the everlasting kingship of Yahweh that Yahweh the king is eternal unlike human kings who rule temporarily. God's power will continue to be revealed and there is no end to Yahweh's kingship. Therefore, the psalmist encourages the worshippers to come before the Lord and worship him. *Secondly,* the psalm talks about having faith in Yahweh who created everything and who controls everything, no power can overtake the sovereignty of God. Yahweh deserves all our praise and worship. This is made clear by addressing the kingship of Yahweh. *Thirdly,* the psalm proclaims the holy nature of Yahweh. Whoever enters the temple of

---

101 George, Ernest Wright, "God the Warrior," in *The Flowering of the Old Testament Theology: A Reader in Twentieth-Century Old Testament Theology, 1930-1990*, edited by David W. Baker (Winona Lake: Eisenbrauns, 1992), 115.

102 Anderson, *Understanding the Old Testament*, 515.

103 Abraham Pezhumkattil, "Israel's Faith Reflected in the Psalms," *Bible Bhashyam,* vol. xvi, no. 3 (September, 1990): 157.

104 Zorn, *Psalms*, 224-225.

105 Claus Westermann, *The Psalms Structure, Content & Message*, translated by Ralph D. Gehrke (Minneapolis: Augsburg Publishing House, 1980), 113.

God needs to maintain holiness in life. Yahweh demands the people to be holy and give their undivided worship.

Looking from above points we can conclude that the psalmist urges people to know the eternal kingship of Yahweh, besides that to have faith in him and be holy and give due adoration to Yahweh the king. Thus this Psalm 93 portrays the kingship of Yahweh above all things.

Chapter 5

Exegetical Study of Psalm 95 Yahweh, the King of all Gods and King of the World

Introduction

Psalm 95 displays the sovereignty of Yahweh's kingship in which we see the faithfulness of Yahweh, who is faithful and continually guides the covenant people throughout their life's journey. Therefore, the text reaffirms Yahweh's kingship, who rules with divine authority. In other words, Yahweh is the King of all gods and King of the world. Reading from a wider perspective, it reveals that Psalm 95 is parallel with Psalms 50 and 80 and this idea is supported by several writers. For example, Jeremias and Weiser claim that Psalm 95 is closely related to Psalms 50 and 81.[1]

The *first* part of this section considers the historical setting of the text. *Secondly,* attention is paid to the literary types that occur in this psalm such as text critical notes, form, structure. *Thirdly,* the study reflects on the exegetical comments of the text and the kingship metaphor of Yahweh. *Fourthly,* I give the comments in relation for worship.

5.1. Historical Analysis

This section explores both the Davidic monarchical and the post-exilic settings. Also considered how Psalm 95 and Psalms 50 and 81 are similar to each other in reflecting the sovereignty of Yahweh.

---

1 Artur Weiser, "The Psalms: A Commentary," in *The Old Testament Library*, edited by Peter Ackroyd (Philadelphia: Westminster John Knox Press, 1962), 625.

5.1.1. Davidic Monarchical Setting

The LXX ascribes Psalm 95 to David (Heb 4:7). In relation to this view Mowinckel and Howard, argue for Davidic monarchical setting. *First,* the enthronement psalms in connection with the New Year festival affirms that such a festival must have existed in pre-exilic or close to monarchical setting.[2] *Secondly,* Zorn states "The psalm is most likely pre-exilic and possibly goes back to the early monarchical period or earlier."[3]

Thirdly, Psalm 95 is similar to the pattern of Psalms 50 and 81. In these Psalms, Yahweh the king is also revealed as God the Creator. According to Eaton, the idea of kingship within Psalm 81 support the view that most probably Psalm 95 comes from the heart of festive celebration as the great procession enters the temple courts to give praises and adoration.[4] So in comparing Psalms 50 and 81, the date or setting of Psalm 95 could be much earlier than post-exilic.[5] *Fourthly,* phrases such as "Yahweh is our God, and we are the people of his pasture, and the sheep of his hand" (Ps 95:6, Ps 23, Lev 26:12, Deut 7:6), lead Schaefer to claims that it is in the Davidic monarchical setting.[6]

As to the date, it is possible that Psalm 95 existed in the monarchical setting with the Davidic dynasty. Thus, as seen above, Mowinckel, Zorn and Eaton support the Davidic monarchical setting.

5.1.2. Post-Exilic Setting

Kraus and Gerstenberger support the post-exilic setting of Psalm 95. *First,* Psalm 95 is in the late monarchy or exilic setting because it reflects a prophetic liturgy.[7] The worship services in Jewish congregations of the fifth and fourth

---

2 Sigmund Mowinckel, *The Psalms in Israel's Worship,Two Volumes in One*, trans. D.R. Ap-Thomas (Grand Rapids: William B. Eerdmans Publishing Company, 2004), 118. See David M. Howard, *The Structure of Psalms 93-100* (Winona Lake: Eisenbrauns, 1997), 115-116. Konrad Schaefer, *Psalms, Berit Olam*: *Studies in Hebrew Narrative & Poetry,* edited by David W. Cotter, (Collegeville: The Liturgical Press, 2001), 236. John Eaton, *The Psalms: A Historical and Spiritual Commentary with an Introduction and New Translation* (London: Continuum International Publishing Group, 2005), 337-338.

3 Walter D. Zorn, "Psalms," in *The College Press NIV Commentary*, vol. 2 (Joplin, MO: College Press Publishing Co, 2004), 202.

4 John Eaton, *The Psalms: A Historical and Spiritual Commentary with an Introduction and New Translation* (London: Continuum International Publishing Group, 2005), 337.

5 Eaton, *The Psalms,* 338.

6 Konrad, Schaefer, "Psalms," *Studies in Hebrew Narrative & Poetry,* edited by David W. Cotter (Collegeville: The Liturgical Press, 2001), 236.

7 Hans-Joachim Kraus, "Psalms 60-150," in *A Continental Commentary*, trans. Hilton C. Oswald (Minneapolis: Fortress Press, 1993), 246. See Erhard S. Gerstenberger, *Psalms, Part 2 and Lamentations: The Forms of the Old Testament Literature*, vol. XV (Grand Rapids: William B. Eerdmans Publishing Company, 2001), 192. Konrad Schaefer,

centuries BCE may have given rise to this kind of public 'introit' in worship.[8] In this account we can think of congregational worship.[9] *Secondly,* this Psalm has often been used in temple worship and it could not have been composed earlier than the late Persian period and probably early in the Greek period.[10] *Thirdly*, Tate affirms, Psalm 95 was originally used in the early post-exilic Israelites communities.[11] It refers to "post-exilic restoration, when services of worship demanded grandiosity as a climax to pilgrimages and processions."[12] *Fourthly,* the internal evidences of Psalm 95 seem to argue for a post-exilic date. The first part of the psalm implies that from the beginning, Israel's God is prominent in Deutero-Isaiah and that this concept is well-established in the mind of the worshippers.

After the exile, the people murmuring against the Lord may reflect their distress about their condition.[13] As a result, it is most likely written in the middle of the fifth century BCE as it is reflected in Trito-Isaiah.[14]

Though LXX assigns this Psalm 95 to David and calls it "a song of praise to David," this point does not bear much weight because it seems to be only a late editorial note.[15] Therefore, although the Psalm may be of pre-exilic origin, most probably it is of a post-exilic date. This is because a post-exilic psalm could be incorporated with the old tradition. As we examine and compare both views in regard to setting, we cannot fully disagree with scholars like Mowinckel and Zorn who have supported the Davidic setting. However, I would support multiple redaction because the people of Israel went astray from God and this is a kind of reminder to the Israelites of how to live as a chosen nation by reminding them of the wilderness experiences.

"Psalms." *Studies in Hebrew Narrative & Poetry Psalms*, edited by David W. Cotter (Collegeville: The Liturgical Press, 2001), 236. Elmer A. Leslie, *The Psalms: Translated and Interpreted in the Light of Hebrew Life and Worship* (New York: Abingdon Press, 1949), 212.

8 Introit which means a composition of vocal music that is appropriate for opening Church services.

9 Gerstenberger, *Psalms, Part 2 and Lamentations*, 185.

10 Charles A. Briggs and Emilie Grace Briggs, "The Book of Psalms," in *The International Critical Commentary*, vol. 1 (Edinburgh: T & T Clark, 1969), 293.

11 Marvine E. Tate, "Psalms 51-100," in *Word Biblical Commentary,* vol. 20, edited by David A. Hubbard, (Dallas: Word Books, 1990), 500.

12 Terrien, *The Psalms: Strophic Structure and Theological Commentary,* 672.

13 William R. Taylor, "The Book of Psalms," in *The Interpreter's Bible,* vol. IV, edited by George Arthur Buttrick (New York: Abingdon Press, 1955), 513.

14 Elmer A. Leslie, *The Psalms: Translated and Interpreted in the Light of Hebrew Life and Worship* (New York: Abingdon Press, 1949), 212.

15 A. A. Anderson,"The Book of Psalms : Psalms 73-150," in *New Century Bible Commentary*, vol. 2, (London: William B. Eerdmans Publishing Company, 1989), 677.

5.2. Literary Analysis of the Text

This section looks into translation, critical notes, form and structure of the text, phrases and repetition which occur in the poem. This helps the reader to understand the text and discover the literary usage which runs through the text.

5.2.1. Translation

1 לכו נרננה ליהוה נריעה לצור ישענו :	1. Come in let us *exult*[16] with joy to the Lord, let us shout for joy to the rock of our *deliverance.*[17]
2 נקדמה פניו בתודה בזמרות נריע לו :	2. Let us come to meet before his face with *thanks giving*,[18] let us raise a shout to him with song.
3 כי אל גדול יהוה ומלך גדיל על־כל־אלהים :	3. For Yahweh is a great God and is a *great King*[19] over all gods.
4 אשר בידו מחקרי־ ארץ ותועפות הרים לו:	4. By whose one's hand are the *depths*[20] of the earth, and to whom the tops of the mountains belong.
5 אשר־לו הים והוא עשהו ויבשת ידיו יצרו :	5. The one to whom the sea belongs, for it was he who made, and his hands formed the dry land
6 באו נשתחוה ונכרעה נברכה לפני־יהוה עשנו:	6. Come in, let us worship and *bow down*,[21] let us *kneel down*[22] to face the Lord our Maker.

16 V.1. רנן 'exult, give a ringing cry.' See A. Philip Brown II and Bryan.W Smith, eds., *A Reader's Hebrew Bible* (Zondervan, 2008), 1204.

17 V.1. ישע Goldingay translated 'delivers.' See Goldingay, *Psalms* 90-150, 87. Weiser translated 'salvation.' I have translated ישע 'deliverance' as Goldingay.

18 V.2. תודה 'song of thanksgiving,' 'song of praise,' thanksgiving in songs of liturgical worship.' See A. Philip Brown II and Bryan.W Smith, eds., *A Reader's Hebrew Bible* (Zondervan, 2008), 1204.

19 V. 3a. ומלך גדול, 'and great king.' The usage of the expression 'a great king' in Pss 47:3, 7, 8, 48: 2-3 indicates clearly that the expressions are definite. Yahweh is not only a great God and a great king but Yahweh is 'the great one.' See Tate, *Psalms* 51-100, 497.

20 V.4. מחקר 'unexplored depths or range.' See A.Philip Brown II and Bryan.W Smith, eds., *A Reader's Hebrew Bible* (Zondervan, 2008), 1204.

21 V. 6a. ונכרעה means 'to bow down,' ו is a particle conjunction כרע is a verb *qal* which is the imperfect 1st person common plural cohortative in both form and meaning 'to bow down or bend the knee.' See Karl Elliger and Wilhelm Rudolph, eds., *Biblia Hebraica Stuttgartensia* (Stuttgart: Biblia Hebraica Stuttgartensia, 1997), 1177.

22 V. 6b. נברכה 'to kneel,' ברך verb *qal* is the imperfect 1st person common plural cohortative in both form and meaning. Some manuscripts were omitted and several manuscripts, the Syriac Version of the OT have ון , Septuagint καιΚλανσωμεν, נברכה. Anderson argues that all these verbs like "worship, bow down and kneel, are probably synonymous and

7 כי הוא אלהינו ואנחנו עם מרעיתו וצאן ידו היום אם־בקלו תשמעו :	7. For he is our God, and we are the people of his pasture, and the sheep of his *hand.*[23] Today, if you hear to his voice.
8 אל־תקשו לבבכם כמריבה כיום מסה במדבר :	8. Do not harden your heart, as at *Meribah,*[24] As in the day of Massah in the wilderness.
9 אשר נסוני אבותיכם בחנוני גם־ראו פעלי :	9. When your ancestors tested me, they tried me, though they had seen my work.
10 ארבעים שנה אקוט בדור ואמר עם תעי לבב הם והם לא־ידעו דרכי :	10. For forty years I loathed with this *generation,* and said they are people whose heart wander about, and they do not know my ways.
11 אשר־נשבעתי באפי אם־יבאון אל־מנוחתי :	11. When I swore in my anger, they shall not come in to *my rest.*[25]

5.2.2. Text Critical Notes

First, קדם 'to meet' (Ps 95:2). The verb form in *piel* talks about 'to meet' or to come whereas in *hiph* it means 'to encounter.' קדם refers to the procession which moves toward the place of worship.[26] In *A Reader's Hebrew Bible,* קדם means 'approach, come to meet.'[27] In a wider perspective, Psalm 95:1-7c begins with a joyful expression. Terrien rightly points out that "the joyful noise is a ritual shout that mobilizes the attention and the cooperation of the whole

---

emphasize the respect and homage due to God." See A. A. Anderson, "The Book of Psalms: Psalms 73-150," in *New Century Bible Commentary,* vol. 2 (London: William B. Eerdmans Publishing Company, 1989), 678. ברך 'kneel down.' See A. Philip Brown II and Bryan. W Smith, eds., *A Reader's Hebrew Bible* (Zondervan, 2008), 1205.

23 V.7c. יד 'hand' is a common noun in the feminine singular construct suffix 3rd person masculine singular. Gunkel, Kraus and BHS suggest the addition of the plural imperative דעו at the beginning, with the reading, 'know today,' (of) his power (literally hand). The change is based on appeal to haplography. We see the syntactical parallels between Ps 79: 13 and Ps 95:7. See Marvine E. Tate, "Psalms 51-150," in *Word Biblical Commentary*, vol. 20, edited by David A. Hubbard (Dallas: Word Books, 1990), 497.

24 V.8. כמריבה 'strife'and מסה 'temptation.' See Arthur G. Clarke, *Analytical Studies in the Psalms* (Grand Rapids: Kregel Publications, 1979), 242.

25 V.11. מנוחה 'my rest,' denotes 'the land of promise' (cf. Num 20:1-13), See Elliger and Rudolph, *Biblia Hebraica Stuttgartensia.*

26 Tate, *Psalms 51-100*, 500.

27 Philip, Brown II, A., and Bryan W. Smith, eds. *A Reader's Hebrew Bible* (Zondervan, 2008), 1204.

assembly." [28] Therefore, because it is found in common plural form מדק invites all people for the worship.

Secondly, פנה 'face or presence' (Ps 95:2). פנה is noun and refers to the face of Yahweh or, in other words, the presence of Yahweh. Goldingay affirms that "the reference to Yahweh's face underlines the reality of meeting, it is as if we actually have seen Yahweh look into Yahweh's eyes, catch sight of Yahweh's smile.[29] Thus, the psalmist is urging people to come before the presence of God.

Thirdly, בוא 'to come' (Ps 95:1, 2, 6). The word בוא may be considered an actual form of entry for worship which motivates the worshippers to prostrate themselves and bow down so that they will be filled with the attitude of worship.[30] Zorn argues that בוא in verse 6 refers to a walk until we meet the one we are looking for, referring to God.[31] Enns claims that what motivates the worshippers now is that God is the creator of the people and that reminds the people to acknowledge the Lord and give due worship to him.[32] Therefore, worshippers recognize the Lord as creator of all and king who is indeed worthy to be worshipped. "We are the people of his pasture, the sheep under God's care" (v.7).[33]

The comparison of God's people to sheep is a common metaphor in the literature of Psalms where it portrays that Yahweh is the one who cares for the people. Here, the psalmist means to say that all things either high or low, small or big, strong or weak, are subject to the Lord's sovereignty. Therefore, it clearly testifies that the Lord's supremacy over the gods and the earth is grounded in the fact that Yahweh is the creator God and nothing else.[34] We are invited to enter into God's presence and worship, and as God's people, we are exhorted to bow down in worship.

Fourthly, מחקר 'range' (Ps 95:4). מחקר is a common noun; a masculine plural construct, meaning 'a range.' The word מחקר does not appear elsewhere and perhaps it means 'places to be explored.' (*BDB,* 350), derives the noun from the verb חקר, meaning to search or to explore. LXX reads περατα means opposite sides and seems to assume מחקרי meaning 'faraway places.' It could also mean 'remote parts of the earth.' In connection to this concept, the power

---

28 Terrien, *The Psalms: Strophic Structure and Theological Commentary*, 669.

29 John Goldingay, "Psalms 90-150," in *Baker Commentary on the Old Testament Wisdomand Psalms,* vol. 3, edited by Tremper Longman III (Grand Rapids: Baker Academic, 2008), 91.

30 Tate, *Psalms 51-100*, 501.

31 Zorn, *Psalms*, 203.

32 Peter E. Enns, "Creation and Re-Creation: Psalm 95 and Its Interpretation in Hebrew 3:1-4:13," *Westminster Theological Journal* 55 (1993): 258.

33 Eugene H.Merrill, *Everlasting Dominion: A Theology of the Old Testament* (Nashville: Broadman & Holman Publishers, 2006), 319–320.

34 Taylor, *Psalms and Proverbs*, 515.

of God expands from the lowest and most unapproachable parts of the earth to the mountain peaks, the whole world is in the hand of God.[35]

Fifthly, עמ מרעיתו וצאן 'His people and the flock of his pasture' (Ps 95:7). The *BHS* suggests the reading עמ מרעיתו וצאן, "His people and the flock of his pasture" and is adopted by Gunkel and Kraus.[36] The change is supported by one Hebrew manuscript, the Syriac and Targum. It seems Anderson supports this phrase as a variation of the covenant concept "I will be their God and they shall be my people" [37] (Jer 31:33, Ex 19:5, Ezek 34:31).

Sixthly, בדור 'with a generation' ב particle preposition דור noun common masculine singular absolute (Ps 95:10). LXX the Greek translation of the Old Testament smoothens out the text with, τηγενεמαεκεινη - ההוא בדור 'with that generation,' so the Syriac version of the Old Testament. M. T. has with a generation. Leslie notes that God made a solemn oath and would not permit that generation to enter into their ultimate heritage.[38] *A Reader's Hebrew Bible* suggests in note 20 מנוחה as 'dwelling place.' This dwelling place refers to the throne of Yahweh which is called a resting place.[39]

Finally, אל־מנוחתי 'into resting place' (Ps 95:11). There are different opinions concerning the meaning of 'resting place.' Terrien claims that 'rest' might be a fitting word for 'green pasture' to parallel with the phrase 'we are the people of his pasture' (Ps 95:7).[40] Anderson argues that it is most probably the 'promised land.'[41] Eaton agrees with Anderson and says this could be compared to the Promised Land which is "God's rest, Yahweh blessed abode" (Deut 12:9, Num 14:30, Ps 132:8, 14).[42] Resting place links with 'coming in' in Psalm 95:6. Therefore, Targum assumes that 'resting place' refers to the sanctuary. In verse 6, people are invited to come and worship the Lord in the temple.[43] However, if we take this view, there is a contrasting use of come or rest in verses 6 and 11. At first, worshippers were invited into God's presence while the conclusion states that 'they shall not enter into my rest.' Therefore,

---

35 Tate, *Psalms 51-100*, 497.

36 Tate, *Psalms 51-100*, 497.

37 Anderson, *The Book of Psalms: Psalms 73-150*, 676.

38 Leslie, *The Psalms: Translated and Interpreted in the Light of Hebrew Life and Worship*, 214.

39 Brown II and Smith, *A Reader's Hebrew Bible*, 1205.

40 Terrien, *The Psalms: Strophic Structure and Theological Commentary*, 672.

41 Anderson, *The Book of Psalms: Psalms 73-150*, 680.

42 Eaton, *The Psalms*, 338.

43 Goldingay, *Psalms 90-150*, 97.

Brueggemann rightly points out that 'rest' originally meant the Promised Land which is God's 'resting place' (Deut 12:10, 25:19, 1 King 8:56).[44]

The psalmist encourages people to come before the Lord and give due reverence to him. The text mentions the phrase 'let us worship' which actually means 'let us prostrate ourselves down.'[45] Kraus argues that people cast themselves down into the dust before Yahweh (cf. Judg 7:5, 1 King 8:54) and 'honour the God of Israel with all shout and praises.'[46] Thus, the psalmist stresses that when people are under the face of Yahweh, they are in the presence of Yahweh.

5.2.3. Form of the Psalm

The form of Psalm 95 is identified as a hymn and a song of thanksgiving. The psalm gives a hymnal call upon the congregation to come before the face of God with songs of praise. It is regarded as a "portion of a liturgy of the autumn festival recited before the festival" congregation entered the sanctuary.[47]

For Taylor the first part of the psalm is a hymn for congregational singing. It may have been a processional hymn sung by the people as they moved to the temple. On the other hand, it could be sung antiphonally, one verse by a priest or a song leader and other verse by the worshippers. But the second part is different as compared to the first part of Psalm 95.[48] According to Terrien, the meter confirms the movement of the poem, verses 1-9 is 3+3 and verses 8-11 is 4+4 in the prophetic oracle.[49] This is how the text indicates the visible characters of form and the use of meter in Psalm 95.

5.2.4. Structure of the Psalm

It is suggested that there are two main structures in Psalm 95. The first part is Psalm 95:1-7a and the second part is Psalm 95:7b-11. Kraus points out the following points through critical analysis. (1) Verses 1-7a talks about singing and giving thanks with two introductions in Verses. 1-2 and 6. (2) Verses 7b-11 reflects the prophetic word of rebuke.[50] Similarly, Weiser argues that the first

44 Walter Brueggemann, *The Message of the Psalms: A Theological Commentary* (Minneapolis: Augsburg Publishing House, 1984), 237.

45 Zorn, *Psalms*, 204.

46 Kraus, *Psalms 60-150*, 247.

47 Weiser, The Psalms: A Commentary, 625-626.

48 Taylor, "The Book of Psalms," 513.

49 Terrien, *The Psalms: Strophic Structure and Theological Commentary*, 669.

50 Kraus, *Psalms 60-150*, 245. Looking at the whole text of Psalm 95, many form critics have argued that Psalm 95 is composed of two songs that were sung in the cult. It seems many scholars support the idea that the congregational praise was followed by prophetic oracles, which Gunkel called *Wechselnde Stimmen.* Hermann Gunkel, *Die Psalmen ubersetzt and erklart.* 6th ed. (Gottingen: Vandenhoeck & Ruprecht, 1986), 418.

part (Psalm 95:1-7a) contains a hymn preparing the congregation for an encounter with God. The second part (Psalm 95:7b-11) is a kind of warning from God and also calling them to obey God.[51]

Eaton agrees with Kraus and Weiser in regards to the function of the structure. However, to some extent Eaton's style of division of the verses is different from theirs (verses 1-7ab is a hymnic style and verses 7c-11 is a call to hear God's voice).[52] To be more specific, we can summarize the Psalm 95 in the following forms. Verses 1-5 deals with God's cosmic creation as a key motivation for worshipping Yahweh and verses 6-7a inspires the faithful to worship Yahweh the great God. Verses 7b-11 concludes the psalm by warning the unfaithful people by citing the example of the incident at Meribah and Massah as a paradigm which is considered to be significant for the worshippers to be true and faithful to God.[53]

5.2.5. Repetition

Repetition is one of the psalmist's special expressions in the context of worship. We see the word גדול 'great' mentioned two times in verse 3. In the history of OT, not only the people of Israel but even the other people, like for instance, the Assyrians claim their god is great (2 Kings 18:19, 28). However, the greatness of Israel's God is incomparable with the great gods of others. The psalmist invites people to acknowledge the great king among the kings. The word great is repeatedly used claiming that Yahweh is a great God and a great king and other gods cannot control the greatness of Yahweh.[54]

The word כי 'for' is found in verses 3 and 7, this 'for' links the ideas from one strophe to another, connecting the kingship metaphor of Yahweh. Brueggemann argues that after the invitation, the first motive is introduced by כי 'for' focuses on the creator. The second motive כי 'for' focuses on the idea that Yahweh is our God and we are his flock.[55] For Gerstenberger, the calls to worship are not motive clauses but true hymnic lines, "sing to the Lord, for Yahweh has triumphed gloriously" (Ex 15:21). Looking into this aspect it seems the song itself has this meaning and as a result, the psalmist puts 'for' before the participants in worship to be endlessly repeated.[56]

This hymn repeatedly uses the word פנה 'face' in verse 2 and 6, the term can refer to seeking or coming into the presence of Yahweh. פנה is used in a metaphorical way for the presence of God and it is appropriate in the context

51 Weiser, *The Psalms*, 625.

52 Eaton, *The Psalms,* 337.

53 Enns, "Creation and Re-Creation: Psalm 95 and Its Interpretation in Hebrew 3:1-4:13," 256.

54 Goldingay, *Baker Commentary on the Old Testament Wisdom and Psalms*, 92.

55 Brueggemann, *The Message of the Psalms: A Theological Commentary*, 236.

56 Gerstenberger, *Psalms, Part 2 and Lamentations*, 183.

of worship.[57] Eaton suggests that the face of Yahweh reflects his holy presence as the worshippers come before him with a song of thanksgiving.[58] Repetition is a literary function and it is beneficial for the worshippers to be reminded again of the Lordship of Yahweh. The usage of repetition has an immense significance for the worshippers.

5.3. Comments in Relation to the Kingship Metaphor

First, ישע 'deliverance' refers to the kingship metaphor of Yahweh (Ps 95:1). Terrien argues that the word ישע or the phrase 'rock of our deliverance' particularly in Psalm 95 demonstrates that "God's presence was sensed with strongest intensity by the devotees of Yahweh" in the context of polytheism.[59] The word צור 'rock' of our deliverance means that through the mighty power of Yahweh, the people were delivered from the enemies' hands. These are several examples of 'rock' referring to God in the book of Psalms (Pss 18:2, 19:14, 28:1, 42:9, 71:3).[60] The royal psalms talk about God as a deliverer, those who called upon the Lord for help, they experienced divine deliverance from enemies.[61] Deliverance implies the ability to defend, rescue, or defeat and is associated with Yahweh's action in bringing the people of Israel out of Egypt, though usually with reference to Yahweh's strong hand (Ps 18:17).[62]

Secondly, צור 'rock' denotes to the kingship metaphor of Yahweh (Ps 95:1) and this is prominent in Deuteronomy 32. Yahweh is described as, "The rock, his work is perfect, and all his ways are just," (Deut 32:4). In Deuteronomy 32, explicitly portrays Yahweh as Israel's rock or their 'creator and protection.' Anderson points out that the metaphor of rock indicates 'reliability and stability' of the divine nature of Yahweh the king.[63] In support of Anderson's point, Flynn also rightly says the word rock is a metaphor which refers to a 'solid foundation' and a 'sure defence.' Yahweh the rock gave birth to Israel. Thus, the rock is their salvation or deliverance (Deut 32:15, 18). This metaphor of rock is used of Christ in the New Testament (1 Cor 10:1-4). Both

57 Tate, *Psalms 51-100*, 501.

58 Eaton, *The Psalms*, 338.

59 Terrien, *The Psalms: Strophic Structure and Theological Commentary*, 669.

60 John H. Walton, Victor H. Matthews, and Mark W. Chavalas, *The IVP Bible Background Commentary: Old Testament* (Downers Grove: IVP Academic, 2000), 515. Briggs suggests that this is the favourite term for God especially in God's relation to the people of Israel from ancient times (Deut 32:15, Ps 62:3, 7, 89:27). See Charles Augustus Briggs, *A Critical and Exegetical Commentary on the Book of Psalms*, vol. I (Edinburgh: T & T Clark, 1969), 294.

61 Peter C. Craigie, "Psalms 1-50," in *Word Biblical Commentary*, edited by David A. Hubbard and Glenn W. Barker (Waco: Word Books, 1983), 173.

62 Goldingay, "Psalms 1-41," 257.

63 Anderson, "The Book of Psalms: Psalms 73-150," 677.

the testaments talk about the metaphor of rock in relation to salvation.[64] Thus, Yahweh is the rock and he alone gives security and protection to the people. His kingship is strong as shown through the metaphor of rock.

Thirdly, גדול יהוה ומלך 'the great God and king' (Ps 95:3). In the light of form critic expression, this figurative phrase denotes the kingship metaphor of Yahweh. The text stresses the great God and king over all gods and the universe. This combination of words is one of the unique characteristics that we see from the psalms of the Yahweh's enthronement.[65]

Fourthly, the word יד 'hand' occurs in Psalm 95 in verses 5 and 7. This imagery indicates the kingship of Yahweh who protects the people. Thus, the hand of Yahweh signifies Yahweh's protection upon the chosen nation. In other words, it also signifies true sovereignty of Yahweh over the whole world as both the sea and dry land are made by Yahweh's hand (Ps 95:5 cf. Ps. 8:3).[66] The works of Yahweh are seen in verse 4 and verse 5 "the depths of the earth are in Yahweh's hand, and the mountain peaks as well." This idea leads into verse 6 once again where the community is invited to come and worship.[67] The royal psalms present Yahweh as the personal deliverer. For example, Psalm 18:2 shows God as a rock or a fortress or a refuge, signifying his trustworthiness and protection and therefore those who are in distress and danger can flee for refuge. Thus, the hands of Yahweh protect all his creatures by his faithfulness.

5.4. Comments in Relation to Worship

The following points are developed to give comments in relation to worship from an exegetical study of Psalm 95. I consider them to be major comments in relation to worship. The facts are linked with the connotations of Yahweh's kingship. They are: *First, the psalmist emphasizes praising Yahweh* in worship because Yahweh the king deserves all our praises. Apparently, the worshippers are called upon to give praises to the king, because Yahweh is the true deliverer. The summons is not just a simple call but a call in an official matter with a purpose and this is what the text rightly indicates. Leslie affirms that "the note of joyous thanksgiving thrills the summons."[68]

---

64 Shawn W. Flynn, *YHWH Is King: The Development of Divine Kingship in Ancient Israel* (Leiden: Koninklijke Brill NV, 2014), 79. See J. A. Thompson, "Deuteronomy," in *Tyndale Old Testament Commentaries* (Leicester: InterVarsity Press, 1974), 298-304. P. C. Craigie, "The Book of Deuteronomy" in *NICOT* (Grand Rapids: William B. Eerdmans Publishing Company, 1976), 376-387. Andrew E. Hill, "רוצ," *Dictionary of Old Testament & Exegesis*, vol. 3, edited by Willem A. VanGemeren (Grand Rapids: Zondervan, 1997), 793-794.

65 Leslie, *The Psalms*, 213.

66 Goldingay, *Psalms 90-150*, 92, 94.

67 Tate, *Psalms 51-100*, 500.

68 Leslie, *The Psalms*, 212-213.

The psalmist says לכו נרננה ליהוה נריעה לצור ישענו "Come let us sing for joy to the Lord and shout to the rock of our deliverance" (Ps 95:1). The call is to worship God with song and music in praise which is the natural overflow of a thankful heart. The praise affirms that all things are in the hands of Yahweh. The psalmist calls for a jubilant exaltation through song declaring that Yahweh is not a deity far away from us. Yahweh is here and Yahweh is our God, our maker and our shepherd. All these give enough reasons to enter in the house of God and praise God with shouting and joyful songs.[69] Anderson rightly notes that worshippers are summoned to acclaim praises because Yahweh is the highest God, who is the king above all kings, who is the creator of the world and Lord of the world.[70] Therefore, Yahweh is hailed by the worshippers as their mighty king and faithful God. Thus, worshippers are summoned to acclaim Yahweh as they have come into the presence of the creator, whose hands made and shaped the land.[71]

Goldingay says that the worship of Yahweh involved the attitude of the heart and must comprise glorifying Yahweh publically.[72] I agree with this point because if worship does not come from the heart, it has no meaning. The inner mind and outward appearance should involve the heart and doing things from the heart is pleasing in God's sight. The mood of the first part of the hymn makes it clear that worship is to be demonstrated in a manner of excitement when the worshippers are called upon to worship God with praises. This type of worship was essential for Israel's worship because they were fond of singing and dancing.

Secondly, the Hebrew word תודה 'thanksgiving or thanks offering' (Ps 95:2) this word is linked worship. Gerstenberger comments that "the תודה was originally a thanksgiving sacrifice." However, it is possible that in worship a thanksgiving song took the place of the animal offering.[73] Mowinckel argues that "both thank offering and thanksgiving psalms are called תודה in Hebrew." Thanksgiving proclaims the mighty deeds of Yahweh and also calls upon the people to give honour and praise to Yahweh.[74] Thanksgiving is an act of worship. תודה which at first meant the gift of thanks (literally, the lifting of hands) and designated "the psalms of thanksgiving, and sacrifice" was completely spiritualized.[75]

69 Zorn, *Psalms,* 201.

70 Anderson, *The Book of Psalms: Psalms 73-150*, 677.

71 Eaton, *The Psalms*, 338.

72 Goldingay, *Psalms 90-150*, 91.

73 Gerstenberger, *Psalms, Part 2 and Lamentations,* 203.

74 Mowinckel, *The Psalms in Israel's Worship*, 27-28.

75 Samuel L. Terrien, *The Psalms and Their Meaning for Today* (New York: The Bobbs-Merrill Company, Inc, 1952), 192.

Watts comments that the Hebrew word for thanksgiving is תודה. The word may apply either to the psalm or to the thanksgiving sacrifice. Probably תודה is used regularly in connection with the offering.[76] Guthrie explains that "תודה denotes thanksgiving, thank offering, thanksgiving sacrifice, and song of thanksgiving."[77] For Gunkel, the thanksgiving psalm belongs originally to the thanksgiving offering. The psalm is related to a celebratory act and is accompanied by calling on the name of Yahweh. This act must have played a significant role in the thanksgiving sacrifice.[78] He further affirms that giving thanks to God who created everything saves people and gathers those who are scattered.[79]

תודה is a song of thanksgiving and thanksgiving psalms are associated with the act of prostration before Yahweh. In Psalm 95, it demands תודה of the entire community.[80]*A Reader's Hebrew Bible* in note 6 suggests that תודה is "Thanksgiving in songs of liturgical worship."[81] Thanksgiving in Israel was a passionate, generous, public response to Yahweh for Yahweh's gift or action and was obligatory for the people of Israel. The word תודה is understood as the completion of petition. When God answers their prayers, Israel offers to Yahweh a song of thanksgiving in response to the act of Yahweh. The act of תודה is clearly a concrete gesture that constitutes an act of worship, an act of devotion and loyalty given to Yahweh.[82]

Thirdly, the psalmist expresses humility in worship which reflects the connotation of kingship metaphor. Yahweh is the king, therefore, the people of God must humble themselves before the highest God. The first part of the hymn encourages the people to come into the presence of God with shouts of praise to Yahweh the king. However, towards the middle, the mood of worship in the text changes (Ps 95:6-7a). The mood of joy and excitement in worship is replaced with that of humility and submission. There are three things that the worshippers are urged to do here: Prostrate themselves, kneel and bow

---

76 John D. W. Watts, "Psalms of Trust, Thanksgiving, and Praise," *Review Expositor* 3, no. 81 (Sum, 1984): 399.

77 Harvey H. Guthrie, *Israel's Sacred Songs: A Study of Dominant Themes* (New York: The Seabury Press, 1978), 147.

78 Hermann Gunkel, *Introduction to Psalms: The Genres of the Religious Lyric of Israel* (Macon, Georgia: Mercer University Press, 1998), 199.

79 Gunkel, *Introduction to Psalms: The Genres of the Religious Lyric of Israel,* 242.

80 Kraus, *Psalms 60-150*, 246.

81 Brown II and Smith, *A Reader's Hebrew Bible*, 1204.

82 Walter Brueggemann, *Worship in Ancient Israel: An Essential Guide* (Nashville: Abingdon Press, 2005), 53–54. Thanksgiving hymns were familiar to the people of Israel. They were usually sung as songs of thanksgiving in response to God's goodness and faithfulness. This is richly demonstrated in that thanksgiving hymns play a vital role in Israel's worship. 54.

down. These gestures express submission and humility in the presence of the awesome king.[83]

Anderson suggests that these three verbs, 'obeisance or prostration,' 'kneeling, and 'bowing down' are probably synonymous and emphasize the respect and homage due to God.[84] The worshippers, as they enter into the temple, must all together prostrate themselves with their faces toward the most holy place which shows their reverence to the most holy God who created everything and who deserves to be worshipped.[85] It implies the acknowledgement of Yahweh's sovereignty in the context of worship because what we do with our bodies expresses our inner being. Goldingay strongly affirms "If there is no self-lowering, there can hardly be inner self lowering."[86] Therefore, for worshippers, humility is an essential part of worship.

Fourthly, the psalmist emphasizes listening to the voice of Yahweh in Worship. The psalmist says "Today if you hear the voice of God, do not harden your heart" (Ps 95:7-8). Here, the psalmist encourages the community to recognize Yahweh's present activities with the 'authority of prophetic charisma' and to listen to the voice of God. The key phrase אל־תקשו לבבכם 'do not harden your hearts' where the psalm warns the community against hardening and hard-heartedness (Ps 95:8). This wilderness generation is described as an example of those with an obstinate attitude to turn away from God's presence.[87] To be more specific, it refers to the examples cited from the wilderness experience of the Israelites. Here the names of two places are mentioned; Meriba and Massah. 'Meribah means strife,' and Massa means 'testing' which indicate the disobedient nature of the Israelites. Therefore, "beware of such error of heart and ignorance of God's way as characterized your ancestors in the forty years of their wilderness wandering" (Ex 16:35).[88]

Brueggemann rightly points out that "worship implies an attitude of listening and right disposition."[89] Psalm 95:7c, alludes to a very significant event in the history of Israel (Ex 34:11, Deut 4:40, 6:6, 9:3). Here, the Lord asks the people of Israel to observe what God commanded them to do because the command is for their own well-being and that of future generations as well. Obey the voice of God so that you will see success and enter into the true life.[90]

83 Samir Massouh, "Exegetical Notes Psalm 95," *TrinJ*, 4 (1983): 85.

84 Anderson, *The Book of Psalms: Psalms 73-150*, 678.

85 Leslie, *The Psalms*, 213.

86 Goldingay, *Psalms: Psalms 90-150*, 93.

87 Kraus, *Psalms 60-150,* 247-248.

88 Leslie, *The Psalms*, 214.

89 Brueggemann, *The Message of the Psalms: A Theological Commentary*, 237.

90 Eaton, *The Psalms*, 338.

For instance, during the time of Amos, Israel's way of worship was not accepted in the sight of God. It is not that the Lord disliked worship, but people did not obey and listen to Yahweh. Formality of worship alone makes no sense before God. Therefore, the Lord said "away with the noise of your songs, I will not listen to the music of your harps (Amos 5:23-24, cf. Isa 1:12-17). It is well-demonstrated that God wants the hearts of the people in worship (Jn 4:24). The psalmist envisions in Psalm 95 how God is to be placed in the centre of their worship.[91]

The psalmist brings in the effectiveness of listening to the voice of God in true worship. The psalmist says 'do not harden your heart as at Meribah and Massah' (Ex 17:1-7; Num 20:1-13) where Israelites tested God and strayed from God due to their rebellious nature. The real danger is that the same thing can happen to the present generation if the people are not mindful of their hearts.[92] Renz states that though the people are resting before the Lord in adoration, unless their hearts are obedient to the Lord, they will be driven out of their rest. Thus, Psalm 95 is a proportional challenge whereby the people are invited to enter into the temple to worship the Lord but are also taught to listen to the Lord and not be disobedient.[93]

This shows that listening to God leads to truthful worship. In the midst of praises in this psalm, the voice of the prophetic admonition burst out using the examples from the wilderness generation where it was expressed that Yahweh excludes from the salvific fulness of 'Yahweh's rest' those whose hearts have been hardened (cf. Heb 3:8, 4:3). Therefore, the true worshippers of Yahweh should and must listen to the voice of God.[94] Even in the NT, the epistle to the Hebrews (Heb 3:7-4:11 quotes Ps 95:7-11) warns against the danger of hardened hearts and urges the belivers to worship God truly. Hence, the psalmist clearly portrays that without obedience, worship becomes meaningless.

5.5. Theological Concerns Pertaining to the Kingship Metaphor of God

This section studies the biblical basis of gestures and postures and why God wants them in worship. Gestures and posture are described in enthronement psalms and they are closely attached with the kingship metaphor of Yahweh in the context of worship. The reason is that worshippers express themselves with an attitude of humility before Yahweh the great king through postures and gestures. The language of gesture and posture are significant elements in communication at the disposal of liturgical worship. Through them, worshippers

91 Zorn, *Psalms*, 205.

92 Brueggemann, *The Message of the Psalms: A Theological Commentary*, 237.

93 Renz, "Come, Let Us Listen to the Voice of the Lord," 146.

94 Kraus, *Psalms 60-150*, 248-249.

involve the whole person in liturgical worship. Therefore, whichever way it may be, liturgical body language is a means of expression and communication with God.[95]

Worship has many facets such as an honouring attitude, symbolic actions and word of praise. Goldingay rightly points out, "It is not surprising that worship involves both acts and words. While acts without words are blind, words without acts are empty." In that sense worship does not just involve the mind or heart. It also equally involves the voice and the body, the hands and the feet. It involves the whole person where worshippers communicate to Yahweh the king.[96]

5.5.1. Shouting

רוע is 'shout' but the term can also refer to the loud sound of a signal, either of a trumpet or a human voice. A variety of reasons or circumstances could lead people to shout, but above all shouting was characteristic of rejoicing especially in the enthronement psalms. Shouts of rejoicing often occurred in contexts where Yahweh's kingship is acclaimed. Psalm 95 is an example of such an instance where worshippers are to worship God with a shout of joy to the rock of our salvation.[97]

This shouting has implication for Israel's worship. The following references occur in the enthronement psalms (Pss 47:1, 95:1-2, 96:12, 98:4, 6). All the nations are called upon to pay homage to the mighty king of the whole world. They shout with joy acclaiming the sovereignty of Yahweh, the king. People shout from the top of their voices, rejoicing to worship and greet Yahweh. The nations accompany their exultant hymns with rhythmic shouting and the clapping of their hands to exalt the king in the highest place.[98] Yahweh is worthy of the praise of the whole universe. Thus, let the universe join in the shouts of joy and praise.

Kurtz suggests that shouting to the Lord is a response to Yahweh the great king. This may refer to any loud vocal or instrumental sound which allows for worshippers to express their emotions to God. In corporate worship, it is

---

95 Jeremy Haselock, "Gestures," in *The New Westminster Dictionary of Liturgy and Worship* (Louisville: SCM Press, 2002), 227-228. Liturgical postures and gestures can also involve different attitudes or characters such as reverence, awe, supplication, penitence and attentiveness. The body expressions are the vehicles which convey the dignity of the human person in the eyes of God. See Jeremy Haselock, "Posture," *The New Westminster Dictionary of Liturgy and Worship*, edited by Paul Bradshaw (Louisville: SCM Press, 2002), 377.

96 John Goldingay, *Old Testament Theology: Israel's Life*, vol. 3 (Downers Grove: InterVarsity Press, 2009), 118.

97 Schäder, "Psalm 47-How Universal Is Its Universalism?," 84-85.

98 Weiser, *The Psalms: A Commentary*, 376.

essential to persuade people to "express emotions that honour the Lord and are under the governorship of a mindfully engaged in truth."[99] Goldingay affirms that worshippers shout in worship with "enthusiasm because Yahweh, is the great king over all the gods and the one to whom the whole cosmos belongs, as its maker."[100] We have noted in the enthronement psalms that Yahweh is exalted as the great king. In connection to this idea, all nations are invited to join in shouts of joy and praise. It is the climax of the Psalter in general and the enthronement psalms in particular "with its outpouring of praise, rises to rhetorical peaks of universality."[101] It is necessary to understand rhetorical expression in the psalms and how it conveys meaning.

All the earth and all its inhabitants, the sea, the rivers and the mountains are summoned to shout for joy and make music to Yahweh.[102] The psalmist talks about shouting in the context of Israel's worship. Both the noise and clamor of shouting and the beauty and order of melody contribute to Yahweh's praise. Goldingay gives two reasons. First, worship need to glorify Yahweh publically, which means he gives special attention to shouting. Another reason is that human beings are "physical beings, with voices."[103] In worship, people express themselves naturally with cries and shouts. Thus, shouting is essential in worship because it involves the whole being of a person. Worship involved with noise means shouting to the Lord. Shouting is not subjected to limitation of heart attitude, it can express freely and loudly with all kinds of emotions.

In the enthronement psalms, all true worshippers are called to join in praise of Yahweh, the king, with joyous shouts sung to the accompaniment of musical instruments. Patterson asserts that although the verbs 'shout' and 'shout for joy' often appear in cries of victory after warfare, they also can be used in connection with joyous praise to God.

Kraus claims that in any case when the "shout is used it is a heralding manifestation of Yahweh's power" especially in the context of worship.[104] Anderson claims that "The reason for shouting is not only a feeling of joy but also the intention to acclaim the divine king" declaring that Yahweh is the King of kings (Pss 47:1, 98:4).[105] Shouting is the characteristic manner of Israel's jubilant cultic celebrations. As we look at 'shouting' in the enthronement

---

99 Kurtz, *God's Word the Final Word on Worship and Music: A Biblical Study*, 149. A shout, wholeheartedly response to God and it is appropriate in worship. A response mentions in the book of Psalms (Pss 41:11, 47:1, 60:8, 65:13, 66:1, 81:1, 95:1-2, 98:4-6, 100:1, 108:9), 149.

100 Goldingay, *Old Testament Theology: Israel's Life*, 177.

101 Wright, *The Mission of God*, 483.

102 Lama, "The Placement of Psalm 145 in Book V: A Compositional Analysis," 286. See (Pss 96:1, 9; 97:5, 9; 98:4; 100:1).

103 Goldingay, *Psalms 90-150*, 91.

104 Kraus, *Psalms 60-150*, 193.

105 Anderson, *The Book of Psalms: Psalms 1-72*, 361.

psalms, we can see that in several places, they mention the essential use of shouting in the worship. The gesture of shouting plays a vital part in Israel's worship. In my opinion, the word 'shout' can be applied in two ways. It can be through singing where the worhippers give their praises to the Lord and on the other hand, worshippers express their joy through shouting, declaring the sovereignty of Yahweh the king.

Therefore, shouting in worship has wide spiritual application and significance for worshippers. As we rejoice, we naturally shout to God expressing our joy and thankfulness.

5.5.2. Bowing

כרע 'to bow down,' this gesture is significant in Israel's worship. Haselock asserts that in the OT, "Bowing is symbolic of the recognition of divine power and of the adoration due to the Almighty God."[106] The psalmist claims, "Come in let us worship and bow down" (Ps 95:6a). Bowing down is considered as one of the most common gestures for worship. Bowing down denotes a humble action and is the most natural approach to the holy presence of God and forms the root idea of worship. Bowing can take the following forms, bending both the knees, bowing the head, bowing like bulrush, bending over double and prostration.[107]

Bowing is a sign of realization that the God who made the universe also cares about the universe. As the body is bowed, the worshippers' mind and will should also bow in submission to Yahweh.[108] Goldingay affirms that worshippers bow down before the presence of Yahweh because Yahweh is the greatest, the mightiest, the most splendid, the most majestic, and the most glorious. Everything in heaven or on the earth belongs to Yahweh the king. The action of bowing down is a sign of exalting the majesty of Yahweh.[109] Kurtz comments that bowing is the posture of meekness, a posture of lowly response that reveals the Lordship of God. This posture of worship is the most common form of worshippers in Israel's worship. The posture usually takes place when the worshipper is overwhelmed in the presence of the Lord. Nevertheless, it is the response of the saints of the ages (Rev 4-5). Humility and submission are hallmarks for the true worshippers of Yahweh, the king.[110]

Olison points out that, "Worship is about God, for God, to God. Worship has nothing to do with pleasing or making ourselves feel good. Worship is

---

106 Haselock, "Posture," in *The New Westminster Dictionary of Liturgy and Worship*, 230.

107 Gentile, "Worship God: Exploring the Dynamics of Psalmic Worship," 194.

108 Wilcock, *The Message of Psalms 73-150,* 93.

109 Goldingay, *Old Testament Theology: Israel's Life*, 176.

110 Kurtz, *God's Word the Final Word on Worship and Music: A Biblical Study*, 149-150.

about making God feel honoured."[111] Besides that, worship is the place where the worshippers bow mentally and physically before the Lord and offer praise to the holy God with reverent awe. Worship is not where worshippers come to meet each other and have a good time. It is where true worshippers to bow before the Lord and honour God.[112] Kraus suggests the unique idea that form-critically Psalm 95:6 calls for a procession, but at the same time, it introduces the act of homage. In fact, this is also a kind of tribute paid to Yahweh. As people come to worship, they cast themselves down before Yahweh, the great king. Probably they honour the God of Israel in praise, thanksgiving and adoration.[113]

Therefore, this metaphor of bowing down is essential in the context of Israel's worship. This bowing down signifies humility before Yahweh, the great King. Thus, bowing is considered a universal sign of respect. Bowing also reflects the fact that we give reverence to God.

5.5.3. Kneeling

ברך is 'kneel,' this is also considered as one of the essential postures presented in the context of Israel's worship. The position clearly signifies adoration. For instance, Jesus used this posture for prayer at Gethsemane (Luke 22:4). The psalmist says, "Let us kneel to face the Lord our Maker," (Ps 95:6). Kneeling is a deliberate act of submission and openly avows God's superiority. It expresses humility and subjugation to the will of God. It makes people totally vulnerable and puts them in a position of surrender (1 Kings 8:54; 2 Chron.6:13).[114]

Psalm 95:6 says, "Come, let us kneel before the Lord our Maker." David frequently bowed before God (Pss 5:7; 45:11). Kneeling is an expression of both humility and honour in the worship of Yahweh. It acknowledges the sovereignty of Yahweh, the king, and also expresses human inability without the help of creator God.[115]

Kneeling in prayer indicates total surrender in the face of God. Therefore, kneeling in worship services has spiritual implications where the worshippers surrender themselves and restore their relationship with God. Therefore, all these gestures are vital in the worship of Yahweh because through different gestures, people can express their needs and desires to Yahweh who is accessible in all situations. Thus, we should use all these principles of gestures to make our worship more fruitful and effective.

111 Kennon D. Olison, *Music in Worship: An Examination of the Contemporary Music in the Churches of Christ* (Bloomington: Kennon D. Olison, 2012), 13.

112 Olison, *Music in Worship,* 33.

113 Kraus, *Psalms 60-150*, 247.

114 Gentile, *Worship God,* 196.

115 Munroe, *The Purpose and Power of Praise and Worship*, 94.

Summary

Following points emerge from the above analysis. *First,* the psalmist describes the theological concerns pertaining to the kingship of Yahweh like postures and gestures in Israel's worship. 'Shouting to God' which indicates joyous acclamation of worship and is a confession of faith in a God who acts in history. On the other hand, postures and gestures are symbolic acts of the body and portray an attitude of submission and humility before Yahweh. God demands worship full of jubilation and worship with submission. In both, our physical gestures and also our inner hearts are required. *Secondly,* we worship because Yahweh created everything and holds everything in his authority. Therefore, the psalmist encourages us to acknowledge God, the creator, giving thanks to him who is the redeemer, merciful, majestic, yet is caring.

Thirdly, in worship listening plays a vital dimension which leads to maturity of faith. Listening leads people to be rooted in the word of God and keeps them from turning away from God as the wilderness generation did (Ps 95:8). *Fourthly,* the psalmist affirms that all worship must come from a sincere and obedient heart. We should not aim to perform external gestures without an inner conviction because that is hypocritical (Ps 95:10). We can conclude that Meribah and Massah incident portrays the consequences of human rebellious nature cannot lead to true worship and applies to disobedient people even today. Thus, a rebellious nature is against the will of God. This has been well exhibited by the psalmist who also brings out the true concept of worship relevant even today through the connotations of Yahweh's kingship.

Chapter 6

Exegetical Study of Psalm 96 Yahweh, the King as Judge of the World

Introduction

Psalm 96 describes the sovereignty of Yahweh who holds divine authority among all the other gods and who will judge the world. The unique feature of Psalm 96 is that it talks about a new song and new governance which played an essential role in Israel's worship as a cultic liturgy. Psalm 96 is parallel with the other enthronement psalms such as Psalms 47, 93 and 97 where it emphasises the connotations about the kingship of Yahweh.[1] The Psalm presents the concept that worship Yahweh should be inclusive in nature. The text affirms that both humans and nature declare the sovereignty of Yahweh through singing and rejoicing about the mighty deeds of God.

Like the previous studies, in this study of Psalm 96, *first,* I focus on its historical analysis and then on its literary aspects. *Secondly,* I focus on the exegetical comments in the text and comments in relation to the metaphor king deriving from it. *Thirdly,* I give comments in relation to worship.

6.1. Historical Analysis

This section deals with Psalm 96 from the historical perspective. It is necessary to evaluate the date and setting of the text. This helps to understand the background of the Psalm before going into the detail of the text. Kraus asserts that Psalm 96 is dependent on Isaiah 40-66 in its formations and

1 Artur Weiser, "The Psalms: A Commentary," in *The Old Testament Library*, edited by Peter Ackroyd (Philadelphia: Westminster John Knox Press, 1962), 628.

images. Therefore, I have focused on the scholarly opinions about how Psalm 96 relates to the book of Isaiah.

6.1.1. Davidic Monarchical Setting

Anderson and Schaefer are in favour of Davidic monarchical setting.[2] *First,* the poetic style has several ancient features and the psalm may well belong to the royal period when the exile prophets were "concerned to make such former festal joy live again, with its message of atonement, its glad tidings of the Lord's salvation."[3] *Secondly,* the account of Psalm 96 portrays that it might have emerged in the context of David's bringing the ark to Jerusalem (1 Chr 16:23-33).[4]

Thirdly, the setting of the enthronement psalms is likely in the feast of tabernacles which was, probably, the Israelite New Year festival. As per the date, this idea is in support of Psalm 96 in a Davidic monarchical setting.[5] I assume that whoever supports Davidic monarchical holds the view that this psalm reflects and has images of monarchical settings.

6.1.2. Post-Exilic Setting

Taylor and Tate place Psalm 96 in the post-exilic setting.[6] *First,* the similarities of Deutero Isaiah and Psalm 96 are so fascinating that the date might be the late exilic period as a kind of hope and restoration or else in post-exilic times with the establishment of the second temple as the new ceremonial place.[7] *Secondly,* the psalm belongs to a post-exilic date because the idea is stressed in Deutero Isaiah and Third Isaiah especially concerning the *nothingness of the*

---

2 A.A. Anderson, "The Book of Psalms: Psalms 73-150," in *New Century Bible Commentary*, vol. 2 (London: William B. Eerdmans Publishing Company, 1989). See John Eaton, *The Psalms: A Historical and Spiritual Commentary with an Introduction and New Translation* (London: Continuum International Publishing Group, 2005), 340-341. Konrad Schaefer, *Psalms, Berit Olam*: *Studies in Hebrew Narrative & Poetry*, edited by David W. Cotter (Collegeville: The Liturgical Press, 2001), 238.

3 John Eaton, *The Psalms: A Historical and Spiritual Commentary with an Introduction and New Translation* (London: Continuum International Publishing Group, 2005), 340.

4 Konrad, Schaefer, "Psalms," *Studies in Hebrew Narrative & Poetry,* edited by David W. Cotter (Collegeville: The Liturgical Press, 2001), 238.

5 Anderson, *The Book of Psalms: Psalms 73-150*, 681.

6 William R. Taylor, "The Book of Psalms," in *The Interpreter's Bible,* vol. IV, edited by George Arthur Buttrick (New York: Abingdon Press, 1955), 517-518. See A. A. Anderson, "The Book of Psalms: Psalms 73-150," in *New Century Bible Commentary*, vol. 2 (London: William B. Eerdmans Publishing Company, 1989), 681. Marvine E. Tate, "Psalms 51-150," in *Word Biblical Commentary*, vol. 20, edited by David A. Hubbard (Dallas: Word Books, 1990), 507.

7 Samuel L. Terrien, "The Psalms: Strophic Structure and Theological Commentary: Psalms 73-150," in *Eerdmans Critical Commentary,* edited by David Noel Freedman, vol. 2 (Grand Rapids: William B. Eerdmans Publishing Company, 2003), 677.

gods and the whole world-wide acknowledgment of the Yahweh's dominion (cf. Isa 40:18-26, 41: 23-24, 44:6-8, 56:6-8, 60:14).[8]

Thirdly, though LXX provides the title as 'A Song of David' which indicates a more ancient origin, however, this psalm seems to be of a post-exilic date. This psalm reflects many points from the book of Isaiah calling nature to give praises to Yahweh (Isa 44:24, 45:12) and the conviction that all nations will worship Yahweh (Isa 45:5, 49:7, 56:3, 66:18).[9] The kingship of Yahweh tradition goes back to early pre-exilic period, however the cultic situations of Psalm 96 is probably in the post-exilic period.[10]

With an analysis of Psalm 96 in both the Davidic monarchical setting and the post-exilic settings, certain scholars are in support of the former like Schaefer while others are in support of the latter like Taylor. However, Gerstenberger developed a wider perspective for the setting of Psalm 96. For him, the origin of Psalm 96 could be in the 'seasonal festivals' (cf. Lev 23; Deut 16) or regular worship services in the exilic and post-exilic era which gave occasion to confess Yahweh as creator of universe and ruler of all the nations.[11]

Hence, looking into the different opinions and perspectives, I would suggest that Gerstenberger's view has contributed a wider aspect to study and understand how Psalm 96 plays a vital role in Israel's worship. Thus, in my opinion the text reflects a post-exilic setting.

6.2. Literary Analysis of the Text

As seen in the previous chapters this section deals with translation, critical notes, form and structure of the text. This helps the reader to know the text and discover the literary usage which runs through the text.

6.2.1. Translation

1 שירו ליהוה שיר הדש שירו ליהוה כל־הארץ :	1. Sing for Yahweh a new song, sing for Yahweh all the earth.
2 שירו להוה ברכו שמו בשרו מיום־ליום ישועתו :	2. Sing for Yahweh, bless his name, and *bear tidings*[12] of his salvation from day to day.

8 Taylor, *Psalms and Proverbs*, 518.

9 Anderson, *Psalms 73-150*, 681.

10 Tate, *Psalms 51-100*, 507.

11 Erhard S. Gerstenberger *Psalms, Part 2 and Lamentations: The Forms of the Old Testament Literature*, Vol. XV (Grand Rapids: William B. Eerdmans Publishing Company, 2001), 190.

12 V. 2. בשר 'tell, announce, or herald as glad tidings.' See A. Philip Brown II and Bryan. W Smith, eds., *A Reader's Hebrew Bible* (Zondervan, 2008), 1205.

3 ספרו בגוים כבודו בכל־העמים נפלאותיו :	3. To recount of his glory among the nations, his wonders among all the peoples.
4 כי גדול יהוה ומהלל מאד נירא הוא על־כל־אלהים :	4. For great is the Lord, and highly to be praised, he is to be *revered* above all gods.
5 כי כל־אלהי העמים אלילים ויהוה שמים עשה :	5. For all the *gods*[13] of the peoples are worthless, but the Lord made the heavens.
6 הוד־והדר לפניו עז ותפארת במקדשו :	6. Majesty and honour are before him, might and *glory are in his sanctuary*.[14]
7 הבו ליהוה משפחות עמים הבו ליהוה כבוד ועז :	7. Ascribe to the Lord, families of the peoples, Give to the Lord glory and strength.
8 הבו ליהוה כבוד שמו שאו־מנחה ובאו להצרתיו :	8. Ascribe to the Lord the glory of his name, carry an offering and come into his courts.
9 השתהוו ליהוה בהדרת־קדש הילו מפניו כל־הארץ :	9. Worship the Lord in holy *attire*;[15] Tremble before Him, all the earth.
10 אמרו בגוים יהוה מלך אף־תכון תבל בל־תמוט ידין עמים במישרים :	10. Say among the nations, "The Lord reigns, the world *established*[16] that shall not be shaken, He will judge the peoples with uprightness."

---

13 V.5[a.] The word אלילים denotes 'worthless thing' cf Job 13:4, Zech 11:7, Lev 19:4 Isa 2:8,10:10, Ezek 30:13. The original meaning may have been 'gods,' used in MT as a term of contempt. LXX uses *daimonia*, "demons," but the word can also mean 'god.' See Marvine E Tate, "Psalms 51-150," in *Word Biblical Commentary*, ed. David A. Hubbard, vol. 20 (Dallas: Word Books, 1990), 510.

14 V. 6[a-a.] few manuscripts and 1 Chr 16:27 has והדוה במפמו 'joy in his place.' Place is a more general term and it could be 'holy place.' Since the material in 1 Chr 16 is attributed to David, the redactor may have wanted to avoid referring to the 'sanctuary' before the temple was built. Tate assumes that honour, majesty, might, and glory form a tetrad of personal divine powers. The word translated glory תפארת is often translated as 'splendour or beauty.' It also refers to Yahweh's glory in Ps 71:8, 1 Chr 29:11, of his name in Isa 63:14, 1 Chr 20:13 and of his arm in Isa 63:12. It is associated with כבוד glory in (Ex 28:2, Isa 4:2, Prov 4:8-9). We can see here that glory is not human glory but the glory of Yahweh. See Marvine E. Tate, "Psalms 51-150," in Word Biblical Commentary, edited by David A. Hubbard, vol. 20 (Dallas: Word Books, 1990), 510-511.

15 V. [9a.] LXX and the Syriac version of the Old Testament have εναυλη, בחצרת 'his court.' See Mitchell Dahood, Psalms 51-100: The Anchor Bible (New York: Doubleday, 1968), 358.

16 V.[10d.] LXX (Symmachus, Syriac version, Cairo Geniza Hier) has κατωρθωσεν-תכן "he has established," compare to Ps 93:1c. See Karl Elliger and Wilhelm Rudolph, eds., Biblia Hebraica Stuttgartensia (Stuttgart: Biblia Hebraica Stuttgartensia, 1997), 1178.

11 ישמחו השמים ותגל הארץ ירעם הים ומלאו׃	11. Let the heavens rejoice, and let the earth be glad, let the sea roar in the fullness.
12 יעלז שדי וכל־אשר־בו אז ירננו כל־עצי־יער׃	12. Then the *field*[17] exults and all that is in it. All the trees of the forest will shout with joy.
13 לפני יהוה כי בא כי בא לשפט הארץ ישפט־תבל בצדק ועמים באמונתו׃	13. *Before*[18] the Lord, for he is coming, *for he is coming*[19] to judge the earth. He will judge the world in righteousness and the peoples in his steadfastness.

6.2.2. Text Critical Notes

First, כל־הארץ 'all the earth' (Ps 96:1). In kingship psalms, this phrase is important because it gives the motif of universalism. This unique phrase כל־הארץ 'all the earth' is addressing all the inhabitants of the earth.[20] It also serves as a poetical inclusion of all, with Yahweh as the creator of the world and God above all gods, which leads people to believe that Yahweh is not only God of Israel but of the whole world.[21] I do agree with Anderson and Tate because this phrase is inclusive of all people and nations.

Secondly, ישועה 'salvation,' is a noun common feminine construct suffix 3rd person masculine singular (Ps 96:2). Here, the psalmist is affirming to the people that salvation needs to be carried over to all people, "bear tidings of his

17 V.[12b.] A few manuscripts and 1 Chr 16:32 have השדה the 'field, land.' See Karl Elliger and Wilhelm Rudolph, eds., Biblia Hebraica Stuttgartensia (Stuttgart: Biblia Hebraica Stuttgartensia, 1997), 1178.

18 V.[13a] 1 Chr 16:33 has מלפני rather than לפני in Ps 96:13. Perhaps מלפני would better mean "because of/ on account of," whereas לפני means "in the presence of/ before." But there is probably little or no difference in meaning. If there is, then we can see a little difference like מלפני going away from the presence of Yahweh and the לפני pointing to the joyful shouting of the trees. See Marvine E. Tate, "Psalms 51-150," in Word Biblical Commentary, edited by David A. Hubbard, vol. 20 (Dallas: Word Books, 1990), 511-512.

19 V. [13b.] כי בא is missing in a multitude of manuscripts. The Syriac version of the Old Testament and I Chr 16:33 have suggested to compare it with Ps 9:9. Delitzsch and Briggs argue that the twofold בא "come" should be read as a participle and not as a perfect. The personal pronoun is expected as the subject is omitted. Gunkel and Kraus read the verbs as expressing an eschatological concept. The commentator Tate supports their view and this idea seems to be more close to the text. See Marvine E. Tate, "Psalms 51-150," in Word Biblical Commentary, edited by David A. Hubbard, vol. 20 (Dallas: Word Books, 1990), 511-512.

20 Anderson, *The Book of Psalms: Psalms 1-72*, 682.

21 Tate, *Psalms 51-100*, 149.

salvation from day to day."[22] Thus, the congregation experiences the presence of God and wants to share the good news to the world.

Thirdly, בכל־העמים 'among all the people' (Ps 96:3). The text affirms that Israelites are called upon to pass on the miraculous saving deeds of God to all people and nations.[23] There is a world-wide summons to adore and give praises to Yahweh the king and the people of God are given the task of spreading the greatness and wonder of Yahweh to all nations.[24]

Fourthly, the word כבוד 'glory' (Ps 96:3). The word כבוד 'glory' refers to the glory of God and this כבוד is parallel to the marvellous works of God. Therefore, in a wider sense, the word פלא, which means 'marvellous,' is associated with the word glory and refers to the mighty acts of Yahweh in creation and deliverance.[25] כי גדול יהוה means 'for great is the Lord' and parallels the marvellous works of Yahweh (Ps 96:4a).[26]

Fifthly, ירא verb *niphal* participle masculine singular absolute (Ps 96:4). Several manuscripts, the Syriac version of the OT and Cairo Geniza have 1 Chr 16:25 ונורא which means "and to be feared." Anderson argues that Yahweh would inspire terror and fear in his enemies, but those who serve Yahweh would have awe and a spirit of praise (cf. Ps 99:3).[27] Kraus[28] translates ירא as 'fear.' Weiser, translates ירא 'terrible.'[29] Goldingay, translates ירא 'revered.'[30] I translate ירא as 'revered' because this has worship implications for my argument.

Sixthly, אלילים 'insufficiency (Ps 96:5). Anderson rightly states that only Yahweh is sufficient; all the gods of the peoples are 'nobodies' and insufficient.[31] אלילים "refers to pagan god, vain, worthless god" (*RHB* notes 15. P.1209). "They are prophesying to you a lying vision, worthless divination, and the deceit of their own minds" (Lev 19:4, Jer 14:14). Idolatry has no divine power because idols are incapable of saving themselves and their worshippers.

---

22 John Hargreaves, *A Guide to Psalms* (Delhi: ISPCK, 1987), 110.

23 Weiser, *The Psalms: A Commentary*, 629.

24 Hans-Joachim, Kraus, "Psalms 60-150," in *A Continental Commentary*, translated by Hilton C. Oswald (Minneapolis: Fortress Press, 1993), 253.

25 Anderson, *The Book of Psalms: Psalms 1-72*, 682.

26 Anderson, *The Book of Psalms*: *Psalms 1-72,* 682.

27 Anderson, *The Book of Psalms: Psalms 73-150*, 683.

28 Hans-Joachim Kraus, "Psalms 60-150," in A *Continental Commentary*, 250.

29 Weiser, *The Psalms: A Commentary*, 627.

30 John Goldingay, "Psalms 90-150," in *Baker Commentary on the Old Testament Wisdom and Psalms*, vol. 3, edited by Tremper Longman III (Grand Rapids: Academic Press, 2008), 100.

31 Anderson, *The Book of Psalms: Psalms 1-72*, 683.

Besides, the hands that made and worshipped idols will also face destruction.[32] Idol worship is incapable of protecting people from Yahweh's judgement, as they are terrified in the presence of his glory and majesty. It is suggested that idolatry destroys the cultic sanctity (Lev 19:4). It is intended to represent Yahweh. Thus, idolatry is a form of worship that has no power and divine revelation.[33]

The gods of the nations have no 'ontological reality,' therefore, in the light of this opinion, the psalmist exhorts the nations to give up their idolatry and worship Yahweh the divine God and to tremble before him, the maker of all.[34] Schaefer comments on the greatness of God is that "God is the greatest, and the universal government is equitable, moreover, God's reign is the motive for all creatures to rejoice"[35] The greatness of other gods cannot be compared to him, therefore, due worship belongs to Yahweh alone (Ps 96:4-5).

Seventhly, משפחות עמים 'families of the people' (Ps 96:7). The phrase of משפחות עמים 'families of the people,' "might suggest the peoples as belonging to different ethnic groups" but it may simply mean the "multitude of the nations."[36] So, when we compare verses 7 and 9, they echo each other in terms of worshiping Yahweh. Therefore, the nations refer to 'the clan of the peoples' and are summoned to enter the temple courts bringing with them their gifts.[37]

Finally, הדרת 'attire' is a noun common feminine singular (Ps 96:9). This expression has more than one interpretation. Traditionally, הדרת is taken from הדרת 'adoration/splendour,' *KJV* 'beauty of holiness.' The reading 'beauty of holiness' was interpreted by older English speaking commentators in a spiritual sense, the beauty of holy deeds and disposition on the part of the worshipper. For Gordon, הדרת refers to Yahweh rather than to worshippers and it is better to take it as splendour with a suffix on קדש with LXX and translate it as 'worship Yahweh in his holy splendour or in his holy attire.'[38]

The text critical notes give guidelines on how to look at the text critically. It is necessary to evaluate their authentic and reliable sources. Besides, they expressed several points which link to the kingship metaphor of Yahweh and bring out the relevant for the theology of worship. Thus, all textual comments contribute several aspects to know the kingship metaphor of Yahweh, the king.

32 Manoja Kumar Korada, "Idolatry: A Problem in the Old Testament," *Bible Bhashyam,* vol. vxxxx, no. 4 (2014): 195-198.

33 Korada, "Idolatry: A Problem in the Old Testament," 205, 209.

34 Merrill, *Everlasting Dominion: A Theology of the Old Testament*, 320.

35 Schaefer, *Psalms: Studies in Hebrew Narrative & Poetry*, 239.

36 Goldingay, *Psalms: Psalms 90-150*, 105.

37 Elmer A. Leslie, *The Psalms: Translated and Interpreted in the Light of Hebrew Life and Worship* (New York: Abingdon Press, 1949), 78.

38 Tate, *Psalms 51-100*, 511.

6.2.3. Form of the Psalm

For Terrien, the visible form of this Psalm is a hymn.[39] This hymn contains four strophes, Psalm 96 verses 1-3, verses 4-6, 7-9, 10-12 followed by an 'Envoi'[40] in verse 13. The horizon of this hymn broadens and covers from 'all the earth' to 'the sea' and the 'forest.' It is clearly shown in this psalm that the blessing of the Lord's name gets linked to the declaration of the Lord's glory.[41]

Kraus suggests that the following visible meters are necessary to be pointed out in Psalm 96: (a) 3+3 meters are shown in verses 1, 3, 6, 13. (b) 4+4 meters are shown in verses 2, 7, 8. (c) Also, 4+3 meters are shown in verses 4, 5, 9, 11, 13 respectively.[42]

6.2.4. Structure of the Psalm

Structurally, Psalm 96 is divided into two main components which are: verses 1-6 and verses 7-13, under these two main strophes, there are five sections: a. (Ps 96:1-3) b. (Ps 96:4-6) c. (Ps 96: 7-9) d. (Ps 96:10) e. (Ps 96:11-13).[43] Zorn claims the structure of this psalm contains the main two strophes beginning from verses 1-6 and verses 7-13.[44]

Kraus claims that Psalm 96 belongs to the category of hymns and its structure can be visualized in the following divisions:[45]

(a) Introduction (Ps 96:1-3)
(b) First main section (Ps 96: 4-6)
(a) Renew introduction (Ps 96:7-9)
(b) Second main section (Ps 96:10-13).

6.2.5. Repetition

The phrase שירו ליהוה 'sing for Yahweh' occurs in v.1 twice and once in verse 2. It affirms that singing plays a vital role in the worship of Yahweh; Yahweh is to be praised at all times because Yahweh alone deserves all our praises.[46] The invitation for worship of Yahweh is followed with the motive introduced by כי

39 Terrien, *The Psalms: Strophic Structure and Theological Commentary*, 674.

40 "Envoi" the word envoi means "A brief stanza concluding certain forms of poetry."

41 Terrien, *The Psalms: Strophic Structure and Theological Commentary*, 674.

42 Kraus, *Psalms 60-150*, 251. The meter is somewhat irregular comparing to some of the enthronement psalms because we see 4+3 occurs in vss.1,5,9,11; 4+4 in vv. 2,4,7,8,10,12; 3+3 in vv. 3,6; and 2+2+2,3+2 in v 13. See William R. Taylor, "The Book of Psalms," in *The Interpreter's Bible,* vol. IV, edited by George Arthur Buttrick (New York: Abingdon Press, 1955), 518.

43 David M. Howard, *The Structure of Psalms 93-100* (Winona Lake: Eisenbrauns, 1997), 147.

44 Walter D. Zorn, "Psalms," *in The College Press NIV Commentary*, vol. 2 (Joplin, MO: College Press Publishing Co, 2004), 210.

45 Kraus, *Psalms 60-150*, 251.

46 Taylor, *Psalms and Proverbs*, 517.

'for' twice, which occurs in verses 4 and 5. With כי the hymnic main section begins. In fact, repeated use of כי in Psalm 96 is to portray the sovereignty of God.[47]

The phrase כל־הארץ 'all the earth' appears twice in verses 1 and 9. Moreover, we see the word ארץ 'earth' in verse 13. We see גוים which means 'nations' is repeated twice, in verses 3 and 10. Therefore, the centre of Psalm 96 focuses on the universality of God in proclaiming the goodness of God to all the earth and nations. It expresses the good news of Yahweh's saving work and that should be spread out to all the earth until all people and nations come to know about the glory of God.[48]

The word כבוד 'glory' is mentioned twice in verses 7 and 8. The repeated use of glory has a unique function in Israel's worship because this word stresses that "every tribe and clan of the world are to acknowledge the worship of the unique glory of the Lord," which is revealed through the characteristic of the kingship of Yahweh.[49] In verse 7, the word 'to give or ascribe' does not mean merely 'ascribe' or 'recognize', but 'give'. The psalmist is affirming that instead of giving due honour to idols, the true worshippers should be able to give honour due to Yahweh the great king.[50] The word שפט 'judge' occurs twice in verse 13. For Anderson, it is both to judge and to rule. God's judgment is not vindictive, but it is considered by righteousness or perfect fairness.[51] Thus, the metaphor of Yahweh as judge symbolizes his faithfulness and absolute authority over all human judges.

6.3. Comments in Relation to the Kingship Metaphor

First, the form critical analysis have identified that the word 'great' is part of the kingship of Yahweh. Gerstenberger suggests that "the designation of גדול 'great' in regard to deities and kings is fundamental for hymnic discourse in the Hebrew Bible at the same time it reveals the kingship metaphor of Yahweh (Ps 96:4).[52] 'Tell of his salvation' mainly talks about Yahweh's victory or triumph which brought about deliverance from chaos. In other words, Yahweh's marvellous works are of supreme quality and are creative acts where Yahweh alone made the heavens and earth.

Hence, the Lord is to be feared above all gods, for they are mere idols things. We see the parallel expression in the book of Isaiah (Isa 40: 25, 44:

---

47 Schaefer, *Psalms*, 238.

48 Tate, *Psalms 51-100*, 512.

49 Eaton, *The Psalms*, 341.

50 Goldingay, *Psalms 42-89*, 105.

51 Anderson, *The Book of Psalms: Psalms 1-72*, 686.

52 Gerstenberger, *Psalms, Part 2 and Lamentations*, 188.

9-20).[53]According to Gerstenberger, "important statement of the hymn is the proclamation and, therefore, acknowledgement of Yahweh, the supreme king's government by all powers and humankind."[54]

Secondly, הוד־והדר 'majesty and honour' this phrase is associated with the kingship metaphor of God. Both הוד־והדר words are nouns common masculine singular absolute (Ps 96:6). This is "the usual pair of words which are used to describe royal dignity" of Yahweh who is above the whole universe and deserves to be adored.[55] Hence, the phrase means that true majesty and honour belong to the living God and no other.

Thirdly, יְהוָה מָלָךְ 'Yahweh reigns' (Ps 96:10). The verbal form מָלָךְ 'reign.' Though this phrase has been discussed earlier, the context here in this Psalm 96 is, probably, different because it is not dealing on the issues of translations but looking at from theological aspect. The psalmist says that Yahweh reigns over all the lands and over all the nations. Thus, the text affirms that the people of God were encouraged to extend the kingship of Yahweh, who is the king and reigns over all the nations. Yahweh is unchangeable and the people are to proclaim the sovereignty of God to others. In regard to the metaphor of the kingship of Yahweh, Kraus notes that two other visible themes come into view from the title of the king: "king is creator and judge of the world."[56]

Fourthly, Yahweh is a righteous judge. This describes a king's task. Yahweh, as a king, has the role of judge, and he governs the nations. He sits on his throne and pronounces judgment over all the wicked.[57] Yahweh, as a righteous judge, is understood by the OT in the framework of the covenant. Divine justice is connected with Yahweh's role as judge. He judges the world with justice (Pss 96:13, 98:9). Justice and judgement are seen as attributes of divine kingship.[58]

Yahweh rules justly for the well-being of the people. When we look at Psalm 96:13, we see the word שפט 'judge' used twice along with דין 'judge' in Ps 96:10. These two words are not negative but have a positive meaning; judicially and theologically both refer to righteous judgment of God. Brueggemann comments, "Rather the terms refer to God's action of intervention to look after the rightful claims of the weak ones who have no power to make their claim or look after themselves" (cf. Isa 1:16-17, Ps

53 Taylor, *The Interpreter's Bible: Psalms and Proverbs*, 518-519.

54 Gerstenberger, *Psalms, Part 2 and Lamentations*, 189.

55 Anderson, *The Book of Psalms: Psalms 1-72,* 683.

56 Kraus, *Psalms 60-150*, 254.

57 Steven J. L. Croft, *The Identity of Individual Psalms* (Sheffield: Sheffield Academic Press, 1987), 84.

58 Aubrey, Johnson, *Sacral Kingship in Ancient Israel* (Cardiff: University of Wales Press, 1967), 90-93.

82:2-4, 72:1-4).[59] Yahweh the king is entirely different from human kings in his function. The two words in verse 13, צדק 'righteousness' and אמונה 'faithfulness are strongly reflect the way God judges the world and its people with the qualities of righteousness and faithfulness or fidelity.[60]

Gerstenberger says, "The creation of the world and the capacity to judge all the nations are the pillars of God's authority."[61] Yahweh the king comes into the human society of injustice and corruption with divine power to makes things right. Therefore, judge is a connotation of Yahweh's kingship. The psalmist demonstrates that the worshippers witnessed God's action of intervention in human situations with faithfulness. Hence, the motif of judge is not punishment but it is right governance.

6.4. Comments in Relation to Worship

These are some of the comments in relation to worship. *First,* שירו ליהוה שיר חדש 'sing to the Lord a new song' (Ps 96:1). This is one of the psalmist's unique way of giving praise to Yahweh. This phrase of a 'new song' is also mentioned by the prophet Isaiah (Isa 42:10). According to Schaefer, the phrase of שירו ליהוה שיר חדש 'sing to the Lord a new song' is liturgical and signifies the 'renewal of praise,' (cf. Pss 33: 3; 40:3, 96:1, 98:1).[62] The psalmist points out the importance of *exalting God through singing in Worship.* All nations are summoned to sing a new song in praise of Yahweh's mighty deeds of victory.[63]

"Sing to the Lord a new song; sing to the Lord all the earth" (Ps 96:1). For Brueggemann, "The praise that articulates this good news of enthronement is a new song. A new song must be sung for a new orientation."[64] It is clear that a new orientation reflects the new circumstances in life. In worship, singing songs signifies the joy of worshipping Yahweh afresh. It is also a sign of the new life which God continues to give to the true believers of Yahweh.[65]

Paul argues that a new song may also be understood as the response to a historical event, a new exodus (Isa 40:9, 41:27, 42:7). A new song could be in

59 Walter Brueggemann, *The Message of the Psalms :A Theological Commentary,* (Minneapolis: Augsburg Publishing House, 1984), 145.

60 Goldingay, *Psalms 42-89*, 107-108. Yahweh judges rightfully, moreover Yahweh judges with truth. The worshippers recognized that Yahweh is always trustworthy which is widely opposite to the judgment of human judges. See in John Hargreaves, *A Guide to Psalms* (Delhi: ISPCK, 1987), 107.

61 Gerstenberger, *Psalms, Part 2 and Lamentations*, 189.

62 Schaefer, *Psalms: Studies in Hebrew Narrative & Poetry*, 238.

63 Charles Augustus Briggs and Emilie Grace Briggs, "A Critical and Exegetical Commentary on the Book of Psalms," in *The International Critical Commentary,* vol. II (Edinburgh: T & T Clark Ltd, 1960), 297.

64 Brueggemann, *The Message of the Psalms : A Theological Commentary*, 144.

65 Hargreaves, *A Guide to Psalms*, 110.

anticipation of what God will do.[66] The views on a new song may differ, but the primary fact is that singing in worship is one of the most vital elements which prepares and inspires the hearts of the worshippers to worship God whole-heartedly. Therefore, singing songs has a great impact for worship.

The psalmist encourages people to come before Yahweh and give him praise the through worship.[67] Patrick D. Miller,[68] and Olley[69] support the idea of exclusivity in the context of worship. The nations have witnessed the true God who controls nature and history. The psalmist asserts an experiential understanding of what is involved in the first commandment and the reciprocity inherent within it.[70] "The hymns of Israel stand in service of the central theological claim of the Old Testament, that the Lord of Israel alone is God and requires the full devotion of all creation."[71]

The kingship of Yahweh shows a clear picture of the full dimension of exclusive worship to God. The psalmist says, 'for all the gods of the people are worthless' (Ps 96:5). This affirms that Yahweh alone deserves to be exalted through singing and to have his name blessed above all names. Here 'singing to the Lord and blessing his name' is an expression of joy.[72]

Secondly, the text emphasizes *bringing an offering in worship.* The poet clearly mentions to "carry an offering and come into his courts" (Ps 96:8). Leslie states, "here the nations, the clans of the peoples are summoned to enter the temple courts bearing their gifts of fealty."[73] The main idea presented here is to establish a living relationship with God. Worshippers are to offer up their gifts in humble adoration, respect and acknowledging to Yahweh and that everything belongs to him.[74] The worshippers are to come into the temple with their offering, which is their mark of respect to Yahweh who deserves

---

66 Mark Sagayam Paul, "*Enthronement Psalms, Psalms of Yahweh's Kingship,*" *Psalms for the People of God*, edited by Mathew Thekkekara (Bangalore: Asian Trading Corporation, 2008), 41.

67 Brevard S. Childs, *Old Testament Theology in a Canonical Context* (London: SCM Press Ltd, 1985), 66.

68 Patrick D. Miller, *Interpreting the Psalms* (Philadelphia: Fortress Press, 1986), 8-15.

69 John W. Olley, "Forensic Connotation of Bos," *Vêtus Testamentum* 26, no. 2 (April, 1976): 231. John W. Olley, "The God of Heaven: A Look at Attitudes to Other Religions in the Old Testament," *Colloquium* 27, no. 2 (1995): 89. John C. Endres, "The Spiritual Vision of Chronicles: Wholehearted, Joy-Filled Worship of God," *The Catholic Biblical Quarterly*, no. 69 (2007): 1-21.

70 Patrick D. Miller, *The Way of the Lord: Essays in Old Testament Theology* (Michigan: William B. Eerdmans Publishing Company, 2007), 114.

71 Miller, *Interpreting the Psalms*, 78.

72 Robert B. Chisholm, "A Theology of the Psalms," in *A Biblical Theology of the Old Testament*, edited by Roy B. Zuck (Chicago: Moody Press, 1991), 303.

73 Leslie, *The Psalms,* 78.

74 Paul, "*Enthronement Psalms, Psalms of Yahweh's Kingship,*" 43.

to be worshipped with all gifts.[75] In Israel's worship, bringing an offering is considered a way of ascribing the sovereignty of Yahweh so as recognize Yahweh's majesty.[76] Thus, offering is an act of worship. It also symbolizes the worshippers' loyalty and relationship with Yahweh. Bringing an offering not only occurs in the OT, but is also an essential part of Christian worship even today.

Thirdly, the psalm exhibits the *ecumenical dimension in worship.* The way the text addresses the audience seems to be worldwide in nature with phrases like 'all the earth' (Ps 96: 1, 9) 'among the nations and people' (Ps 96: 3, 7, 10). Looking into all these perspectives, Gerstenberger points out that with the emphasis on "proclamation and the wide horizon of addressees the psalm from the outset has a universal and extroverted character."[77] The poem expects people to "bless the name of God and bear tidings of the salvation of Yahweh from day to day." And to recount of his glory among the nations, his wonders among all the peoples" (Ps 96:2-3). Yahweh's greatness needs proclaiming among the peoples and nations because of the feeble nature of the gods of the people and they need to know the true God.[78]

As we see here, there is a great *missionary task* which needs to be emphasized even in worship. Israelites are to tell the good news, the saving deeds of Yahweh who defeated chaos and made the world of life. The nations who worship other gods are to hear the gospel and to know that supreme glory belongs to God alone. Across the world, the good news is to be proclaimed that Yahweh is king over all the kings and a true God to be adored.[79] Okoye affirms, "The wholeness of all creation belongs to the vision of the reign of God, and it is to this reign that the church witnesses in its mission to preach the gospel to every creature."[80] God's kingship is over humankind, the heavens, the earth,

---

75 James Chukwuma Okoye, *Israel and the Nations: A Mission Theology of the Old Testament* (New York: Orbis Books, 2006), 106.

76 Goldingay, *Psalms 42-89*, 105.

77 Gerstenberger, *Psalms, Part 2 and Lamentations*, 187. See Erhard S. Gerstenberger, *Psalms, Part I, with An Introduction to Cultic Poetry: The Forms of the Old Testament Literature*, vol. XIV (Grand Rapids: William B. Eerdmans Publishing Company, 1988), 197. Bernhard W. Anderson, *Out of the Depths: The Psalms Speak for Us Today* (Louisville: Westminster John Knox Press, 2000), 156. Christopher J. H. Wright, *Old Testament Ethics for the People of God* (Leicester: InterVarsity Press, 2004), 130. Mascarenhas, *The Missionary Function of Israel in Psalms 67, 96, and 117*, 169-170. Eaton, *The Psalms: A Historical and Spiritual Commentary with an Introduction and New Translation*, 343. Mark Sagayam Paul, *"Enthronement Psalms, Psalms of Yahweh's Kingship" Psalms for the People of God*, edited by Mathew Thekkekara (Bangalore: Asian Trading Corporation, 2008), 43.

78 Goldingay, *Psalms: Psalms 90-150*, 104.

79 Eaton, *The Psalms,* 340-341.

80 James Chukwuma Okoye, *Israel and the Nations: A Mission Theology of the Old Testament* (New York: Orbis Books, 2006), 105.

the sea, the field and all the trees (Ps 96:11-12). This is directed to the different churches as well as to people of other faiths showing that we are partners with all the families of people.[81]

Psalm 96 asks all the people to come and join in adoration of Yahweh. God's greatness and his saving deeds of good news need to be proclaimed to all humankind and creatures. A *multi-religious* participation in the worship of Yahweh is well highlighted in this psalm. Therefore, the implication for worship is to proclaim the saving deeds of Yahweh to all.

Fourthly, rejoicing is linked to the kingship of Yahweh. Yahweh rules over the whole world with right authority. He has done great things. Therefore, the people of the earth rejoice under his divine kingship. גיל 'rejoice' (Ps 96:11). גיל is one of the psalmist's usual expressions in the enthronement psalms. גיל 'rejoice' is associated with the kingship metaphor of Yahweh. Goldingay affirms that the first part of the invitation is to rejoice based on a declaration of the kingship of Yahweh and is also incorporated with the idea of praise to honour Yahweh. The second part of the invitation is to rejoice on the basis of what Yahweh has done.[82]

In verse 11 the hymnical idea of rejoicing from the phrase ותגל הארץ ישמחו השמים "Let the heavens be glad and let the earth be rejoice." It expresses that both heaven and earth and everything in them would rejoice in the eyes of God. The seas and trees of the forest resound like the congregation.[83] That everything in the universe will rejoice and praise Yahweh the sovereign God. Heaven and earth, the sea, the trees and its fullness all are to praise and worship the king and creator God. We see a parallel expression in the book of Isaiah (cf. Isa 44:23, 49:13).[84]

The worshippers and nature rejoice in the presence of God as they have witnessed the divine nature of God. This indicates that even nature declares the greatness of God in its own way. Psalm 96 demonstrates the future universal rule of God. The Lord will come and the world will see righteousness and equity for all people in Yahweh's kingship; this reflects how all creature are to give reverent to Yahweh the God.

6.5. Theological Concerns Pertaining to the Kingship Metaphor of God

The diversity of the psalms poses a challenge when sketching a theology of the psalter. However, the theme of Yahweh's kingship in the enthronement psalms

81 Paul, *Enthronement Psalms,* 43.

82 Goldingay, *Psalms 42-89*, 110.

83 Goldingay, *Psalms 42-89*, 107.

84 Kraus, *Psalms 60-150*, 278.

is the basis for the theology. Here, I deal with the theology of connotations of the kingship metaphor of Yahweh on transcendence and rejoicing.

6.5.1. Kingship and Transcendence

Transcendence is aconnotation of the kingship metaphor of Yahweh. Transcendence is a state of excelling. When we talk about God's transcendence, it represents his sovereignty over creation and his ability to excel beyond human imagination and power and to be exalted above all creation. Yahweh's power is manifested to all people and in all nature, and as a result, Yahweh is declared as king of all the earth.[85] Glory is a concept that aptly portrays his transcendence.[86] Glory is a state of high honour and is associated with reverence. This is applied to God in the OT. The God of glory occupies a high position indicative of the kingship of Yahweh.[87] The concept of glory carries a great weight of honour or excellence.

The historical-literary analysis reveals that the word כבד 'glory' plays a significant role in showing the concept of Yahweh's superiority among all the people and gods (Ps 96:3).[88] Glory is the mark of honour and respect to Yahweh. The psalmist affirms that righteousness and glory denote that Yahweh righteously rules the universe with the power of authority and, therefore, deserves all honour and glory.[89]

In public worship, it is not surprising that the Psalter in general and the enthronement psalms in particular use this term to convey the power of Yahweh. For instance, God's glory and strength are in the sanctuary (Ps 63:3). In the place of the dwelling of your glory (Ps 26:8) and looks forward eschatologically when 'all people will see God's glory' (Ps 97:6 cf. Isa 40:5).[90]

Yahweh is ascended above all gods. The people must know that Yahweh is in control of everything with divine authority. This shows Yahweh's transcendence over all. The text points out 'Yahweh is to be worshiped above all gods' (Ps 96:4). This portrays that Yahweh is more powerful than all other gods. The appearance of Yahweh causes all the idol worshippers to observe what kind of gods they worship. The worshipers of images are judged.

---

85 Lama, "The Placement of Psalm 145 in Book V: A Compositional Analysis," 284.

86 Robert L. Saucy, "Doctrine of God," in *Evangelical Dictionary of the Theology,* edited by Walter A. Elwell (Grand Rapids: Baker Book House, 1984), 461.

87 C. John Collins, "כבד," in *New International Dictionary of Old Testament Theology & Exegesis,* vol. 2, edited by Willem A. VanGemeren (Grand Rapids: Zondervan, 1997), 579-580.

88 Ludwing Koehler and Walter, *The Hebrew and Aramaic Lexicon of the Old Testament*, vol. 1 (Leiden: Koninklijke Brill NV, 2001), 455-457.

89 Ludwing Koehler and Walter Baumgartner, *The Hebrew and Aramaic Lexicon of the Old Testament*, vol. 1 (Leiden: Koninklijke Brill NV, 2001), 457.

90 Collins, "כבד," 582.

Therefore, all powers are subjected to the powerfulness of יהוה עליון because the kingship of Yahweh is far above all gods.[91]

God has absolute control over all forms and reveals himself to the people. Therefore, Yahweh is worthy to be praised and worshipped with honour and reverence. The connotation of *transcendence* denotes that Yahweh is ascended above all and reveals himself to the world. Therefore, transcendence is linked to the kingship of Yahweh.

6.5.2. Kingship and Rejoicing

Rejoicing refers to the connotation of Yahweh's kingship. People and nature rejoice and declare the kingship of Yahweh because Yahweh is the true king. Why should the whole world rejoice? Ollenburger brings out important ideas in the relation between 'kingship and rejoicing.' According to him 'rejoicing' is a characteristic motif of these enthronement psalms.[92] The verb גיל 'to rejoice' occurs directly in Psalms 96:11, 97:1, 8, 12. Thus to rejoice is based on a declaration of Yahweh, the great king, over all the earth.[93] Gunkel asserts that Yahweh's kingship is a realm of justice and grace and lasts forever (Pss 98:2, 99:4). This kingship is perhaps welcomed with a loud shout which connotes 'rejoicing.' The enthronement psalms declare that the kingship of Yahweh encompasses all nations. All gods bow before the one who has now proven to be the highest in the entire world.[94]

Ollenburger affirms that often the announcement of Yahweh's kingship is followed by an exhortation towards heaven and earth to rejoice (Ps 96). The terrifying glory of Yahweh causes people to rejoice and even Zion hears the declaration and rejoices. This rejoicing is to occur because Yahweh is God over all the earth and all gods.[95] Goldingay affirms, that "It is Israel in its worship that hears the psalm's declaration that the creation is to rejoice and its bidding to the earth and its people" (Ps 96).[96]

The concept of rejoicing in Psalm 97 corresponds to a similar concept in Psalm 96:11. Therefore, the continuity of the whole set of rejoicing carries on to the enthronement psalms. The description of Yahweh's kingship gives the reason for people to rejoice. The fact that Yahweh reigns is good news and causes not just all people but the whole universe to rejoice.[97] In worship, the

91 Kraus, *Psalms 60-150*, 260.

92 Ollenburger, *Zion the City of the Great King*, 34.

93 Goldingay, *Psalms 42-89*, 110.

94 Hermann Gunkel, *Introduction to Psalms: The Genres of the Religious Lyric of Israel* (Macon, Georgia: Mercer University Press, 1998), 69.

95 Ollenburger, *Zion the City of the Great King*, 34.

96 Goldingay, *Psalms 42-89*, 108.

97 Goldingay, *Psalms 90-150*, 111-112, 117.

people of Israel rejoice in God's steadfastness and saving power and proclaim his kingship and faithfulness to other nations as well. Ollenburger rightly points out that the themes of rejoicing and of the new song are associated with the notion of Yahweh's kingship.[98]

For instance, Psalm 96 begins with a phrase 'to sing a new song' and declares Yahweh's sovereignty among all the nations (96:1, 10-13). Again, Psalm 98 begins with the same phrase to 'sing a new song' and further declares the righteousness of Yahweh the king. He affirms that 'rejoicing' talks about the celebration of Yahweh's kingship. This is how a connection is made among the new song, rejoicing, Yahweh's kingship and royal rule.[99]

When the worshippers exhort, "Rejoice, the Lord is king," they declare the promise of the kingdom. Though unseen in fullness, the kingdom of God is more real and powerful than any other powers. Therefore, the psalmist declares to the people to rejoice for the wonders that Yahweh, the king, has done and, urges the worshippers to shout to the Lord who rules. The whole earth and distant shores are exhorted to rejoice in Yahweh's awesomeness and sovereignty.[100] In fact, Psalms 97 and 99 are a similar pair "launching their call to praise with the affirmation the Lord reigns and call upon the earth and the distant shores to rejoice. The greatness, justice, holiness and forgiveness of Yahweh are the main reasons for anticipating such responses."[101]

There is no king who exhibits firmness like Yahweh. Therefore, all the creatures rejoice because the righteousness of Yahweh's kingship. Here, rejoicing is a universal event which includes nature herself. The poet declares that the heavens, earth, sea and everything should rejoice in the kingship of Yahweh who is in control of the cosmos with divine power. It is clear that rejoicing emphasizes God's kingship. Thus, rejoicing is attached to the worship of Yahweh's kingship, because Yahweh deserves all our praises, rejoicing, shouting and worship. The purpose of rejoicing and excitement is to worship Yahweh.

Summary

Following points emerge from the above analysis. *First,* singing a new song expresses the renewal of hope and spiritual re-energizing in the mighty power of God. Psalm 96 mentions the words save, make, reign, judge, righteous and truth which demonstrates to the people that the Israelites believed and

98 Ollenburger, *Zion the City of the Great King*, 35.

99 Ollenburger, *Zion the City of the Great King*, 35.

100 Eugene H. Merrill, *Everlasting Dominion: A Theology of Old Testament* (Nashville: Broadman & Holman Publishers, 2006), 320.

101 Christopher J. H. Wright, *The Mission of God: Unlocking the Bible's Grand Narrative.* (Illinois: InterVarsity Press, 2006), 480.

worshipped the true God.[102] *Secondly,* the psalmist expresses that Yahweh is to be revered or feared above all gods (Ps 96:4). At this point, the psalmist encourages the people to worship Yahweh with the right attitude by coming before him with trembling. *Thirdly,* God's glory needs to be proclaimed to all the nations and people. *Fourthly,* the worshippers and nature rejoice in the presence of God. *Lastly*, psalmist affirms that not only people but even nature ought to give all praises to the sovereign God. The Psalm has both particular and universal motifs. Both Israel and nations are called to worship Yahweh. Thus, Psalm 96 has *ecumenical* motifs.

102 Hargreaves, *A Guide to Psalms*, 107.

Chapter 7

Exegetical Study of Psalm 97 Yahweh, the Righteous and Just King

Introduction

Psalm 97 contains many figures of speech and examples of parallelism, all of which point to the kingship of Yahweh. The figures of speech are considered vital characteristics of Psalm 97 because they help the Israelites to understand Yahweh. The hymn in its own way reveals the sovereignty of God who deserves all our worship and praise. Besides that, Psalm 97 places special emphasis on the Lord's righteous judgment to the world. In other words, Yahweh is the righteous and just king. Additionally, this psalm is a worship hymn that concisely declares a God-centred worldview. Therefore, the psalmist calls upon the people to 'rejoice' in the worship of Yahweh.

First, I focus on the historical analysis in Psalm 97. *Secondly,* deals its setting, translation and textual argumentation. *Thirdly*, explains the structure and form of the Psalm and, *finally*, I give the comments in relation to the kingship metaphor and to the worship.

7.1. Historical Analysis

In this section, I have analysed the historical setting of Psalm 97 in both the Davidic monarchical setting and the post-exilic setting. With regard to the setting of the Psalter, there are different opinions which have emerged from different schools of interpretation. Therefore, it is important to study and explore it from different aspects.

7.1.1. Davidic Monarchical Setting

Johnson[1] and Eaton,[2] support the monarchic setting of this psalm. *First,* Psalm 97 is set in the pre-exilic festival which means a Davidic monarchical setting as it refers to a festival in the early period. The psalm begins with a summons to the world at large to rejoice that Yahweh is king, and that he continues to manifest his kingship and that the whole world, has seen his mighty acts. *Secondly,* it indicates that Psalm 97 is an ancient section, as shown from the beginning as verses 1-6. It is a visible manifestation of a pre-exilic enthronement psalms.[3]

I believe the commentators like Eaton support the Davidic monarchical setting on the basis of reference to the daughters of Judah found in the text. However, in my opinion there are few evidences for Davidic monarchical setting. We cannot ignore the Davidic monarchical setting because this is part of the study of the Psalter.

7.1.2. Post-Exilic Setting

Westermann, supports the post-exilic setting. *First*, Psalm 97 is a late origin because the imperative call to praise appears at the end of the psalm and this is considered to be a sure sign of late origin.[4] *Secondly,* Psalm 97 is a post-exilic psalm which honours Yahweh as king and also expands the theme of justice, in the book of Isaiah, especially from Isaiah 40-55. There are several references that show how Isaiah and Psalm 97 to be parallel. For instance, "let the earth rejoice and many isles be glad" (Isa 49:13, 42:10.51:5) and all the worshippers of images are put to shame (Isa 42: 17, 45:16).[5] *Thirdly,* another possible reason for suggesting the post-exilic setting for Psalm 97 is possibly that the hymn has so many links with the message of Deutero-Isaiah, or Trito-

1 Aubrey Johnson, *Sacral Kingship in Ancient Israel* (Cardiff: University of Wales Press, 1967), 104-105.

2 John Eaton, *Psalms of the Way and the Kingdom: A Conference with the Commentators* (Sheffield: Sheffield Academic Press, 1995), 95.

3 Eaton, *Psalms of the Way and the Kingdom,* 95-96, 102.

4 Claus Westermann, *The Praise of God in the Psalms*, translated by Keith R.Crim. (Virginia: John Knox Press, 1965), 149. Carroll Stuhlmueller, *Psalm: A Biblical Theological Commentary* (Wilmington: Michael Glazier, 1983), 88. Hans-Joachim Kraus, "Psalms 60-150," in *A Continental Commentary*, translated by Hilton C. Oswald (Minneapolis: Fortress Press, 1993), 257-258. Samuel L. Terrien, "The Psalms: Strophic Structure and Theological Commentary: Psalms 73-150," in *Eerdmans Critical Commentary,* vol. 2, edited by David Noel Freedman (Grand Rapids: William B. Eerdmans Publishing Company, 2003), 618.

5 Carroll Stuhlmueller, *Psalm: A Biblical Theological Commentary* (Wilmington: Michael Glazier, 1983), 88.

Isaiah. Psalm 97:8 clearly identifies the setting of Psalm 97 as a cultic song which makes it natural to think of a post-exilic expression.[6]

Therefore, there is visible connection between Psalm 97 and Second Isaiah because "Psalm 97 shows the influence of Second Isaiah. It is noted that the early post-exilic period is probable."[7] The above discussions are some of the views which support the post-exilic setting. In the opinion, the Psalm might have originated during the monarchical period but was used widely in the post-exilic setting. Therefore, it is necessary to look at the redaction history, how the Psalm was formed. It also broadens the scope of how the hymn was used and which historical setting is suitable to the text.

7.2. Literary Analysis of the Text

This section analysed the literary function of Psalm 97. It is useful to understand the text and bring out new insights. Thus, I emphasize the critical notes, form, structures and the repeated words as well as repeated phrases in the text in order to investigate the unique characteristics of the Psalm.

7.2.1. Translation

1 יהוה מלך תגל הארץ ישמחו איים רבים :	1. The Lord reigns, let the earth be rejoice, many *islands*[8] be glad.
2 ענן וערפל סביביו צדק ומשפט מכון כסאו:	2. Clouds and darkness all around him, righteousness and judgment are the foundation of his throne.
3 אש לפניו תלך ותלהט סביב צריו:	3. A *fire*[9] goes before him, and burn up his oppressors all *around*.[10]
4 האירו ברקיו תבל ראתה ותחל הארץ :	4. His lightning causes to shine up the world, the earth saw and tremble.

6 Hans-Joachim, Kraus, "Psalms 60-150," in *A Continental Commentary*, translated by Hilton C. Oswald (Minneapolis: Fortress Press, 1993), 257-258.

7 Samuel L. Terrien, "The Psalms: Strophic Structure and Theological Commentary: Psalms 73-150," in *Eerdmans Critical Commentary,* vol. 2, edited by David Noel Freedman (Grand Rapids: William B. Eerdmans Publishing Company, 2003), 618.

8 V.1. אִי 'distant islands and shores, coast-lands and islands.' See A. Philip Brown II and Bryan.W Smith, eds., *A Reader's Hebrew Bible* (Zondervan, 2008), 1206.

9 V.3. אֵשׁ 'fire' which represents of destructive and also refining power. See Arthur G. Clarke, *Analytical Studies in the Psalms* (Grand Rapids: Kregel Publications, 1979), 244.

10 V.3a. few manuscripts have סביביו 'around him.' See Karl Elliger and Wilhelm Rudolph, eds., *Biblia Hebraica Stuttgartensia* (Stuttgart: Biblia Hebraica Stuttgartensia, 1997), 1178.

5 הרים כדונג נמסו מלפני יהוה מלפני אדון כל־הארץ :	5. The mountains melted like wax at the face of the Lord, At the *face*[11] of the Lord of the whole earth.
6 הגידו השמים צדקו וראו כל־העמים כבודו:	6. The *heavens declare*[12] his righteousness, And all the peoples have seen his glory.
7 יבשו כל־עבדי פסל המתהללים באלילים השתחוו־לו כל־אלהים :	7. Be ashamed who serve graven images, who boast themselves of idols, *worship*[13] him all you gods.
8 שמעה ותשמח ציון ותגלנה בנות יהודה למען משפטיך יהוה :	8. Zion heard and was glad, And the *daughters of Judah*[14] have rejoiced because for your judgments, Lord.
9 כי־אתה יהוה עליוןעל־כל־הארץ מאד נעלית על־כל־אלהים :	9. For you, Lord, Most High over all the earth, you are ascended more above all gods.
10 אהבי יהוה שנאו רע שמר נפשות חסידיו מיד רשעים יצילם :	10. The Lord loves those who *hate* evils, *who keeps*[15] the souls of his glory ones, He rescued them from the hand of the wicked.
11 אור זרע לצדיק ולישרי־לב שמחה :	11. Light is sown for the righteous, and joy for the upright in heart.
12 שמחו צדיקים ביהוה והודו לזכר קדשו :	12. Be glad you righteous in the Lord, and praise for the remembrance of his holiness.

11 V.5b is missing in the Syriac version of the Old Testament. See Karl Elliger and Wilhelm Rudolph, eds., *Biblia Hebraica Stuttgartensia* (Stuttgart: Biblia Hebraica Stuttgartensia, 1997), 1178.

12 V.6. נגד 'declare' it is in verb *hiphil* perfect 3rd person common plural. This implies that they have witnessed Yahweh's great act of liberating the nation of Israel. See Arthur G. Clarke, *Analytical Studies in the Psalms* (Grand Rapids: Kregel Publications, 1979), 244.

13 V.7a LXX, Syriac have imperative חוה 'to bow down, to worship.' השתחוה is usually taken as *hithpael* imperative rather than as indicative. The form of the verb is the same, and therefore the imperative reading would be appropriate. It would be "bow down to him, all your gods." See Marvine E. Tate, "Psalms 51-150," in *Word Biblical Commentary*, vol. 20, edited by David A. Hubbard, (Dallas: Word Books, 1990), 517.

14 V.8. 'daughter of Judah' refers daughter cities. See Arthur G. Clarke, *Analytical Studies in the Psalms* (Grand Rapids: Kregel Publications, 1979), 245.

15 V.10c. LXX and Cairo Geniza added κυριοζ 'Lord.' see Karl Elliger and Wilhelm Rudolph, eds., *Biblia Hebraica Stuttgartensia* (Stuttgart: Biblia Hebraica Stuttgartensia, 1997), 1178.

7.2.2. Text Critical Notes

First, איים רבים means *'many islands'* (Ps 97:1). There is a contrast in view among the commentators of the phrase איים רבים *many islands.* Phillips, do not give attention to איים רבים from the universal worship of Yahweh, they just point out that this is referring to foreign countries. The word איים is in noun common masculine plural absolute, means 'land or coast' denotes a land that is surrounded by water. In the text, it appears in the noun common masculine plural. Therefore, it generally refers to the sea girth; meaning 'surrounded by the sea' or the lands beyond the shores of Israel. איים refers to foreign coasts and not merely islands. In a wider context, the psalmist is referring to the Gentile Nations.[16] Eaton refers to the countries on the other side of the Mediterranean, such as Greece, pointing to the ends of the earth.[17] The word איים could refer to a new era for all the world to the utmost bounds.[18] Thus, commentators only suggest nations and give no further explanation on *many islands.*

On the other hand, Kraus, Spickard and Cragg, support that איים refers to the universal worship of Yahweh. The use of איים רבים 'many islands' means all the world should join in homage and praise of Yahweh's kingship (Isa 97:1, Isa 42: 12).[19] The islands or distant shores enhance the universal scope of Yahweh's reign.[20] איים רבים refers generally to the most remote coastlands of the whole world. The expression of rejoicing of the whole world demonstrates the world-wide significance of the glad tidings of the beginning of the kingdom of God

16 John Philips, *Exploring Psalms: An Expository Commentary*, vol. 2 (Grand Rapids: Kregel Publications., 2002), 78. See John Goldingay, "Psalms 90-150," in *Baker Commentary on the Old Testament Wisdom and Psalms*, vol. 3, edited by Tremper Longman III (Grand Rapids: Academic Press, 2008), John Goldingay, "Psalms 90-150," in *Baker Commentary on the Old Testament Wisdom and Psalms*, vol. 3, edited by Tremper Longman III (Grand Rapids: Academic Press, 2008), 112–113. John Eaton, *The Psalms: A Historical and Spiritual Commentary with an Introduction and New Translation* (London: Continuum International Publishing Group, 2005), 343-344.

17 John Goldingay, "Psalms: Psalms 90-150", in *Baker Commentary on the Old Testament Wisdom and Psalms*, vol. 3, edited by Tremper Longman III (Grand Rapids: Baker Academic, 2008), 112.

18 Eaton, *The Psalms*, 343.

19 Kraus, *Psalms 60-150*, 258.

20 Paul R. Spickard and Kevin M. Cragg, *A Global History of Christians: How Everyday Believers Experienced their World* (Grand Rapids: Baker Academic, 1994), 518. Artur Weiser, "The Psalms: A Commentary," in *The Old Testament Library*, edited by Peter Ackroyd (Philadelphia: Westminster John Knox Press, 1962), 632-633. A. A. Anderson, "The Book of Psalms: Psalms 73-150," in *New Century Bible Commentary*, vol. 2 (London: William B. Eerdmans Publishing Company, 1989), 687. Erhard S. Gerstenberger, *Psalms, Part 2 and Lamentations: The Forms of the Old Testament Literature*, vol. XV (Grand Rapids: William B. Eerdmans Publishing Company, 2001), Erhard S. Gerstenberger, *Psalms, Part 2 and Lamentations: The Forms of the Old Testament Literature*, vol. XV (Grand Rapids: William B. Eerdmans Publishing Company, 2001), 192.

relating to universal worship.[21] Yahweh, being the universal and even cosmic overlord, איים is the global expression in the Yahweh kingship hymns. This means that a universal reign of Yahweh is intended and confessed against all other claims.[22] The coastlands or isles denote the Mediterranean Sea, but in this verse, it probably refers to the remotest parts of the earth and it speaks of the universal homage which will be rendered to Yahweh the king.[23]

I am in agreement with Kraus and others who talk about universal worship. איים רבים 'many islands' has wide implications for universal worship as it focuses on the whole world worshiping Yahweh. Therefore, the contrast in their view is that earlier scholars merely talk about the nations, but the phrase איים רבים does not end from there, but talks about the nations in the context of worship. The little contrast in ideas makes a huge difference in its meaning and in the implications. To me, this has a great implication for the universal worship of Yahweh.

Secondly, ענן וערפל 'cloud and heavy cloud or darkness' (Ps 97:2). The metaphorical expression of talks about the 'awe and mystery which surrounds God.' ענן 'cloud' is the 'sign of Yahweh's presence' (Ex 19: 9, 16, 24: 15-16) and so is ערפל 'darkness' (Ex 20:21, Deut 4:11, 5:22). Cloud and darkness indicate the presence of Yahweh, because it signifies that this real presence was a protective shield covering the chosen people.[24] In a wider aspect, the OT idea of God as one who is surrounded by the impenetrable darkness of clouds reverently maintains the mystery of God's nature and impressively indicates the threateningly serious character of God appearing.[25] The two Hebrew words ענן 'clouds' and ערפל 'darkness' are implied as theophanies of God. As we talk about the sovereignty of Yahweh, the clouds and darkness express majesty and splendour of Yahweh.[26]

Thirdly, הגידו 'declare' is in verb *hiphil* perfect 3rd person common plural (Ps 97:6). The psalmist stresses that the handy work of God declares the sovereignty of God. The earth and heavens are embodied as the earth sees and trembles, the heavens declares God's righteousness (Ps 97: 6). Schaefer comments, the heavens become the messenger of Yahweh and exalt his righteousness and glory to all peoples. As it says "heaven heralds God's

21 Artur Weiser, "The Psalms: A Commentary," in *The Old Testament Library*, edited by Peter Ackroyd (Philadelphia: Westminster John Knox Press, 1962), 632.

22 Erhard S. Gerstenberger, *Psalms, Part 2 and Lamentations: The Forms of the Old Testament Literature*, vol. XV (Grand Rapids: William B. Eerdmans Publishing Company, 2001), 192.

23 A.A. Anderson, "The Book of Psalms: Psalms 73-150," in *New Century Bible* Commentary, vol. 2 (London: William B. Eerdmans Publishing Company, 1989), 687.

24 Goldingay, *Psalms 90-150*, 112.

25 Weiser, *The Psalms,* 632.

26 Hermann Gunkel, *Introduction to Psalms : The Genres of the Religious Lyric of Israel* (Macon, Georgia: Mercer University Press, 1998), 61.

righteousness to which all people are witness."[27] The heavens ring out with the testimony of how Yahweh established a right order and the majesty of Yahweh was manifest to all people and nations.[28] Yahweh's awesomeness is seen in his hiddenness as well as in his blazing glory as manifestation of his kingship that is so compelling that even the gods should worship him.[29] Broyles points out that these two attributes of צדק 'righteousness' and משפט 'justice' are revealed from heavens to earth and all the people behold his glory.[30]

Fourthly, בוש 'shame' (Ps 97:7). The verb בוש connotes humiliation by the failure of human endeavour.[31] Olley points out that בוש means 'be shown to be in the wrong,' "let me not be shown to have been in the wrong to have trusted in you."[32] The word strongly affirms to giving due honour to Yahweh and not to idols. The heavens herald God's righteousness to which all peoples and nations witness the sovereignty of Yahweh and before which idolaters are shamed. John W. Olley, and Avrahami comment on בוש 'shame.' For Olley it is possible that בוש *bos* had its original use within a forensic setting, although its use in Biblical Hebrew is more general.[33]

The root בוש 'to be ashamed' appears mostly in poetic contexts. The appearance of a verb within literature provides the opportunity to understand its meaning in the light of common associations that are demonstrated in word pairs, parallels and clues of words. The meaning of בוש is determined within a semantic field rather than looking at the comparative philology.[34] The book of Psalms shows that the meaning of בוש has to do with the experience of a disconnection between expectations and reality which is an experience of disappointment. Its primary meanings are frustration, failure and lack of trust.

---

27 Konrad Schaefer, *Psalms*: *Studies in Hebrew Narrative & Poetry*, edited by David W. Cotter (Collegeville: The Liturgical Press, 2001), 240.

28 Eaton, *The Psalms*, 343.

29 Eugene H.Merrill, *Everlasting Dominion: A Theology of the Old Testament* (Nashville: Broadman & Holman Publishers, 2006), 320.

30 Craig C. Broyles, "The Psalms and Cult Symbolism: The Case of the Cherubim-Ark," in *Interpreting the Psalms: Issues and Approaches*, edited by Philip S. Johnston and David G. Firth (England: InterVarsity Press, 2005), 150.

31 Marvine E. Tate, "Psalms 51-150," in *Word Biblical Commentary*, vol. 20, edited by David A. Hubbard (Dallas: Word Books, 1990),519. See John W. Olley, "The God of Heaven: A Look at Attitudes to Other Religions in the Old Testament," *Colloquium* 27, no. 2 (1995): 89. Yael. Avrahami, "בוש in the Psalms-Shame or Disappointment?" *JSOT* 34, no. 3 (2010): 299-309.

32 John W. Olley, "Forensic Connotation of *Bos*," *Vêtus Testamentum* 26, no. 2 (April, 1976): 231.

33 Olley, "Forensic Connotation of *Bos*," 232. See Yael. Avrahami, "בוש in the Psalms –Shame or Disappointment?" *JSOT,* vol. 34, no. 3 (2010): 295-313.

34 Yael. Avrahami,"בוש in the Psalms-Shame or Disappointment?" *JSOT,* vol. 34, no. 3 (2010): 299.

The word בוש describes failure subsequent to a reliance on other nations or gods (Jer 14.2; Job 6.20; Hos 13.5).[35]

Fifthly, אלהים 'gods' (Ps 97:7). This is a common masculine plural absolute noun. LXX and Syriac read *οἱ ἄγγελοι αὐτοῦ* meaning 'all you his angels.' Gerstenberger and Goldingay argue that *ἄγγελοι* probably refers to 'all the other gods.'[36] For Tate, this represents 'idols,' all these gods are compelled to join in the worship of Yahweh and bow down before the Most High God.[37] Terrien claims that it probably refers to "foreign gods, they must submit to the Most High."[38]

Sixthly, בנות 'daughters,' refers to the cities (Ps 97:8). The daughters of Judah rejoice. Weiser and Smith affirm that "daughters is (provincial cities) of Judah."[39] Dahood affirms that Daughters of Judah talks about "the towns and villages of Judah."[40]

Seventhly, אהב 'love' (Ps 97:10). This is the concrete covenantal motif. The Lord describes intimate relationship with humankind as shown in the word אהב 'love' (Ps 97:10). Gerstenberger comments that this is a "comforting assurance of God's guaranteed help" (Ps 97: 10-11).[41] True worshippers truly love the Lord and hate evil and as a result they share a bond with the Lord.[42]

Eighthly, שנאו 'hate to' (Ps 97:10), to be read in several manuscripts, Syriac שנא 'haters of.' Gunkel, Kraus and others, insist that the context does not allow the reading, "O Lovers of Yahweh, hate evil." They insist that Yahweh must be the subject of the verb 'love' and thus change שנאי 'lovers of,' to אהב, participle, which means 'one who loves.' Tate continues to affirm that the change of the imperative שנאו 'hate to' שנאי 'haters of,' Yahweh loves the haters of evil. Minor changes provide a smoother agreement in the text. Perhaps, LXX agrees with MT and MT does not present any excessive difficulty, supported by Howard.[43]

The psalmist encourages true worshippers not to compromise with evil activities but to hate them. 'Hate evil' is from the covenantal love of justice (cf. Amos 5:15). Yahweh's faithfulness and sovereign justice by the punishment

---

35 Avrahami, "בוש in the Psalms–Shame or Disappointment?" 308-309.

36 Gerstenberger, *Psalms, Part 2 and Lamentations*, 193.

37 Tate, *Psalms 51-100*, These references give clear picture what is all about the other gods or angels (Isa 42:17, 44:9-11, 45:16, Jer 10:14, Ex 20:4-5), 519.

38 Terrien, *The Psalms: Strophic Structure and Theological Commentary*, 680.

39 Tate, *Psalms 51-100*, 519.

40 Mitchell Dahood, *Psalms 51-100: The Anchor Bible* (New York: Doubleday, 1968), 362.

41 Gerstenberger, *Psalms, Part 2 and Lamentations*, 193.

42 Eaton, *The Psalms,* 344.

43 Tate, "Psalms 51-150," 517.

of evil is visibly manifested in the sight of whole world.[44] Leslie remarks that "If you hate evil, you are in the love and care of the king"[45] (Ps 97:10).

Ninthly, צִיּוֹן 'Zion' is a proper name and has no gender (Ps 97:8). Mohol, asserts that Zion means fortress, and metaphorically it refers to the people of Jerusalem and believing community at large.[46] It is noticed that the name Zion occurs in the cultic context in the OT (1 Chr 11:5). In many passages, Zion indicates the city of Jerusalem and the two names are often used interchangeably (Isa 2:3, 4:3, 30:19). Salem is also considered to be a variant of the city Jerusalem which parallels צִיּוֹן (Ps 76:3). Also, Judah is occasionally mentioned with Zion (Jer 14:19, Ps 69:36).[47] In particular, "Zion designates Jerusalem as the city of Yahweh and his dwelling temple." 'My holy mountain' parallels Zion (Ps 2:6). Israel worships Yahweh on Zion. Here the nation can see God's mighty deeds (Ps 84:8).[48]

Finally, אור זרע לצדיק 'light is sown for the righteous' (Ps 97:11). The psalmist declares that the verb זרע mean to 'sow,' it is *Qal* passive participle masculine singular absolute. The metaphor of 'sow' refers that righteous people are always in the eyes and sight of God. Eaton argues that, "Light is often a symbol of salvation."[49] For Goldingay, "Light stands for life, deliverance and blessing." When God's light shines on the righteous, joy is produced in the life of humans.[50]

These text critical comments are relevant and supportive to the argument of my thesis, because this helps me to have a wider understanding of the text and in bringing out the kingship metaphor from its theological significance for worship.

7.2.3. Form of the Psalm

The form critical analysis reveals that Psalm 97 has a 'hymnic form' and it is also considered to be a descriptive praise of Yahweh.[51] For Anderson, the hymn consists of two main parts: 1. a description of the sovereignty and majesty of Yahweh (Ps 97:1-6). 2. A description of the effects of Yahweh's rule over Israel

44 James E. Smith, *The Wisdom Literature and Psalms* (Joplin, Missouri: College Press, 2007), 377.

45 Leslie, *The Psalms,* 81.

46 Eliya Mohol, "Zion," in *Dictionary of Mission Theology* (Illinois: InterVarsity Press, 2007), 447.

47 F. Stolz, "צִיּוֹן," in *Theological Lexicon of the Old Testament,* vol. 2, edited by Ernst Jenni and Claus Westermann (Peabody: Hendrickson Publishers, Inc, 1997), 1071-1072.

48 Stolz, "צִיּוֹן," 1074.

49 Eaton, *The Psalms,* 690.

50 Goldingay, *Psalms 42-89*, 116-117.

51 Tate, *Psalms 51-100*, 518.

and all the peoples and (Ps 97:7-12).[52] In regard to the metre of the hymn, there are several observations. Kraus identifies the following 3+3 meter takes over in verses 2-6 and 11-12. In addition, there are long verses 4+3 in verse 1 and 4+4 in verse 9. Also 3+3+3 are visible in the following verses 7, 8, and 10.[53]

But Anderson comments that the metre of the hymn is mainly 3+3.[54] This is how different opinions were developed among the psalms scholars like Anderson and Kraus. However, to me Anderson's view gives the idea to see what the whole text is all about.

7.2.4. Structure of the Psalm

Philips divides the structure of Psalm 97 into two parts: 1. The Lord who is celebrated as the reigning one (Ps 97:1-9) 2. The righteous one (Ps 97:10-12). Both points are inseparable.[55] Philips' way of breaking the verses is different from Anderson's. Whereas Limburg comments that the psalm is divided not only into two but three segments: 1. The earth is called to rejoice and be glad (Ps 97:1-5). 2. Zion is glad and rejoices (Ps: 6-9). 3. The righteous experience joy and are called to rejoice (Ps 97:10-12).[56]

Howard also divides Psalm 97 into three according to the strophe but not the same as Limburg. 1. Psalm 97:1-6, 2. Psalm 97:7-9, 3. Psalm 97:10-12.[57] Anderson, Philips, Limburg and Howard do not fully agree with each other regarding the structure of Psalm 97. I support Howard because his division is more coherent than the others. Looking into the form-critical genre, structure and metre, there is no solution for solid arrangement but the unity and diversity contributes to the unique poetical characteristic of Psalm 97.

7.2.5. Repetition

The word גיל means 'rejoice' and is repeated both in verses 1 and 8. It indicates the rhetorical nature of the text. Rejoicing is always connected with the enthronement psalms and it invites 'all the land' to rejoice in the kingship of Yahweh. Psalm 97 declares that the universal reign of Yahweh is not only for the Israelites but it is intended that all nations rejoice in worshipping the true God.[58] The word שמח 'glad' occurs in verses 1, 8 and 11. The appearance and mighty works of Yahweh brings שמח 'glad' "to those who live in Yahweh's

52 Anderson, *The Book of Psalms: Psalms 73-150*, 686.

53 Kraus, *Psalms 60-150*, 257.

54 Anderson, *The Book of Psalms: Psalms 73-150*, 687.

55 John Philips, *Exploring Psalms: An Expository Commentary*, vol. 2 (Grand Rapids: Kregel Publications., 2002), 77.

56 James Limburg, "Psalms," in *Word Biblical Commentary*, edited by Patrick D Miller and David. L. Bartlett (Louisville: Westminster John Knox Press, 2000), 302.

57 David M. Howard, *The Structure of Psalms 93-100* (Winona Lake: Eisenbrauns, 1997), 73.

58 Gerstenberger, *Psalms, Part 2 and Lamentations*, 192.

covenant." Therefore, the psalm repeatedly mentions the word שמח to reveal a heart of gladness and rejoice in the Lord.[59]

The word צדק 'rightness or righteousness' is mentioned in verses 2 and 6 whereas צדק 'just or righteous' is mentioned in verses 11 and 12. Righteousness is one of the unique characteristics of Yahweh's nature and kingship. Brueggemann affirms that, "The actual substance of governance is characterized by righteousness and justice."[60] In Israel's worship, it always relates to covenantal relationship of God; that is, to love God (Ps 97:10) and live a righteous life. Brueggemann argues that "new orientation is a life of disciplined response to God's will for justice."[61] Here, a new situation in human life talks about new life in a person.

The word אור 'light' occurs in verses 4 and 11 and affirms the mighty power of God and which also brings new life. The hymn of Psalm 97 is a response to the manifestation of the Lord which is signified by the action of worship. Therefore, the psalmist depicts the Lord as radiant in majesty, perhaps for the worshipers, and his light has brought transformation upon their own encounter with God.[62] The word פנה 'face' occurs twice in verse 5. It is noted that פנה here symbolizes the presence of the Lord. The mountains which are a symbol of stability melt before the presence of the Lord. The face of the Lord reveals that Yahweh is the ruler and master of the whole universe.[63] All these repetitions refer their usefulness in the context of Israel's worship as it becomes a reminder for the people to rely on Yahweh the king.

7.3. Comments in Relation to the Kingship Metaphor

In this section I concisely discussed and give comments to the text in relation to the kingship metaphor looking from historical literary approach. *First,* מָלָךְ יְהוָה *'The Lord reigns'* (Ps 97:1).[64] The psalm begins with a declaration, and Kraus describes this as a 'formula of obeisance.' Yahweh is honoured as king and this 'obeisance all the world is to join.' Yahweh is the ruler of the whole world and nobody can take away his kingship.[65] For Knight, the context shows that Israel had just returned from exile. At that time, the Israelites had listened to the comforting words of Isaiah the prophet. They have heard the great voice

59 Kraus, *Psalms 60-150*, 260.

60 Walter Brueggemann, *The Message of the Psalms: A Theological Commentary* (Minneapolis: Augsburg Publishing House, 1984), 146.

61 Brueggemann, *The Message of the Psalms: A Theological Commentary,* 147.

62 Eaton, *The Psalms*, 341-342.

63 Anderson, "The Book of Psalms, 688.

64 Here, I used vowels along with Hebrew consonants, because this clearly distinguishes between "Yahweh the king and Yahweh reign." Here מָלָךְ is verb *Qal* and is in perfect third person masculine, so it is translated according to the verb and not the noun.

65 Kraus, *Psalms 60-150*, 258.

of encouragement (Isa 40:1-6) and they declare in faith 'the Lord reigns.'[66] The declaration of Yahweh's reign brings joy to the world and jubilation to the coastlands.[67] The proclamation of Yahweh's reign offers hope to the righteous over their opposition.

Secondly, highest is a connotation of Yahweh's kingship which is stressed in Psalm 97. The full form of the divine name עליון על is attested in Gen 14:18-20 and Ps 78:35, it appears in parallel with אלהים, a usage that corresponds precisely to Gen 14. Here, Yahweh is identified with עליון על where Abram swears, "I raise my hand to Yahweh." It means Yahweh and עליון are not identical.[68] The relation of the phrase ןוילע לא to creation and to the Davidic kingship is evident in Gen 14 and in some other texts such as 2 Sam 22: 14, Ps 47:2. The use of עליון is addressed mostly to God when the universal claims for Israel's God appear.[69] In the enthronement psalms, particularly in Psalm 97, עליון appears in the context of a hymn celebrating Yahweh's kingship and it is logically connected with the universal dominion of the highest God over all the earth.[70]

Kraus explicitly supports the motif of עליון 'Most High God' in enthronement psalms. The highest God refers to the God of Israel.[71] As the highest God, he plays the role of the highest authority revealing his divine kingship to the world to let the people know the true God and worship him. לא is a common name for Israel's God. This is prominent in the pre-Mosaic era (Gen 12-50).

Fretheim affirms that the God whom Israel's ancestors worshiped under the name אל is none other than Yahweh the king. אל אלהי ישראל 'God of Israel,' (Gen 33:20). For instance, Abram addressed Yahweh with אל עליון 'God Most High,' indicating that יהוה is the same as אל. This is the name with which Melchizedek addressed God.[72] According to Genesis 14:19, עליון על is

66 George, A. F. Knight, *Psalms: The Daily Study Bible Series*, edited by John C. L. Gibson (Edinburgh: Saint Andrew Press, 1983), 114.

67 Sebastian Kizhakkeyil, *The Psalms: The Prayer Book of the Bible* (Ruhalaya, Ujjain: Ruhalaya Publications, 2005), 362.

68 H.J. Zobel Greifsward, "עליון," in *Theological Dictionary of the Old Testament,* vol. XI, edited by G. Johannes Botterweck (Grand Rapids: William B. Eerdmans Publishing Company, 2001), 125.

69 Terrence E. Fretheim, "אל." in *New International Dictionary of Old Testament Theology & Exegesis,*vol. I. edited by Willem A. VanGemeren (Grand Rapids: Zondervan, 1997), 400-401.

70 Greifsward, "עליון,"This meaning implies the notion of dominion over the universe. The one who is exalted far above all gods is also Most High over all the earth (Ps 97:9). He is sovereign over the national gods of the various lands and peoples (cf. Deut 32:8-9). 126.

71 Kraus, *Psalms 60-150*, 247.

72 Terrence E. Fretheim, "אל," in *New International Dictionary of Old Testament Theology & Exegesis,* vol. I, edited by Willem A. VanGemeren (Grand Rapids: Zondervan, 1997),

described as creator of heaven and earth. Beyond doubt, all the text references to עליון refer to Yahweh.

The poet portrays the greatness of God through the divine title of God יהוה עליון which means the 'Most High God' (Ps 97:9). Therefore, Yahweh asserts authority over the nations and the peoples' gods like, for instance, in relation to Egypt or Canaan, Philistia, Assyria and Babylon.[73] No other gods can compare with the majesty and the kingship of God (Ps 96: 4-5).

Thirdly, dominion is a connotation of the kingship of Yahweh and it refers to the ruling power of God. The text mentions כסא 'throne' which refers to the power of Yahweh who is above all the kings and gods. Anderson affirms that כסא "signifies the rule or dominion of God."[74] The throne of Yahweh is founded on two pillars; they are 'righteousness and justice' which mark the characteristic of Yahweh's dominion based on righteousness.[75] Yahweh's government can never depart from righteousness.[76] Here, the word כסא symbolizes the power and stability of Yahweh's kingship and all other gods will come under God's mighty throne one day.

Fourthly, אש *fire* (Ps 97:3). The metaphor of אש plays a significant role in the theophanies of God (cf. Ex 19:18, 24:17 Deut 5:4, Ps 50:3). Goldingay and Philips support that the metaphor of fire symbolizes God's power or presence. 'Fire consumes Yahweh's foes,' this is certainly good news for the true worshippers of Yahweh. It wipes out Yahweh's oppressors and the wrongdoers. The fire is reflected in lightning and it shows the power of Yahweh which makes the earth tremble for injustice.[77] Yahweh came into an unjust world to play the role of a righteous king. Fire and lightning symbolize the weapons of God. As Yahweh demonstrates divine authority, all the people see Yahweh's faithfulness and thus Yahweh deserves all honour and sincere adoration.[78]

Genesis 14, is the only text where these words אל עליון are juxtaposed, however they are usually in par (Ps 73:11, 107:11). In poetic books, עליון is often in par with Yahweh. 400.

73 Goldingay, *Psalms 42-89*, 115.

74 Anderson, *The Book of Psalms: Psalms 1-72*, 687.

75 Limburg, *Psalms*, 329.

76 Phillips, *Exploring Psalms,* 78.

77 Goldingay, *Psalms 90-150*, 113. Fire symbolizes Yahweh's wrath which goes before God to consume the enemies of the true God. The manifestation of Yahweh's power is described in terms of the great theophanies of the past. Yahweh's lightning lights up the world. The mighty mountains melt in the presence of God who is lord of all the earth (Ps 97:5, cf. Micah 1:4). See Hans-Joachim Kraus, "Psalms 60-150," in *A Continental Commentary*, translated by Hilton C. Oswald (Minneapolis: Fortress Press, 1993), 260-261. John Philips, *Exploring Psalms: An Expository Commentary*, vol. 2 (Grand Rapids: Kregel Publications, 2002), 77-78. James E. Smith, *The Wisdom Literature and Psalms* (Joplin, Missouri: College Press, 2007), 377.

78 Goldingay, *Psalms 90-150*, 114.

The nature of God cannot be graphically portrayed in static terms as something which is objective and static in essence, but must be experienced in a personal encounter as in the case of fire it is a dynamic in its effect as fire.[79] Thus, fire illustrates the 'mystery of God's appearance.'[80] The power of Yahweh burns the enemies of Yahweh. The power of Yahweh shines in the world. The whole world sees and trembles. The mountains melt like wax at the presence of the Lord.[81] The psalm rejoices over the Lord's righteousness that reigns over the whole earth. All people can see the outcome of the nature of God's rule in the universe, and even the clouds, darkness, fire and lightning are associated with God's presence among human beings (Ex 19:9, 16-18).

7.4. Comments in Relation to Worship

These are some of the essential points in relation to the true worshippers of Yahweh and need to be emphasized. The points are: *First, the psalmist expresses rejoicing in worship*. The psalm begins with the declaration that the Lord is king and invites the earth to rejoice in worshipping the Lord.[82] The earth trembles, the mountains erupt; the heavens declare Yahweh righteousness; and bear the news to all the lands to rejoice and worship Yahweh the King of kings (Ps 97:1-6).[83] The psalmist calls upon the people to rejoice in the awe-inspiring power of God. Mount Zion rejoices and the cities of Judah are glad for the authority of Yahweh over idolatry. This rejoicing happened in Judah and this can also happen elsewhere as Yahweh is all in all.[84] In my view, true worship needs a heart of rejoicing and this is demanded by the Almighty God. All the adversaries of Yahweh are burned up in the flame of fire. So also idol worshippers are put to shame. But in the community of Zion, the congregations of Yahweh are exalting and rejoicing in worship of the true God.[85] According to Smith, the righteous should rejoice at every mention of the name of the Lord which brings to remembrance all that Yahweh has done."[86] We also see the distinction between those who love the Lord and who love evil. Any nation or people who love God truly have a cause for rejoicing. The one who keeps the

79 Weiser, *The Psalms: A Commentary,* 632-633.

80 Kraus, *Psalms 60-150*, 261.

81 Philips, *Exploring Psalms: An Expository Commentary*, 78.

82 Kraus, *Psalms 60-150: A Continental Commentary*, 260.

83 Elmer A. Leslie, *The Psalms: Translated and Interpreted in the Light of Hebrew Life and Worship* (New York: Abingdon Press, 1949), 80.

84 Goldingay, *Psalms 90-150*, 116.

85 Kraus, *Psalms 60-150*, 260.

86 Smith, *Psalms*, 377. Yahweh lightens the world, the heavens proclaim the righteousness of God, and Yahweh is victorious over all the worthless idols or gods, exalted far above all gods. See Marie Burns, *The Poetic Books Part II: Psalms 73-150 & Proverbs* (Bloomington: Author House, 2005), 126.

covenant of God and does Yahweh's will delight in God's presence and rejoice in him.[87]

Rejoicing in the worship of Yahweh has an implication for worship in a universal aspect. For this reason, the psalmist urges the whole earth to rejoice and praise in the worship of Yahweh. Yahweh demonstrates the truth in everything and the world witnesses that nothing can control the mighty power of Yahweh. The psalmist portrays that the worshipping community of Israel rejoice in the Lord because Yahweh is the king who is more powerful than all other gods and has performed mighty deeds. The spirit of rejoicing holds the power that motivates the worshippers. True worshippers of God should worship and rejoice with the indwelling presence of God. As the people of Israel rejoiced in the Lord, even today the worshippers of God are to rejoice in the Lord and worship him faithfully.

Secondly, the psalmist *expresses submission in worship.* The psalmist urges the nations to submit in true worship to the Lord. If they ignore worshipping the true God and persist in idolatry, they will certainly be put to shame as Yahweh is superior over those who worship idols and gods. The whole earth, all the people and all the gods, therein pay attention and bow down and submit to the Most High God.[88] The text denotes the phrase יהוה עליון כי־אתה, '*For you, Lord, Most High* (Ps 97:9). The great king over all the earth, Yahweh, being the Most High, impacts other nations and not merely the nation of Israel. Thus, the title Most High witnesses the supremacy of God and it also gives the perspective of God who is to be worshipped by humankind with fear and respect.[89] Tate affirms "The psalm is focused on the exalted position of Yahweh above the earth and all other gods."[90] The existence of foreign gods is not denied as in other hymns, but here it clearly portrays that they must submit to the Most High. That shows that idols are insufficient compared to the power of Yahweh.[91]

The entire world stands before the face of God and all nations are subjects in Yahweh's empire. Additionally, the text indicates that all gods bow down and worship Yahweh who is a living God.[92] All people can see the splendour of

87 Brueggemann, *The Message of the Psalms: A Theological Commentary*, 147.

88 Gerstenberger, *Psalms, Part 2 and Lamentations*, 192.

89 Goldingay, *Psalms 42-89*, 77. See Erhard S. Gerstenberger, *Psalms, Part 2 and Lamentations: The Forms of the Old Testament Literature*, vol. XV (Grand Rapids: William B. Eerdmans Publishing Company, 2001), 193.A. A. Anderson, "The Book of Psalms: Psalms 73-150," in *New Century Bible Commentary*, vol. 2 (London: William B. Eerdmans Publishing Company, 1989), 689.

90 Tate, *Psalms 51-100*, 518.

91 Terrien, *The Psalms: Strophic Structure and Theological Commentary*, 680.

92 Gunkel, *Introduction to Psalms: The Genres of the Religious Lyric of Israel*, 69.

the Lord and anyone with some other god is shamed.[93] Leslie argues, "In keen irony the psalmist calls upon their gods to worship God" (Ps 97:7).[94]

The insufficient gods fall down in obeisance to acknowledge the supremacy of Yahweh. Anything as most important in our life, or anything that takes all our time and devotion rather than God, tends to become our idol.[95] Smith comments that true worshippers "must abhor all that is antagonistic to this holy God."[96] The people of God are taught to worship the Lord sincerely. The lovers of Yahweh are those who are committed to Yahweh's call and are faithful to God in all circumstances. The lovers of Yahweh are the people of pure heart and pure devotion.[97]

This is an essential point and reminder for the true worshippers of Yahweh not to be tempted by anything else that takes the place of God in life. In a broader sense, the word 'submission' implies that Yahweh is superior to any other gods. Therefore, other gods are required to submit themselves to the true God. On the other hand, the psalmist urges worshippers to submit themselves before the sovereignty of God. Hence, submission has unique aspect in the worship of Yahweh the king. When we surrender and submit ourselves to God, we can worship God with the right attitude and mind.

7.5. Theological Concerns Pertaining to the Kingship Metaphor of God

In this section I deal theological concerns which are reflecting to the kingship metaphor of Yahweh in the light of connotations which emerge from the exegetical study. They are particularity and deliverance. All these points denote the kingship metaphor of Yahweh.

7.5.1. Kingship and Particularity

As already discussed in the exegetical study, the metaphor of Yahweh as king shows that he has a prerogative to demand exclusive worship. Loyalty to any other god is an abomination to him.[98] The psalmist strongly affirms that Yahweh desires true worship over and above all gods. "Worship constitutes the activity that maintains the relationship between God and Israel. Israel has the duty to worship God continually, wholeheartedly and exclusively."[99] Believing

93 Limburg, *Psalms*, 329.

94 Leslie, The Psalms: Translated and Interpreted in the Light of Hebrew Life and Worship, 80.

95 N. J. Paul, *Effortless Prayers through Psalms* (Madurai: Word of Christ, 2003), 90-91.

96 Smith, *The Wisdom Literature and Psalms*, 377.

97 Tate, *Psalms 51-100*, 520.

98 Eliya Mohol, "Metaphors of Zion Traditions and Their Relevance for Mission," *UBS Journal,* vol.5, no. 1 (March, 2007): 88.

99 John C. Endres, "The Spiritual Vision of Chronicles: Wholehearted, Joy-Filled Worship of God," *The Catholic Biblical Quarterly*, no. 69 (2007): 12. Israel is not to worship other gods or even to worship the Lord alongside other gods. Israel was also highly required to

in one God makes Israel's worship distinctive from other nations (Pss 96:4-5, 97:9).[100]

Olley asserts that the Hebrew Bible condemns worship of anything other than the worship of Yahweh.[101] Clifford and Goldingay emphasize the singularity of Yahweh. Nothing can compare with Yahweh who is all-powerful and all-knowing, and he does not require human labour in the way that other deities usually do. Monotheism also forbids images for no single being can represent the creator of all. Therefore, the word *imageless* is significant in Israel's worship (Deut 4:10-12).[102] We find this especially when we look at what the psalms have to tell us about Yahweh's relationship to other gods. The God of Israel is portrayed as the only God who ought to be acknowledged as the true God. It implies that Israel itself ought to worship Yahweh alone.[103]

The enthronement psalms present that Yahweh is the creator who made all humanity and who owns the depths of the earth, mountain peaks, seas, and the land. Therefore, as the master of all, Yahweh claims exclusive worship.[104] In the deliberation of the exclusive worship of Yahweh, the enthronement psalms agree with the Deuteronomistic writer.[105] Thus torah, prophets and Psalter are in line with the Deuteronomy ideology that there is only one holy God (Deut 6:4, 23:39, Ex 20:3, Isa 46:9). The psalmist declares that those who boast and worship other gods will be ashamed; that means they will be proven wrong (Pss 97:7, 115:3-8).

As seen in the exegetical study בוש 'to be ashame' as found in the enthronement psalms refer to idol worshippers who have forsaken God. Idol worship implies the violation of the relation of trust with Yahweh, thus idol worshippers will encounter בוש (Ps 97:7, Isa 45: 15-16).[106] בוש refers to humiliation, the worshippers of idols, faced humiliation because they could not receive sufficient help from their gods.[107] The proclamation made in Zion

understand with their whole heart that the Lord is one and demands a love of God from the heart. See Gordon McConville, "Deuteronomy," *New Bible Commentary 21st Century*, Edition Consulting, edited by D. A. Carson (Leicester: InterVarsity Press, 2002), 200-201.

100 Clifford, *Psalms 1-72: Abingdon Old Testament Commentaries*, 28.

101 Olley, "The God of Heaven," 89, 93, 94.

102 Clifford, *Psalms 1-72*, 28.

103 Goldingay, *Psalms 42-89*, 108. (Deut 4:35, 5:7, 6:4).

104 Ajoy K. Lama, "The Placement of Psalm 145 in Book V: A Compositional Analysis" (Doctor of Philosophy, Thesis, Trinity International University, 2002), 281-282.

105 Endres, The Spiritual Vision of Chronicles," 201.

106 Philip J. Nel, "בוש," in *New International Dictionary of Old Testament Theology & Exegesis*, vol. I, edited by Willem A. VanGemeren (Carlisle: Paternoster Press, 1997), 624-625.

107 Tate, *Psalms 51-100*, 519.

echoes throughout even Judah and elsewhere (Ps 97:7-8).[108] The condition and experience of forgetting God is qualified as בוש. In that way בוש refers to the painful experience of guilt because of their sinful acts this experience of shame is often complemented with disgrace in OT.[109]

The Lord is over all of the earth and all humankind is urged to worship Yahweh. Idols bring false hope whereas Yahweh offers true love and true hope to the true worshippers. Idols have nothing to offer their makers. The idol has no voice, does not answer, and pays no attention (1 Kings 18:29). The maker of the idol is only a human. The artisans themselves are merely human, let them stand up; let them tremble; they shall surely put to shame (Isa 44:11). When the idol maker carves an image, he brings shame upon himself, and he will become as deceitful as his idol. The makers of the idols become like their idols, they are deceivers. False images will disappear, only God can bring true hope (Jer 10:11).[110]

Olley remarks that whenever בוש occurs "generally the context is a cry for deliverance from enemies who ill-treat the suppliant. Thus the suppliant cries not only for deliverance, but also for vindication, that the enemy be put to shame."[111] He affirms they will be shamed, shown to have been in the wrong to have trusted in those gods or lords for security.[112] He argues that the context portrays that the one who is incensed against Yahweh shall come for judgement and 'be put into shame.'[113]

Mowinckel expresses connection between the words בוש 'shamed' and אלילים 'nothing or non-entities' which portray nothingness of images or idols compared to Yahweh. For Mowinckel, Yahweh's appearance is a 'horror' to all the gods, these אלילים prostrate themselves before Yahweh and pay homage to him.[114] אלילים 'insignificant, worthless' 'non-entities,' the gods of the other nations are worthless and ineffective. אלילים have no power over God. The

108 Schaefer, *Psalms*, 240. The Decalogue prohibits Israel's making or serving images and also bowing. So the prophets and even the psalmist declare that certainly the nations are going to be shamed by their images, because their gods are insufficient and empty (Isa 42:17, 44:9-11, Jer 10:14, Ps 97:7). See Goldingay, *Psalms 42-89*, in *Baker Commentary on the Old Testament Wisdom and Psalms,* vol. 2 (Grand Rapids: Baker Academic, 2007), 114.

109 Nel, "בוש," 624.

110 Kidd, *Stones of Grace*, 35.

111 Olley, "Forensic Connotation of *Bos*," 231-232.

112 Olley, "The God of Heaven," 90.

113 Olley, "Forensic Connotation of *Bos*." 232.

114 Mowinckel, *The Psalms in Israel's Worship*, 148. See Artur Weiser, "The Psalms: A Commentary," in *The Old Testament Library*, edited by Peter Ackroyd (Philadelphia: Westminster John Knox Press, 1962), 635-635. James Chukwuma Okoye, *Israel and the Nations: A Mission Theology of the Old Testament* (New York: Orbis Books, 2006), 106. John Goldingay, *Old Testament Theology: Israel's Life*, vol. 3, (Downers Grove: InterVarsity Press, 2009), 31-32.

psalmist invites people to turn from their idols and worship the true God alone.[115] Exclusivity claims that only Yahweh has the real power. Yahweh is Israel's faithful God and deliverer, 'there is no one but me' (Isa 45:21).[116]

Ugaritic myth Baal becomes the king of gods after his resurrection and victory over *Mot*. According to the Babylonians' epic of creation, Marduk had become king; however in the Israelites' view he is nothing before Yahweh the king. This shows the Israelites that the "other gods have been put to shame" (Ps 97:7). "In true Yahwism the other gods had been Yahweh's enemies ever since the struggles of the immigration and the fights for independence against the natives."[117] Weiser argues, all the worshippers of images lose confidence in their idols. They are ashamed before the mighty power of Yahweh and they must acknowledge the reality that they are defeated.[118]

The enthronement psalms expresses that the other gods are struck with horror at the very presence of Yahweh, they tremble and pay homage to him who is above them. This also means shame and defeat to all 'image worshippers' who put their confidence in םילילא but the appearance of Yahweh the king puts all the other gods to shame.[119] The psalmist urges people to rely on God alone for deliverance.[120] "Yahweh has ascended above all gods" (Ps. 97:9). All the other gods of the people are worthless" (96:5). Therefore, on this basis, the psalmist claims exclusive worship of Yahweh. Being Yahweh's personal possession, Israel has no right to worship other gods.[121]

All gods and nations bow down and worship Yahweh who is a living God (Ps 96:4). Goldingay affirms that, in the Israelite worship, Yahweh alone is to be honoured and there are no images of Yahweh to help their worship.[122] The announcement of the rule of Yahweh seated upon the cherubim is accompanied by typical theophanic phenomena, the trembling of the peoples and quaking of the earth show execution of Yahweh's sovereignty over gods.[123] Israel must worship Yahweh alone in order to be a witness to other nations.

The exclusiveness of Yahweh is clearly denoted from this phrase **יהוה אלהינו יהוה אחד** 'Yahweh is our God, Yahweh one' (Deut 6:4). This reinforces the fact that Yahweh is the one and only God whom Israel must worship. 'God is one means he alone is truly real,' this signifies that Yahweh

115 Okoye, *Israel and the Nations: A Mission Theology of the Old Testament*, 106.

116 Goldingay, *Old Testament Theology: Israel's Faith*, 31-32.

117 Mowinckel, *The Psalms in Israel's Worship*, Two Volumes in One, 148.

118 Weiser, *The Psalms: A Commentary*, 634.

119 Mowinckel, *The Psalms in Israel's Worship*, 149.

120 Goldingay, *Old Testament Theology: Israel's Faith*, 733.

121 Goldingay, *Old Testament Theology: Israel's Faith*, 71, 75.

122 Goldingay, *Old Testament Theology: Israel's Life*, 120.

123 Ollenburger, *Zion the City of the Great King*, 48-49.

is divine and there is no one besides him (Isa 43:10-14, Isa 45:5, 6, 18).[124] Chisholm points that the people of God are not to place their faith in the gods of the nations but in Yahweh.[125] Similarly, Wright points out that the root of the faith of Israel is to worship Yahweh alone. The defining characteristic of the covenant people is a faith of 'one Lord, one love, one loyalty.' This point brings out the ideology of exclusive worship.[126] True worship belongs to God alone, therefore, the psalmist calls upon the nations to come and offer worship Yahweh, the king of the universe and renounce idolatry.[127] No other gods can compare with Yahweh who has clearly pronounced "I am the Lord and I give my glory to no other" (Isa 42: 8, 11). This is because the text projects that the worshippers of idols are put to shame. The worshippers of Yahweh will continue to rejoice, therefore worshippers are urged to give all praise and adoration exclusively to Yahweh.

7.5.2. Kingship and Deliverance

Deliverance is a connotation of the kingship of Yahweh. He rules overall and therefore he must rescue righteous people. The deliverance motif is found in the enthronement psalms and also the psalms of lament. This becomes the basis of Israel's relationship with Yahweh. There are two aspects in relation to Yahweh as a deliverer. *First,* Yahweh possesses the power to deliver the people from their sinful nature. *Secondly,* Yahweh possesses the power to deliver the oppressed people who are deprived of their rights. The main focus in this section is the power of Yahweh to deliver the oppressed. According to House, the deliverer God enters the human world, establishes a relationship with the people and intervenes to deliver the oppressed.[128]

The text explicitly points out the words אשׁ 'fire,' אור 'light,' and ברק 'lightning,' indicating that Yahweh appears as a great God to fight and deliver the righteous in the midst of difficulties. The psalmist uses אשׁ 'fire' and אור 'light' as a metaphor of Yahweh's theophany which reveals the presence of Yahweh and overtakes all the oppressors of Yahweh (Ps 97:3-4).[129] The use of ברק 'lightning' in the OT relates to the presence of Yahweh which is usually in

124 Goldingay, *Old Testament Theology: Israel's Faith*, 38.

125 Robert B. Chisholm, "A Theology of the Psalms," *A Biblical Theology of the Old Testament*, edited by Roy B. Zuck (Chicago: Moody Press, 1991), 263.

126 Christopher J. H. Wright, *Knowing Jesus through the Old Testament* (Chennai: UESI Publication Trust, 2001), 186.

127 James Chukwuma Okoye, *Israel and the Nations: A Mission Theology of the Old Testament* (New York: Orbis Books, 2006), 106.

128 Paul R. House, *Old Testament Theology* (Downers Grove: InterVarsity Press, 1998), 498.

129 Martin J. Selman, "אור," in *New International Dictionary of Old Testament & Exegesis*, vol. 1, edited by Willem A. VanGemeren (Carlisle: Paternoster Press, 1997), 324.

the context of divine judgment, retribution, or warfare and it pertains to God's awesome presence and "describes God's avenging judgment" (Ps 97:4).[130]

The word ברק refers exclusively to manifestations of God's wrathful interaction with people on earth (Ps 97:4). God's threatening theophany in lightning is accompanied by descriptions of terrifying forms such as the storm, clouds, darkness, fire, wind and smoke. Besides that ברק serves as a kind of reminder of the divine warfare of Yahweh. The psalmist rightly states, "God of Israel manifests himself with frightening and dramatic phenomena to protect his people and to defeat the enemy" (Ps 144). ברק 'lightning' is a phenomenon from heaven associated with glittering. For example, the presentation of God's law from Mt Sinai (Ex 19:16). God's avenging judgment with a lightning sword in his hands (Deut 32: 41) and several indications are found in the Psalter of how Yahweh manifests himself and saves the people (Pss 18:14, 97:4, 135: 7, 144).[131] The context of the text denotes that Yahweh the king himself appears in the form of light and fire to save the righteous.

The psalmist points out מיד רשעים יצילם 'he delivers them from the hand of the wicked' (Ps 97:10). The Psalter in general and the enthronement psalms in particular point out that the chosen people come before God's presence to be rescued from violent, dangerous hands and lying tongues. Some of them plead for deliverance from their transgressions. Also, in some incidents, people praise God for delivering them from the hands of the wicked. Yahweh rescues his people and the people praise him. This shows Yahweh's kingship is associated with the mighty power as rescuer and defender. This phrase reveals that significance of deliverance occurs in the enthronement psalms and Yahweh is portrayed as the superior defender and deliverer.[132]

The various acts of Yahweh's deliverance experienced by the community and individuals are indicated in the Psalter (Pss 4:4, 107:24, 118:23). The acts of wonder and deliverance in the OT relate to God's historical action for the covenant people. The concrete experience of deliverance of God's acts are indicated in the hymns.[133] For example, the wonders he has done during the crossing of the sea, the wilderness journey (Ps 78:12), and his saving acts towards the people (Pss 9:1, 40:5-6, 71:17, 107:15).[134]

---

130 William Koopmans, "ברק," in *New International Dictionary of Old Testament Theology & Exegesis,* vol. I, edited by Willem A. VanGemeren (Carlisle: Paternoster Press, 1996), 769.

131 Koopmans, "ברק," 769.

132 Ben C. Ollenburger, *Zion the City of the Great King: A Theological Symbol of the Jerusalem Cult* (Sheffield: Sheffield Academic Press, 1987), 58. (Cf. Pss 7:1, 25 :20, 31:15, 109:21, 120:2, 142:6).

133 R. Albertz, "פלא," in *Theological Lexicon of the Old Testament,* vol. 2, edited by Ernst Jenni and Claus Westermann, translated by Mark E. Biddle (Peabody: Hendrickson Publishers,Inc, 1997), 982-984.

134 Albertz, "פלא." 984-985.

Yahweh the warrior is addressed as the one who alone does wonders (Pss 136:4, Neh 9:17, Ps 72:18, 86:10, 98:1, 105:5, 106:22). The context indicates that all the works, statutes, rules and judgments of Yahweh in the world have the characters of divine marvel (Ps 119:129, Isa 25:1). It is noteworthy that the term אלפ is prominent in the hymnic parts of the OT which mostly occur in the Psalter, especially in Psalm 97.

Summary

The following points emerge from the above analysis. *First,* the psalm proclaims the kingship of Yahweh and invites the earth to rejoice. *Secondly,* the psalmist urges the nations to submit to the true worship of the Lord. The psalmist expresses that due worship belongs to Yahweh and not to idols. Yahweh reigns over the whole world, gods, peoples, and nature and all are called upon to worship. *Thirdly,* the sovereign Lord invites all humankind to worship the Lord because of the blessedness of the Lord's reign. *Fourthly,* whoever hates evil practices and loves the Lord are preserved in the kingship of God. The holiness of Yahweh is remembered throughout the generations and it is worthwhile to worship the holy God.

Thus, the whole Psalm 97 presents the nature of Yahweh's kingship to the universe and invites all nations to participate in the worship of Yahweh. Psalm 97 uses the poetic devices of imagery and parallelism. The figures of speech portray God's glory pictorially. Images like fire, lightning and mountains melting reveal the sovereignty of Yahweh's power over the earth. Psalm 97 brings out essential aspects of worship such as rejoicing and submission, enhancing worship and encouraging worshippers all over to worship him in holiness.

Chapter 8

Exegetical Study of Psalm 98 Yahweh, the Victorious Warrior over Chaotic Power

Introduction

Psalm 98 is a joyful hymn of praise and expresses how the worshippers shout before Yahweh the victorious king along with their instruments. This is an excellent example of how Israelites praise God for their deliverance. The event of Psalm 98 is referred to as the jubilant celebration of the marvellous deliverance that Yahweh accomplished for the covenant people. The hymn reflects the usefulness of musical instruments in Israel's worship. This gives us a picture of how Israelites used different types of musical instruments in their worship. Psalm 98 resembles with Psalm 96 in many ways, for instance, in both the psalms we find the same phrase "singing a new song" (Pss 96:1, 98:1). Psalm 98 invites all the earth and nature to offer their praises to Yahweh. And this concept expresses the thought of universal worship. Therefore, my focus in this chapter is to show how in this Psalm singing along with instrumental music relates to universal worship.

First, I attempt a historical analysis of Psalm 97. *Secondly,* I look at the literary aspects and *thirdly,* I give a textual argumentation and interpretation. *Fourthly,* I discuss the comments to the kingship metaphor in relation to worship and theological concerns pertaining to the kingship metaphor of Yahweh.

8.1. Historical Analysis in Psalm

In this section, I deal with the historical aspects of both the Davidic monarchical setting and the post-exilic setting. It is important to know the historical background because it helps in understanding why the individual text has been written and how it can be applied.

8.1.1. Davidic Monarchical Setting

Firstly, the setting of Psalm 98 is, probably, from the pre-monarchical period or exilic- period as the psalm emphasizes to give praise and worship Yahweh at his stool, which denotes the idea of how Yahweh delivered his people from the danger of life.[1] *Secondly,* the text mentions about Yahweh's relationship with the chosen people and provides assurance for those who call on the name of Yahweh. Thus, the setting of this psalm is pre-exilic occurring during the monarchical period.[2] There are many similarities between Psalm 96 and Psalm 98, for instance the settings of both seen to be the same. Psalm 98 is likely to be pre-exilic speaking of the Lord coming as creator king for the people and the worshippers see the sovereign Lord.[3]

8.1.2. Post-Exilic Setting

Stuhlmueller and Longman place Psalm 98 in the post-exilic setting. *First,* "The occasion for the original composition seems to have been the return from exile but the psalm extends to all God's redemptive acts or marvellous things for his covenant people."[4] *Secondly,* "Psalm 98 emerged from the early post-exilic period, when the second temple had been erected."[5] *Thirdly,* Kraus observes that the *Sitzim Leben* of Psalm 98 is from the worship of the post-exilic time, especially for the act ofprostration before Yahweh. He argues that in the "cultic celebrations of post-exilic times the exodus event and the eschatological theophany of Yahweh are strongly emphasized."[6] *Fourthly,*

---

1 Marvine E. Tate, "Psalms 51-150," in *Word Biblical Commentary*, vol. 20, edited by David A. Hubbard (Dallas: Word Books, 1990), 506.

2 Walter D. Zorn, "Psalms,"in *The College Press NIV Commentary*, vol. 2 (Joplin, MO: College Press Publishing Co, 2004), 230.

3 John Eaton, *The Psalms: A Historical and Spiritual Commentary with an Introduction and New Translation* (London: Continuum International Publishing Group, 2005), 263-264.

4 Carroll Stuhlmueller, *Psalm: A Biblical Theological Commentary* (Wilmington: Michael Glazier, 1983), 99. See Hans-Joachim Kraus, "Psalms 60-150," in *A Continental Commentary*, translated by Hilton C. Oswald (Minneapolis: Fortress Press, 1993), 263-264. Tremper Longman III, "Psalm 98: A Divine Warrior Victory," *JETS* vol. 27, no. 3 (September, 1984): 272. Samuel L. Terrien, "The Psalms: Strophic Structure and Theological Commentary: Psalms 73-150," in *Eerdmans Critical Commentary,* vol. 2, edited by David Noel Freedman (Grand Rapids: William B. Eerdmans Publishing Company, 2003), 684.

5 Samuel L. Terrien, "The Psalms: Strophic Structure and Theological Commentary: Psalms 73-150," in *Eerdmans Critical Commentary,* vol. 2, edited by David Noel Freedman (Grand Rapids: William B. Eerdmans Publishing Company, 2003), 684.

6 Hans-Joachim Kraus, "Psalms 60-150," in *A Continental Commentary*, translated by Hilton C. Oswald (Minneapolis: Fortress Press, 1993), 264.

Psalm 98 was not recited as a remembrance of an historical deliverance in the ancient period, but probably was structured in such a way that it could be "recited after any of the numerous deliverances that Israel experienced during her history."[7]

There are different views among the commentators as to whether Psalm 98 refers to Yahweh's act of deliverance at the time of the exodus, or to restoration from exile or no specific deliverance event. To my understanding, this psalm does not necessarily look into the exodus event but reflects the sovereignty of Yahweh in any period of human history. Thus, this hymn suits the post-exilic setting as supported by Terrien and Kraus when it is analysed from the redaction and rhetorical perspective.

8.2. Literary Analysis of the Text

In this section, I analyse the literary function of Psalm 98 with an emphasis on translation, critical notes, form of genre, structures and repeated words and phrases in the text in order to investigate the unique characteristic of the psalm.

8.2.1. Translation

<table>
<tr><td>1 מזמור שירו ליהוה שיר חדש כי־נפלאות
עשה הושיעה־לו ימינו וזרוע קדשו :</td><td>1. A *Psalm.*[8] Sing to the Lord a new song, for he has done *wonders*,[9]</td></tr>
<tr><td>2 הודיע יהוה ישועתו לעיני הגוים
גלה צדקתו :</td><td>2. The Lord had made *known his salvation*;[10] he has uncovered his righteousness in the sight of the nations.</td></tr>
<tr><td>3 זכר חסדו ואמונתו לבית ישראל ראו
כל־אפסי־ארץ את ישועת אלהינו :</td><td>3. He has remembered his kindness and steadfastness to the house of Israel. All the ends of the earth have seen the saving work of our God.</td></tr>
<tr><td>4 הריעו ליהוה כל־הארץ פצחו ורננו
וזמרו :</td><td>4. Raise a shout to Yahweh, all the earth, break forth and shout joyfully, and sing praise.</td></tr>
</table>

7 Tremper Longman III, "Psalm 98: A Divine Warrior Victory," *JETS* vol. 27. no 3 (September, 1984): 272.

8 V.1. מזמור is suggested as 'Psalm or melody.' See Karl Elliger and Wilhelm Rudolph, eds., *Biblia Hebraica Stuttgartensia* (Stuttgart: Biblia Hebraica Stuttgartensia, 1997), 1178.

9 V.1. נפלאות shows the cosmic wonders done by God as well as the historical achievement on behalf of the covenant people. See Mitchell Dahood, Psalms 51-100 : *The Anchor Bible*, vol. II (New York: Doubleday, 1968), 365.

10 V.2. ידע 'to know' "Yahweh gave historical proof of his conquest over his cosmic rivals by giving Israel victory over the nations." To let people know the mightiness of Yahweh. See Mitchell Dahood, Psalms 51-100: *The Anchor Bible*, vol. II (New York: Doubleday, 1968), 365.

5 זמרו ליהוה בכנור בכנור וקול זמרה :	5. Make music to the Lord with a lyre, with the lyre voice of a song.
6 בחצצרות וקול שופר הריעו לפני המלך יהוה :	6. With *trumpets*[11] and the sound of the *horn,*[12] raise a shout before the king, Yahweh.
7 ירעם הים ומלאו תבל וישבי בה :	7. The sea and its fullness roar, the world and those who dwell in it.
8 נהרות ימחאו־כף יחד הרים ירננו :	8. The *rivers*[13] *clap their hands*,[14] the mountains shout together for joy.
9 לפני־יהוה כי בא לשפט הארץ ישפט־תבל בצדק ועמים במישרים :	9. Before the Lord, for he is coming to judge the earth, he will judge the world with righteousness and the peoples with justly.

8.2.2. Text Critical Notes

First, שירו ליהוה שיר חדש 'sing to Yahweh a new song' (Ps 98:1). How did the sing to Yahweh a new song arise and what does it imply? It is necessary to consider what was said about the *new song* by commentators. These are the references made to the new song (Pss 33:3, 40:3, 96:1, 98:1, 144:9, 149:1, Isa 42:10, Rev 5:9, 14:3).

11 V.6. חצצרות 'trumpets' is in noun common feminine plural absolute form. "The trumpets were metal instruments of either bronze or silver. The tone was probably high with a limit range of four or five notes" (Num 10: 2-10, 2Kgs 12:14, 2Chr 5:12-13). See Marvine E. Tate, "Psalms 51-150," in *Word Biblical Commentary*, vol. 20, edited by David A. Hubbard (Dallas: Word Books, 1990), 523.

12 V. 6. שופר 'horn' this instrument is usually used for signaling (cf. Judg 3:27, 6:34, Neh 4:18-20, 1 Kgs 1:34, 2 Kgs 9:13, Isa 27:13). Marvine E. Tate, "Psalms 51-150," in *Word Biblical Commentary*, vol. 20, edited by David A. Hubbard (Dallas: Word Books, 1990), 523.

13 V.8. נהר 'stream or river' noun common masculine plural absolute. I have translated in plural form as rivers. Here, the rivers represent "kinds of refreshment and channels of blessing from a source known and unknown." See Arthur G. Clarke, *Analytical Studies in the Psalms* (Grand Rapids: Kregel Publications, 1979), 244. Cf. Karl Elliger and Wilhelm Rudolph, eds., *Biblia Hebraica Stuttgartensia* (Stuttgart: Biblia Hebraica Stuttgartensia, 1997), 1179.

14 V.8. מחא 'clap' verb qal imperfect 3rd person masculine plural. As mentioned rivers, hills, mountains in the text clap hands, indicating the waves striking against one another with a sound of applaud. See Arthur G. Clarke, *Analytical Studies in the Psalms* (Grand Rapids: Kregel Publications, 1979), 246. Dahood suggested, 'their hands' refers to "the name of a part of the body" through which they expressed the joy of Yahweh who triumphed over the heathen gods. Mitchell Dahood, *Psalms* 51-100: *The Anchor Bible*, vol. II (New York: Doubleday, 1968), 365-366.

Verhoef, and several scholars support 'new song' as an act of deliverance and salvation for the ends of the earth.[15] The covenant people respond to both the experienced and the expected saving deeds of Yahweh in the new song. In all these occurrences, the new song talks about how God's people acknowledge God's revelation and the experience of a *new act of deliverance.* חדש 'new' here has the meaning of fresh, adapted to the occasion. It does not mean that the old songs are being replaced by the 'new ones.' In the psalms, the new song generally refers to the *deliverance* that the psalmists actually experienced.[16] This 'new song' is parallel to the *new thing of deliverance* in the history of Israel, which Yahweh has done for them as mentioned in Deutero-Isaiah (Isa 42:10, 43:18-19).[17] Therefore, this new song recalls Yahweh's *saving works* reveal his righteousness to the nations and his enduring love and faithfulness toward his own people in Israel.[18]

"The new song is a *new act* on God's part, which completely corresponds to Deutero-Isaiah's proclamation, I will make a new thing known to you."[19] Oswalt says that it is particularly noteworthy that the entire earth with all its peoples is enjoined to give this praise in a new song. "It is because God's servant will *make God's salvation* available to the whole earth that the prophet is caught up in a whirlwind of joy and praise and calls on earth's inhabitants to join him."[20] The phrase 'new song' indicates that the main emphasis is on the salvation of God for the world. God has shown himself faithful to Israel so he will be faithful to the whole world.[21]

R. North Rome and others support 'new song' as an *eschatological* motif. Rome sees an eschatological motif in the following verses. 'He put a new song in my mouth' (Ps 40:3). 'Sing to the Lord a new song all the earth' (Ps 96:1).

---

15 Pieter A. Verhoef, "חדש," in *New International Dictionary of the Old Testament Theology & Exegesis,* vol. 2, edited by Willem A. VanGemeren (Grand Rapids: Zondervan, 1997), 36. Robert E. Wallace, *The Narrative Effect of Book IV of the Hebrew Psalter* (New York: Peter Lang Publishing, Inc, 2007), 44-45. John N. Oswalt, "The Book of Isaiah Chapters 40-66," in *The New International Commentary on the Old Testament*, edited by R. K. Harrison (Grand Rapids: William B. Eerdmans Publishing Company, 1998), 6-10.

16 Verhoef, "חדש," New talks about Yahweh coming to do justice upon the earth Ps 149:7, to continue and complete his work of creation Ps 33:6, 15, to let heavens and earth rejoice Ps 96:11 and to show his salvation to the ends of the earth (Ps 98:3, 8), 36-37.

17 Robert E Wallace, *The Narrative Effect of Book IV of the Hebrew Psalter* (New York: Peter Lang Publishing, Inc, 2007), 45.

18 Tate, "Psalms 51-100," in *Word Biblical Commentary,* 524.

19 Claus Westermann, *Isaiah 40-55: A Commentary* (Philadelphia: The Westminster Press, 1969), (Isa 42:10-13, 44:23, 45:8, 48:20, 49:13, 52:7-10), 103.

20 John N. Oswalt, "The Book of Isaiah Chapters 40-66," in *The New International Commentary on the Old Testament*, edited by R.K. Harrison (Grand Rapids: William B. Eerdmans Publishing Company, 1998), 123.

21 Oswalt, "The Book of Isaiah Chapters 40-66," 123-124.

'Sing to Yahweh a new song, for he has done marvellous things, his right hand and his holy arm makes him victorious' (Ps 98:1). 'I will sing a new song' (Ps 144:9). The context of all these appearances join into "a consistent image of *eschatological* newness." He asserts that Psalm 98 focuses on newness.[22] The new song denotes eschatology because it is a song that surpasses time and space.[23] Primarily, the phrase 'new song' presupposes a new experience of God in action. The 'New Song' is generally used in *eschatological* hymns, anticipating by faith the final work that God's salvation is to accomplish.[24]

I support the first view that 'new song' refers to the saving act of Yahweh and this has an implication for all nations to share in the salvation of God. Though a New Song is considered the historical account of deliverance from exile, it implies more than merely deliverance; it depicts the grace of salvation from a universal perspective. Thus, this has essential implications in the context of worship.

Secondly, כנור 'lyre' is a noun common masculine singular absolute (Ps 98:5). כנור is with strings of equal length and most probably differs from a harp, likely a rectangular shaped stringed instrument used to accompany singing. It was a popular instrument throughout the Ancient West Asia. This instrument is used in worship and it gives melody and harmony in singing.

Thirdly, חצצרות 'trumpets' is a noun common feminine plural absolute (Ps 98:6). חצצרות were metal instruments of either bronze or silver. A trumpet is a long, straight instrument of metal for signaling, used in worship to get people's attention.[25] The tone was, probably, high with a limited range of four or five notes (cf. Num 10:2-10, 2 Kgs 12:14, 2 Chr 5:12-13).

Fourthly, שופר 'horn' is a noun common masculine singular absolute (Ps 98:6). שופר is a curved and conical shape made from the horns of wild goats or rams, capable of two or three notes and mostly used for signalling as well as indication[26] (cf. Judg 3:27, 6:34, Neh 4:18-20, 1 Kgs 1; 34, Isa 27:13, Ex 19:16, Ps 47:6). Horns are instruments used for gaining people's attention

---

22 R. North Rome, "חדש," in *Theological Dictionary of the Old Testament,* vol. 1V, edited by G. Johannes Botterweck and Helmer Ringgren, translated by David E Green (Grand Rapids: William B. Eerdmans Publishing Company, 1980), 239. Leslie C. Allen, "שִׁיר," in *New International Dictionary of Old Testament Theology & Exegesis,* vol. 4, edited by Willem A. VanGemeren (Grand Rapids: Zondervan, 1997), 99-100.

23 Kraus, *Psalms 60-150*, 264.

24 Leslie C. Allen, "שִׁיר," in *New International Dictionary of Old Testament Theology & Exegesis,* vol. 4, edited by William A. VanGemeren (Grand Rapids: Zondervan, 1997), 90. (cf. Pss 96:1, 98:1, 147:1, Isa 42:10, Rev 20:22, Rev 5:9).

25 John Goldingay, "Psalms: Psalms 90-150," in *Baker Commentary on the Old Testament Wisdom and Psalms,* vol. 3, edited by Tremper Longman III (Grand Rapids: Baker Academic, 2008), 122.

26 Tate, *Psalms 51-100*, 523.

rather than being strictly a musical instrument. Both trumpet and horn were usually used to announce the arrival of a human king but were also used in worship for praising Yahweh.[27]

Finally, מחא 'strike' or 'clap' verb *qal* imperfect third person masculine plural (Ps 98:8). The word מחא strike' occurs in *qal* only here and also in Isa 55:12 with כף 'palm/hand' 'all the trees of the field will clap their palm(s).' The parallel verses also indicate the word כף appears with תקע thrust or clap" in Ps 47:2 and with נלה smite or strike in 2 Kgs 11: 12 with שסק/ספק "slap or clap" in Num 24:10 (in anger) and in Job 27:23 (in mockery). The *piel* of מחא with יד 'hand' is found in Ezek 26:6.[28]

Schaefer suggests that the rivers are constantly rolling with heavy noise and the fast moving water produces a sound like clapping hands. This seems to be a poetical way of expression. Perhaps it reflects the climactic presence of Yahweh the king.[29] According to Ellen F. Davis "Psalm 98 Rejoicing in Judgment," *Interpretation* 46 (1992). "The principle here is that God is to be glorified in every aspect of creation, and God's glory is magnified as each creature human animal, cultivated field, or uninhabited mountain does, becomes the thing for which it was made."[30]

These critical notes help me to draw light on musical instruments and how music is made and draw implications for worship. Whenever the psalmist talks about singing, it is always linked with instruments. Thus, it shows that instruments along with singing has a vital implication for Israel's worship as well as for worship today.

8.2.3. Form of the Psalm

Looking at from the perspective of form critical study Gerstenberger and Kraus claim that in Psalm 98 the visible genre is a hymn.[31] Therefore, Psalm 98 comes under the category of a hymn. Brueggemann and Bellinger observed that Psalm 98 continues as series of hymn (93-100) on the reign of YHWH. Probably, the setting of the enthronement psalms likely come from a common

---

27 Goldingay, *Psalms: Psalms 90-150*, 122.

28 Tate, *Psalms 51-100*, 523.

29 Konrad Schaefer, *Psalms: Studies in Hebrew Narrative & Poetry,* edited by David W. Cotter (Collegeville: The Liturgical Press, 2001), 243.

30 Ellen F. Davis, "Psalm 98 Rejoicing in Judgment," *Interpretation* no. 46 (April, 1992): 174.

31 Erhard S. Gerstenberger, *Psalms, Part 2 and Lamentations: The Forms of the Old Testament Literature*, vol. XV (Grand Rapids: William B. Eerdmans Publishing Company, 2001), 197. Kraus also notes that "the psalm belongs to the category of songs of praise." Thematically, the psalm is dominated by the concept of the kingship metaphor of Yahweh; as a result, naturally it is counted among the kingship hymns of Yahweh. See Hans-Joachim Kraus, "Psalms 60-150," in *A Continental Commentary*, translated by Hilton C. Oswald (Minneapolis: Fortress Press, 1993), 263.

festival setting that focuses on the divine kingship. It is suggested that the festival celebrated and re-enacted the enthronement of Yahweh over all the earth for the sake of order and justice.[32] Thus, Psalm 98 portrays how the people of Israel give praise and worship to Yahweh.

8.2.4. Structure of the Psalm

With regard to the structure of the psalm, Weiser[33] and Longman divide the hymn into three strophes. They are: 1. Praise Yahweh who has delivered Israel in the past (Ps 88: 1-3); 2. Praise Yahweh who rules over the world (Ps 98:4-6); 3. Praise Yahweh who will judge the universe (Ps 98: 7-9).[34] Evidently, Zorn also supports the three divisions but his division is slightly different from the others. In the first strophe, Ps 98:1-4 talks about the Israelites praising Yahweh for her victory. In the second strophe, Ps 98: 5-6, the mood of praising has expanded to the whole world. In the third strophe, Ps 98: 7-9, the praise is expanded in a much wider aspect, inviting the creation, nature and all the inanimate world to join in the praise of the victorious King.[35]

On the other hand, Kraus and Goldingay support the idea that Psalm 98 is divided into two strophes. For Kraus, Psalm 98 is divided into two parts, the first part is Ps 9:1-3 and the second part is Ps 98:4-9.[36] Goldingay argues that Ps 98: 1-3 apparently address Israel and Ps 98: 4-9 addresses the whole earth. The first division refers to Yahweh's commitment and faithfulness which have already been exercised in delivering the people of Israel. The second division refers to Yahweh's authority that will be demonstrated in due time.[37] In my opinion, the threefold division gives a clear idea of how to understand the text.

8.2.5. Repetition

The word זמר means 'to make music' which is repeated twice in Psalm 98:4, 5. The repetitions support intended effects within the hymn, thus it offers opportunity for much 'joyful noise or singing from inner being' as a result Yahweh is well pleased.[38] In verse 5, we see the phrase בכנור which means 'with a lyre.' Possibly, the psalmist indicates the essential use of singing along with instrumental music in worship. These repeated words presumably belong

32 Walter Brueggemann and W.H. Bellinger, "Psalms," in *New Cambridge Bible Commentary*, edited by Ben Witherington III (New York: Cambridge University Press, 2014), 420.

33 Weiser, *The Psalms: A Commentary*, 637.Vv.1-3, speaks of Yahweh's marvellous deeds and calls in vv. 4-6 and speaks to the whole and vv. 7-9 calls upon nature to pay homage to God with shouts of joy.

34 Longman III, "Psalm 98: A Divine Warrior Victory," 268-269.

35 Zorn, *Psalms*, 226.

36 Kraus, *Psalms 60-150*, 263.

37 Goldingay, *Psalms: Psalms 90-150*, 119.

38 Gerstenberger, *Psalms, Part 2 and Lamentation*, 197.

to the context of Israelite worship, and also rhetorically address the world where everyone is invited to make music to Yahweh the King.[39] The word רנן, which means 'shout with joy,' occurs twice and is found in verses 4 and 8. The word רנן expresses a joyful shout to God which is not just from the world's human inhabitants, but also from all its creatures, for Yahweh has done marvellous things.[40] The word רוע which means 'to raise a shout' and occurs in both verses 4 and 6 in the imperative form. For Anderson, the word רוע signifies "a cry is not simply a wish, but also recognition of the royal authority and a submission to it."[41] The text clearly indicates that along with all kinds of musical instruments the worshippers shout before Yahweh (Ps 98: 6).

The word ארץ 'earth' appears in verses 3, 4 and 9 and the word תבל 'world' occurs in verses 7 and 9. This signifies that all parts of the earth thunder forth praise to the enthroned King of the whole world.[42] In verse 9 itself, we see the word שׁפט 'judge' appear twice. Yahweh, the king of the world, is enthroned above all nations as judge of the world.[43] Yahweh establishes a "rule marked with righteousness and equity."[44] The word שׁפט reflects the nature of Yahweh the king, who has authority to judge the universe. Therefore, in the context of Israel's worship, the divine nature and mighty works of Yahweh enables worshippers to give due homage to the Lord.

8.3. Comments in Relation to the Kingship Metaphor

As seen in the other psalms, even in this section, I briefly give the comment to the words which are associated with the metaphor of kingship. *First;* חסד '*steadfast love,*' Yahweh the king extends his steadfast love to all generations. This is associated with the connotation of Yahweh's kingship. As a king, he continues to show his faithful love to the people while promoting and straightening their lives. At the same time, the history of Israel reveals that Yahweh, in his kindness, led and guided the covenant people. For instance, in the deliverance from Egypt, Yahweh demonstrated his kingship through חסד to the people of Israel.[45]

39 Goldingay, *Psalms 90-150*, 119-120.

40 Goldingay, *Psalms 90-150*, 123.

41 A. A. Anderson, "The Book of Psalms: Psalms 73-150," in New *Century Bible Commentary*, vol. 2 (Grand Rapids: William B. Eerdmans Publishing Company, 1985), 692.

42 Elmer A. Leslie, *The Psalms: Translated and Interpreted in the Light of Hebrew Life and Worship* (New York: Abingdon Press, 1949), 82.

43 Kraus, *Psalms 60-150*, 265.

44 Walter Brueggemann, *The Message of the Psalms: A Theological Commentary* (Minneapolis: Augsburg Publishing House, 1984), 148.

45 H.-J. Zobel Greifsward, "חסד," in *Theological Dictionary of the Old Testament,* edited by G. Johannes Botterweck and Ringgren, Helmer, translated by Green, David E, vol. V (Grand Rapids: William B. Eerdmans Publishing Company, 1986), 55.

Yahweh's kindness is shown by the nouns used in parallel with חסד. Yahweh's חסד is expressed as an act of strength, victory or salvation, justice and righteousness (Ex 15:13, Ps 98:2). Thus, Yahweh's חסד is an expression of his divine mercy.[46] Yahweh's steadfast love is found in Yahweh's promises to individuals and the community at large. It is also revealed through Yahweh's forgiveness, providence and sustaining grace. Therefore, from the theological aspect, Yahweh's חסד and goodness are parallel in the function of kingship. Besides, Yahweh זכר 'remembers' the promise of his חסד which means 'love' and אמונה 'faithfulness' to the לבעת ישראל 'house of Israel' and God have been fulfilled.[47] The word זכר is related to the relationship between God and Israel. The world recognizes God's faithfulness and saving power, as a result, they worship the true God. Thus, God's main purpose in *Heilsgeschichte* (salvation history) is to reveal God's salvation to the whole world through חסד.[48]

Secondly, righteousness is the connotation of Yahweh's kingship. God is holy, therefore, Yahweh is a righteous king and the righteous king acts righteously for the benefit of all the people. In connection to Yahweh as a righteous king, the terms צדקה 'righteousness' and משפט 'justice' are often used in parallel to each other and seem to be synonymous in their functions. The king is to judge the people with righteousness. In other words, Yahweh the king is one who administers or exercises with משפט 'justice' and צדקה 'righteousness.' The psalmist says, by the function of justice and righteousness, Yahweh is exalted and shows his divine nature to the world (Ps 98: 2).[49]

The ways of the Lord are upright because he is a righteous God and who acts justly. The principle of משפט 'justice' focuses on decision, judgement and law while צדק righteous mostly focuses on the principle of what is right and what is correct. צדק is often used in connection with correct speech or judgment (Pss 9:9, 98: 9, Prov 8:6 Isa 11:4, 45:19). Thus, צדק is an action which follows with the right measure of doing things.[50] צדק includes the aspect of claiming what is rightfully due as a legitimate claim. The psalmist says, "Yahweh will judge the world with righteousness and equity" (Ps 98:9). The context of Psalm 98 describes Yahweh as a righteous king. The holiness of God is disclosed through the deeds of his righteousness. Thus, Yahweh acts and rules in righteousness.

---

46 Greifsward, "חסד," God's kindness finds expression in his endless reconciling love and forgiveness. Merciful and gracious is Yahweh, slow to anger and of great kindness (Ex 34:6, Ps 145:8, Num 14:18). 55.

47 Schaefer, *Psalms*, 242.

48 Weiser, *The Psalms: A Commentary*, 638.

49 B. Johnson, "צדק," in *Theological Dictionary of the Old Testament,* vol. XII, edited by G. Johannes Botterweck (Grand Rapids: William B. Eerdmans Publishing Company, 2003), 247.

50 Johnson, "צדק," 247-248.

8.4. Comments in Relation to Worship

I deal with two points of comments in relation to worship. *First, making music and the importance of musical instruments in worship* this is emerge out of my exegesis. This is related to the worship of Yahweh the king. The establishment of Yahweh's kingship causes a universal rejoicing and praising of Yahweh through singing songs.[51] The psalmist turns to the whole created world, and to all its creatures, and amazingly, they all make music to Yahweh.[52] This idea shows that music is part and parcel of Yahweh's kingship as people and nature all give praises to Yahweh. As we see, the first strophe mentions that Israel is singing and exalting Yahweh as they look in retrospect to the deliverances which Yahweh has performed. In the second stanza, God is being praised as king of the earth. In the third stanza, not only animate but also inanimate creation cries out for joy in the Lord who is the coming Judge.[53]

Weiser affirms that God has the power to harmonize both humankind and nature in "the exultant chorus of the whole world singing praises to the glory of God."[54] The 'sea contributes its thunder, the rivers clap their hands and the mountain sings to the rhythm' so, all creatures in their own way offer their praise to Yahweh, the king.[55] The 'entire created world is moved' looking at the marvellous deeds of Yahweh. The expressions of the sea, rivers and mountains give due honour with shouts of joy.[56] Thus, the psalmist exhorts all the earth to sing and praise Yahweh because Yahweh is the everlasting king.

The psalmist stresses the essential use of musical instruments in the worship community (Ps 98:5-6). Terrien refers to "musical instruments that support the voice and the ritual shouts."[57] Phillips argues that "instruments of music are brought to add to the ever growing volume of sound."[58] Psalm 98 mentions three musical instruments; the *lyre, trumpets*, and *horn* all of which

---

51 Brueggemann, *The Message of the Psalms: A Theological Commentary*, 148.

52 Goldingay, *Psalms: Psalms 90-150*, 123.

53 Longman III, "Psalm 98: A Divine Warrior Victory," 271.

54 Weiser, *The Psalms: A Commentary*, 639.

55 Eaton, *The Psalms*, 345.

56 Kraus, *Psalms 60-150*, 265. In OT times, singing and worship were inseparably linked to the joy of the Lord. As we see here, when Pharaoh was finally overthrown at the Red Sea, Moses and the children of Israel sang (Ex15:1) cried out, "Sing ye the Lord, for he hath triumphed gloriously." In relation to this, it seems that king David's psalms picked up the theme and amplified it in numerous ways, encouraging hymns calling people to come before Yahweh's presence with singing. No doubt this glorious musical synthesis makes the "Psalter into a singing sword of truth." See Ernest B Gentile, *Worship God: Exploring the Dynamics of Psalmic Worship* (Portland: City Bible Publishing, 1994), 148.

57 Terrien, *The Psalms: Strophic Structure and Theological Commentary*, 638.

58 John Philips, *Exploring Psalms: An Expository Commentary*, vol. 2 (Grand Rapids: Kregel Publications., 2002), 87.

are used for worship services. According to Gerstenberger, the lyre and harp serve predominantly in psalms; it seems that in small group services, these two instruments are usually used (Pss 33:2, 71:22). Nevertheless, Psalm 98 mentions the trumpet and horn which are used apparently for worship in larger communities.[59] "Lyre is the chief instrument of the psalmists."[60]

Kraus affirms that the "musical instruments" mentioned are to accompany the hymn of homage before God in worship.[61] Music, whether vocal or instrumental, always has played an important role in all kinds of religious rituals throughout all known cultures. Sounds and melody, rhythm and movement are integral to many forms of worship.[62] Adding musical instruments to corporate or individual worship enriches the worship experience. Instrumental accompaniments have a calming, liberating and peaceful effect (Ps 71: 22).[63] When we look into Israel's religious history, it seems that the Israelites usually approached Yahweh through a variety of religious ceremonies, not only by sacrifices and offerings, but also by singing and playing instruments. Thus, the Israelites were fond of singing and playing instruments.

Secondly, the gesture of clapping hands in worship. Kraus and Anderson suggest that applause or clapping hands is obviously an expression of enthusiastic joy, as it was customary at enthronements (Ps 47:1, 98:8). The seas roar, the rivers or floods clap their hands so as the mountain shout to the Lord.[64] Anderson seems to support that the sea, river and mountains are a form of "a poetical description for the whole world.[65] Goldingay claims that "rivers can clap hands as they tumble over rocks, throwing up spurts of spray that intermingle with one another like hands joining. Likewise, the mountains resound as the wind roars over them. "The mountains and the hills before you shall burst into song, and the trees of the field shall clap their hands" (Isa 55:12b).

We found that the rivers lift up their voice in the psalms where as in Isaiah the trees clap their hands. Hence, in the parallelism, they all together offer their praise and worship the Lord.[66] The sea 'roars' and the 'rivers' clap their hands. This demonstrates that they become artists in the "dramatic

59 Gerstenberger, *Psalms, Part 2 and Lamentation*, 179.

60 Eaton, *The Psalms*, 345.

61 Kraus, *Psalms 60-150*, 265.

62 Erhard S. Gerstenberger, "Singing a New Song: On Old Testament and Latin American Psalmody," *Word & World* 2, no. 5 (Spr, 1985): 155.

63 Ernest B. Gentile, *Worship God: Exploring the Dynamics of Psalmic Worship* (Portland: City Bible Publishing, 1994), 178.

64 Kraus, *Psalms 60-150*, 265.

65 Anderson, "The Book of Psalms : Psalms 73-150," 693.

66 Goldingay, *Psalms 90-150*, 123.

display of divine power."[67] In a magnificent and poetical personification of nature, the psalmist discerns in the roaring of the sea a sound comparable to the 'clapping of hands' (cf. Isa 55:12).[68] Clapping hands is considered to be an authentic mode of worship expression. Clapping in congregational worship has a spiritual application. In fact, it signifies reaffirmation of the covenant between God and human.[69]

The psalmist describes amazingly how the rivers applause and delight before Yahweh. Looking into this context, it has vital implications for worship. When a worshipper is inspired with the word and divine power of God, it is natural that, physical gestures such as clapping hands or raising hands will happen. Singing and playing instrumental music, even clapping hands, has immense implications for worship.

8.5. Theological Concerns Pertaining to the Kingship Metaphor of God

In general, the enthronement psalms talk about the use of music, and particularly in psalm 98, both celebratory and meditative, in the acknowledgement of Yahweh's kingship. It shows that music is linked with the connotation of Yahweh's kingship.

8.5.1. Kingship and Music

The word music is derived from an ancient Greek word μουσική 'art of the *Muses*' which means any of the arts or sciences governed by the Muses.[70] Musical forms of the ancient Greeks are known to have existed from around 500 BCE. During the classical age (450-325 BCE) there was a peak of the musical movement, mainly due to the "development of annual festivals and

---

67 Terrien, *The Psalms: Strophic Structure and Theological Commentary*, 684.

68 Weiser, *The Psalms: A Commentary*, 639.

69 Gentile, *Worship God: Exploring the Dynamics of Psalmic Worship*, 184.

70 Chrysostom Nassis, "The Use of Music in Christian Worship: Background and Early Evidence," *Phronema*no. 22 (2007): 24. Originally a term used comprehensively for the various art forms attributed to the god Apollo, the mythological musician Orpheus and other deities, most particularly the Muses "who were believed to inspire all artists, especially poets, philosophers, and musicians." (Nine goddesses - daughters of the god Zeus, king of the gods, and of Mnemosyne, the goddess of memory). Cf. Panagiotis Trembelas, *The Origins and Character of Christian Worship* (in Greek), (Athens: Soter, 1962), 1. Pelosi comments that the significance of *mousike* has undergone Platonic investigation. Plato contributed to the musical phenomenon and its association with philosophy. He described the ethical and philosophical values traditionally linked to the musical experience in ancient Greece. Certainly "many of Plato's musical observations have been interpreted as examples of the characteristic ancient Greek way of understanding music and living music, as a phenomenon with extraordinary persuasive and ethical qualities." See Francesco Pelosi, *Plato on Music, Soul and Body* (New York: Cambridge University Press, 2010), 1-2.

contests of vocal and instrumental music."[71] The word for music in modern Hebrew is מוסיקה. The Hebrew word for music is not exactly found in the Old Testament. The absence of the term, however, does not mean that music had no role to play in ancient Israel's worship. We find expressions of vocal music like singing, praising, shouting and chanting in the Psalter. We also find mention of different musical instruments used in Israel's worship as recorded in the Psalter. All these are indications that music, both vocal and instrumental, played an important role in ancient Israel's worship.

The Hebrew word שיר 'song' refers to the cultic song. This term is often used with מזמור in the headings of the psalms. The difference between שיר and רומזמ is not noticeable. The song is often accompanied by musical instruments. שיר always appears in connection with the temple worship and it is also considered to be a specific designation for the temple song in which worshippers give praises to Yahweh[72] Mowinckel suggests that שיר is rendered as music or as hymns.[73] Terrien comments that the "word מזמור translated 'Psalm' designates a sacred song accompanied by stringed instruments."[74] For Anderson, the Hebrew word זמר is connected with מזמור Psalm.[75] Goldingay claims that the Hebrew word זמר means "make music," giving emphasis to both singing and playing. The word psalm מזמור comes from the root word of זמר which means a religious song.[76] Probably the word רמז and its meaning is associated with the Greek usage of μουσική in its expressions.

Music is an artistic form of auditory communication incorporating instrumental or vocal tones. Music was important in all aspects of life in the Ancient West Asia for instance in work, war, entertainment, love, where it probably contributed as a basic element in worship.[77] Gerstenberger remarks that "Music, be it vocal or instrumental, always has played an important role in all kinds of religious rituals throughout all known cultures. Sound and

---

71 Nassis, "The Use of Music in Christian Worship: Background and Early Evidence," 25. Theories on the nature, function, and origin of music are discussed extensively in the writings of Philosophers and Mathematicians such as Pythagoras, Plato, Aristotle, Aristoxenus and Euclid. They claimed that music influences human thoughts, emotions, and behaviour. Cited from Plato*: Five Great Dialogues,* edited byLouise Ropes Loomis (Roslyn, New York: 1969), 289.

72 Kraus, *Psalms 1-59*, 21, (Amos 6:5, I Chr 15:16, 16:42, 2Chr 5:13, 23:13, 18, 34:12).

73 Mowinckel, *The Psalms in Israel's Worship*, 8.

74 Samuel Terrien, *The Psalms: Strophic Structure and Theological Commentary,* 28. The title is sometimes accompanied by its synonym song or canticle (Pss 30, 48, 65-68, 75-76, 83, 87-88, 92), 29.

75 A.A. Anderson, "The Book of Psalms: Psalms 73-150," 363–364.

76 John Goldingay, *Songs from a Strange Land: Psalms 42-51* (Illinois: InterVarsity Press, 1978), 73.

77 John W. Hilber, "Psalms," in *Zondervan Illustrated Bible Backgrounds Commentary*, edited by John H. Walton, vol. 5 (Grand Rapids: Zondervan, 2009), 403.

melody, rhythm and movement are integral to many forms of worship."[78] Music, probably, came out of rites, ceremonies, and hymns and chants used in Canaanite festivals, and out of nomadic songs used for pilgrimages. One way or the other, music grew from these influences collectively and were adapted into the liturgical customs of Yahweh worship. In the early stage music had become a mark of Israelite faith. Israelites were approaching Yahweh the king, in a great variety of religious ceremonies, for instance, in sacrifices, offerings and in singing hymns and lamentations.[79]

The role of music plays a vivid part in Israel's community life from the very beginning. We see in the Genesis account that Jubal is the father of all who play the harp and flute (Gen 4:21). In OT times, song and worship were inseparably linked to the joy of the Lord. For example, when Pharaoh was finally overthrown at the Red Sea, Moses and the children of Israel sang. Moses cried out "Sing to the Lord, for he has triumphed gloriously." (Ex 15:1-17). We see the roles of Miriam and Deborah. Trained musicians eventually appear around the time of David and Solomon which mark a distinctive stage in the history of OT.[80] Eaton points out, "Singing itself was the heart of the music, while the instruments appropriately known as instruments of song, had deep significance as joined with the voices in a common endeavour" (Amos 6:5, I Chron15:16).[81] The psalms were composed to be sung along with musical instruments. These instruments occur in the enthronement psalms. The lyre is among the stringed instruments, the horn and the trumpet among wind instruments (Pss 47:5, 98:6).[82]

Routledge claims that music and singing played an important part in the life and worship of Israel. People celebrated God's mighty acts through music. Singing songs with musical instruments was a vital part of Israel's worship.[83] Adding musical instruments to corporate or individual worship enriches the worship experience. The various types of musical instruments are mentioned in the Psalter. For instance, Psalm 150 mentions several musical instruments like *harp, trumpet, horn, lyre, timbrel, string-instruments, flute, and cymbals*

78 Gerstenberger, Singing a New Song, 155.

79 Gerstenberger, Singing a New Song, 156.

80 Harold M. Best, "Music in Israelite Worship," in *The Biblical Foundations of Christian Worship*, vol. I. edited by Robert E. Webber (Peabody: Hendrickson Publishers, Inc., 1993), 228. Israel's temple music was professionally organized (1 Chron 15: 16-22, 16: 42, 25: 1-8).

81 Eaton, *The Psalms,* 9.

82 John Day, *Psalms* (New York: T & T Clark International, 2003), 16. Scripture references that describe singing in public worship (Ps 98:1, Rev 5:7, Mat 26:30, Neh 12:27, 46, Acts 16:25, Ephe 5:19, Colo 3:16).

83 Robin Routledge, *Old Testament Theology: A Thematic Approach* (England: InterVarsity Press, 2008), 206–207.

used in Israel's worship. The musical character of Israel's worship is perhaps profoundly demonstrated in Psalm 150 and interestingly calls for vocal outpourings of praise.[84] It is possible that the composer of this particular hymn of praise takes delight in the musical instruments which accompany the words of the psalms and help the worshippers to praise God joyfully.[85] Goldingay and Leslie claim that the horn was usually played by the priests; harp, lyre and cymbals by the Levites and tambourine, strings and pipe by lay people.[86] Gerstenberger claims that musical instruments provided the melody and rhythm for the songs and were used for the worship of Yahweh (Pss 57:8, 147:7).[87] Three musical instruments שופר 'horn' כנור 'lyre' and חצצרה 'trumpet' are mentioned in the enthronement psalms.[88]

שופר is a horn for blowing. This instrument is considered one of the most frequently mentioned biblical instruments. The various usages of שופר can put it as a signaling instrument (Pss 47:6, 98:6). The special function of שופר instrument is that it was sounded in both war and peace. It has a ritual usage, it carried the cries of the people to God.[89] Goldingay strongly affirms "horns are 'natural' instruments made from the actual horn of an animal. They were more an instrument for gaining people's attention than a strictly musical instrument" (Pss 47:7, 81:3, 150:3).[90] Eaton is also in line with Goldingay's view on the description of horns; he asserts that the horn was made from a wild goat or ram. The horn instrument is suitable for solemn signals or marks the coming of God.[91] Terrien rightly points out that it was "blown before and after solemn occasions."[92] The horn was one of the most ancient musical instruments used in temple worship and it was significant particularly at the new moons and Sabbaths when the worshippers proclaimed the Lord is king (Num 29:1, Ps 47:5, 81:3). The Lord is to be praised with the blast of a horn in worship.[93]

כנור is a lyre. It is a stringed instrument (Ps 98: 5). The instrument has a sound box at its base and two side-arms rising to join a crossbar. Strings,

---

84 Jonathan L. Friedmann, *Music in Biblical Life: The Roles of Songs in Ancient Israel* (Jefferson, North Carolina: McFarland & Company, Inc., Publishers, 2013), 150.

85 Leslie, *The Psalms*, 30.

86 Goldingay, *Psalms 90-150*, 748.

87 Gerstenberger, *Psalms, Part I, with An Introduction to Cultic Poetry,* 18.

88 Day, *Psalms*, 16. Scripture references that describe singing in public worship (Ps 98:1, Rev 5:7, Mt 26:30, Neh 12:27, 46, Acts 16:25, Eph 5:19, Col 3:16).

89 E. Werner, "Music," in *The Interpreter's Dictionary of the Bible: An Illustrated Encyclopedia,* vol. 4, edited by George Arthur Buttrick (Philadelphia: Westminster John Knox Press, 1962), 473.

90 Goldingay, *Psalms 90-150*, 122.

91 Eaton, *The Psalms,* 11.

92 Terrien, *The Psalms: Strophic Structure and Theological Commentary*, 929.

93 Leslie, *The Psalms*, 30.

that number from four to eleven, are stretched from the crossbar to the sound box.[94] This instrument was played with the hands and accompanied by a song in the worship of Yahweh.[95] It is a melodious instrument which is employed to accompany vocals in the worship of Yahweh by exalting Yahweh the king through praises.[96] The association of the כנור with singing is ancient and greatly significant in the psalms material (Gen 31: 27, 2 Sam 6:5, Isa 23:16, Pss 57:9, 98:5, 147:7, 149:3, 150:3). It remained a cultic instrument in the developed pattern of the second temple worship and was seen in continuity with the prophecy of pre-exilic times (1 Chr 25:4).[97] The lyre was regularly used in Israel's worship. This indicates that singing was incorporated with musical instruments in praising Yahweh the king.

חצצרה is a trumpet, a long straight instrument of metal for signaling (Ps 98:6). In length, it is a little short of a cubit. It is a narrow tube with flared ends slightly thicker than a flute, with a mouthpiece wide enough to admit the breath and a bell-shaped extremity. As mentioned earlier, the trumpet is played by priests rather than by the Levites. Trumpet is considered as the instrument of the priest par excellence.[98] The trumpet was used for summoning the congregation in worship (Num 10:2).[99] Gerstenberger argues that "trumpet and horn are added as proper instruments, apparently for worship in larger communities."[100] Goldingay comments that Israel's musical instruments were mostly rhythmic, stringed instruments like the harp, lyre or tambourines. The Israelites' way of singing was similar to chanting.[101]

Instrumental accompaniment has a soothing, liberating and peaceful effect. David sang and played his harp for King Saul (1 Sam 16: 23). During the time of Zerubbabel, when they laid the foundation of the restoration temple, the Levites ministered with trumpets and cymbals to praise the Lord (Ezra 3:10). When the kingdom was divided, priests always reinstituted psalmic worship methods with the instruments of David.[102] Song and instrumentation clearly played a vital part in Israelite worship. "Music is an important way of

---

94 Eaton, *The Psalms,* 9.

95 Leslie, *The Psalms*, 30.

96 Gerstenberger, *Psalms, Part 2 and Lamentations*, 459.

97 Ivor H. Jones, "Musical Instruments," in *The Anchor Bible Dictionary,* vol. 4, edited by David Noel Freedman (New York: Doubleday, 1992), 937.

98 Jones, "Musical Instruments," 936.

99 Eaton, *The Psalms,* 11.

100 Gerstenberger, *Psalms, Part 2 and Lamentations,* 197.

101 John Goldingay, *Old Testament Theology: Israel's Life*, vol. 3 (Downers Grove: InterVarsity Press, 2009), 174–175.

102 Gentile, *Worship God: Exploring the Dynamics of Psalmic Worship*, 178.

approaching the mystery of God and of expressing the joy of being in God's presence."[103]

Music played the central role in all other aspects of Israelites' life, not just worship. It played a part in their worship, work, merrymaking and military activities. Thus, music is connected with specific acts of God where the sovereignty of God is revealed.[104] King David's psalms picked up the theme and amplified it in numerous ways, encouraging hymns calling people to come before Yahweh's presence with music. This glorious musical synthesis of all the OT makes the Psalter into a singing sword of truth.[105] Anderson rightly points out that the music or hymn is a song that extols God's greatness and goodness manifest in history and creation. In Psalms, this type generally begins with an "imperative call to worship" 'Come let us sing to the Lord' (Ps 95:1).[106]

The psalmist's invitation is extended to all nature. It is very striking to see the poetical expression of the personified aspects of nature like the sea, the river; the mountains are to join the universal worship in praising Yahweh.[107] It is in praise, more than any other human act, where the name of God is proclaimed in fullness and glory. In other words, music is more than any other act which fully expresses devotion and worship to Yahweh the great king.[108] Miller affirms that, "All the works of God, the whole creation, the heavenly beings, praise God. They testify to God's greatness and pass the word on in order that others may hear, praise and worship."[109]

Goldingay points out that making music in worship glorifies Yahweh as the one who is deserving of all praises. Unless we learn how to sing, unless we know how to love, we will never learn how to understand and worship Yahweh the great king.[110] Prabhakar claims that, "Song and music are counted as symbols of life." He further affirms that when we talk about music, it is linked

103 Best, "Music in Israelite Worship," 226.

104 Best, "Music in Israelite Worship," *The Biblical Foundations of Christian Worship*, 227. These are some of the examples how music is linked with the mystery of God. The fall of the walls of Jericho (Josh 6:4-20), the enthronement of kings (11:14, 11 Chron 13:14, 20:28), music for the court (2 Sam 19:35, Eccles 2:8) and feasting (Isa 5:12, 24:8-9), as well as for the restoration of the prophetic gifts (2 Kings 3:15) and soothing the personality disturbances (1 Sam 16: 14-23, Gen 31:27, Ex 32:17-18, Nun 21:17, Judg 11:34-35, Isa 16:10, Jer 48:33).

105 Gentile, *Worship God: Exploring the Dynamics of Psalmic Worship*, 148.

106 Anderson, *Understanding the Old Testament*, 505.

107 Richard D. Patterson, "Singing the New Song: An Examination of Psalms 33, 96, 98 and 149," *Bibliotheca Sacra,* vol. 656, no. 164 (October-December, 2007): 421.

108 Patrick D. Miller, *Interpreting the Psalms* (Philadelphia: Fortress Press, 1986), 67.

109 Miller, *Interpreting the Psalms*, 73. The following references clearly indicates (Pss 29, 69:34, 97:6, 98:7-8, 148, 19:1-4, 97;6, 145:10-11, and Isa 42:10-11, 44:23, 49;13, Joel 2:21-22).

110 Goldingay, *Old Testament Theology: Israel's Life*, 176.

with sound. Sound is believed to have the function of mediation between the profane and the sacred and between the divine and the human. Music gives an opportunity to the worshippers to offer the best sound they can produce to offer to God.[111] Besides that music allows us to express an intensity of emotion through multiplicity. For instance, pitch, volume, harmony make for greater expressiveness through singing.[112]

The Hebrew Bible portrays that singing is accompanied by plucked strings, percussion and wind instruments similar to that of neighbouring peoples and how they have also used musical instruments in their songs[113] Music moves people to experience God. It profoundly nourishes the spirit of true worshippers and also reveals the mighty deeds of God.[114] Songs are directed to God and they glorify and declare the sovereignty of God. Possibly psalms included all the hymns and canticles that were common to Jewish worship in the tabernacle, the temple, and the synagogue. Looking into all these aspects, I would say that worship with music brings the mind, soul and body together to glorify God. Here, the total being is involved in the worship of Yahweh. Music helps us to focus our attention on God alone and also prepare the heart to receive God from within. Music has always been at the centre of the worshiping community of the Israelites. The song reflects what is going on in both our hearts and minds together. We are affirming and expressing our faith in Yahweh through singing. I believe that through music, a wider intensity of feeling can be expressed by worshippers to Almighty God.

8.5.2. Clapping

תקע is 'to clap,' the gesture of clapping hands appears in the enthronement psalms in two incidents (Pss 47:1, 98:8). The Hebrew word for clap is usually rendered 'smite or strike.' This was used as a gesture of triumph over the enemy or as an expression of thankfulness. Clapping of hands demonstrates the joyous acclamation of the people who rejoice in Yahweh's kingship as the mighty God seated on the holy throne.[115] Giuliano, points out the difference

111 Prabhakar, "Christian Worship: A Dalit Perspective," 28.

112 Prabhakar, "Christian Worship: A Dalit Perspective," 28.

113 Eaton, *The Psalms,* 10.

114 David Breckbill, "Love, Music, and the Bible: In Praise of Interpretive Flexibility," *UBS Journal,* vol. 8, no. 2, vol. 9.1 (2015): 130–131.

115 Perdue, "Yahweh Is King over All the Earth," 92. See Erhard S. Gerstenberger, *Psalms Part I With An Introduction to Cultic Poetry: The Forms of the Old Testament Literature*, vol. XIV (Grand Rapids: William B. Eerdmans Publishing Company, 1988), 196. Walter Brueggemann, *Worship in Ancient Israel: An Essential Guide* (Nashville: Abingdon Press, 2005), 45. R. Mark Giuliano, "Psalm 47: A Note on Clapping in Worship," *Encounter,* vol. 72, no. 2 (Winter-Spring, 2012): 83-84.

between clapping hands and applause in worship. He argues that hand clapping is an action of worship and applause is a reaction to performance.[116]

Schäder, states that clapping hands indicates jubilation or a celebration (Ps 98:8), a similar action is mentioned at the coronation of Josiah as the king of Judah (2 Kings 11:12).[117] In the act of clapping, worshippers are not "simply reacting to a performance but are themselves engaging in act of worship." In worship we are invited to participate in the action of worship, to use our hands as musical instruments in expressing our faith, whereas applause is a kind of congregational response of appreciation and encouragement to the performers.[118] Clapping hands is a sign of approval and appreciation. Human hands and feet contain nerves that are attached to every organ, so as we clap, the nerves in our palms and fingers stimulate the whole body that energises us to express our whole being to the Lord. Praising God by clapping hands gives honour to God and enhance the worshippers' spiritual life.[119] At the same time, the worshipping community and the righteous are encouraged to express contentment, joy and exultation.

Wright mentions that clapping hands is fairly universal and a collective sign of approval. Those who clap are in a sense acknowledging something that has brought them happiness, joy or benefit. It speaks of appreciation and gratitude. It is a form of physical and audible thanksgiving that supplements or replaces words. The nations ought to clap for Yahweh because God defeated them through Israel.[120] Goldingay rightly points out that psalmists urge all people to clap hands and also challenges them to recognize their real king Yahweh.[121]

Clapping hands is an indication of happiness in success and signifies joy in the relationship with Yahweh, the creator God. The same metaphor of clapping hands occurs in the book of Isaiah, "all the trees of the field shall clap their hands," (Ps 98:8 cf. Isa 55:12). The psalmist calls to the nations to join in applause to Yahweh, God of Israel. When people focus on God with their voices, naturally they find fulfilment in clapping unto God in appreciation for all the mighty deeds of God. Therefore, clapping hands has a spiritual significance in worship. Dudley rightly points out that "worship involves the

116 R. Mark Giuliano, "Psalm 47: A Note on Clapping in Worship," *Encounter*vol. 72, no. 2 (Winter-Spring, 2012): 83.

117 Jo-Marí Schäder, "Psalm 47 – How Universal Is Its Universalism? An Intra-, Inter- and Extra textual Analysis of the Poem" (Magister Artium in Ancient Languages and -Cultural Studies in the Faculty of Humanities Thesis, University of Pretoria, 2008), 44.

118 Giuliano, "Psalm 47: A Note on Clapping in Worship," 84.

119 Myles Munroe, *The Purpose and Power of Praise and Worship* (Shippensburg: Destiny Image, 2000), 95.

120 ChristopherJ.H. Wright, *The Mission of God* (Illinois: InterVarsity Press, 2006), 474.

121 Goldingay, *Psalms 42-89*, 61.

body as well as the mind and spirit." Through the physical expression, the worshippers find meaning and acceptability.[122] Body language involves in offering worshippers the whole being to Yahweh, the king. Even God makes gestures, for instance, God smiles and looks upon the people and nations (Num 6:25, Ps 37:13). The symbols in worship are powerful. They can free the soul to laugh and rejoice in the Lord. Postures and gestures signify worshippers' humility, submission and exaltation before the face of the sovereign God. To me they are considered as important elements of worship in the context of Israel's worship.

Summary

Following points emerge from the above analysis. *First,* the psalmist portrays the kingship metaphor of Yahweh from all kinds of dominion aspects. Yahweh has the authority to judge the world with righteousness. *Secondly,* Psalm 98 functions as a victory song and expands the circle of praise to a universal arena. *Thirdly,* the chosen nation as they worship Yahweh confess his marvellous deeds and declare the salvation of God to all the nations (Ps 98:2). *Fourthly,* Yahweh is the king for the whole world including creatures. The psalmist calls for all the earth to praise the Lord. Also, the psalmist calls all creation to offer their praises to God. That shows music plays an essential part in corporate worship with universal purpose. *Finally,* each one of God works is designed for the glorification of Yahweh. Thus, all these points carry huge principles for the worship of Yahweh in the contemporary context.

---

122 Martin Dudley, "Movement in Worship," in *The New Westminster Dictionary of Liturgy and Worship*, edited by Paul Bradshaw (Louisville: SCM Press, 2002), 325.

Chapter 9

Exegetical Study of Psalm 99 Yahweh, a Just Ruler and Compassionate King of the World

Introduction

Psalm 99 begins with the glorious trust that the יְהוָה מָלָךְ 'Lord reigns' over all things. In this psalm, the psalmist expresses the historical relation of Yahweh to the community of Israel. The hymn also presents Yahweh who hears the cry of the people and answers them. Moreover, the text reflects the divine character of holiness in Yahweh which is different from all the other gods. The psalmist encourages the congregation to worship and give due homage and praises to Yahweh, who is King of kings. Besides that, the hymn also portrays Yahweh as having an intimate saving relationship with Israel throughout her history. Thus, the psalm declares Yahweh's reign to the earth.

First, I attempt a historical analysis of Psalm 99. *Secondly,* I look at the literary aspects and functions of the psalm. *Thirdly,* I give the textual argumentation and interpretation of the text. *Inally,* I deal with the comments in relation to the kingship metaphor and the comments in relation to worship.

9.1. Historical Analysis in Psalm

This section explores the historical setting of Psalm 99 in order to understand how this hymn has emerged. It is important to look at the text from both the Davidic monarchical setting and the post-exilic setting. The significance of historical analysis enables us to know the history of the text and its application to the particular historical background.

9.1.1. Davidic Monarchical Setting

Weiser, and Eaton place Psalm 99 in the Davidic monarchical setting. *First,* the song testifies to a fundamental characteristic of the OT revelation of God. The allusions to the sacred ark like cherubim, footstool in verses 1 and 5, indicate that the psalm originated in the pre-exilic era.[1] *Secondly,* the setting states that Psalm 99 is pre-exilic and celebrates Yahweh's constant reign. As a result, 'there is nothing against a pre-exilic origin of the song.' Psalm 99 could be dated in the time of the kings that is monarchical period.[2] By looking at the content of the text, Anderson agrees that Psalm 99 is a 'pre-exilic origin' especially.[3] *Thirdly,* Psalm 99 begins with the phrase 'the Lord's reign' and this phrase is usually applicable to a pre-exilic date, in that sense it is from the Davidic monarchical setting.[4]

With the Davidic monarchical setting, Psalm 99 uses symbols to describe the footstool which reflects an early form of Israel's tradition. Thus, the footstool plays a significant role in the Israelites' religious life during the monarchical period.

9.1.2. Post-Exilic Setting

Terrien and Gerstenberger support the setting as the post-exilic period. *First,* the most likely date for this particular psalm is the Persian period, when the second temple was erected and solemn ceremonies were held there.[5] *Secondly,* the psalmist is "letting the congregation participate with hymns and shouts of adoration." Worship assemblies in the post-exilic age developed this type of hymn similar to the Davidic monarchical setting.[6] Looking into the broader perspective, Terrien and Gerstenberger's view has a wide scope in understanding the text. We cannot totally ignore the Davidic monarchical

1 Artur Weiser, "The Psalms: A Commentary," in *The Old Testament Library*, edited by Peter Ackroyd (Philadelphia: Westminster John Knox Press, 1962), 641. See Hans-Joachim Kraus, "Psalms 60-150," in *A Continental Commentary*, translated by Hilton C. Oswald (Minneapolis: Fortress Press, 1993), 269. A. A. Anderson, "The Book of Psalms: Psalms 73-150," in *New Century Bible Commentary*, vol. 2 (London: William B. Eerdmans Publishing Company, 1989), 694.

2 Hans-Joachim Kraus, "Psalms 60-150," in *A Continental Commentary*, translated by Hilton C. Oswald (Minneapolis: Fortress Press, 1993), 269.

3 A.A. Anderson, "The Book of Psalms : Psalms 73-150," in *New Century Bible Commentary*, vol. 2, (London: William B. Eerdmans Publishing Company, 1989), 694.

4 John Eaton, *The Psalms: A Historical and Spiritual Commentary with an Introduction and New Translation* (London: Continuum International Publishing Group, 2005), 347.

5 Samuel L. Terrien, "The Psalms: Strophic Structure and Theological Commentary: Psalms 73-150," in *Eerdmans Critical Commentary,* vol. 2, edited by David Noel Freedman (Grand Rapids: William B. Eerdmans Publishing Company, 2003), 688.

6 Erhard S. Gerstenberger, *Psalms, Part 2 and Lamentations: The Forms of the Old Testament Literature*, vol. XV (Grand Rapids: William B. Eerdmans Publishing Company, 2001), 202.

setting, however, Psalm 99 was possibly used in worship during the post-exilic period.

9.2. Literary Analysis of the Text

Literary analysis focuses on the following aspects: translation of the text, text critical notes, form and structure and use of repetitions in Psalm 99 in order to explore the characteristic of the psalm.

9.2.1 Translation

1 יהוה מלך ירגזו עמים ישב כרובים תנוט הארץ :	1. The Lord reigns, the people *tremble*,[7] he sits on the Cherubim, the earth shake.
2 יהוה בציון גדול ורם הוא על־כל־העמים :	2. The Lord is great in Zion;[8] he is high above all the *peoples.*[9]
3 יודו שמך גדול ונורא קדוש הוא :	3. Let them praise your great name and to be revered, holy is he.
4 ועז מלך משפט אהב אתה כוננת מישרים משפט וצדקה ביעקב אתה עשית :	4. *Mighty King*[10] *loves justice,*[11] you have established uprightness, you have made justice and righteousness in Jacob.

7 V.1. רגז mentions as 'tremble with emotion,' or 'with terror.' See A. Philip Brown II and Bryan.W Smith, eds., *A Reader's Hebrew Bible* (Zondervan, 2008), 1207.

8 V. 2. ציון 'Zion.' "Zion is the seat of His visible glory and universal sovereignty on earth." See Arthur G. Clarke, *Analytical Studies in the Psalms* (Grand Rapids: Kregel Publications, 1979), 247.

9 A. R. Hulst, "עמ," in *Theological Lexicon of the Old Testament*, edited by Ernst Jenni and Claus Westermann, (Peabody: Hendrickson Publishers, Inc, 1997). The word עמ is often translated as people. The word עמ occurs in several Sem. Language. It is one of the terms of relationship and means the paternal uncle. Also, the word soon came to mean tribe in a collective sense. Most likely, the meaning paternal uncle is original Hebrew meaning and tribe is a later development, whichever way the meaning may be, עמ emphasizes the relationship of humans. Thus, עמ is commonly translated as people. In this sense, people and tribe are used interchangeably. The singular עמ may refers to the covenant people of Israel as the actual cultic community while the plural form עמים may refer to the peoples of the earth (Ex 19:5, Deut 2:25, 4:19, Pss 49:2, 96:3, 98:9, 2 Chr 6:33). 896, 915-916.

10 V. 4. ועז מלך 'mighty king' Kraus prefers ועז מלך as 'a strong one is king.' See Hans-Joachim Kraus, "Psalms 60-150," in *A Continental Commentary*, translated by Hilton C. Oswald (Minneapolis: Fortress Press, 1993), 267. For Dahood, ועז מלך translates as the 'strongest king. 'See Mitchell Dahood, Psalms 51-100: *The Anchor Bible* (New York: Doubleday, 1968), 378. See Weiser 'mighty one become King.' See Artur Weiser, "The Psalms: A Commentary," in *The Old Testament Library*, edited by Peter Ackroyd (Philadelphia: Westminster John Knox Press, 1962), 640. I have translated ועז מלך 'mighty king' because Yahweh alone deserves to be called the Mighty King, whose kingship will never end.

11 V.6 משפט אהב 'who loves just action.' See Mitchell Dahood, Psalms 51-100: *The Anchor Bible* (New York: Doubleday, 1968), 369.

5 רוממו יהוה אלהינו והשתחוו להדם רגליו קדוש הוא׃	5. Exalt the Lord our God, and worship at his footstool, holy is he.
6 משה ואהרן בכהניו ושמואל בקראי שמו קראים אל־יהוה והוא יענם׃	6. Moses and Aaron were among his *priests* and Samuel was among those who called on his name, They called upon the Lord, and he answered them.
7 בעמוד ענן ידבר אליהם שמרו עדתיו וחק נתן־למו׃	7. He spoke *to them*[12] in the pillar of clouds, they kept his testimonies, and the decrees he gave them.
8 יהוה אלהינו אתה עניתם אל נשא היית להם ונקם על־עלילותם׃	8. Lord our God, you answered them, you were a forgiving God to them, though avenged their misdeeds.
9 רוממו יהוה אלהינו והשתחוו להר קדשו כי־קדוש יהוה אלהינו׃	9. Exalt the Lord our God, and worship at his holy mountain for holy is the Lord our God.

9.2.2. Text Critical Notes

First, כרובים 'Cherubim' is a noun common masculine plural absolute (Ps 99:1). The word is also attached to the reign of Yahweh. Goldingay's interpretation is that "cherubim are winged beings of partly animal and partly human appearance. Yahweh sits on heavenly cherubim when transported about the cosmos to take action on earth and also sits enthroned above the cherubim in the sanctuary."[13] The psalmist portrays that יהוה בציון גדול means 'Yahweh is great in Zion' (Ps 99:2). Anderson affirms that "Yahweh is the only true world king whose kingdom is the whole universe" and the earthly centre of Yahweh's reign is Zion.[14] Kraus notes the God of heaven is present in Zion, in the sanctuary of the temple and the ark. The great king rules over the world kingdom. Therefore, all nations are subjected to Yahweh the great king.[15]

Secondly, העמים 'the strong ones' (Ps 99:2). Dahood support העמים 'the strong ones looking into the root word םימע 'strong ones,' and considers םימע

12 V.7. למו 'them' here is different comparing to v.6. It למו refers to the nation of Israel. See Mitchell Dahood, Psalms 51-100: *The Anchor Bible* (New York: Doubleday, 1968), 249.

13 John Goldingay, "Psalms 90-150," in *Baker Commentary on the Old Testament Wisdom and Psalms*, vol. 3, edited by Tremper Longman III (Grand Rapids: Academic Press, 2008), 127. (Cf. Ps 80:1, I Sam 4:4, II Sam 6:2). Cherubs are mysterious celestial beings, guarding the Garden of Eden (Gen 3:24) and sometimes they were regarded as personifications of winds or storm-clouds (2 Sam 2:11, Ezek 41:18). These mysterious creatures may have formed the cherub-throne of Yahweh which is associated with the Ark of the Covenant. See Anderson, *The Book of Psalms: Psalms 73-150*, 694.

14 Anderson, *The Book of Psalms: Psalms 73-150*, 694.

15 Kraus, *Psalms 60-150*, 270.

to be a term used for pagan deities. He claims that Yahweh is too great for Zion and beyond all the "strong ones."[16] Kraus and Gunkel say that העמים refers to nations. 'Yahweh is great in Zion and uplifted above all the nations (Ps 99:2).[17] All the nations are subjects of his empire (Ps 99:2).[18]

Tate and Goldingay support העמים as referring to 'peoples.' Yahweh is in Zion and is the great one. He is exalted and he reigns over all the peoples. Therefore, peoples are called to praise Yahweh.[19] Yahweh's rule as the great king does not mean he rules over deities as seen in Pss 95 and 96 but overall the peoples. 'Enthroned in Zion' signifies that Yahweh is in a position definitively standing over the peoples of the region (Ps 99:2).[20] To me, though עמים is translated as peoples or nations, the context of the text in Psalm 99:2 does not mention the word עמים 'nations.' Therefore, after looking all the parallel verses, I am convinced that העמים should be used as 'peoples.' This supports my argument of the universal aspect of Yahweh being exalted.

Thirdly, שמך 'name' (Ps 99:3). The word שמך is usually read as an attributive adjective by modifying 'name' as 'your great and awesome name' or more probably, 'your name is great and awesome.'[21] Yahweh's name is great and thus reflects his holiness. Besides that, the name of Yahweh is above every name and he deserves due worship.[22]

Fourthly, ועז מלך משפט אהב 'mighty king loves justice' (Ps 99:4). This is considered to be complicated, and variations in interpretation are numerous. *KJV* "The king's strength also loveth judgment" follows a tradition in LXX, Jerome, Peshitta and Quila, but it likely to be incorrect with עז as the subject of the verb אה, supported by Eaton. According to *RSV* translation, 'Mighty king, lover of justice' and *NEB* translation, 'he is holy,' follows Gunkel in transposing מלך עז reading 'he is holy a mighty king.'[23] However, Kraus prefers ועז מלך 'a

16 Mitchell Dahood, *Psalms 51-100: The Anchor Bible* (New York: Doubleday, 1968), 367-368.

17 Kraus, *Psalms 60-150*, 260.

18 Hermann Gunkel, *Introduction to Psalms: The Genres of the Religious Lyric of Israel* (Macon, Georgia: Mercer University Press, 1998), 69.

19 Marvine E. Tate, "Psalms 51-100, "in *Word Biblical Commentary*, vol. 20, edited by David A. Hubbard (Dallas: Word Books, 1990), 525–526. Artur Weiser, "The Psalms: A Commentary," in *The Old Testament Library*, edited by Peter Ackroyd (Philadelphia: Westminster John Knox Press, 1962), 640. John Goldingay, "Psalms 90-150," in *Baker Commentary on the Old Testament Wisdom and Psalms*, vol. 3, edited by Tremper Longman III (Grand Rapids: Academic Press, 2008), 127.

20 Goldingay, *Psalms: Psalms 90-150*, 127.

21 Tate, *Psalms 51-100*, 526.

22 Goldingay, *Psalms 90-150*, 128.

23 Tate, "Psalms 51-150," in *Word Biblical Commentary*, 527.

strong one king, he loves justice.' In my opinion, Kraus' interpretation works in the context of Psalm 99:4 as we focus upon the divine kingship of Yahweh.

Fifthly, בכהניו 'priests' particle preposition כהן noun common masculine plural construct suffix 3rd person masculine singular. Johnson argues that Moses is not incorporated along with the priests. He argues that בכהניו involves a *beth essentiae*, which means 'as' and that his priests and callers on his name are plurals of excellence. He means to say that "with Aaron and Samuel as priest and prophet par excellence respectively." The argument seems to be correct though the Masoretic apparently wanted Moses and Aaron read together. I assume that Moses could be one of the priests in his time, so we cannot ignore the Masoretic' version.[24] These are the text critical notes that I have discussed. When we explore the textual notes, it brings out new insights and implications for worship.

9.2.3. Form of the Psalm

Howard, comments that Psalm 99 is a hymn.[25] Kraus argues that Psalm 99 belongs to the category of songs of praise. Psalm 99 is counted among the 'Yahweh as king hymns.'[26] "This hymn is made up of three strophes and *Envoi*.[27] The strophes contain three stichoi each, and the envoi summarizes the whole in a threefold stichos."[28] As we look at the psalm, it is probably described as a hymn to the God of holiness. It was intended to be used in the temple (Ps 99: 5, 9). The psalm also reveals the name of Moses and Aaron, who played the role of ambassador for Yahweh. Moses and Aaron are termed Levites in Ex 2:1, 4:14 but this psalm is the only place in the OT where Moses is called a priest. Whatever termed it may be the fact is that they were the religious leaders for the people of God.[29] Therefore, the temple worshippers might have used this psalm in the temple and expressed their devotion to Yahweh the king.

---

24 Karl Elliger and Wilhelm Rudolph, eds., *Biblia Hebraica Stuttgartensia* (Stuttgart: Biblia Hebraica Stuttgartensia, 1997), 1179.

25 David M. Howard, *The Structure of Psalms 93-100* (Winona Lake: Eisenbrauns, 1997), 164.

26 Kraus, *Psalms 60-150*, 268.

27 *Envoi* which iscalled as a short stanza or an author's concluding remarks.

28 Terrien, *The Psalms: Strophic Structure and Theological Commentary: Psalms 73-150*, 686.

29 William R.Taylor, *The Interpreter's Bible: Psalms and Proverbs*, vol. IV, edited by George Arthur Buttrick (Nashville: Abingdon Press, 1955), 528. We also see the special focus in concluding verse in the second and third strophes that is in verse 5, 9 where it is a little longer than the corresponding verse in the preceding strophe. The meter is irregular. 531.

9.2.4. Structure of the Psalm

The hymn comprises of three strophes, (Ps 99: 1-3, 4-5, 6-9). Strophe I. Ps 99: 1-3, strophe II. Ps 99: 4-5 both end with the same phrase "for he is holy" and strophe III. Ps 99: 6-8 with envoi verse 9 slightly enlarge the phrase "for holy is the Lord our God."[30] Weiser is also in favour of threefold strophes, I strophe (Ps 99: 1-3) God's holiness is praised. II strophe indicates God's holiness is praised in the establishment of righteousness and III strophe praises for Yahweh's holiness in judgments.[31] Anderson claims that "the structure of the Psalm is problematic" because like Terrien, Eaton prefers a threefold division. On the other hand, there is some sort of refrain in verses 5 and 9. Nevertheless, he is in support of two strophes, verses 1-5 and verses 6-9.[32] I suggest that two-fold strophes give a better picture in understanding the text.

9.2.5. Repetition

Here, the intention is to explore how the writer uses repetition in this hymn. The text explicitly portrays the sovereignty of God whose kingship is far above anything else. We see the personal name of God יהוה is used seven times in verses 1, 2, 5, 6, 8 and twice in verse 9.[33] The word עמים is found in verse 1 and 2 which means 'peoples' is in noun common masculine plural absolute. The analysis of the word עמים shows that the text and context say it peoples rather than people. Probably, the whole world is in the mind of the psalmist.[34] The phrase קדוש הוא which means 'holy is he' is repeated twice in the hymn, in verses 3 and 5, this signify that 'true divinity, fullness of godhead' belongs to Yahweh the king.[35] This may refer to Yahweh or the name of Yahweh. In fact, קדוש portrays God's awe-inspiring power and also God's moral majesty.[36] The word ענה means 'to answer' and occurs in both verses 6 and 8. This signifies that God answers the prayers of his people throughout the history of Israel.[37] השתחוו the root word is חוה which means 'to bow down' or worship is found in verses 5 and 9 both talk about the same thing. Anderson claims that this means to "fall prostrate in humility before the divine king."[38]

The hymn expresses the remarkable pronouncement יהוה אלהינו which means 'Lord our God' in both verses 5 and 9. Gerstenberger suggests 'Lord

30 Terrien, *The Psalms: Strophic Structure and Theological Commentary*, 686.

31 Weiser, *The Psalms: A Commentary*, 641.

32 Anderson, *The Book of Psalms: Psalms 73-150*, 694.

33 Zorn, *Psalms*, 230.

34 Taylor, *Psalms and Proverbs*, 529.

35 Eaton, *The Psalms*, 347.

36 Anderson, *The Book of Psalms: Psalms 73-150*, 695.

37 Goldingay, *Psalms 90-150*, 131.

38 Anderson, *The Book of Psalms: Psalms 73-150*, 696.

our God' may have significance in terms of congregational activities. The phrase Yahweh our God refers to the "quality of a popular shout within the worship liturgy."[39] For Kraus, the phrase יהוה אלהינו is considered to be the title of Yahweh the king and this "divine name is associated with the potency of the covenant promise."[40] The word רום which means 'to be lifted up,' or 'to raise' occurs twice in both verses 5 and 9. This word is parallel to the phrase 'Lord our God.' The Israelite community is called to exalt Yahweh. Yahweh is high over all peoples. Therefore, Israel is to lift Yahweh high, exalt and worship Him.[41] Tate argues, "the use of the verb רום is one of the features which ties the psalm together."[42] Looking at the repeated phrases and words, I suggest that it has incredible significance in the context of worship. In fact, rhetorical criticism or repetition of the words imply exalting God again and again in worship.

9.3. Comments in Relation to the Kingship Metaphor

First, יְהוָה מָלָךְ 'Yahweh reigns' (Ps 99:1). Psalm 99 begins with the phrase 'Yahweh reigns' like in Psalms 93:1, 97:1. Goldingay suggests יְהוָה מָלָךְ refers to Yahweh's victory over Egypt and also over Canaan (Ex 15:15, 18, Deut 2:25).[43] Eaton claims that the phrase יְהוָה מָלָךְ conveys that Yahweh sits in the majesty of his new reign above all the kings and this expresses the "cosmic reality of the Creator, ascended as victorious and supreme over all."[44] 'Yahweh reigns' is an enthronement cry and here it portrays that the Lord's seat is above the cherubim.[45] The reign of God is connected with the phrase ירגזו עמים 'the people tremble.' Brueggemann[46] and Anderson[47] suggest that עמים ירגזו refers to the whole world and not to a single nation.

Secondly, להדם 'for footstool' (Ps 99:5). Tate says that by adding *lamedh* to להדם the phrase becomes "bow down at his holy mountain."[48] Ollenburger

39 Gerstenberger, *Psalms, Part 2 and Lamentations,* 200.

40 Kraus, *Psalms 60-150*, 270.

41 Goldingay, *Psalms 90-150*, 129.

42 Tate, *Psalms 51-100*, 529.

43 Goldingay, *Psalms 90-150*, 127.

44 Eaton, *The Psalms,* 347.

45 Elmer A. Leslie, *The Psalms: Translated and Interpreted in the Light of Hebrew Life and Worship* (New York: Abingdon Press, 1949), 83.

46 Walter Brueggemann, *The Message of the Psalms: A Theological Commentary* (Minneapolis: Augsburg Publishing House, 1984), 148.

47 Anderson, *The Book of Psalms: Psalms 73-150*, 694. The word רגז means tremble and it is in verb *qal* imperfect 3rd person masculine plural jussive in meaning, but no unique form of jussive is based on this. For Anderson, 'people tremble' refers to "the whole world and all that in it."

48 Tate, *Psalms 51-100*, 527.

argues להדם is 'to the footstool of Yahweh' or 'to the holy mountain of Yahweh.'[49] In Jer 3:16-18, Zion is identified as Yahweh's crown and Yahweh's footstool. Hence, in the exilic period, Zion itself could be identified with the throne of Yahweh which itself signifies the presence of God.[50] The word הדם which means 'footstool' is linked with the word 'worship.' The imagery of footstool appeared in both enthronement psalms and royal psalms. The psalmist affirms that worshippers prostrate themselves before Yahweh's footstool (Ps 132:7).[51]

In Howard's view, 'footstool' is either the ark or Mt. Zion itself.[52] Yahweh's footstool has two forms. The earth is Yahweh's footstool (Isa 66:1). The phrase in Psalm 99 shows a synonymous parallelism with Isaiah, "The heaven is my כסא 'throne' and the earth is my הדם 'footstool. 'This indicates that the feet of the enthroned person is used symbolically. Yahweh the king, is said to have a footstool which may be either Zion or the Ark, referring to his indwelling power in the temple.[53] In addition to that, Jerusalem or the sanctuary is also Yahweh's footstool (Ps 132:7, Lam 2:1). Thus, Yahweh's footstool becomes Yahweh's הר קדש 'Holy Mountain.'[54] In that sense הר קדש 'holy mountain' represents the temple that offers opportunities for worship.[55] In my opinion, it makes sense there is a close association with the Ark and Zion with the presence of God. The text shows that worshippers of Yahweh are to bow down before the footstool which represents the kingship of Yahweh. All the points above portray the kingship metaphor of Yahweh in the context of Israel's worship.

Thirdly, justice is the connotation of Yahweh's kingship. משפט 'judgment or justice 'exhibits a variety of semantic variants. The focal point of Psalm 99 lies in the realm of justice and judgment. Yahweh, exercises authority with

---

49 Ben C. Ollenburger, *Zion the City of the Great King: A Theological Symbol of the Jerusalem Cult* (Sheffield: Sheffield Academic Press, 1987), 186.

50 Tate, *Psalms 51-100*, 527.

51 Terrien, "The Psalms: Strophic Structure and Theological Commentary: Psalms 73-150," 848.

52 Howard, *The Structure of Psalms 93-100*, 89.

53 I. Cornelius, "הדם," in *New International Dictionary of Old Testament Theology & Exegesis,* vol. I, edited by Willem A. VanGemeren, (Carlisle: Paternoster Press, 1997). 1011. See John Goldingay, "Psalms 90-150," in *Baker Commentary on the Old Testament Wisdom and Psalms*, edited by Tremper Longman III, vol. 3 (Grand Rapids: Academic Press, 2008), 129. The call to exalt the Lord continues as a summons to fall down in obeisance towards Yahweh's footstool. In a wider sense, the image applies to the temple or mount Zion (Isa 66: 13, Ezek 43:7). And also refers to the ark (I Chr 28:2). See John Eaton, *The Psalms: A Historical and Spiritual Commentary with an Introduction and New Translation* (London: Continuum International Publishing Group, 2005), 347.

54 Goldingay, *Psalms 90-150*, 131-132.

55 Brueggemann, *The Message of the Psalms: A Theological Commentary*, 149.

justice. He gives stability to the people and nations.[56] The kingship of Yahweh is fully committed to the role of justice. משפט denotes the right or authority of rule and include which is right, proper and righteous and ensures a well ordered society. Yahweh loves justice because he dispenses justice.[57]

Yahweh's role as king of the world involves justice and righteousness; he ministers to the nations with justice. Thus, justice is considered to be an essential part of Yahweh's kingship. The psalmist explicitly mentions that the king's role is the execution of justice. Therefore, the royal kingship of Yahweh establishes justice and reveals his just rule to the ends of the world (Pss 97:2, 99:4, 98:9).[58] The creator God and ruler of all creation also acts in both mercy and justice which indicates that his kingship is based on justice and not partiality.[59] It is worth noting that the psalmist explicitly talks about Yahweh's rule with justice and it is associated with the work of righteousness, peace, prosperity and harmony.

Fourthly, holiness is associated with the connotation of Yahweh's kingship. In connection with this, the holy God operates the universe in a manner of holiness which is a unique characteristic of God. "Yahweh is set apart in the sense of being incomparable, different and unlike any other. This God is not set apart from the world, however, but rather set apart for the world. Yahweh relates to the world unlike any other divine king" (Ps 99:5, 9).[60] Through holiness he reveals himself to the world (Isa 6:3). This phrase refers the divine being of Yahweh and also shows the heavenly ones were expressing their joy in God's holiness.[61] Motyer points out that "Holiness is God's hidden glory; glory is God's all-present holiness."[62] God's holiness shows itself not only in his sovereign power but also in his character of rightousness. Therefore, the congregation bows down before the God whose holiness is manifested in righteousness (Isa 5:16).[63]

---

56 B. Johnson, "משפט," in *Theological Dictionary of the Old Testament,* vol. IX, edited by G. Johannes Botterweck, translated by David E Green (Grand Rapids: William B. Eerdmans Publishing Company, 1998), 87.

57 Johnson, "משפט," in *Theological Dictionary of the Old Testament,* 92-93.

58 J.Clinton McCann, "Righteousness, Justice and Peace: A Contemporary Theology of the Psalms," *Horizon Biblical Theology,* vol.23, no. 2, December (2001): 115–116.

59 Walter Brueggemann and W. H. Bellinger, "Psalms," in *New Cambridge Bible Commentary*, edited by Ben Witherington III (New York: Cambridge University Press, 2014), 426.

60 Brueggemann and Bellinger, *Psalms*, 425.

61 H. C. Leupold, *Exposition of Isaiah: Chapters 1-39,* vol. I (England: Baker Book House Company, 1986), 130.

62 J.A. Motyer, *The Prophecy of Isaiah* (Leicester: InterVarsity Press, 1993), 77.

63 Weiser, *The Psalms: A Commentary*, 642-643. A. A. Anderson, "The Book of Psalms: Psalms 73-150," in *New Century Bible Commentary*, vol. 2 (London: William B. Eerdmans Publishing Company, 1989), 695.Walter Brueggemann, *Worship in Ancient Israel: An*

9.4. Comments in Relation to Worship

Here, I discuss the following points in relation to worship. *First,* אל נשא *'God of forgiveness'* (Ps 99:8). God forgives as the phrase אל נשא indicates. God also holds 'vengeance against the godless to hold sway' as the word נקם meaning avenge, punish suggests.[64] Brueggemann claims that the two-sidedness of the awesome kingship are "God forgives and God punishes," and he refers to God who "saves and the one who judges."[65] Thus, God's holy presence is experienced most intensely in forgiveness and punishment where God demonstrates divine authority upon human beings. God disciplines people, erases sinful conduct and offers people the privilege to worship and participate in God's holiness.[66]

Secondly, קראים אל־יהוה *'call upon the Lord'* (Ps 99:6). The text mentions some of the religous figures in Israel with references to Moses, Aaron and Samuel and explains the issue of intercession. Anderson claims that they are portrayed as exercising intercessory functions.[67] Schaefer notes that Moses is the mediator of the law, Aaron represents the priesthood and Samuel the prophets. They all exercise an intercessory role between God and the people.[68] On behalf of the people, they called upon the name of Yahweh and their prayers were answered.[69] The phrase 'call upon the Lord' expresses how the worshipers must present themselves before Yahweh who is worthly to be adored.

Essential Guide (Nashville: Abingdon Press, 2005), 73. John Goldingay, "Psalms 90-150," in *Baker Commentary on the Old Testament Wisdom and Psalms*, edited by Tremper Longman III, vol. 3 (Grand Rapids: Academic Press, 2008), John Goldingay, "Psalms 90-150," in *Baker Commentary on the Old Testament Wisdom and Psalms*, vol. 3, edited by Tremper Longman III (Grand Rapids: Academic Press, 2008), 128.

64 Kraus, *Psalms 60-150*, 271.

65 Brueggemann, *The Message of the Psalms: A Theological Commentary*, 149.

66 Konrad Schaefer, "Psalms,"*Studies in Hebrew Narrative & Poetry,* edited by David W. Cotter (Collegeville: The Liturgical Press, 2001), 245. God's holiness manifests itself in the fact that God punishes the sin of humankind and also offers forgivenes. This signifies the "innermost core of God's holiness before which the congregation falls down and worships." See Artur Weiser, "The Psalms: A Commentary," in *The Old Testament Library*, edited by Peter Ackroyd (Philadelphia: Westminster John Knon Press, 1962), 644.

67 Anderson, *The Book of Psalms: Psalms 73-150*, Moses in Ex 14:15, 17:11, 32:11, Num 12:13, 14:13. Aaron along with Moses in Num 16:41-50. In regard to Samuel and his role we see in I Sam 7:8, 12:16), 696.

68 Schaefer, *Psalms*, 245. The psalmist selects these three great figures, Moses, Aaron, and Samuel as representatives of Israel's priesthood. They function in the psalm as mediators of the work of Yahweh. See James A. Durlesser, "Trishagion Und Gottesterrschaft: Psalm 99 Als Neuinterpretation von Tora Und Propheten," *Jewish Biblical Literature* 3, no. 110 (1991): 520.

69 Goldingay, *Psalms 90-150*, 130.

The psalmist stresses the importance of intercession in worship. The psalmist reveals that when Israel's ancestors offered intercession on behalf of the community, they received answers from God. For instance, Moses, Aaron and Samuel cried out to the Lord not for themselves but for others (I Sam 12:16-25, Nun 14:13-19).[70] They are people in Israel's history who are powerful in prayer. All of them are addressed as great intercessors.[71] God spoke to Moses and Aaron out of the pillar of cloud. The poet refers to the incident when God spoke to Samuel from above the sacred ark (I Sam 3:3-14). These people of God reminded the community of Israel to keep God's commandments.[72] Briggs argues that Israel as a whole was forgiven because of the intercession of these heroes of faith and their priestly meditation.[73] On this theological issue, Tate, having a wider perspective, says that even though people encounter the punishment of God due to their wrong-doings, nevertheless Yahweh responds to their prayers with forgiveness.[74] The character of this section recieves special emphasis from the fact that the hymn now turns to the prayer style of dialogue with God.[75]

The text claims that Israel's worship has taken the form of intercession. Schaefer argues "God's distant holiness is accessible through human intermediaries."[76] Intercession makes a bridge where worshippers can talk with God. Weiser, Knight, and Goldingay point out that intercession is one of the unique elements in the worship of Israel. Additionally, intercession helps the community to grow spiritually and also to bring healing to human society. Therefore, as Moses, Aaron and Samuel did, we have to continue with the element of intercession to support one another and make worship more meaningful.

Thirdly, the psalmist stresses the importance of *congregational hymns* in worship. The psamist calls the "congregation to the adoration and praise of God."[77] The hymn expresses, "may they praise your great name and tremble for God is holy" (Ps 99:3). Yahweh's name is great, holy and deserves due worship which indicates that Yahweh is in fact "distinctive, supernatural,

70 George, A. F. Knight, *Psalms: The Daily Study Bible Series*, edited by John C. L. Gibson (Edinburgh: Saint Andrew Press, 1983), 122. These men had cried passionately and God had answered them passionately. God had spoken to them in the pillar of cloud (Ex 13:21 Nun 12:5, 14:14 Deut 31:15).

71 Tate, *Psalms 51-100*, 529.

72 Weiser, *The Psalms: A Commentary*, 644.

73 Francis, S. R. Driver, Brown, and Charles A Briggs. *Hebrew and English Lexicon of the Old Testament* (Oxford: Oxford University Press, 1907), 310.

74 Tate, *Psalms 51-100*, 530.

75 Weiser, *The Psalms: A Commentary*, 542.

76 Schaefer, *Psalms*, 245.

77 Weiser, *The Psalms: A Commentary*, 642.

transcendent, heavenly."[78] Wright suggests that the affirmation of 'the Lord reigns' in based on qualities such as the "greatness, justice, holiness and forgiveness of Yahweh." All these reasons make the psalmist call upon the congregation to give praises to Yahweh.[79] The psalmist expresses that a community that assembles in worship must praise Yahweh. The earth trembles and yet not in fear, terror and torture which cause destruction, but in awe of Yahweh's presence which is, therefore, harmonious with "let them praise the great and awful name.[80] In connection to this view, the text leaves no doubt that the congregations are involved in praise and adoration. Congregations praising together in worship leads to the acknowledgement of the sovereignty of Yahweh.[81] This is a call to all the congregations to give glory to God and accept the kings who reigns above all.

The hymn indicates a call upon all the congregations to praise the holy name of God. In relation to this, the people bow down before God whose holiness is manifested in righteousness (cf. Isa 5:16). The peoples praise God with awe and thanksgiving and in a joyous manner for the righteous rule of their God over the whole world.[82] The congregations praise the holiness of God in the temple. The congregational hymns are considered to be an influential element in Israel's worship. Looking into this issue today, congregational hymns play a vital role in corporate worship. The congregational hymns have extensive implications for worship. Therefore, I affirm that although congregational hymns are an integral part of worship, they also give spiritual application by creating a worshipful atmosphere and preparing the minds of people for receiving God's direction.

9.5. Theological Concerns Pertaining to the Kingship Metaphor of God

In this section, I deal with theological concerns in association to the kingship metaphor of Yahweh based in Psalm 99. They are: Kingship and Supremacy, Kingship and Refuge and also Kingship and Holiness.

9.5.1. Kingship and Supremacy

Psalm 99 mentions about footstool of Yahweh and this refers to the dominion power of Yahweh who is seated above everything else and that, therefore, due

78 Goldingay, *Psalms 90-150*, 128.

79 Christopher J. H. Wright, *The Mission of God* (Illinois: InterVarsity Press, 2006), 480.

80 Charles Augustus Briggs, and Emilie Grace Briggs. "A Critical and Exegetical Commentary on the Book of Psalms." In *The International Critical Commentary*, vol. II (Edinburgh: T & T Clark Ltd, 1907), 308.

81 Gerstenberger, *Psalms, Part 2 and Lamentations,* 200, 202.

82 Weiser, *The Psalms: A Commentary*, 642-843.

reverence belongs to him. The Hebrew Bible mentions that הדם 'footstool' refers to the temple (Isa 60:13). It also refers to the ark (1 Chron 28:2, Lam 2:1). But Kraus and Weiser comment that the ark should not be separated from the cherubim throne.[83] At the same time, Zion is parallel to the Holy Mountain. God was worshipped at his הדם 'footstool' (Ps 99:5). When the ark was brought into the temple, the worshippers prostrated themselves before his footstool (1 Chron 28:2).[84] Tate suggests that it was most probably refers to the ark, because a footstool was used for the enthroned divine king. In the ancient world, kings are portrayed as "sitting on thrones with their feet on footstools."[85] Whatever the opinion may be, symbolically הדם 'footstool' refers to the dominion of God, and therefore, the psalmist is exalting Yahweh above all.

The text points out ורם הוא על־כל־העמים 'he is exalted above all the peoples' (Ps 99:2). Also, רוממו יהוה אלהינו והשתחוו להדם רגליו 'Exalt the Lord our God, and worship at His footstool' (Ps 99:5). From the literary aspect, both the phrases focus on the kingship of the Lord, which is reinforced by the symbol of his footstool.[86] 'Let us go to his dwelling place; let us worship at his footstool' (Ps 132:7). In this context, the psalmist affirms the dominion rule of Yahweh who holds the authority and, as a result, is worthy to be worshipped. The concept of highest God also points to the dominion rule of Yahweh the king, which refers to the God of Israel.[87] As the highest God, he plays the role of the highest authority, revealing his divine kingship to the world to let people know the true God and worship him.

Gerstenberger, and others support the supremacy of Yahweh among all kings and gods. The text points out into this phrase, the participle preposition of על 'above 'over' or in other words 'height' means Yahweh is higher than all gods. Again גדיל 'great' adjective masculine singular absolute, represents the greatness of Yahweh. The greatness of Yahweh is over all peoples. The text, especially in verse 3, expresses the dominion rule of Yahweh.[88] Both the

---

83 Tate, *Psalms 51-100*, 529. See Hans-Joachim Kraus, "Psalms 60-150," in *A Continental Commentary*, translated by Hilton C. Oswald (Minneapolis: Fortress Press, 1993), 853. Artur Weiser, "The Psalms: A Commentary," in *The Old Testament Library*, edited by Peter Ackroyd (Philadelphia: Westminster John Knox Press, 1962), 33-34, 39-40.

84 I. Cornelius, "הדם," in *New International Dictionary of Old Testament Theology &Exegesis*. vol. I. edited by Willem A. VanGemeren (Carlisle: Paternoster Press, 1997), 1011.

85 Tate, *Psalms 51-100*, 529.

86 Craig C. Broyles, "The Psalms and Cult Symbolism: The Case of the Cherubim-Ark." *Interpreting the Psalms: Issues and Approaches*, edited by Philip S. Johnston and David G. Firth. (England: InterVarsity Press, 2005), 147.

87 Kraus, *Psalms 60-150*, 247.

88 Gerstenberger, *Psalms, Part 2 and Lamentations,* 183. See Leslie, *The Psalms: Translated and Interpreted in the Light of Hebrew Life and Worship*, 213. A. A. Anderson, "The Book

words על 'over' and גדיל 'great' are associated with the kingship of Yahweh (Ps 99:2-3). The Lord has demonstrated not only his authority, but also his dominion over all other gods, which the psalmist talks about.[89] The psalmist claims that Yahweh rules above the gods of the Canaanites. The Assyrians spoke of their great and mighty kings, however, Yahweh is the greatest king above all. Yahweh is the king of kings over the whole world (2 Kings 18:19, 28).[90] The highest God is the one who made the universe. Phrases like 'the depths of the earth' and 'the heights of the mountains' show that all things belong to God. Exalt the Lord our God, and worship at his holy mountain for holy is the Lord our God.

9.5.2. Kingship and Refuge

ציון 'Zion' is a symbol of *refuge*, this is connected with the kingship metaphor of Yahweh. Zion also stands for Jerusalem and is the throne of Yahweh (Deut 12:5).[91] Gunkel and Rad point out that ציון 'Zion' is Yahweh's residence (cf. Ps 9:12).[92] Yahweh has chosen Zion as the place of his resting.[93] It is a place of worship with a special focus on the community of God's people which can be widened to the community of worshippers.[94] Ollenburger and Mohol affirm

---

of Psalms: Psalms 73-150," in *New Century Bible Commentary*, vol. 2 (London: William B. Eerdmans Publishing Company, 1989), 678. Eugene H. Merrill, *Everlasting Dominion: A Theology of Old Testament* (Nashville: Broadman & Holman Publishers, 2006), 573. John Goldingay, "Psalms 90-150," in *Baker Commentary on the Old Testament Wisdom and Psalms*, vol. 3, edited by Tremper Longman III (Grand Rapids: Academic Press, 2008), 92-93.

89 Merrill, *Everlasting Dominion: A Theology of the Old Testament*, 573.

90 Goldingay, *Psalms: Psalms 90-150*, 92.

91 Howard, *The Structure of Psalms 93-100*, 159. See David A. Rausch "Zionism," in *New 20th Century Encyclopedia of Religious Knowledge*, edited by J. D. Douglas (Grand Rapids: Baker Book House, 1991), 893-894. See above 'Zion' in pages 79-80.

92 Gunkel, *Introduction to Psalms: The Genres of the Religious Lyric of Israel*, 69. See Ben C. Ollenburger, *Zion the City of the Great King: A Theological Symbol of the Jerusalem Cult* (Sheffield: Sheffield Academic Press, 1987), 66-87. Eliya Mohol, "The Covenantal Rational for Membership in the Zion Community Envisaged in Isaiah 56-66" (Unpublished PhD Thesis, Coventry: Coventry University, 1998), 105-108. Roberts, "The Enthronement of Yhwh and David: The Abiding Theological Significance of the Kingship Language of the Psalms," 685–686. John Eaton, *The Psalms: A Historical and Spiritual Commentary with an Introduction and New Translation* (London: Continuum International Publishing Group, 2005), 343.

93 Gerhard von Rad, *Old Testament Theology: The Theology of Israel's Historical Traditions*, vol. 1 (Louisville: Westminster John Knox Press, 2001), 46. See Anderson, *The Book of Psalms: Psalms 1-72*, 689. Bernhard W. Anderson, *Out of the Depths: The Psalms Speak for Us Today* (Louisville: Westminster John Knox Press, 2000), 147-149.

94 Geoffrey W. Grogan, *Psalms: The Two Horizons Old Testament Commentary Psalms* (Grand Rapids: Wm. B. Eerdmans Publishing Co, 2008), 270.

that ציון is a symbol of sanctuary which is grounded in the presence of Yahweh. Yahweh reigns in Zion as the most powerful God who defeated the power of chaos and is exalted above all the peoples (Ps 99:2).[95] Zion tradition talks about subjugation, where Yahweh rules, protects, and fights against the nations. It is also a place from where blessing flows out. Both Israel and nations come to worship Yahweh in Zion.[96] The enthronement psalms, especially Psalms 97:8 and Psalm 99:2, emphasize that Zion is the centre of Yahweh's rule. Ollenburger[97] points out five points of Zion tradition:

1. Zion is the peak of Zaphon, the highest mountain (Ps 48:3-4).
2. The river of paradise flows from it (Ps 46:5).
3. Yahweh triumphed over the flood of chaos waters (Ps 46:3).
4. Yahweh triumphed over the kings and their nations (Pss 46:7, 48:5-7, 76:4).
5. The pilgrimage of the nations comes to Zion (Ps 72:8-9).

The temple in Jerusalem symbolizes Yahweh's earthly dwelling place, the centre of God's rule on earth. Jerusalem and the temple both symbolize God's dwelling place. The sanctuary was located on a raised area of Jerusalem, which was known as the temple Mount. This is often referred to as Mount Zion.[98] The psalmist says, "I have set my king on Zion, my holy hill" (Ps 2:6). Israel worships Yahweh on Zion and from this place the nations can see God's mighty deeds (Ps 84:8).[99] The theology of Zion denotes both particularity and universality. Particularity refers to the notion that Zion is Yahweh's place and his protection for the chosen people. Universality points to Yahweh's purpose in choosing Zion to bless all other nations. Additionally, Zion theology talks about the *centripetality* which refers the nations moving towards Zion, and *centrifugality* which denotes messengers from Zion towards to the nations. "The centrifugality thus leads to centripetality: the gathering and bringing of the nations to Zion."[100] Thus, Zion plays a significant role in the context of worship and in the mission of Yahweh for reaching out to all nations (Pss 46,

95 Ollenburger, *Zion the City of the Great King*, 66-67.

96 Eliya Mohol, "The Covenantal Rational for Membership in the Zion Community Envisaged in Isaiah 56-66." Unpublished PhD Thesis, Coventry University, 1998), 105-106.

97 Ollenburger, *Zion the City of the Great King,* 15.

98 Thomas Hale, *The Applied Old Testament Commentary: Applying God's Word to Your Life*(Eastbourne: David C. Cook, 2007), 18.

99 F. Stolz, "ציון," in *Theological Lexicon of the Old Testament,* vol. 3, edited by Ernst Jenni and Claus Westermann (Peabody: Hendrickson Publishers, Inc, 1997), 1072, 1074.

100 Mohol, "Zion," 448. See Eugene H. Merrill, *Everlasting Dominion: A Theology of Old Testament* (Nashville: Broadman & Holman Publishers, 2006), 582-584. John H. Hayes, *Introduction to the Bible* (*Philadelphia:* Westminster John Knox Press, 1971), 131-133.

48, 122, Isa 1:21, 27). It shows that Zion does not just stand for a particular group of people, but it symbolizes the believing community for the whole world.[101]

Mohol claims that in "Isaiah 56:1-8 are giving the right to membership in Yahweh's community on the basis of allegiance and holiness."[102] Anderson claims that the kingdom of Yahweh is the "whole universe and the earthly centre of his reign is Zion."[103] It is important to note that Zion functions as the instrument of blessing to the nations and parallels can be found in Genesis 12:1-3 and Isa 60:1-3, 16.[104] Yahweh has assigned Israel into the mission of God to all the earth and all the families of the nations to those who turned to the guidance of Yahweh.[105]

Zion's mission is not limited; it embraces all nations. Thus, Zion has a missional significance as the kings and nations come to Zion to acknowledge Yahweh the king (Ps 72:8-9). The context of Psalm 97 denotes that Yahweh receives Israel's praise in Zion (Ps 65: 2, 97: 8, 147:12). As seen in the above discussion, the OT refers to Zion as Yahweh's throne where his kingship is shown to the whole world (Isa 8:18, Pss 74:2 cf. 135:21). As Ollenburger and Mohol suggest, in particularity there is universality in order to bless all the nations. Zion is used metaphorically as the 'river of paradise' which refers to the presence of Yahweh that flows from Zion to all the earth.

Thus, universality is visible in the theology of Zion because it is from Zion that Yahweh's rule extends to the nations, and all the nations, in turn, come to express their submission and give due worship to the Lord in Zion.

---

101 Mohol, "Zion," 448, 450. See A. James Rudin, "Zionism," in *The Encyclopedia of Christianity*, vol. 5, edited by David A. Fahlbusch (Grand Rapids: William B. Eerdmans Publishing Company 1986), 856-860. A. A. Anderson, "The Book of Psalms: Psalms 73-150," in *New Century Bible Commentary*, vol. 2 (London: William B. Eerdmans Publishing Company, 1989), 694-695. F. Stolz, "צִיּוֹן," *Theological Lexicon of the Old Testament,* edited by Ernst Jenni and Claus Westermann (Peabody: Hendrickson Publishers, Inc, 1997), 1072-1074.

102 Eliya Mohol, "The Confessional Community of Isaiah 56-66," in *Missiology for the 21st Century: South Asia Perspectives*, edited by Roger E. Hedlund and Paul Joshua. Bhakiaraj (Delhi: ISPCK, 2004), 31. See B. Sundkler, the World of Mission (Grand Rapids: Eerdmans, 1965, David J. Bosch, *Transforming Mission: Paradigm Shifts in Theology of Mission* (New York: Orbis Books, 1992), 28.

103 Anderson, *The Book of Psalms: Psalms 73-150*, 694.

104 Mohol, "The Covenantal Rational for Membership in the Zion Community Envisaged in Isaiah 56-66," 64, 105. Cf. B. Sundkler, Zulu Zion and Some Swazi Zionists (Oxford: Oxford University Press, 1985)

105 Arthur F. Glasser, *Announcing the Kingdom: The Story of God's Mission in the Bible* (Grand Rapids: Baker Academic, 2003), 22.

9.2.3. Kingship Metaphor and Holiness

The word קדש 'holy' denotes *God's holiness* which contrasts with worldly things. Holiness is an expression of God's perfection or wholeness, and it refers the idea of separation from darkness because God is holy and separated from moral imperfection common to humanity (Hos 11:9, Ps 99:3).[106] Divine holiness is not merely moral purity, it is separated by elevation above all that is finite and imperfect.[107] In other words it is the otherness, of God from all his creation.[108] None of the gods are holy as Yahweh. Therefore, the holy God calls his people to be holy, providing for them the standard of obedience whereby that holiness may be maintained (Lev 19:2). The call of Israel to holiness was based on the fact that they had become God's possession.

Holiness should characterize Israel's distinctiveness in relation to the nations with regard to purity laws (Lev 11: 44-45) or moral behaviour (Lev 19, Deut 7:6, 14:2, 26:19).[109] Ross rightly argues that God "demanded that Israel be set apart to his holy law and not live like the nations of the world."[110] Mohol affirms that Yahweh called Israel עם קדוש 'holy people' and exhorts them to live a holy life, distinct from the neighbouring nations (Isa 62:12, Deut 20:8).[111] Thus, they were urged to forsake idols and give exclusive worship to him. Holiness is considered as a significant feature in Old Testament ethics.[112]

Holiness is one of the distinctive characteristics of Yahweh, the king. As a holy God, he sits on a *holy throne* (Ps 47:2, 8). The characteristic of holiness is exhibited in his kingship. Therefore, holiness is central to Yahweh in contrast to other gods. The point is that the divinity of Yahweh is the quality that represents the uniqueness of divine kingship. The Lord is holy "in

---

106 Jackie A. Naude, "קדש," in *New International Dictionary of Old Testament & Exegesis*, vol. 3, edited by Willem A. VanGemeren (Grand Rapids: Zondervan, 1997), 879. See Eliya Mohol, "The Covenantal Rational for Membership in the Zion Community Envisaged in Isaiah 56-66" (Unpublished PhD Thesis, Coventry University, England, 1998), 80-85.W. Kornfeld, Vienna, "קדש," in *Theological Dictionary of the Old Testament,* vol. XII, edited by G. Johannes Botterweck, translated by Douglas W. Stott (Grand Rapids: William B. Eerdmans Publishing Company, 2003), 523.

107 Arthur G. Clarke, *Analytical Studies in the Psalms* (Grand Rapids: Kregel Publications, 1979), 247.

108 Williams, J. R. "Holiness," in *Evangelical Dictionary of the Theology,* edited by Walter A. Elwell (Grand Rapids: Baker Book House, 1984), 515.

109 Naude, "," קדש 882-883.

110 Allen P. Ross, *Holiness to the Lord: A Guide to the Exposition of the Book of Leviticus* (Grand Rapids: Baker Academic, 2002), 45.

111 Mohol, "The Covenantal Rational for Membership in the Zion Community Envisaged in Isaiah 56-66," 105.

112 Walter C. Kaiser, *Toward Old Testament Ethics* (Grand Rapids: Zondervan Publishing House, 1983), 139. John Barton, *Understanding Old Testament Ethics: Approaches and Explorations* (Louisville: Westminster John Knox Press, 1984 reprint 2003), 1-100.

supreme majesty, in justice and in responsibility."[113] The holiness of Yahweh is different from that of Ancient West Asian kingship. Though Ancient West Asian kingship is considered to be holy, it does not encompass all the aspects of the holiness of Yahweh the king. Clarke observes that holiness is the central and eternal principle of Yahweh's kingship.[114]

The word holiness refers to the radical uniqueness of Yahweh, who may not be easily approached and also may not be confused with anyone else. Holiness is one of the incompatible characteristics of Yahweh who is beyond and above everything.[115] Israel celebrates Yahweh's holy name (Pss 103:1, 105:3,111:9, 145:21). In these doxologies, the worshippers give glory to the holy, sacred and awesome name of Yahweh. The worshippers recognize with full acknowledgement Yahweh's peculiar claim and its holy character.[116] The prophet Isaiah says "Holy, holy, holy is the Lord of hosts" (Isa 6:3). Holiness becomes a concept that means more than the fearful and fascinating. The people experience the character of holiness of Yahweh in their experience of Yahweh's kingship. The nature of sacredness covers the rule of Yahweh in all dimensions.[117]

Here, sanctity refers to the holiness of the most holy God who has established justice and is revealed as the true judge. It is through the act of justice and judgment that the true divine nature of Yahweh is manifested and it has a universal validity and power.[118] Goldingay suggests the following points as the primary aspects in knowing the holiness of Yahweh. *First,* holiness is fundamentally about the distinctive authority and majesty of Yahweh. Yahweh's name as the "expression of Yahweh's being is therefore to be acknowledged as holy." *Secondly,* uprightness and faithfulness are associated with the holiness of Yahweh.[119] The holiness of Yahweh is incomprehensible to the human mind, and it is the real nature of God that makes the congregation bow down and worship.[120] Holiness comes out powerfully in the enthronement psalms particularly in Psalm 99. Yahweh's holiness is present in all the decrees of Yahweh the king. "As the community seeks to carry out these decrees, it

113 Mays, *Psalms: Interpretation a Bible Commentary for Teaching and Preaching*, 316.

114 Clarke, *Analytical Studies in the Psalms*, 247.

115 Brueggemann, *Theology of the Old Testament*, 288. Holiness is one of the characteristic used with reference to Yahweh. The covenant people testify the holiness of Yahweh because Yahweh is holy and nothing can compare with the holiness of Yahweh. For instance, "Who is like you, O Lord, among the gods? who is like you, majestic in holiness awesome in splendour, doing wonders" (Ex 15:11). Once for all I have sworn by my holiness (Ps 89:5).

116 Brueggemann, *Theology of the Old Testament*, 290.

117 Mays, *Psalms: Interpretation a Bible Commentary for Teaching and Preaching*, 316.

118 Kraus, *Psalms 60-150*, 272.

119 Goldingay, *Psalms 90-150*, 132.

120 Weiser, "The Psalms: A Commentary," 644.

brings God's holiness out of the sanctuary and into the world."[121] The holy God requires holiness in the life and action of the people. The call to holiness is essential for the people of God as it has always been.[122]

Extol and worship Yahweh because he is holy. All these qualities encourage and lead the world to the place of worship. In addition, Yahweh, the holy king has answered the cry of the people. The holy nature of Yahweh is reflected in majestic rule, in giving law and in administering justice and mercy.[123] Konkel argues that "everything else derives from it, leans upon it, and can be understood with reference to it and only it."[124] If we are to understand God in the light of Israelites worship, we need to distinguish the distinctive Israelite concept of the divine God and how he is worshipped as the greatest king.[125]

Yahweh possesses the nature of holiness and this characteristic sets him apart from human kings. The concept of holiness is considered to be the basic foundation of Israelite religious belief in Yahweh. Holiness is part of kingship as Yahweh demonstrates the character of holiness in exercising and maintaining the nation and people. Thus, he graciously intervenes in the lives of the people to make his worshippers holy because 'Yahweh is holy' (Ps 99:3, 5, 9).

Summary

The following points emerge from above discussion. *First,* Psalm 99 strongly reaffirms the concept that the Lord reigns. The Psalm demonstrates the divine character and mighty works of God. Thus, the kingship metaphor denotes Yahweh's sovereignty and implies that all must worship Yahweh alone. *Secondly,* as described in the introduction, the character of Yahweh's holiness has applications for the worship of God who is holy and just. *Thirdly,* the invitation to praise God's great and awesome name implies worship where the worshippers are worshipping God through congregational hymns. *Fourthly,* trembling before God denotes Yahweh's majesty and implies that all must fear God and worship Yahweh truthfully. *Finally,* calling upon the name of God implies that all must come before God through prayer. Thus, Psalm 99 demonstrates the greatness of Yahweh and implies that his people must bow down and worship Yahweh sincerely.

---

121 Pleins, *The Psalms: Songs of Tragedy, Hope, and Justice*, 132.

122 Michael Wilcock, "The Message of Psalms 73-150: Songs for the People of God," in *The Bible Speaks Today*, edited by Alec Motyer, (Nottingham: InterVarsity Press, 2001), 105.

123 Schaefer, *Psalms*, 244.

124 August. Konkel, "The Exaltation of the Eternal King." *Διδασκαλία* (1990): 14.

125 Konkel, "The Exaltation of the Eternal King," 15. The following references talk about the holiness of Yahweh Ps 33:21, 1 Sam 2:2, Isa 40:25, 57:15, Hos 11:9, Hab1:12.

Chapter 10

Exegetical Study of Psalm 100 Yahweh, the King as Shepherd of the People of Israel

Introduction

Although, Psalm 100 lacks explicit reference to the kingship metaphor, Anderson and Howard suggest that it expresses the universal nature of God's kingship.[1] Brueggemann calls it a short benediction to the Pss 93, 95-100 and a doxology which closes with the imagery use of Yahweh as king (Pss 93-99).[2] Similarly, Eaton says that this psalm is related to the preceding series (93, 95-99) in its main features.[3] In this way, it fits with the kingship psalms 93-99[4] and

1 A.A. Anderson, "The Book of Psalms: Psalms 73-150," in *New Century Bible Commentary*, vol. 2 (London: William B. Eerdmans Publishing Company, 1989), 698. See David M. Howard, *The Structure of Psalms 93-100* (Winona Lake: Eisenbrauns, 1997), 196.Michael Wilcock, "The Message of Psalms 73-150: Songs for the People of God," in *The Bible Speaks Today*, edited by Alec Motyer, 2 (Nottingham: InterVarsity Press, 2001), 107-108.

2 Walter Brueggemann, "Psalm 100," *Interpretation* 1, no. 39 (1985): 65.

3 John Eaton, *The Psalms: A Historical and Spiritual Commentary with an Introduction and New Translation* (London: Continuum International Publishing Group, 2005), 349. Tate affirms that psalm 100 does not directly follow a kingship of Yahweh psalm, but obviously there are certain points, for instance, calling people to give homage and praise to Yahweh. All these forms make it similar to Pss 96-99. Psalm 100.1 talks about all the earth and this is with a universal focus and is parallel to Pss 96-99. See Marvine E. Tate, "Psalms 51-150," in *Word Biblical Commentary*, vol. 20, edited by David A. Hubbard (Dallas: Word Books, 1990), 535.

4 Michael Wilcock, "The Message of Psalms 73-150: Songs for the People of God," in *The Bible Speaks Today*, edited by Alec Motyer, 2 (Nottingham: InterVarsity Press, 2001), 107-108.

is occasionally classed with the enthronement psalms.[5] Psalm 100 functions with Psalm 95 to frame the core kingship of Yahweh (96-99).[6] The visible kingship metaphor of Yahweh in relation to worship and the expressions that we see in Psalms 47, 93-99 and Psalm 100 have coherence.

Analysing all these similarities, I agree that Psalm 100 has much to say on the concept of the kingship metaphor of Yahweh based on the theme of thanksgiving in Israel's worship. Worship, thus, begins in the reality of thanksgiving and finds its expression in prayer, song and offering sacrifice.

10.1. Historical Analysis

This section explores both the Davidic monarchical and the post-exilic settings in order to understand how this particular hymn has emerged and redacted.

10.1.1. Davidic Monarchical Setting

The setting of Psalm 100 shows it to be a hymn which accompanies worshippers to the front of the temple gates where people were called upon to enter inside the sanctuary with shouts and songs of praise. Terrien and Howard hold the view that the setting of Psalm 100 is the Davidic monarchical setting.[7] *First,* "it is impossible to determine the date of Psalm 100 accurately."[8] As a result, "it is difficult to suggest a date of composition for the final product." However, this hymn might have been used on several occasions during the Davidic monarchical setting.[9] *Secondly,* though Psalm 100 is parallel with Isaiah 40-66, it does not necessarily demand a late date just because of the connection with Isaiah 40-66. Therefore, Howard rightly states that "a pre-exilic date for Psalm 100 is a reasonable guess."[10]

---

5 Anderson, *The Book of Psalms: Psalms 73-150*, 698.

6 David M. Howard, *The Structure of Psalms 93-100* (Winona Lake: Eisenbrauns, 1997), 164.

7 Marvine E. Tate, "Psalms 51-150," in *Word Biblical Commentary*, vol. 20, edited by David A. Hubbard (Dallas: Word Books, 1990), From the literary aspect, Psalm 100 is close to Psalm 95 because both psalms say 'with a cry for shouts of joy' (Pss 95:1b, 2b, 100:1b) using the same verb 'shout. 'And both the psalms also emphasize "thanksgiving," 535. See Samuel L. Terrien, "The Psalms: Strophic Structure and Theological Commentary: Psalms 73-150," in *Eerdmans Critical Commentary,* edited by David Noel Freedman, vol. 2 (Grand Rapids: William B. Eerdmans Publishing Company, 2003), 690. David M. Howard, *The Structure of Psalms 93-100* (Winona Lake: Eisenbrauns, 1997), 192.

8 Weiser, Artur Weiser, "The Psalms: A Commentary," in *The Old Testament Library*, edited by Peter Ackroyd (Philadelphia: Westminster John Knox Press, 1962), 645.

9 Samuel L. Terrien, "The Psalms: Strophic Structure and Theological Commentary: Psalms 73-150," in *Eerdmans Critical Commentary,* vol. 2, edited by David Noel Freedman (Grand Rapids: William B. Eerdmans Publishing Company, 2003), 690.

10 Howard, *The Structure of Psalms 93-100*, 192.

The commentators likeTerrien and Howard who are in support of the Davidic monarchical setting, probably, relate the worship pattern into the monarchical period. Besides that, a tradition-historical approach is centred on the tradition of the Davidic setting. Hence, we cannot totally ignore the Davidic monarchical setting for Psalm 100.

10.1.2. Post-Exilic Setting

Kraus[11] and Taylor and Tate place Psalm 100 in the post-exilic setting. *First,* worship is the most significant why the people of Israel come to the temple, lift up their voice and make a joyful noise to the Lord. Therefore, Taylor strongly suggests the date of Psalm 100 is "postexilic, for worship is centred at the one temple into whose gates and courts the Lord's people seek entrance."[12] *Secondly,* the psalm, probably, applies to Jerusalem, but it relates the practices that lead to the post-exilic period of time.[13] According to Tate, Psalm 100 is short, it is difficult to bring out enough evidence regarding the date. Nevertheless, it is composed for some liturgical purpose in the post-exilic period.[14]

These are some of the commentators' opinions regarding the date of Psalm 100 to a post-exilic setting. However, looking into a broader aspect, Psalm 100 probably has a message that relates to both the exilic and the post-exilic period. According to me this Psalm, it is more likely used in the post-exilic period.

10.2. Literary Analysis of the Text

A literary analysis focuses on the following aspects: text critical notes, form, structure and repetitions. All these aspects enlighten us to understand the unique characteristics of the text.

10.2.1. Translation

1 מזמור לתודה הריעו ליהוה כל־הארץ׃	1. A Psalm of *Thanksgiving*.[15] Raise a shout to the Lord all the earth.

---

11 Hans-Joachim Kraus, "Psalms 60-150," in *A Continental Commentary*, translated by Hilton C. Oswald (Minneapolis: Fortress Press, 1993), 274.

12 Taylor, William R, "The Book of Psalms," in *The Interpreter's Bible,* vol. IV, edited by George Arthur Buttrick (New York: Abingdon Press, 1955), 533. See Marvine E. Tate, "Psalms 51-150," in *Word Biblical Commentary*, edited by David A. Hubbard, vol. 20 (Dallas: Word Books, 1990), 535.

13 Kraus, *Psalms 60-150*, 274.

14 Tate, *Psalms 51-100*, 536.

15 V.1. Kraus renders תודה 'Is a song of Thanksgiving.' See Hans-Joachim Kraus, "Psalms 60-150," in *A Continental Commentary*, translated by Hilton C. Oswald (Minneapolis: Fortress Press, 1993), 274. Goldingay translates תודה as 'confession.' John Goldingay, "Psalms 90-150," in *Baker Commentary on the Old Testament Wisdom and Psalms*, edited by Tremper Longman III, vol. 3 (Grand Rapids: Academic Press, 2008), 133. Weiser, translates תודה as

2 עבדו את־יהוה בשמחה באו לפניו ברננה׃	2. *Serve*[16] the Lord with gladness, come in before his presence *with exultation.*[17]
3 דעו כי־יהוה הוא אלהים הוא־עשנו ולא אנחנו עמו וצאן מרעיתו׃	3. Know that the Lord is God, it is he himself made us, and *not we ourselves,* we are his people and the flock of his pasture.
4 באו שעריו בתודה חצרתיו בתהלה הודו־לו ברכו שמו׃	4. Come into his gates with *thanksgiving*,[18] and his courts with praise. Be thankful unto him, *worship*[19] his name.

'praise.' Artur Weiser, "The Psalms: A Commentary," in *The Old Testament Library*, edited by Peter Ackroyd (Philadelphia: Westminster John Knox Press, 1962), 645. Mays, renders תודה as 'thank offering.' See James L Mays, "Worship, World and Power: An Interpretation of Psalm 100," *Interpretation* 23, no. 3 (1969): 315. *A Reader's Hebrew Bible* innote 2 mentions 'sacrifice of thanksgiving, offering of thanks.' See A. Philip Brown II and Bryan W. Smith, eds., *A Reader's Hebrew Bible* (Zondervan, 2008), 1208. I translated תודה as thanksgiving because Psalm 100 is considered to be a doxology for enthronement psalms. Therefore, translating תודה as 'thanksgiving' conveys the theological significance for the whole kingship psalms.

16 V.2. עבדו 'serve' verb qal imperative masculine plural. It is giving homage to Yahweh with submission. Serve the Lord with fear, with trembling (Ps 2:11). See Arthur G. Clarke, *Analytical Studies in the Psalms* (Grand Rapids: Kregel Publications, 1979). 249.

17 V. 2. ברננה 'with shout,' noun common feminine singular absolute. Weiser translates 'with shouts of joy.' See Weiser, "The Psalms: A Commentary," in *The Old Testament Library*, edited by Ackroyd (Philadelphia: Westminster John Knox Press, 1962), 648. Dahood, translates, 'With joyful song.' See Mitchell Dahood, Psalms 51-100: *The Anchor Bible* (New York: Doubleday, 1968), 370. Kraus ברננה 'with jubilation.' See Hans-Joachim Kraus, "Psalms 60-150," in *A Continental Commentary*, translated by Hilton C. Oswald (Minneapolis: Fortress Press, 1993), 273. Goldingay, translates ברננה 'with resounding' See John Goldingay, "Psalms 90-150," in *Baker Commentary on the Old Testament Wisdom and Psalms*, edited by Tremper Longman III, vol. 3 (Grand Rapids: Academic Press, 2008), 133. Tate, translates ברננה 'with joyful songs.' He argues that the long form רננה (joyful songs or jubilation, Cf. Psalm 63:6) in the plural rather than the normal form of רנה. Thus, Tate, took ברננה as a plural form and he translates it as 'with joyful songs similar to Weiser's view. *A Reader's Hebrew Bible*, Psalm 100 note 5 mentions רננה as 'exultation, rejoicing, and joy.' See A. Philip Brown II and Bryan. W Smith, eds., *A Reader's Hebrew Bible* (Zondervan, 2008), 1208. I take it as exultation because this exultation refers to the feeling of triumphant elation or jubilation. The word ברננה mentions in BHS, ב particle preposition and רננה is in noun common feminine singular absolute which means 'with shout of joy.'

18 V.4. תודה, *A Reader's Hebrew Bible*, Psalm 100 note 9 suggests תודה as 'Thanksgiving in songs of liturgical worship. See A. Philip Brown II and Bryan. W Smith, eds., *A Reader's Hebrew Bible* (Zondervan, 2008), 1208.

19 V.4. ברכו שמו 'to bless his name.' Kraus, translates 'honour his name' See Hans-Joachim Kraus, "Psalms 60-150," in *A Continental Commentary*, translated by Hilton C. Oswald

5 כי־טוב יהוה לעולם חסדו ועד־דר ודר אמונתו׃	5. For the Lord is good, his loving kindness is everlasting and his *steadfastness*[20] to generation after generation.

10.2.2. Text Critical Notes

First, כל־הארץ 'all the earth' (Ps 100:1). Like the preceding enthronement psalms, Psalm 100 stresses on the universal aspect as the phrase כל־הארץ 'all the earth' clearly indicates. For Kraus, כל־הארץ means that Yahweh is the Lord of all the world, so as to Yahweh is "due the praise of all lands."[21] Anderson argues כל־הארץ may refer to the chosen people of God who "represented all the peoples of the world."[22] However, I support Kraus's view and my argument is that all the earth refers to the whole world.

Secondly, דעו *qal* imperative masculine plural from the root ידע 'to know' (Ps 100:3). The verb ידע 'know' implies to recognizes that the Lord is God. Anderson states that ידע implies to acknowledge that Yahweh is God in heaven above and on the earth beneath (Deut 4:39).[23] Thus, the phrase 'know that the Lord is God' seems extraordinary for a summons to worship.[24]

(Minneapolis: Fortress Press, 1993), 273. Dahood and Tate translate 'bless his name.' SeeMitchell Dahood, Psalms 51-100: *The Anchor Bible* (New York: Doubleday, 1968), 371. Marvine E. Tate, "Psalms 51-150," in *Word Biblical Commentary*, edited by David A. Hubbard, vol. 20 (Dallas: Word Books, 1990), 533. Weiser translates 'praise his name.' See Artur Weiser, "The Psalms: A Commentary," in *The Old Testament Library*, edited by Peter Ackroyd (Philadelphia: Westminster John Knox Press, 1962), 645. Goldingay translates 'worship his name.' See John Goldingay, "Psalms 90-150," in *Baker Commentary on the Old Testament Wisdom and Psalms*, edited by Tremper Longman III, vol. 3 (Grand Rapids: Academic Press, 2008), 133.

20 V.5. Terrien translates 'truth.' See Samuel L. Terrien, "The Psalms: Strophic Structure and Theological Commentary: Psalms 73-150," in *Eerdmans Critical Commentary*, edited by David Noel Freedman, vol. 2 (Grand Rapids: William B. Eerdmans Publishing Company, 2003), 689. Mays translates 'faithfulness.' See James L. Mays, "Worship, World and Power: An Interpretation of Psalm 100," *Interpretation* 23, no. 3 (1969): 315-330. I translate 'steadfastness' as it reflects the unchanging faithfulness of Yahweh and moreover as the source of all of the goodness of Yahweh toward his people.

21 Kraus, *Psalms 60-150*, 274.

22 Anderson, *The Book of Psalms: Psalms 1-72*, 698.

23 Anderson, *The Book of Psalms: Psalms 1-72*, 699.

24 Erhard S. Gerstenberger *Psalms, Part 2 and Lamentations: The Forms of the Old Testament Literature*, vol. XV (Grand Rapids: William B. Eerdmans Publishing Company, 2001), 203. This gives the true nature of the hymn. Perhaps it "serves the purpose of representing God as a living reality and of imparting the knowledge associated there with." See Artur Weiser, "The Psalms: A Commentary," in *The Old Testament Library*, edited by Peter Ackroyd (Philadelphia: Westminster John Knox Press, 1962), 646.

Thirdly, עשה 'to make' (Ps 100:3). Mays, says, the verb עשה 'to make' does not refer to the creation of the world and its creatures, but rather the historical fashioning worshipping community.[25] Tate points out, "the verb עשה is related to Israel's history of redemption and Israel is the making of Yahweh" (1 Sam 12: 6, Isa 29:23, 43:7,44:2, Deut 32:6, Ps 95:6-7).[26] It implies that God cares for all humanity according to a freely bestowed covenant and thus human destiny is with God.[27] The metaphor of 'making' for the historical tradition of Yahweh's deeds leads logically to the recognition that the congregation is the people of Yahweh.[28] It portrays Israel as the people of Yahweh and Yahweh is the protector and redeemer of the covenant people of Israel.

Fourthly, ולא אנחנו which means 'not with ourselves.' There is problem in regard to the interpretation of the phrase ולא אנחנו. The *Ketiv* of MT reads ולא אנחנו 'and not we (ourselves),' but the Qere reads ולא אנחנו , 'and we are his.' LXX, Symn, and Syr suggest reading 'and not we ourselves,' but 'and we are his' has good support from some manuscripts, Aquila, Jerome, and Targum (cf Ps 95:7). Also, the Masoretic tradition reckons some fifteen passages in which לא (not) is written but which should be read as is לו (to him).[29] His people and the flock of his pasture, 'were nothing' (cf. BDB, 520).[30]

Fifthly, ברך 'to bless' verb *piel* is in the imperative masculine plural (Ps 100:4). Anderson[31] and Weiser comment that ברך means to 'praise.' Praise God for all his blessings.[32] And Taylor,[33] and Terrien[34] translate ברך as 'bless' because to bless God means to praise him for all the mighty deeds. The *piel* form of ברך expresses respect, gratitude and appreciation which are linked with worship.[35] Gerstenberger strongly claims that ברך is from the *piel* stem,

25 Mays, "Worship, World and Power: An Interpretation of Psalm 100," 324. The psalm speaks from within the fellowship of God's people. It refers to the making, not of humanity, but of Israel, when God constituted his nation at Sinai. See Michael Wilcock, *The Message of Psalms 73-150.* (England: InterVarsity Press, 2001), 108.

26 Tate, *Psalms 51-100*, 537.

27 Konrad Schaefer, *Psalms*: *Studies in Hebrew Narrative & Poetry*, edited by David W. Cotter (Collegeville: The Liturgical Press, 2001), 247.

28 Mays, "Worship, World and Power: An Interpretation of Psalm 100," 329.

29 Tate, "Psalms 51-150," 533.

30 Dahood, *Psalms 51-100: The Anchor Bible*, 371.

31 Anderson, *The Book of Psalms: Psalms 1-72*, 699.

32 Weiser, *The Psalms: A Commentary*, 631.

33 Taylor, *The Interpreter's Bible: Psalms and Proverbs*, 535.

34 Terrien, *The Psalms: Strophic Structure and Theological Commentary*, 689. See Marvine E. Tate, "Psalms 51-150," in *Word Biblical Commentary*, edited by David A. Hubbard, vol. 20 (Dallas: Word Books, 1990), 533.

35 Tate, *Psalms 51-100*, 534.

meaning actively 'blessing God,' a formula of intense liturgical use.[36] Kraus translates ברך as 'honour.'[37] Goldingay uses 'worship' in his translation because ברך has a sense of worship. These are the variations of the translations of the word ברך.

I support Goldingay's translation because the text definitely speaks about worshipping Yahweh. Looking at Psalm 100, it is clear that worship is the main idea presented by the psalmist. Additionally, ברך represents the usual acts of worship. Therefore, I translate ברך as 'worship.'

Finally, the phrase כי־טוב יהוה 'for the Lord is good' (Ps 100:5). This phrase expresses the sovereign and divine characters which are in Yahweh the true God. The words חסד 'loving kindness' and אמונה 'faithfulness, trustworthiness,' are qualities associated with the phrase 'the Lord is good.'[38] There are several translations for the word חסד, nevertheless, according to the Hebrew Bible the primary meaning of חסד is directed to Yahweh's relationship with the Israelites and particularly with worshippers of Yahweh.[39] Yahweh's goodness is everlasting and for all people. Therefore, the psalmist expresses that Yahweh deserves our sincere worship and thanksgiving.

10.2.3. Form of the Psalm

Howard asserts that Psalm 100 is in the form of a hymn.[40] Leslie notes that "the psalm is in the form of a liturgical hymn and is rendered antiphonally" and it reflects the procession of pilgrims and the priestly choir. He said that as the pilgrims enter the outer court of the temple, they sing summons to praise. It is a called to the worshippers. Worshippers are to raise the glad cultic shout unto God, worshipping God in the mood of rejoicing.[41] Psalm 100 belongs to the group of songs of praise.[42]

In form, it consists of two short hymns, verses 1-3, 4-5 with the usual hymnal parts, i.e., the call to worship and the ground for the call. The meter is irregular: 3+3+3 (Ps 100:1-2), 4+4+3 (Ps 100:3), 3+2+3 (Ps 100:4) 2+2+3 (Ps 100:5).[43] Kraus notes that the meter of this psalm is clearly evident being

---

36 Gerstenberger, *Psalms, Part 2 and Lamentations,* 204.

37 Kraus, *Psalms 60-150*, 273.

38 John Goldingay, "Psalms 90-150," in *Baker Commentary on the Old Testament Wisdom and Psalms*, edited by Tremper Longman III, vol. 3 (Grand Rapids: Academic Press, 2008), 137.

39 Pravan Paul, *Power and Love in the Book of Hosea: A Postcolonial Reading* (Delhi: Living Insight Translators & Publisher Pvt. Ltd, 2015), 24.

40 Howard, *The Structure of Psalms 93-100*, 164.

41 Elmer A. Leslie, *The Psalms: Translated and Interpreted in the Light of Hebrew Life and Worship* (New York: Abingdon Press, 1949), 191.

42 Kraus, *Psalms 60-150*, 274.

43 Taylor, *The Interpreter's Bible: Psalms and Proverbs*, 532-533.

3+3+3.[44] Anderson argues that this is a hymn and the metre is 3+3+3.[45] Tate also suggests that Psalm 100 is almost universally classified as a hymn.[46]

10.2.4. Structure of the Psalm

Regarding the structure, the pattern is the same as Psalm 95. Generally, the structure is indicated in the following pattern; call to praise in verses 1-3, the reason why in verse 3; another call to praise in verse 4 and the reason why in verse 5.[47] The structure is meant to be used as liturgy as the context reflects, with the first stanza of the hymn sung by those at the head of procession as they move up to the temple gates. And, then, the second hymn sung as a response from another choral group within the temple. This helps the worshippers to enter the temple courts.[48]

10.2.5. Repetition

The word תודה means 'thanksgiving' and occurs twice, once in verse1 and once in verse 4. Originally, תודה was a 'thanksgiving sacrifice.'[49] As the text is repeated in two verses, it indicates that Psalm 100 has a significant role in the context of worship. It also assumes that this is a "congregational act rather than to a private thank-offering or thanksgiving."[50] The verb בוא 'to come in' is repeated in both verse 2 and verse 4 and it is an imperative invitation to come before the presence of God for worship. Weiser asserts that the psalmist gives a call to the worshippers' בוא to come into the sanctuary in order to worship and give praise to Yahweh.[51] The conjunction כי means 'for, that' and occurs in both verses 3 and 5. Analysis of the usage of the word כי usually appears in the praise contexts. Gerstenberger points that כי used as part of the hymn that the choir or congregation repeatedly sang (cf. Psalms 33:4, 96:4-5).[52]

---

44 Kraus, *Psalms 60-150*, 274.

45 Anderson, *The Book of Psalms: Psalms 73-150*, 698.

46 Tate, *Psalms 51-100*, 534. Many scholars classify Psalm 100 as an entry hymn like A. A. Anderson, "The Book of Psalms: Psalms 73-150," in *New Century Bible Commentary*, vol. 2 (London: William B. Eerdmans Publishing Company, 1989), 698. Hans-Joachim Kraus, "Psalms 60-150," in *A Continental Commentary*, translated by Hilton C. Oswald (Minneapolis: Fortress Press, 1993), 203-204. Artur Weiser, "The Psalms: A Commentary," in *The Old Testament Library*, edited by Peter Ackroyd (Philadelphia: Westminster John Knox Press, 1962), 647.

47 Eaton, *The Psalms*, 349.

48 Taylor, *The Interpreter's Bible: Psalms and Proverbs*, 532.

49 Gerstenberger, *Psalms, Part 2 and Lamentations*, 203.

50 Anderson, *The Book of Psalms: Psalms 1-72*, 698.

51 Weiser, *The Psalms: A Commentary*, 647.

52 Gerstenberger, *Psalms, Part 2 and Lamentations,* 204.

The noun דור 'generation' is mentioned twice in verse 5. Anderson affirms that 'it is unending' refers to the loving kindness of Yahweh.[53] The noun דור is repeatedly used in the worship of Yahweh it is the Lord who made us. The word עשה which means 'made' is used in the sense of a divine making, fashioning, forming, particularly for the people. It seems that עשה is a metaphor for God's election and salvation of Israel as a people of God.[54] Briggs comments 'it is Yahweh who made us' reflects that we are God's own creatures, belonging to God over and above as God's rightful creation.[55] In my opinion, all these repetitions have a point for implications of worship. When words or phrases are repeated, it is a way of demanding worshippers to exalt or praise Yahweh. Thus, repeated words and phrases are a special characteristic of Hebrew poetry.

10.3. Comments in Relation to the Kingship Metaphor

First, the word מרעית means 'shepherding' (Ps 100:3). And רעה 'shepherd' means to tend or to pasture and also refers to govern (2 Sam 7:7). The shepherd is applied to Yahweh and refers to his authorities. Therefore, *shepherding* is a connotation of the kingship metaphor of Yahweh. The shepherding image reflects one who "watches over, guards, feeds and protects a flock."[56] Along with the concept of Yahweh, the maker of the universe, the image of the מרעית 'shepherding' and צאן 'flock' which reflects the Ancient West Asian conception of the king and his people. Yahweh is the maker and also the shepherd of the flock. This metaphor is also associated with calling Yahweh the king who creates and also has the power to care.[57]

Shepherding is an essential part of Yahweh's kingship because as king, he has to tend people, and show care towards his flock. The title of shepherd has significant effect, especially to the community which depends primarily on farming and rearing livestock.[58] Shepherd is a common term used for a king

53 Anderson, *The Book of Psalms,* 700.

54 Walter D. Zorn, in "Psalms," *The College Press NIV Commentary*, vol. 2 (Joplin, MO: College Press Publishing Co, 2004), 238. (cf. Ps 95:6-7, Deut 32:6, 15, Isa 43:1, 21, 44:2).

55 Charles Augustus, Briggs and Emilie Grace Briggs, "A Critical and Exegetical Commentary on the Book of Psalms," in *The International Critical Commentary*, vol. II (Edinburgh: T&T Clark Ltd, 1907), 311.

56 Louis Jonker, "רעה," in *New International Dictionary of Old Testament Theology & Exegesis,* vol, 3, edited by Willem A. VanGemeren (Grand Rapids: Zondervan, 1997), 1141.

57 Kraus, *Psalms 60-150*, 247.

58 J. A. Soggin, "רעה," in *Theological Lexicon of the Old Testament,* edited by Ernst Jenni and Claus Westermann, vol. 3, translated by Mark E. Biddle (Peabody: Hendrickson Publishers, Inc, 1997). 1247. The classical expression Yahweh as a shepherd, is found in several passages (Ps 23: cf. 28:9, 80:2, Gen 48: 15, 49:24, Isa 40:11, Hos 4:16, Mic 7:14).

throughout the Ancient West Asia. In this context, the imagery of the shepherd denotes the covenant between Yahweh and Israel (cf. Pss 74:1, 79:13, 80:2).

Secondly, maker connotes the kingship of Yahweh (Ps 100:3). Anderson rightly says, עשה 'to make' is not giving reference to the creation of human and universe but it talks about the formation of the people of Yahweh and how he continues to lead them through.[59] The עשה 'to make' denotes that Yahweh is the king who makes things possible which indicates God's action in all realms of his activity in history and nature, both in the world and in creation, in past, present, and future. It explains his saving activity in Israel at the beginning of history (Gen 12:2).[60] The word עשה relates to well-being, victory and deliverance. It also expresses the power of Yahweh who is able to make things according to his purpose. Hence, עשה describes Yahweh's creative activity in all its dimensions.[61] The psalmist says it is he who made us and we are his, this statement denotes that the creature speaks of their Lord on whom they depend on in everything and to whom alone they put their trust and hope.[62]

Additionally, the verb עשה shows that Yahweh is in control over history and over individual lives. Yahweh demonstrates who he is in his עשה. Therefore, the psalmist portrays that Yahweh's power is manifest in the word עשה. 'Yahweh does what he says' he will do (Gen 21:1, Num 23:19). 'Yahweh does what he wants' (Ps 115:3)[63] Yahweh is the king and also the maker who makes everything.

Thirdly, faithfulness or truth connotes the kingship of Yahweh (Ps 100:5). Yahweh is a faithful God, and, therefore, truth belongs to him. In connection to the noun אמת 'truth' is considered to be one of the keys in the kingship of Yahweh, and this is also parallel with his divine love and goodness. The theological significance of אמת is derived from its frequent usage in describing the character of Yahweh (Ex 43:5-7). אמת represents the heart of God's self-

---

There are several passages which speak of the people as the flock (Ps 68; 8, 74:1, 77:21, 78; 52, 79:13, 95:7, 100:3, 121:4), 1248.

59 Anderson, "The Book of Psalms: Psalms 73-150," 699. (Cf. Isa 29:23, 43:1, 21, 44:2, 60:21). See Charles Augustus Briggs and Emilie Grace Briggs, "A Critical and Exegetical Commentary on the Book of Psalms," in *The International Critical Commentary,* vol. II (Edinburgh: T &T Clark Ltd, 1907), 311. Artur Weiser, "The Psalms: A Commentary," in *The Old Testament Library*, edited by Peter Ackroyd (Philadelphia: Westminster John Knox Press, 1962), 645.

60 J. Vollmer, "עשה," in *Theological Lexicon of the Old Testament,* vol. 2, edited by Ernst Jenni and Claus Westermann, translated by Mark E. Biddle (Peabody: Hendrickson Publishers, 1997), 949.

61 Vollmer, "עשה,"949.

62 Weiser, *The Psalms: A Commentary*, 646.

63 Vollmer, "עשה," 950.

revelation to the people. He is abounding in love and faithfulness.'[64] The understanding of God as a God of faithfulness is often celebrated in Israel's worship. This motif is explicitly expressed in the enthronement psalms. God's graciousness and faithfulness is continuously expressed toward Israel through his sovereignty. Therefore, the people of Israel are expected to be faithful to a faithful God (Jos 24:14).[65]

The faithfulness of Yahweh functions in the form of *deliverance and protection.*[66] Yahweh is a God of אמונה 'faithfulness' therefore he acts faithfully to the world (Deut 32:4).The psalmist asserts that his faithfulness is in the sense of "integrity, trustworthiness, and dependability" and Yahweh displays all these qualities in his kingship.[67] Unfaithful kings execute their government in evil ways and people suffer under them. However, the psalmist shows that Yahweh executes his power faithfully and does things that are good for all.

10.4. Comments in Relation to Worship

First, תודה 'songs of thanksgiving' (Ps 100:1). The root meaning of the verb is ידה in *hiphil* which means to confess and declare. There is no word in Hebrew 'to thank.' The praise being either declarative, referring to what God has done, or descriptive, referring to what he characteristically does. The Hebrew word תודה can also mean a thank offering or thank sacrifice.[68] Schaefer points out that Psalm 100 תודה refers to both the "thanksgiving sacrifice and accompanying praise."[69] For Crüsemann, תודה could be sacrifice which is offered in a thanksgiving ceremony, and then became a song of praise to accompany with the sacrifice. However, Tate does not fully agree with Crüsemann because he maintains the traditional view by considering it to mean 'thanksgiving,' but he also affirms that the double meaning of the word should

64 R. W. L. Moberly, "אמן," in *New International Dictionary of Old Testament & Exegesis*, vol.1, edited by Willem A.VanGemeren (Carlisle: Paternoster Press, 1997), 428.

65 Moberly, "אמן," 429.

66 Robert B. Chisholm, "A Theology of the Psalms," in *A Biblical Theology of the Old Testament*, edited by Roy B. Zuck (Chicago: Moody Press, 1991), 300.

67 Moberly, " אמן," 229-430.

68 Tate, *Psalms* 51-100, 533.

69 Schaefer, *Psalms*, 245. See Bernhard W. Anderson, *Out of the Depths: The Psalms Speak for Us Today* (Louisville: Westminster John Knox Press, 2000), 102. Erhard S. Gerstenberger, *Psalms, Part 2 and Lamentations: The Forms of the Old Testament Literature*, vol. XV (Grand Rapids: William B. Eerdmans Publishing Company, 2001), 203. Walter Brueggemann, *Worship in Ancient Israel: An Essential Guide* (Nashville: Abingdon Press, 2005), 54. John Eaton, *The Psalms: A Historical and Spiritual Commentary with an Introduction and New Translation* (London: Continuum International Publishing Group, 2005) 349.John Goldingay, "Psalms 90-150," in *Baker Commentary on the Old Testament Wisdom and Psalms*, edited by Tremper Longman III, vol. 3 (Grand Rapids: Academic Press, 2008), 134.

not be ignored. He further mentions that the English word for 'thanksgiving' has a double degree of 'praise' and the 'act of giving thanks' may possibly 'involve a worship service.'[70] Crüsemann focuses on 'thanksgiving' and with slight modification it means thanksgiving along with praise. I agree with the assessment. Thanksgiving still makes sense in the interpretation, particularly in the context of worship.

The psalmist claims that when the community uses the hymn that extols God's saving or mighty acts, it is called a thanksgiving hymn.[71] Psalm 100 is an acknowledgment that life is a gift and should refer back to the giver through praising God.[72] Leslie points out that "the praise of God is one of the deepest human impulses in worship."[73] The psalm is a summons 'to shout for joy to the Lord all the earth' (Ps 100:1). The hymn begins with thanksgiving to praise the Lord and it is an inclusive call. I agree with individual praises to God, yet, the text here more clearly focuses on community thanksgiving praise.

Thanksgiving and homage to Yahweh is the purpose of entering into the sanctuary for worship, implying that in every way God deserves all honour and praises[74] In fact, singing thanksgiving hymns turns into proclamation of good news to others and also becomes a sort of invitation to let others respond to the reality of the good news (Ps 103:20-22). Thanksgiving hymns have a spiritual dimension for both individuals as well as the community. The psalmist explicitly talks about the use of the thanksgiving hymn in Israel's worship. Thanksgiving hymns had a great impact with regard to true worship during those days and as well as today.

Secondly, עבד means 'to work or to serve' (Ps 100:2). Tate, Kraus, and Schaefer point out עבד in relation to worship. The verb עבד conveys a variety of meanings like in being military service, or to serve a god or even to worship Yahweh.[75] Looking at the context of the text as the worshipping

70 Tate, *Psalms 51-100*, 533.

71 Anderson, *Out of the Depths: The Psalms Speak for Us Today*, 111. The theme of the hymn in Psalm 100 reflects the acts of God in saving and sustaining the covenant people. See A. A. Anderson, "The Book of Psalms: Psalms 1-72," in *New Century Bible Commentary*, vol. 1 (London: William B. Eerdmans Publishing Company, 1985), 699.

72 Brueggemann, "Psalm 100," 65.

73 Leslie, *The Psalms*, 192.

74 Kraus, *Psalms 60-150*, 275.

75 Tate, *Psalms 51-100*, 536. The verb on one side means to function as a servant or as a slave, mainly to work for someone (Ezek 29: 18, Judg 9:28, I King 5:1). On the other hand, the verb is used for worship of other gods rather than Yahweh (Deut 7:4, 8:19, 11:16, 28:36, 30:17). It is also used in the worship of Yahweh (Deut 6:13, 10:12, 11:13, Ex 23:25), to worship or serve Yahweh alone is the basic requirement for all Israelites, 536-537. See John Goldingay, "Psalms 90-150," in *Baker Commentary on the Old Testament Wisdom and Psalms*, vol. 3, edited by Tremper Longman III, (Grand Rapids: Academic Press, 2008), 135. Erhard S. Gerstenberger, *Psalms, Part 2 and Lamentations: The Forms of the Old*

community enters the sanctuary, Kraus claims עבד expresses the performance of a celebration of worship.[76] עבד points to the "fact that worshipping Yahweh involves a serious submission of the whole self." The verb עבד implies that "worship is done for God's sake and not for ours; servants serve their master, not themselves."[77] עבד in the expression of 'worship or serve the Lord' may refer to the peoples' homage toward God, or more specifically the liturgy.[78]

The word serves as a technical term for performing as servants or subjects what is proper in worship (cf. Ex 3:12, Mal 3:14).[79] The royal psalms mention serving the Lord with fear and with trembling this affirms both service and reverence and that the nations are invited into this adoration of Yahweh (Ps 2:11).[80] Jacobson is right when he says, "The Lord God was proclaimed as Israel's king from the beginning of Israel's existence as a people."[81] Therefore, the nation of Israel is called to serve the Lord single heartedly. The text indicates a royal setting. The usage of עבד in the Psalter shows that it specializes in one of its possible functions, denoting the conduct appropriate for relation to a royal figure (Yahweh the king). 'To serve' can be used a political context, however, here the text talks about honouring, rather than the other way around. The context indicates the cultic activities.[82] Analyzing the context, the summons to serve Yahweh is a call to worship of Yahweh. Thus, 'serve' is another word used for worship.

The text clearly portrays that people should "serve the Lord with gladness" (Ps 100:2). For Anderson, 'with gladness is the right mood' that befits the blessings which God bestows upon the people.[83] Similarly, Goldingay asserts that gladness means coming into Yahweh's presence with 'enthusiasm.'[84] The aim and spirit of worship is gladness in God's presence.[85] Gladness is the sign of delighting and rejoicing in the worship and service of God. The characteristic of a hymn is to praise; all the praises and worship are to submit

---

Testament Literature, vol. XV (Grand Rapids: William B. Eerdmans Publishing Company, 2001), 203. See A. Philip Brown II and Bryan. W Smith, eds., *A Reader's Hebrew Bible* (Zondervan, 2008), 1208.

76 Kraus, *Psalms 60-150*, 274.

77 Goldingay, *Psalms 42-89*, 135.

78 Schaefer, *Psalms*, 246.

79 Taylor, *The Interpreter's Bible: Psalms and Proverbs*, 533.

80 Goldingay, "Psalms 1-41," 102.

81 Jacobson, *The Royal Psalms and Jesus Messiah*, 192.

82 Mays, "Worship, World and Power: An Interpretation of Psalm 100," 321.

83 Anderson, *The Book of Psalms: Psalms 1-72*, 698.

84 Goldingay, *Psalms 42-89*, 135.

85 Schaefer, *Psalms*, 246.

to the presence of Yahweh."[86] As worshippers come into the presence of God, they are to raise the glad cultic shout unto God, worship God in the mood of rejoicing and with the resounding cry of singing voices.[87]

Worshipping with gladness implies outbursts of delight. The word 'gladness' is related to 'enthusiasm in function.' Therefore, the psalmist talks about an enthusiastic spirit in the presence of God. We see two aspects from the word 'gladness' in the context of worship. The hymn affirms that God wants worshippers to come and worship the true God with a heart of gladness. Gladness is also reflected in worship, revealing the joy and blessing of living in a right relationship with God who is the Shepherd and king and, who is good, merciful and faithful. Therefore, gladness is very significant for Israel application for Israel's worship and also vitally significant for our worship today.

Thirdly, the verb בוא 'to come' (Ps 100:2, 4). The word בוא is attached to a noun שער 'gate' which implies coming to the sanctuary for worship (Ps 100:4). The psalmist invites the whole world to come into Yahweh's presence, right through the gates into the very heart of the family of Yahweh for worship. The people are to come with a song of praise with thanksgiving.[88] "The aim in both praise and thanksgiving is to exalt and glorify God and the two belong together."[89]

Fourthly, the psalm emphasizes the use of *thank-offering* in worship. This psalm is present as a liturgy of entrance for the procession of pilgrims into the sanctuary bringing their thanks offerings to the Lord.[90] In a broader sense, thank offering can be an expression of gratitude to God not just limited through songs of thanksgiving, but also include as the offering of sacrifices to God. Anderson argues that Psalm 100 expresses that thanksgiving is an act of the whole worshipping community. The community has received and are blessed, and as such they offer their thanks and bless the name of the giver God.[91] Here, the psalmist conveys that the Lord is the object for worship.

Kraus claims that the cultic community is called to recognize and praise Yahweh in different forms because Yahweh sustains, leads and is kind and merciful to the people. The psalm strongly talks about the self-understanding of

---

86 Brueggemann, "Psalm 100," 65.

87 Leslie, *The Psalms: Translated and Interpreted in the Light of Hebrew Life and Worship*, He further comments that the "glad song" is threefold: 1) The Lord is conceived of as one, the clearly implied belief in monotheism. 2) The Lord as the Creator who created everything. 3) The Lord is the Shepherd who leads and provides. Thus the Lord deserves all praises and worship with a delightful spirit. 191.

88 Goldingay, *Psalms 42-89*, 136.

89 Tate, *Psalms 51-100*, 538.

90 Leslie, *The Psalms*, 191.

91 Anderson, *The Book of Psalms: Psalms 1-72*, 699.

the worship community.[92] It means that we need to understand that everything belongs to God and in return we need to acknowledge Yahweh as the only true and living God. He is the giver and provider. This is something the people of Israel often forgot (Jer 31:34). Therefore, the psalmist is expressing how self-understanding is deeply important for the worshippers of God. The psalmist says "Know that the Lord is God, it is he himself made us, and not we ourselves are his people and the flock of his pasture" (Ps 100:3). This statement refers to the awareness of God which awakens in the worshipper the sense of creaturehood, and thus human self-sufficiency vanishes."[93] Zorn argues that "know that Yahweh is God" literally means a recognition formula that acts as a confessional faith. For instance, Yahweh is God, there is no one like Yahweh the Lord (Ex 7:5, 8:10).

The form critical analysis shows that this is not simply talking about theory. It is "Israel's experience to know Yahweh as the only true and living God."[94] As the people of Israel experience the mighty works of God, they return to worship, offering their thank offering and blessing the name of Yahweh the king. This is how Psalm 100 depicts the importance of thanks offering in the form of sacrifices and blessings to the name of the Lord. Once a person know who the Lord is, they would definitely want to offer gifts to God. Looking into all these aspects, thank offerings enhance Israel's worship in various ways. As the Lord provides for our needs, we need to acknowlege the greatness of God with our offerings as a symbol of our faith to Yahweh the king.

10.5. Theological Concerns Pertaining to the Kingship Metaphor of God

In this section, I deal with the theological concerns which are linked to the kingship metaphor of Yahweh in the light of connotations which emerge from the exegetical studies of Psalm 100. They are: shepherding, and faithfulness. All these points denote the kingship metaphor of Yahweh.

10.5.1. Kingship and Shepherding

As shown in the text study, the role of the shepherd is to guide and feed the sheep and lead them to safety. The use of the metaphor of מרעית 'shepherding' in Psalm 100 speaks not only of the shepherd, but the relationship of both the shepherd and the sheep. The text mentions "Know that the Lord is God, it is he himself made us, and not we ourselves, we are his people and the flock of his pasture" (Ps 100:3[c]). Thus, shepherd imagery gives affirmations

92 Kraus, *Psalms 60-150*, 275.

93 Schaefer, *Psalms*, 247.

94 Zorn, *Psalms*, 238.

to the relationship between Yahweh and people.[95] The figurative language of the sheep and the shepherd expresses God's loving kindness toward the people (Ps 23, Isa 40:11). Shepherds are given the task to maintain welfare of the people. Shepherding is part of Yahweh's responsibility as he devotes himself to care for the sheep.[96] In Ancient West Asia, shepherding was the occupation of nomads and settled people alike. In support of this opinion, even in Mesopotamia and Egypt, shepherd was a title given to the king.[97] Eichrodt points out, "Alongside power, the ancient oriental ideal of kingship includes the protection the true shepherd gives to his flock, by leading the needy to pasture, providing food and drink, and establishing pasturages and places of safety."[98]

The prophet Ezekiel speaks about human shepherds. They were selfish shepherds who fed themselves, even at the expense of the sheep.[99] They ruled over the sheep with force and harshness (Eze 34:2-6). Whereas Yahweh, the king, who is the good shepherd, rescues and feeds the wandering sheep which refers to the relationship between God and human. God, the supreme shepherd, is tender and loving and is concerned about the welfare of the sheep.[100]

The metaphor of God as a shepherd is implied in several contexts. The depiction of Yahweh as a shepherd originated in Israel's life, especially in the desert. It is clear from several contexts that he should be understood as a shepherd who looks after the need of the people (Gen 33:13, Isa 40:11).[101] In the exilic context, the shepherd metaphor became meaningful. As the flocks scattered, Yahweh the king had to gather them as a shepherd would do. In response to this situation, major attention is given to the rescue of the flock and also to the harshness faced by the flock. Psalm 23 gives a full metaphor for Yahweh as *life-giving* which means to lead, restore and offer what they cannot secure for themselves.[102]

The acknowledgement that Yahweh is the shepherd of Israel grew in the religious experience of the people. For instance, people seek Yahweh's help and guidance in worship through praises and prayers for forgiveness. He is also described as a powerful leader who drives out the other nations and

95 Walter Brueggemann, *Theology of the Old Testament* (Minneapolis: Fortress Press, 2005), 260-261.

96 Allen, "שִׁיר," 161-162.

97 George Kaniarakath, "The Merciful God of the Prophets," *Bible Bhashyam,* vol. XXX1, no. 1 (March-December, 1981): 22.

98 Walter Eichrodt, "Ezekiel: A Commentary," in *The Old Testament Library* (Philadelphia: The Westminster John Knox Press, 1970), 469.

99 Kaniarakath, "The Merciful God of the Prophets," 22.

100 Kaniarakath, "The Merciful God of the Prophets," 23.

101 Jonker, "רעה," 1141.

102 Brueggemann, *Theology of the Old Testament*, 259-561.

makes place for his own flock (Pss 78:52-55, 70-72). For example, the return from the Babylonian exile is described in a similar way. Yahweh exercises the function of a shepherd who will pasture his people.[103] The fullest illustration of shepherding is found in Ezekiel 34. This text points out 'Israel's past and future' and also shows how irresponsible shepherds neglect their flocks. As a result, they encounter oppression and suffering. Therefore, responding to the context, Yahweh will act as a responsible shepherd and bring back what has been lost.[104] The Lord says, 'I will be the shepherd, "I will bring them out from the peoples and gather them from the countries, and will bring them into their own land, and I will feed them on the mountains of Israel, by the watercourses, and in all the inhabited parts of the land" (Ezek 34:13). The psalmist speaks of the Lord as a good shepherd on whom they depend on for everything and to whom alone they can turn for help.[105]

The worshippers realize that they are safe in the care of God, the faithful shepherd. People run to Yahweh seeking protection in time of crises. This saving act of Yahweh portrays a shepherd who leads his flock to safe pastures (Ex15:13, 17).[106] Even in the NT, the shepherding image functions meaningfully, "Jesus is the good shepherd who calls his own sheep by name and leads them out" (Jn 10:3). "I am the good shepherd, the good shepherd gives his life for the sheep" (Jn 10:11). Jesus had compassion for the crowd because they were like sheep without a shepherd.

The connotation of *shepherding* portrays the caring role of Yahweh the king. I will seek the lost, and I will bring back the strayed, and I will bind up the injured, and I will strengthen the weak (Ezek 34: 13, 16). Thus, shepherding denotes that the king protects and guides the people from danger and provides for their need.

10.5.2. Kingship and Faithfulness

Faithfulness refers to Yahweh's kingship metaphor. The qualities of loyalty, reliability and dependability are linked with the kingship of Yahweh. As the righteous king, he is faithful towards the covenant people through which the faithful act of Yahweh is declared to the world.

The text points out זחסדו ואמונתו לבית ישראל he (Yahweh) has remembered his kindness and steadfastness to the house of Israel' (Ps 98:3[a]). The psalmist

---

103 Jonker, "רעה," 1141. (Isa 40:11, 49: 9-13, Jer 23:1-8, 31: 8-14).

104 Brueggemann, *Theology of the Old Testament*, 260.

105 Weiser, *The Psalms: A Commentary*, 646-647. See Obert B. Chisholm, "A Theology of the Psalms," in *A Biblical Theology of the Old Testament*, edited by Roy B. Zuck (Chicago: Moody Press, 1991), 298. Bernhard W. Anderson, *Out of the Depths: The Psalms Speak for Us Today* (Louisville: Westminster John Knox Press, 2000), 46.Walter Brueggemann, *Worship in Ancient Israel: An Essential Guide* (Nashville: Abingdon Press, 2005), 44.

106 Jonker, "רעה," 114.

lays emphasis on the words like זכר 'remember' and אמונה 'steadfastness' which portray the true faithfulness of Yahweh towards the covenant people. Yahweh the king, has shown his אמונה 'faithfulness' to the house of Israel.[107] Chisholm suggests that one of the important attributes of Yahweh the king, is אמונה 'faithfulness' which is found in heaven and continues to surround him as he rules from above. As a result, Yahweh's faithfulness is described through his words and deeds and his promises are reliable. Yahweh's reliability and faithfulness are revealed in his protection and deliverance to the house of Israel.[108]

Yahweh's faithful actions play an important role in his divine kingship. As it is portrayed in Israel's history, Yahweh shows forgiveness to those who acknowledge him and trust in him in times of need. The psalmist says, לנו ופדנו למען חסדך 'redeem us for the sake of your kindness' (Ps 44:27). The psalmists normally sought Yahweh's faithfulness and mercy when they were overwhelmed by powerful enemies or by their sinfulness.[109] The history of Israel reveals Yahweh's faithfulness towards the nation of Israel.

Goodness corresponds to the faithfulness of Yahweh. Yahweh, the Most High God, is also a good God who possesses the divine quality of excellence to rule. "Goodness is the very essence of God's nature."[110] The term טוב 'good' is the designation of God. The root word can supplement the word חסד 'steadfast love.'[111] God as טוב acquires the meanings of blessing and salvation (Pss 27:3, 65:5, 128:5, Neh 9:25, 35). It is also considered as well-being. טוב comes to mean goodness and thereby is related to the meaning of חסד (Ex 33:19, Isa 63:7).[112] The word 'good 'points 'to do good things.' Therefore, the king's role is to do good things for the people. The Psalter mentions the phrase *God is good* in several places (Pss 86: 5, 100:5, 106: 1, 107: 1, 118: 29, 145:9). Frequent references elsewhere indicate the goodness of God in the OT (1 Chron 16:34, Ezra 3:11, Jer 33:11). The Lord said, "I will make all my goodness pass before you" (Ex 33:19).[113] God is the one who works wonders and he even provides all good things to all creatures. The psalmist attributes to Yahweh good qualities like faithfulness, mercifulness and protection. This is

107 Kizhakkeyil, *The Psalms: The Prayer Book of the Bible*, 363.

108 Chisholm, "A Theology of the Psalms," 298.

109 Chisholm, "A Theology of the Psalms," 298.

110 Weiser, *The Psalms: A Commentary*, 647.

111 H. J. Stoebe, "טוב," in *Theological Lexicon of the Old Testament,* vol. 2, edited by Ernst Jenni and Claus Westermann, translated. Mark E. Biddle (Peabody: Hendrickson Publishers, Inc, 1997), 494. See Bernhard W. Anderson, *Out of the Depths: The Psalms Speak for Us Today* (Louisville: Westminster John Knox Press, 2000), 144.

112 Stoebe, "טוב," 495. (Cf. Hos 3:5, Pss 23:6, 68:11).

113 Robert P. Gordon, "טוב," in *New International Dictionary of Old Testament Theology & Exegesis,* vol. 2, edited by Willem A. VanGemeren (Carlisle: Paternoster Press, 1997), 355.

the way the psalmist reveals the goodness of God (Pss 71:22, 78:41, 89:19).[114] טוב יהוה לכל 'the Lord is good to all' (Ps 145:9). The psalmist affirms that Yahweh is worthy of praise because of his greatness and goodness. Yahweh has compassion on all he has made.

The priestly blessing in the Qumran initiation ceremony includes the prayer that "God will bless you with all good and keep you from evil" (1QS 2:2-3). Also 1QS 11: 14 mentions that God covers the iniquities of the psalmist by his great goodness.[115] Truly, God is good to Israel. The goodness of Yahweh is demonstrated by caring for the flock. All these features, Yahweh is טוב 'good' and his הסד 'steadfast love' and אמונה 'faithfulness' to all generations explicitly portray the highest quality of God.[116] The goodness of Yahweh is linked with his enduring truthfulness and love as shown in his protection and provision for the people. God's goodness also incorporates all the things that he created. The psalmist says כי־טוט יהוה 'for the Lord is good' (Ps 100:5).

The psalmist says טוב־יהוה לכל ורחמיו על־כל־מעשיו 'The Lord is good to all, and His mercies are over all His works' (Ps 145:9). God's goodness is like a fountain from where all good things spring forth.[117] The goodness of God, his grace and faithfulness are the unshakable foundations on which the community's experience of his steadfast love is built.[118] This concept illustrates co-existence, the fact that the goodness of God and his love are always to be an expression of his power.

The connotation of Yahweh's faithfulness refers to Yahweh's loyalty, goodness and loving kindness toward the people, to those who love him and keep his commandments (Deut 7:9). The faithfulness of Yahweh indicates the goodness of God. The psalmist declares that Yahweh is faithful and merciful. The faithfulness of God is demonstrated through his grace; and goodness. Thus, the faithfulness of Yahweh has a great significance because he exercises humility and kindness in his kingship.

Summary

We can conclude that Psalm 100 summarizes the preceding enthronement psalms. Dahood claims that though this hymn does not specifically refer to God as king, its phraseology sufficiently resembles that of the preceding psalms celebrating Yahweh's kingship.[119] In support of Dahood, Wilson suggests that this 'thanks psalm' enjoins the people to serve and praise in the kingly courts

114 Pezhumkattil, "Israel's Faith Reflected in the Psalms," 164.

115 Gordon, "טוב," 356.

116 Kizhakkeyil, *The Psalms: The Prayer Book of the Bible*, 367.

117 Chisholm, "A Theology of the Psalms," 297-298. (cf. Pss 106:1, 107:1, 136:1, 34:8, 54:6).

118 Weiser, *The Psalms: A Commentary*, 647.

119 Dahood, *Psalms 51-100: The Anchor Bible*, 371.

of Yahweh. Therefore, Psalm 100 is a fitting conclusion to the litany of praise expressed in the proceeding psalms particularly Pss 96-99.[120]

The metaphor of shepherd is explicitly mentioned in the text. Shepherd is a connotation of 'king'. In fact, 'king' is called as shepherd in Ancient West Asia context. Looking into the whole argument of Psalm 100, the following points emerge from the above analysis. *First,* though the text fails in emphasizing the kingship metaphor as compared to other enthronement texts, the psalmist expresses the nature of Yahweh as king which is parallel to the kingship psalms. *Secondly,* the psalm calls the entire world to worship and honour Yahweh by the phrase 'shout to the Lord all the earth' (Ps 100:1). *Thirdly,* the significance of thanksgiving and its implication for Israel's worship are explicitly mentioned in the text of Psalms 100. *Fourthly,* the word 'goodness' is drawn from concrete acts marked with the two nouns of steadfast love and faithfulness which portray Yahweh's unconditional commitment to the Israelites and also to the entire world at large. Thus, Psalm 100 is inclusive in nature in the sense that all people are invited to worship.

120 Gerald Henry Wilson, *The Editing of the Hebrew Psalter* (Chico: Society of Biblical Literature, 1985), 217.

Chapter 11

Kingship of Yahweh and Its Implications for Early Christian Worship and in a Pluralistic Context

Introduction

In chapters 3 to chapter 10, I looked at the kingship metaphor following historical literary exegesis of all the enthronement psalms and elaborated the theological themes pertaining to the kingship metaphor. This chapter focuses on the implications of the kingship metaphor for early Christian worship and a pluralistic context. As seen in the previous chapters, the enthronement psalms declare the kingship of Yahweh, and this becomes significant for worship. Yahweh, who delivers humans in times of trouble, is also the God whom humans are called to worship, acknowledge and give thanks to.[1] Gunkel,[2] and Westermann[3] talk about particularity and universality of worship, and elements of worship like praise, hymns and thanksgiving as being essential for

---

1 Patrick D. Miller, "Him Only Shall You Serve Reflections on the Meaning of Old Testament," *Andover Newton Quarterly,* vol. 11, no. 3 (Jan, 1971): 141-142.

2 Hermann Gunkel, *Introduction to Psalms: The Genres of the Religious Lyric of Israel* (Macon, Georgia: Mercer University Press, 1998), 48-49.

3 Claus Westermann, *The Praise of God in the Psalms*, translated by Keith R. Crim (Virginia: John Knox Press, 1965), 31. (1). The ideas of descriptive praise (talks about giving praises to God through hymns for the mighty actions of Yahweh). (2). Declarative praise (talks about the song of thanks and praises to God for a specific deed).

worship. Eaton,[4] and Brueggemann,[5] however, stress the significance of music and gestures in worship (Pss 98:5-9, 148, 150).

The above scholars discussed some of the implications inadequately. Also, they focused on the Psalter in general, but did not give special attention to the enthronement psalms. My focus is to bring together the major implications of the kingship metaphor in the enthronement psalms which linked to New Testament and Christian history. The *first* section focuses on the use of kingship metaphor in the New Testament worship. The *second* section deals with the use and implications of the kingship metaphor from Church history. I have dealt with the first two points before coming to the Indian context because they provide the bridge methodologically to the Indian context as lordship denotation flows from kingship metaphor. *Thirdly,* I focus on the denotation, connotations and their implications for worship in the Indian context.

11.1. Kingship Metaphor in New Testament Worship

This section focuses on how the kingship of Yahweh is a link between the OT and NT. New Testament continues to express the importance of the kingship metaphor in the context of worship based generally on the OT and in particular in the enthronement psalms. Moritz[6] and Watts[7] suggest that NT frequently cites the OT, especially the book of psalms. Thus, I focus on the kingship of Jesus and worship of the early Christian.

11.1.1. Kingship of Jesus and Worship

The phrase *King of kings* is not only mentioned in the OT but occurs even in NT. King of kings is parallel to some other titles in the NT like 'Jesus king of the Jews' (Mat 27:37, Jn 18:28-40, Mk 15:2, 12, 18). Bruner comments that the Roman sign placed over the head of Jesus was, *this is Jesus the king of the Jews meaning King of believers.*[8] The nature of the crucified Jesus demonstrates the

4 John Eaton, *The Psalms: A Historical and Spiritual Commentary with an Introduction and New Translation* (London: Continuum International Publishing Group, 2005), 13.

5 Walter Brueggemann, *Worship in Ancient Israel: An Essential Guide*(Nashville: Abingdon Press, 2005), 20. See John Goldingay, "Psalms 90-150," in *Baker Commentary on the Old Testament Wisdom and Psalms*, vol. 3, edited by Tremper Longman III (Grand Rapids: Academic Press, 2008), 137.

6 Thorsten Moritz, *A Profound Mystery: The Use of the Old Testament in Ephesians* (Leiden: E. J. Brill, 1996), 13.

7 Rikk Watts, "The Psalms in Mark's Gospel," in *The Psalms in the New Testament* (London: T & T Clark International, 2004), 42. See Hughes Oliphant Old, *Worship: Reformed According to Scripture* (Louisville: Westminster John Knox Press, 2002), 35-36.

8 Frederick Dale Bruner, "The Churchbook Matthew 13-28," in *Matthew: A Commentary*, vol. 2 (Grand Rapids: William B. Eerdmans Publishing Company, 2004), 735.

kingship of God. All who believe in Christ as king are circumcised in hearts by true faith in Christ.[9]

Several places in NT mention the use of the enthronement psalms and draw parallel expressions. Moyise remarks that when the trumpet blows, people will hear the victory of the Lord (Rev 11:15). This reference especially runs parallel with the enthronement psalms (Ps 99:1). John borrows the idea of Yahweh's reign and the rage of the nations.[10] The dominion and rule of this world have been given to God, Jesus Christ, who shall "reign forever and ever."[11] It is a promise of victory for the Lamb in the battle, the Lamb will overcome all the adversaries for he is Lord of lords and King of kings. This phrase emphasizes on the sovereignty of God which is described in the enthronement psalms (Rev 17:14, 19:16).[12] The enthronement psalms clearly denote Yahweh as king sitting on a throne (Ps 47:9). This idea is reflected in the NT when John uses the expression "seated on throne" in several places (Rev 4:2-3, 9-10, 22:1). In all these references, Jesus is also seated on the throne which recalls the idea that the son of man will sit on the throne of glory (Mt 19:28, 25:31).[13]

Worship and singing were a vital part in the life and ministry of Jesus, the king of the Jews. This is illustrated in Mark's account of the last supper. "After singing hymns, they went out to the Mount of Olives" (Mk 14:26). Averbeck suggests that seeking and worshipping God in spirit means worship should come from within us, with the inspiration of the Holy Spirit. Also, seeking and worshipping God in truth means worship must be truthful and founded in the word of God which refers to Jesus Christ, king of the Jews. The point is that spirit and truth go together in authentic worship (Jn 4:24).[14] A principle of worship in spirit combines two areas, the human spirit and God as spirit. The Holy Spirit renews us and stimulates us to worship God in spirit since God is spirit. Here, the connection of human beings to God's spirit leads us to worship God in truth. The truth about God inspires true worship.[15]

---

9 Bruner, "The Church book Matthew 13-28," 735.

10 Steve Moyise, "The Psalms in the Book of Revelation," in *The Psalms in the New Testament,* edited by Steve Moyise and Maarten J. J. Menken (London: T & T Clark International, 2004), 240.

11 Robert H. Mounce, "The Book of Revelation," in *The New International Commentary on the New Testament* (Grand Rapids: William B. Eerdmans Publishing Company, 1998), 226.

12 Mounce, "The Book of Revelation," 319.

13 Moyise, "The Psalms in the Book of Revelation," 243.

14 Richard E. Averbeck, "Worship God in Spirit," in *Authentic Worship: Hearing Scripture's Voice, Applying Its Truths*, edited by Herbert W. Bateman (Grand Rapids: Kregel Publications, 2002), 82.

15 Averbeck, "Worship God in Spirit," 102.

Dunn argues that the gospel of John is against a growing "formalism and institutionalization" in the context of worship. God seeks "a worship which is living, the ever new response to God who is spirit as prompted and enabled by the spirit of God in the light of the truth of Jesus."[16] Jesus invites believers to worship in spirit and in truth. Many of the psalms contain prophetic oracles that reveal the reign of the Christ.[17] Throughout the ministry of Jesus, it reveals his kingship to the people.

The Lord of lords will strike down the nations, and all the nations are subject to the righteous king.[18] The white horse is called faithful and true, and John is using this thought in Revelation to express that Jesus will judge the world with righteousness.[19] "Who will not fear and bring glory to God? For you alone are holy. All nations will come and worship before you" (Rev 15:4). Here, the universal recognition of the Lord as the one true God is clearly indicated as seen in enthronement psalms. This echoes the belief that "during the Messianic age the nations of the world will worship the God of Israel" (cf. Phil 2:9-11). The nations shall come and give praise and glorify the name of God because God alone is holy and deserves homage from all the nations. The ways of God the king are just and true. The divine kingship of God is fully manifested through all the wonders and righteous acts (Rom 15:9-12).[20]

11.1.2. Kingship and Early Christian Worship

It is logical that early Christian worship was connected to Jewish worship in their use of psalms, especially the kingship psalms of the synagogue. The worship of the early Christians would have been influenced by Jewish worship (Acts 24:5).[21] Early Christian worship copied many of the worship traditions of the synagogue like scripture reading, sermon, prayers and psalmody. Christians gathered for prayer and their prayer meetings began with the whole congregation singing psalms, probably, including the enthronement psalms (Acts 4:23-31). Paul states that whenever they were to gather together for worship, they were to sing psalms (1 Cor 14:26).[22]

Early Christians maintained the tradition of Jewish worship. They attended worship daily and spent much time together in worship (Acts 2:46-

16 James D. G. Dunn, *Unity and Diversity in the New Testament: An Inquiry into the Character of Earliest Christianity* (London: SCM Press, 1993), 131.

17 Hughes Oliphant Old, *Worship: Reformed According to Scripture* (Louisville: Westminster John Knox Press, 2002), 37.

18 Mounce, *The Book of Revelation*, 356.

19 Moyise, "The Psalms in the Book of Revelation," 244.

20 Mounce, *The Book of Revelation*, 287.

21 Barry C. Johnson, *A Change is Gonna Come: The Transformation of a Traditional to a Contemporary Worship Celebration* (Bloomington: Author House, 2008), 17.

22 Old, *Worship: Reformed According to Scripture*, 36.

47, 3:1, 5:12). It is also suggested that they continued offering their gifts at the altar (Mt 5:23).[23] The pattern of worship was not exclusive to the temple or synagogues, but it was also present in the family home. They gathered in private houses for prayer and worship, followed by teaching, similar to the pattern of the synagogue service, while also including other elements like fellowship meals, and the singing of psalms in a more spontaneous manner (Acts 2:42, 5:42). House church worship was important for Paul's mission because more gentiles were believers but were not welcome to worship in synagogues (Rom 16:5, 1 Cor 16:19, Col 4:15). Paul retained the basis of worship as expressed in the OT and in the enthronement psalms and expressed Christ's presence through mutual relationships and ministries. The "body of Christ comes to visible expression pre-eminently in and through worship" (1 Cor 12-14).[24]

The early Christians loved singing in their worship. Even in prison, Paul and Silas sang hymns in their devotion despite persecution. Believers of Christ sang psalms and hymns and spiritual songs in praising the Lord (Eph 5:19, Col 3:16).[25] The gospels provide several psalms of praise from the worship of early church (Lk 2:13-14, 1:46-55, 1:68:79, 2:29-32). The singing of these hymns in the common meal was probably imitated in the worship of the early Christian church.[26] Similarly, McKinnon suggests that they sang the Hallel Hymns from Psalms 113-18 and identified it with the Passover meal (Mt 26:30 Mk 14:26).[27] All these indicate that the early Christians used psalms in their worship. The hymns and psalms that were used in worship were spiritual songs which means that they were songs of the Holy Spirit exalting the kingship of Yahweh through Jesus Christ (Acts 4:25, Eph 5:19). Christian worship was inspired and empowered by the Holy Spirit. Thus, early Christian worship indicates spirit filled worship.[28] Paul expressed that everything in the service of worship should emphasize kingship of Christ and thereby edify the Church of Christ (1 Cor 14:1-6).

11.2. Kingship Metaphor for Worship in the Church History

Here, I look at the use of psalms from the perspective of Church history because psalms and kingship metaphor continued to be important throughout Church history. The psalms and kingship metaphor of Yahweh helped church

23 Dunn, *Unity and Diversity in the New Testament,* 127.

24 Dunn, *Unity and Diversity in the New Testament,* 129.

25 Johnson, *A Change is Gonna Come,* 18.

26 Johnson, *A Change is Gonna Come,* 17.

27 James McKinnon, *Music in Early Christian Literature: Cambridge Reading in the Literature of Music* (Cambridge: Cambridge University Press, 1987), 13.

28 Old, *Worship: Reformed According to Scripture*, 5.

fathers and the reformers, particularly, Martin Luther, John Calvin and Zwingli to propagate the message to the people and also to enhance worship.

11.2.1. Kingship and Church Fathers in Worship

The psalms in general and enthronement psalms in particular remained important through the Christian generations. Many of the fathers like Origen and Saint Jerome wrote commentaries on the book of Psalms. Especially in the fourth century, psalms were sung everywhere, during worship and even while walking. Jerome claims that farmers sang the psalms even when they were working.[29] Clement of Alexandria insisted on Christians praising Yahweh in the Psalter by giving reference to Psalm 150. He suggested the use of musical instruments in worshipping Yahweh the king which are given "allegorical meaning in the psalms" but not to use the instruments that were used in idolatry.[30]

Jerome revised the Old Testament Latin version of some Old Testament books including the Psalms (*Psalterium Vetus*). He included elements of Jewish scholarship in his Old Testament commentaries, which included the book of Psalms.[31] Augustine talked about the distinctiveness of the Psalms among the other books of the Bible. He claimed that "Music is honourably placed in many passages of the sacred Scriptures."[32] Therefore, psalms were effectively used in worship by giving due praises to Yahweh the king.

Thomas Aquinas used psalms to enlighten the life of the prayer in his *Postilla Super Psalmos*. His commentaries discuss how the psalms are related to prophecy and can be interpreted at two levels-the Davidic narrative and prophetic role of Christ.[33] The Church fathers gave an important place to the Psalter and the singing of hymns exalting Yahweh's kingship. This corresponds to the use of music in enthronement psalms and kingship metaphor for the worship.

11.2.2. Kingship and Reformers in Worship

Luther argues the idea of *iustitia Dei* (latin) translated as the 'righteousness of God.' The righteousness of God is a recurrent phrase in both the Psalms and Romans. Yahweh the king, acts justly. Luther believed that righteousness of God refers to the idea that God judges impartially. God judges everybody

29 Michael Barber, *Singing in the Reign: The Psalms and Liturgy of God's Kingdom* (Steubenville: Emmaus Road Publishing, 2001), 24.

30 Bruce K. Waltke and James M. Houston, *The Psalms as Christian Worship: A Historical Commentary* (Grand Rapids: William B. Eerdmans Publishing Company, 2010), 40.

31 Waltke and Houston, *The Psalms as Christian Worship: A Historical Commentary*, 46.

32 James McKinnon, *Music in Early Christian Literature: Cambridge Reading in the Literature of Music* (Cambridge: Cambridge University Press, 1987), 165.

33 Waltke and Houston, *The Psalms as Christian Worship: A Historical Commentary*, 65-57.

with complete justice.[34] The concept of the righteousness of God is parallel with the enthronement psalms. The enthronement psalms clearly address the righteousness of God (Pss 96:10-13, 97: 10-12). Luther claimed that all Christians were priests and needed no mediator other than Christ before God, neither priests nor other human power possesses divine power but God alone.[35] "He is a God of majesty and power, inscrutable, terrifying, devastating, and consuming in his anger. Yet the All Terrible is All Merciful too."[36] 'God is holy, he is mighty,' has an 'energetic power' and 'always active.'[37] This refers to the kingship of Yahweh, who has the authority over all. The enthronement texts explicitly mention the mightiness of Yahweh the king.

It is mentioned in Calvin's commentaries that God governs his people by his hands and all others who are given responsibility to rule over the Church are subject to him. This affirms the kingship of Yahweh.[38] Calvin viewed the psalms as the canonical manual of piety. The Psalter perfectly taught the right manner of praising and worshipping God. The psalms provide a vehicle for communal worship. They move us to trust and praise God (cf. Pss 96, 98, 99, 100).We are God's flock (Ps 100:4). The psalms, in general, and enthronement psalms, in particular, present to us a mirror in which we are led to praise God and find rest in Yahweh's sovereignty.[39]

Calvin's concern for the liturgy was part of the building of the Church. In his ministry, he advocated the singing of psalms. Calvin suggested three important elements in the structure of "public worship service preaching, prayers (including singing) and the administration of the sacraments."[40] Through singing hymns, worshippers exalt the sovereignty of God in worship. Psalm singing is considered a significant vocal contribution of people in the worship service. During the Reformation period, Calvin gave importance to the Psalter linking it to the text that was preached to the congregation. "Psalm-

---

34 Alister E. McGrath, *Reformation Thought: An Introduction* (Oxford: Blackwell Publishing, 1999), 106-107.

35 Paul R. Spickard and Kevin M. Cragg, *A Global History of Christians: How Everyday Believers Experienced their World* (Grand Rapids: Baker Academic, 1994), 177.

36 Roland H. Bainton, *Here I Stand: A Life of Martin Luther* (New York: Abingdon Press, 1950), 385.

37 Bernhard Lohse, *Marthin Luther's Theology : Its Historical and Systematic Development*, trans. Roy A. Harrisville (Minneapolis: Fortress Press, 2006), 212.

38 Joseph Haroutunian, "Calvin: Commentaries," in *The Library of Christian Classics*, vol. XXIII (London: SCM Press Ltd, 1958), 362.

39 Joel R. Beeke, "Calvin on Piety," in *The Cambridge Companion to John Calvin*, edited by Donald K. McKim (Cambridge: Cambridge University, 2004), 137. See Joseph Haroutunian, "Calvin: Commentaries," in *The Library of Christian Classics,* vol. XXIII edited by (London: SCM Press Ltd, 1958), 361-365.

40 Wulfert de Greef, "Calvin's Writings," in *The Cambridge Companion to John Calvin*, Donald K. McKim (Cambridge: Cambridge University, 2004), 53.

singing disciplines the heart's affections in the school of faith and lifts the believer to God. Psalm-singing amplifies the effect of the word upon the heart and multiplies the spiritual energy of the Church. The Psalms can stimulate us to raise our hearts to God."[41] Psalms-singing is associated with the kingship metaphor as people give praises to Yahweh the king.

Bromiley points out that Zwingli and Bullinger were of the opinion that God gives his message to humans in a gentle and attractive way, through parables, proverbs and riddles and bring humans to the knowledge of God.[42] "God's word has its own clarity and its own ability to convinced people."[43] Potter comments that the reformer Zwingli said, "Scripture has its own interpreter. Every chapter of the Old Testament foreshadowed the coming of Christ; the poetry of the psalms contained Christian education."[44] He claims the "absolute sovereignty of God" over all the people.[45] This is also indicated in the enthronement psalms where psalmists strongly claim the absolute sovereignty of Yahweh over all the creation (cf. Pss 95: 4-5, 97:7). Thus, the kingship metaphor plays a significant role during Reformation period as the reformers portray Yahweh as the king who controls all human authority.

11.3. Denotation and Connotations of the Kingship for Worship in the Indian Context

As seen in the previous chapters, the Psalmists call upon all people to give due worship to Yahweh because he is the king, the creator, the sustainer and the owner of all things. Thus, our worship should be a spontaneous expression of creatures to their Creator.[46] The kingship metaphor of Yahweh is the central aspect of Christian worship. Therefore, in this section, I deal with the denotation and connotations of kingship metaphor and implications for today's worship as it has immense relevance for worship in the Indian context.

11.3.1. Kingship and Sovereignty in Worship

Sovereignty is a denotative meaning of Yahweh the king because he alone possess the power to rule. The sovereignty of Yahweh is demonstrated in the enthronement psalms. The psalmist stresses that Israel's worship declares the sovereignty of God to the world. The sovereignty of God stands for the

41 Beeke, "Calvin on Piety," 138.

42 G. W. Bromiley, "Zwingli and Bullinger," in *The Library of Christian Classics,* vol. XXIV (London: SCM Press, 1958), 72-73.

43 Jaques Courvoisier, *Zwingli: A Reformed Theologian* (Virginia: John Knox Press, 1963), 36.

44 G. Richard Potter, *Zwingli* (Cambridge: Cambridge University Press, 1976), 295.

45 McGrath, *Reformation Thought: An Introduction*, 133.

46 Phillip G. Kayser, *Delighting in God's Kingship Over Worship* (Omaha: Biblical Blueprints. Org, 2009), 11.

supremacy of God, the kingship of God and the godhead of God. Leslie comments that the pagan nations of the world tremble under the sovereignty of God. The psalmist summons upon the nations to exalt the dominant power of Yahweh.[47]

Mays asserts the following points on the sovereignty of God. *First,* Yahweh is the ruler of the gods (Ps 95:3). The true worshippers of Yahweh cannot worship these gods. All the other gods worship and exalt Yahweh above all (Ps 97:7, 9). *Secondly,* Yahweh rules over the world and all existence. Yahweh's majesty is superior to the mighty waters (Ps 93:3-4). The depths and heights of the earth, sea and dry land belong to Yahweh. *Thirdly*, Yahweh rules over all the nations and this kingship is to be proclaimed to all the nations (Pss 47:2, 99:2, 96:5, 97:6-7).[48] The action of Yahweh's sovereignty indicates that the rule of Yahweh is powerful, awesome and effective, and that it expounds the reign of Yahweh over the universe in all its existence.[49] Yahweh is honoured objectively and directly as the supreme God over all powers in all the enthronement texts.[50] The concept of the sovereignty of Yahweh is addressed and elaborated, for instance, in phrases like 'Yahweh is our God' and 'we are the people of God's pasture' (Pss 95:7, 100:3) which the Israelite congregations possibly shouted out.

None, can defeat the counsel of Yahweh, for sovereignty belongs to Yahweh, who rules and who is the governor over the nations (Pss 22: 28, 93:1, 95:3, Dan 4:35).[51] The immovability of the world points out the authenticity of Yahweh's reign. The trustworthiness of Yahweh's decrees and holiness parallel Yahweh's sovereignty over the primeval chaos. Yahweh is a divine warrior. The appearance of Yahweh overwhelms earth and the peoples in its acts of righteous judgement of the world, and in maintaining the rule of highest sovereignty.[52] The psalmist brings out the mightiness of God through verses like 'by the word of the Lord, the heavens were made' and 'all the hosts by the breath of Yahweh's mouth' (Pss 33:6, 96:5). The word and breath signify and symbolize the sovereignty of God.[53] The sovereignty of God over all the gods has great implications in the context of Indian Christian worship. When

47 Elmer A. Leslie, *The Psalms: Translated and Interpreted in the Light of Hebrew Life and Worship* (New York: Abingdon Press, 1949), 83.

48 James Luther May, *The Lord Reigns: A Theological Handbook to the Psalms* (Louisville: Westminster John Knox Press, 1994), 14.

49 Mays, *The Lord Reigns: A Theological Handbook to the Psalms*, 15.

50 Erhard S. Gerstenberger, *Psalms, Part 2 and Lamentations: The Forms of the Old Testament Literature*, vol. XV (Grand Rapids: William B. Eerdmans Publishing Company, 2001), 175.

51 James P. Arthur, *God Deserves Our Worship* (Mustang: Tate Publishing & Enterprises, 2010), 51.

52 Mays, *The Lord Reigns: A Theological Handbook to the Psalms*, 15.

53 Arthur, *God Deserves Our Worship*, 51.

we say that God is sovereign, in an actual sense, we declare that God is God and worthy of worship. When we declare the sovereignty of God, it means Yahweh is the Most High, Almighty, and the possessor of all power in heaven and earth.

11.3.2. Kingship and Exclusive Worship

Exclusive worship is an integral part of the connotation of kingship metaphor and it has implications for worship in the Indian context. What does exclusive worship mean in the context of Christian worship today? What part does our worship play in the totality of our relationship with God? "Yahweh our God, Yahweh one" (Deut 6:4). This central confession of Israel's faith makes it clear enough that God is one; it is an affirmation that Yahweh has exclusive allegiance and that Israel will have no other gods besides Yahweh.[54] The worship of Yahweh by the covenant people is set apart as exclusive. Allegiance to Yahweh alone is considered the primary command in the context of Israel's worship. The psalmist comments that cultic infidelity and graven images provoke God's wrath (Ps 78:56-62).[55] Israel's worship is exclusively focused on God who is greatly exalted as the King of kings and the Lord of the whole world.[56]

The concept of monotheism in Israel's worship shows that the Psalter maintained exclusive worship. For Kumar, Israelite worship is focused on Yahweh alone.[57] Though there are different opinions in regard to exclusive worship, the enthronement psalms clearly portray the theological significance of worshipping of Yahweh alone. There is only one holy God and one rock of refuge. Therefore, the psalmist stresses worshipping the highest and the only Yahweh. Lucas argues that the Israelites were commanded to worship no god other than Yahweh. The enthronement psalms focus on Yahweh's incomparability without denying the existence of other gods.[58] The psalmist claims that Yahweh presides in the council of the gods and sentences all the other gods to death for failing to uphold justice (Ps 82). This is a way of emphasizing the absolute exclusive worship of Yahweh; Yahweh is the only God (Ps 115:4-7). The Psalms express the experience of a special sense of

54 John Goldingay, *Key Questions about Christian Faith: Old Testament Answers* (Grand Rapids: Brazos Press, 2010), 9.

55 Stephen L. Cook, *The Social Roots of Biblical Yahwism* (Atlanta: Society of Biblical Literature, 2004), 36.

56 John Goldingay, *Songs from a Strange Land: Psalms 42-51* (Illinois: InterVarsity Press, 1978), 81.

57 Rathna Kumar, "The Role of the Environment in the Worship of Israel," *ABS Journal,* vol. 3, no. 1 (April, 2011): 68.

58 Ernest C. Lucas, *Exploring the Old Testament: A Guide to the Psalms & Wisdom Literature*, vol. 3 (Downers Grove: InterVarsity Press, 2003), 52.

God's presence in worship which means the one and only true God speaks to true worshippers.[59]

The Psalter gives a clear picture of the full dimension of God's exclusive claim. God rebukes imperfect worship (Ps 50). The psalmist asserts an experiential understanding of what is involved in the first commandment and the reciprocity inherent within it.[60] Therefore, the psalmist urges the worshipper to give honour to Yahweh with a clean heart (Pss 29:1-2, 96:7-8). Israel is Yahweh's personal possession, meaning it has no right to worship other gods but only the holy God.[61] Yahweh the king demands exclusive worship from the chosen people. This concept has significance for Christian worship in the multi-religious context of India. What is religious pluralism? According to S.J. Samartha "Religious pluralism is a part of the larger plurality of races, peoples, and cultures, of social structures, economic system and political patterns, of languages and symbols, all of which are part of the total human heritage. Religious pluralism, that is, the fact that different religions respond to the Mystery of Ultimate Reality or *sat* or *theos* in different ways…."[62]

What did the psalmist says in the context of religious pluralism? In response to religious pluralism, the psalmist affirms that "there shall be no strange god among you; you shall not bow down to a foreign god. I am the Lord your God, who brought you up out of the land of Egypt" (Ps 81:9-10). It implies that if Israel turns to the gods of Canaan in worship, they violate their commitment to Yahweh. Mohol claims that Israel's religious tradition strongly affirms that Yahweh alone is God and this opposes any rival claim of divinity and establishes the concept of universality as God of all.[63] Each of these texts (Ex 20:2-3, Deut 5:7, Ps 81:9) indicates that Yahweh commanded Israel to have 'no other gods' besides their sole authentic God. Their main message is the exclusive worship owed to Yahweh. Yahweh is the sole Lord over all the earth.[64] Eaton asserts that Yahweh is the holy one who alone is to be worshipped. This exclusive role is marked with the phrase that Yahweh

59 Lucas, *Exploring the Old Testament*, 56. (cf. Pss 24:6, 27:4, 42:1-2, 84:7).

60 Patrick D. Miller, The *Way of the Lord: Essays in Old Testament Theology* (Michigan: William B. Eerdmans Publishing Company, 2007), 114.

61 John Goldingay, *Old Testament Theology: Israel's Faith*, vol. 2 (Illinois: InterVarsity Press, 2006), 71, 75.

62 S. J. Samartha, *One Christ Many Religions: Toward a Revised Christology* (Bangalore: *SATHRI*, 1992), 4.

63 Eliya Mohol, "Prophetic and Popular Responses to Religious Pluralism in Jeremiah," *UBS Journal,* vol. 6, no. 2 (2009): 42.

64 Stephen L. Cook, *The Social Roots of Biblical Yahwism*. Atlanta: Society of Biblical Literature, 2004), 91-92.

reigns and no other (Pss 93:1, cf. 23:1).[65] There are many gods and goddesses, but there is only one true God who deserves to be revered. In my opinion, the context of religious plurality, and the affirmation that besides Yahweh there is no true god is a great challenge for the true worshippers of Yahweh. Hence, the connotative of exclusive worship which was a part of the OT now becomes pertinent in religious pluralistic worship in the Indian context.

11.3.3. Kingship and Universal Worship

Universality denotes the connotation of the kingship metaphor of Yahweh. The nations belong to Yahweh; they are destined to come and bow down to honour Yahweh (Ps 86:9).[66] Glasser asserts that Yahweh demands that the whole earth and all the families of the nations worship Yahweh.[67] At the same time, Flynn also affirms that the kingship of Yahweh is not limited to the temple. The kingship of Yahweh is not even limited to Israel. Rather, the families of the peoples are invited to come and worship Yahweh (96:7-10). כל הארץ 'all will bow down and worship Yahweh and thus reinforce the scope of the kingship (Ps 96:9). The psalmist emphasizes universalistic kingship twice with the rhetorical expression of Yahweh as judge especially in Psalm 96 (Ps 96:13).[68] In a wider context, the enthronement psalms link Yahweh's kingship to salvific acts (Pss 95:1, 96:2, 97:10).

The whole universe is invited to come and worship in the presence of Yahweh. They can come right through the gates into the very courtyard of the house of Yahweh where the householder receives and welcomes guests into the heart of the family (Ps 100:3-4).[69] The invitation to the world to join the covenant people in worship and confession shows that the psalmist knows that God's way with Israel is God's way with the whole world. Thus, the universalism claim is explicitly indicated in the invitation of the worship of Yahweh. In other words, the invitation has universal scope (Pss 47; 1, 66:1, 96:1, 98:4).[70] God's kingly rule is identified with a particular people, the seed of Abraham, with whom Yahweh had established a special covenantal

---

65 Eaton, *The Psalms,* 28. See Paluri Wilson, "Religious Convergense and Globalization in the Indian Context" *Journal of Mission and Intercultural Studies,* vol. 1, no. 1 (April, 2014): 77-87. Plamthodathil S. Jacob, *JMIS* "Doing Mission in the Pluralistic Context of India" vol.1, no. 1 (April, 2014): 7-23.

66 Goldingay, *Old Testament Theology: Israel's Faith*, 733.

67 Arthur F. Glasser, *Announcing the Kingdom : The Story of God's Mission in the Bible* (Grand Rapids: Baker Academic, 2003), 22.

68 Shawn W. Flynn, *YHWH is King: The Development of Divine Kingship in Ancient Israel* (Leiden: Koninklijke Brill NV, 2014), 41.

69 Goldingay, *Psalms: Psalms 90-150*, 136.

70 James Luther Mays, *Psalms: Interpretation A Bible Commentary for Teaching and Preaching* (Louisville: John Knox Press, 1994), 319.

relationship. God is disclosed as the King of kings through mighty acts and authoritative words.[71]

God did not abandon the nations. The universal note in the enthronement psalms stresses that all the nation's clap in the worship of Yahweh. The nations have actually become one with the people of Abraham's God through the worship of Yahweh. This is how worship becomes the key to draw the attention of all the people to come into the presence of Yahweh. The God of Israel is the God of all the world. "The world becomes one in the oneness of Israel's God."[72] Israel is called a holy people (Ex 33:12). Through Israel, other people receive the grace of Yahweh. The enthronement psalms present the nation of Israel in יהוה מלך worshipping Yahweh the king with the rest of the peoples without distinction.[73] This shows that the entire universe is in the hands of God. Yahweh's dominion extends beyond the covenant people in order to embrace the whole world.

God anticipated and commanded the worldwide spread of biblical faith. God blessed Abraham and promised that all peoples on earth will be blessed through him (Gen 12:3). Wright asserts that "Abraham's response of faith and obedience not only moves God to count him as righteous but also enables God's promise to move forward toward its universal horizon."[74] The content of Psalm 47 indicates that the nations become part of the nation of the God of Abraham and that the rulers of the earth (princes or kings of the nations) belong to God (Ps 47:10).[75] Leslie comments that "The nations of the earth, the pagan peoples, recognize the superiority of Israel's God. In order to share in the blessings of Israel, they join themselves to Abraham's God."[76] Israel had a certain responsibility with regard to the nations. Israel being God's people are to witness the reality of Yahweh to the nations through word and deed and cause the nations to come and worship. Israel's witness has a universal goal as Yahweh is the only God in all of creation.[77] God's sovereign rule ultimately brings all people to light. Yahweh is the source of all authority and victory over

71 Glasser, *Announcing the Kingdom : The Story of God's Mission in the Bible*, 22.

72 Christopher J. H. Wright, *The Mission of God: Unlocking the Bible's Grand Narrative* (Illinois: InterVarsity Press, 2006), 232.

73 Wallace, Robert E. *The Narrative Effect of Book IV of the Hebrew Psalter* (New York: Peter Lang Publishing, Inc., 2007), 81-82.

74 Wright, *The Mission of God*, 206.

75 Jo-Marí Schäder, "Psalm 47- How Universal Is Its Universalism? An Intra-, Inter- and Extratextual Analysis of the Poem." Magister Artium in Ancient Languages and -Cultural Studies in the Faculty of Humanities, Thesis, University of Pretoria, 2008. 98.

76 Elmer A. Leslie, *The Psalms: Translated and Interpreted in the Light of Hebrew Life and Worship* (New York: Abingdon Press, 1949), 67.

77 Eckhard J. Schnabel, "Israel, the People of God, and the Nations" *Journal of the Evangelical Theological Society,* 45, no. 1 (March, 2002): 40.

all things. The psalmist asserts "All the ends of the earth shall remember and turn to the Lord and all the families of the nations shall worship before him. For dominion belongs to the Lord, and God rules over the nations" (Ps 22: 27-28, Dan 7:18).

The people of God declare his glory among the nations, and his marvellous deeds among the peoples (Ps 96:3). God is not concerned solely with individuals, but with families, peoples, and nations. God delights to dwell in their midst, that through them, his rule might extend to all aspects of life. God is opposed to racism, nationalism, sexism and all other *isms* that humiliate people.[78] Schnabel comments that the concept of the 'people of God,' defined as the membership in God's people, is no longer dependent upon biological descent (Isa 56:3-8). Nations are given privileges that had been reserved for the Israelites (Isa 66:21). They are to be integrated into God's people.[79] All the foreign powers are to unite in singing the song of praise of the assembled worshippers of Israel. The motive of this universal worship and exaltation is given in the fact that through history, Yahweh has already proved to be the sovereign Lord in the world of nations.[80]

God, who is lord of all, hears the praise and sees the worship of all that is created. In fact, the worship of Israel stands in the service of the central theological claim of the Old Testament in general and Psalter in particular. This is the claim that the Lord of Israel alone is God and requires the full devotion of all creation.[81] The psalmist directly addresses the earth and its people, inviting the whole world to come to the worship of Yahweh (Ps 96).[82] The God of Israel unlocks the doors of salvation and liberation for all those who choose to follow.[83] In the spirit of the universal nature of adoration of Yahweh, it is denoted that Israel's worship knows no bounds. The psalmist projects that heaven and earth belong to God, so the nations must worship Yahweh. Israel's religious tradition strongly affirms that Yahweh alone is God and this counters any rival claim of divinity while establishing the concept of the universality of God of all. Faced with fresh challenges from religious pluralism, the psalmist affirms the true divinity of Yahweh.[84]

78 Glasser, *Announcing the Kingdom: The Story of God's Mission in the Bible*, 25.

79 Schnabel, *Israel, the People of God, and the Nations*, 41-42.

80 Kraus, *Psalms 1-59*, 470.

81 Patrick D. Miller, "Enthroned on the Praises of Israel: The Praise of God in Old Testament Theology,"*Interpretation* 39, no. 1 (January, 1985): 19.

82 Goldingay, *Psalms: Psalms 90-150*, 108.

83 Pravan Paul, "Being Light and Salt: Meaning and Mission of the Bible in Multi-Cultural and Multi-Religious Contexts of India," *UBS Journal,* vol. 8, no. 9 no. 1 (September, 2013, March, 2015): 33.

84 Eliya Mohol, "Prophetic and Popular Responses to Religious Pluralism in Jeremiah." *UBS Journal,* vol. 6, no. 2 (2009): 42.

Therefore, inclusive worship has a significant role for Indian Christians because the God of Israel is the God of Indians. In the worship of Yahweh there is no distinction between the rich or poor or between the classes. All are invited to worship Yahweh the king. Israel's worship always involves the whole world and whoever claims Yahweh as the true God. Israel's God is confessed as the God of all the earth and everyone is invited to participate in the worship of Yahweh. Therefore, Yahweh's relationship with the nation of Israel has wide implications for worship in the Indian context.

11.3.4. God Centredness in Worship

God centredness is part of the connotation of kingship metaphor because Yahweh, the king, plays the dominant role in both heaven and the earth. What is the main focal point in worship? For whom is worship? Who is the God we worship, and what kind of worship is appropriate to that God? God should be placed in the centre of worship. The main theme of worship is to focus on God and ascribe glory to God. The whole concept here is that the worship of God should be God-centred and God-directed or else it may lead the worshippers into inappropriate worship. The psalmist's concept of worship was 'theocentric' not 'anthropocentric.' They held that nothing on earth is worthwhile unless it is properly related and directed to the creator of the universe, giver of life, master, and saviour.[85]

God is the infinite centre of worship that enables the worshippers to spend time with God in all the fullness of God's splendour.[86] Miller comments that Israelites worship rejects attempts to control or manipulate the place of Yahweh in a magical way, whether it is by some ritual activity or the use of representations of the deity in the context of worship.[87] Therefore, worshippers ought to focus on God and have God-centred worship. This is an essential principle of worship. As the king of worship, Yahweh has the authority to lead a meaningful worship.[88] True worship begins with God and involves the worshippers' hearts, mind and strength. What is important in true worship is not observance of rules and regulations, but, how we worship.

Dawn observes that worship that is based on God-centeredness begins with a prelude offering worshippers an opportunity to move away from the distractions of their workday and family matters and lead them into the presence

---

85 Ralph L. Smith, *Old Testament Theology: Its History, Method, and Message* (Nashville: Broadman & Holman Publishers, 1993), 312.

86 Marva J. Dawn, "Worship to Form a Missional Community," *Direction*vol. 28, no. 2 (1999): 149. See Kumar, "The Role of the Environment in the Worship of Israel," 64.

87 Miller, "Him Only Shall You Serve Reflections on the Meaning of Old Testament," 143.

88 Phillip G. Kayser, *Delighting in God's Kingship Over Worship* (Omaha: Biblicalblueprints.org, 2009), 11.

of God.[89] It is possible that some Christians just attend worship to receive a blessing rather than to make an offering to God. However, every act of worship should be understood as part of an offering to God. Worship that involves the entire person and focuses attention on God's graciousness glorifies and reflects God's truth. This is essential for true worship and spiritual adventure. Therefore, worship that effectively reinforces the image of God's truth in the minds of the people can contribute greatly to the growth of a person toward maturity.[90] Worship directed to God allows God to be the central point. In other words, the whole point of worship is to bring forth the kingship of God as the subject and object in the heart of worshippers. The enthronement psalms also contain references to the deeds of Yahweh and all the divine characteristics of Yahweh like justice and fairness which give reasons for worship. All these reasons are connected with the kingship of Yahweh. It is essential that the Church keeps God as the subject and object of worship. God-centred worship has an immense impact on the life of the worshippers especially in the Indian context. It is the one God, the true and only God, who has graciously revealed life to us. It is this inner life of God that shapes Christian worship.[91] It emphasizes total submission to the authority of God and allows God to rule in the hearts of the people. Thus, the goal of the worshippers is to allow God to be the centre of the whole being of the people and the worship. The psalmist strongly emphasizes that what pleases God is our attitude in worship. When worshippers engage with God in their hearts and in all their struggles and happiness, God becomes the centre of worship.

Worship should not be based on secular ideals which destroy the atmosphere of true worship. There is a need for Indian Christians to allow God to be the centre of their worship. It is likely that today we see human centeredness trying to control the whole picture of worship. Therefore, it is a great challenge to allow God to be the centre of worship because failure to do so will lead us away from God-centred worship.

11.3.5. Glorifying God in Worship

We have seen glorifying God is connected with kingship metaphor; God is the king who deserves to be elevated above all gods and kings. The worshippers assemble together and magnify the greatness of God. The theology of worship is to glorify God and also to participate in the life of God. True worship

89 Marva J. Dawn, *Reaching Out without Dumbing Down: A Theology of Worship for the Turn-of-the-Century Culture* (Grand Rapids, Michigan: William B. Eerdmans Publishing Company, 1995), 77.

90 Edward M. Curtis, "Ancient Psalms and Modern Worship," *Bibliotheca Sacra*vol. 154, no. 615 (July-September, 1997): 285-286.

91 Roland R. Byars, *Christian Worship: Glorifying and Enjoying God* (Louisville: Westminster John Knox Press, 2000), 17.

motivates us to offer our heart, soul, and mind to God faithfully. When a person is in God, he or she reflects the likeness of God in all dimensions of life. Worship is not just asking a blessing from God, but it is glorifying God for all his faithfulness and righteousness. The enthronement psalms portray that Yahweh triumphs over enemies, for the gods of others are nothing but Yahweh is the one true God (Ps 96:4). Thus, the people of Israel rely on Yahweh and glorify the incomparable God who is all in all through their gestures.[92] As seen in exegetical study, the enthronement texts mention the God of Israel as highest God, king, creator and judge of the world.

One of the visible patterns of Israel's worship is calling the people to glorify Yahweh who delivers and fulfills his promises. The deliverance of the community as well as the individual draws the congregation as a whole into grateful confession that glorifies Yahweh.[93] Israel's worship is conducted in the confidence that Yahweh deserves all glory. The psalms give evidence of Israel joyously entering into the presence of Yahweh to glorify and lift up the name of Yahweh above everything else (Pss 95:1-2, 118:19, 122:1).[94] The psalmist invites the community of worshippers into the complete range of life in God and glorifies the Most High God who rules all.[95] The psalmist responds "bless the Lord, O my soul, and all that is within me, bless the name of God" (Ps 103:1). It refers to the joy and glory of God that should be the deepest desire of God's people in worshipping and glorifying the name of Yahweh. The biblical idea of glorifying God is letting the worthiness of God be manifest. The main intention of this idea is that the whole world is an arena for God's glory to be revealed. For instance, the heavens and all nature declare the glory of God. The whole earth is full of the glory of God (Ps 19:1, Isa 6:3). Through their expression of the mighty acts of Yahweh, the worshippers glorify and uphold his kingship.[96]

True worship is all about magnifying the greatness of Yahweh the king. In worship, we offer praise to God because it is our duty as worshippers and also because it is our delight. It is in worship that God creates inner joy in the worshippers. It is this inner life of God that shapes Israel's worship to grow in God.[97] The worshippers assemble together to glorify God through their worship. Hence, this is significant for present day worship because

92 Praven, "A Search for a Theology of the Psalter," 15.

93 Goldingay, *Key Questions about Christian Faith: Old Testament Answers*, 102.

94 Walter Brueggemann, *Worship in Ancient Israel: An Essential Guide* (Nashville: Abingdon Press, 2005), 73.

95 Brueggemann, *Worship in Ancient Israel: An Essential Guide*, 79.

96 William Dyrness, *Themes in the Old Testament Theology* (Illinois: InterVarsity Press, 1977), 167-168.

97 Byars, *Christian Worship: Glorifying and Enjoying God*, 10.

worshippers should be able to glorify God in the way they worship. Thus, true worship starts as an act of obedience and giving glory to God.

11.3.6. Listening to God in Worship

Listening to God's voice is linked with Yahweh's kingship because Yahweh is the king and we ought to listen to him rather than listening to worldly power. In other words, listening serves as a call to pay attention to the one who is the authority. As shown in exegetical study the Hebrew word שמע is translated as 'to hear, to listen and pay attention.' The main meaning of שמע is to hear sounds with the ear. Where words are heard, it involves an engagement with the mind and comes to mean 'listen' (Gen 18:10).[98] The whole text of the enthronement psalms first calls for attention to hear the word of God in worship. Hearing is often used as a substitute for taking heed and acting on what is heard. To hear, in this sense, is to obey "Hear O Israel the Lord our God is one Lord" (Deut 6:4).[99]

"To love the Lord God with all your heart and with all your soul and with all your strength and keep the commandment in the heart" (Deut 6:5-6). This affirms that God's people are called to attend to God's word so that we might know and remember Yahweh who is the king.[100] שמע is also used in the sense of learning about the greatness of God and proclaiming his actions to others (Isa 66:19). In other words, שמע also expresses the idea of listening attentively which means to set the heart and mind to God (Ps 49:2, Deut 27:9, Job 29:21). Thus, שמע is closely associated with teaching and learning where the psalmist urges the covenant people to learn how to listen to the voice of Yahweh. For example, at Mount Horeb, Israel gathered together to listen to God's words so they might learn to fear God (Deut 4:10). The concept is reflected in Israel's worship (Pss 34:11).[101] Yahweh reminded the people of deliverance and urged them to listen to the voice of Yahweh. Goldingay affirms that "Worship involves both noise and attentiveness. Both are responses to what Yahweh has done."[102] The psalmist says "I shall listen for what Yahweh will speak" (Ps 85: 8). To listen is viewed as Israel's response to God's teaching. God reminds the covenant people to listen and obey. One of the primary aspects is that God communicates with people in worship through the ages. Worship

98 K. T. Aitken, "שמע," in *New International Dictionary of Old Testament Theology & Exegesis,* vol. 4, edited by Willem A. VanGemeren (Carlisle: Paternoster Press, 1996), 175.

99 William Dyrness, *Themes in the Old Testament Theology* (Illinois: InterVarsity Press, 1977), 93.

100 Johnson, H. Wayne, "Practicing Theology on a Sunday Morning: Corporate Worship as Spiritual Formation." *TRINJ*, no. 31 (2010): 35.See Antonio Dongshi, *Words and Gestures in Liturgy* (Collegeville: Liturgical Press, 2009), 13.

101 Aitken, "שמע," 176-177.

102 Goldingay, *Old Testament Theology: Israel's Faith*, 132-133.

begins by listening to God. The enthronement psalms reveal what a sincere heart of worship looks like. For example, Psalm 95 demonstrates both a call to praise and an exhortation to listen to God's voice in worship. "For he is our God, and we are the people of his pasture, and the sheep of his hand. Today, if you hear his voice" (Ps 95:7). It emphasizes the listening dimension suggesting the prophetic oracle of Ps 95: 7-11 as one of the ways to prepare the people for proper worship. The sheep listen to the shepherd, so the Israelites must listen to Yahweh and worship.[103]

The psalmist stresses that the worshippers must heed the voice of God because the Lord is the great king, maker and ruler of the universe. What people owe to their king is to hear the voice of God.[104] The phrase "heed to the voice of the Lord" is an exhortation to the Church not to fall away from God's commands but rather to invite the congregation to authentic worship. The hymn identifies God as sovereign overall and then teaches that true worship is the devotion of life; listen to God, trust and obey God alone.[105]

Worship requires obedience and listening. Worship is a call to acknowledge God; it is also the acknowledgment of how Yahweh helps people. The idea of listening to God's voice is connected with exhortation, recognizing the kingship of God and giving due worship to God.[106] Listening is so profound an act of worship that worshippers desperately need the help of the spirit in order to have a submissive attitude of listening to God. Only when a person hears the voice of God and responds to the word of God, his or her heart will be renewed to worship and glorify God.[107] One of the factors which could be lacking in contemporary worship is calling God's people to listen and obey God's instruction.[108] The psalmist expresses this idea: "To listen and to learn is to walk the way that leads to life."[109] Listening begins with devoted obedience and follows from hearing, knowing and worshipping Yahweh wholeheartedly. We see that love, obedience and worship are an appropriate affirmation of faith in God.[110] Listening leads to personal enrichment and

---

103 Christopher Renz, "Come, Let Us Listen to the Voice of the Lord." *Worship,* vol. 70, no. 2 (1996): 140–145.

104 Mays, *Psalms: Interpretation a Bible Commentary for Teaching and Preaching*, 305-306.

105 Mays, *Psalms: Interpretation a Bible Commentary for Teaching and Preaching*, 307.

106 Renz, "Come, Let Us Listen to the Voice of the Lord," 152.

107 Johnson, "Practicing Theology on a Sunday Morning: Corporate Worship as Spiritual Formation," 36.

108 Shirley Ho and Feng Yi Lin, *Psalms 73-150*: *Asia Bible Commentary Series,* edited by Bruce J. Nicholls (Manila: Asia Theological Association, 2013), 88.

109 J. Clinton McCann, "The Hope of the Poor: The Psalms in Worship and Our Search for Justice." *Touching the Alter: The Old Testament for Christian Worship*, edited by Carol M Bechtel (Grand Rapids, Michigan: Wm. B. Eerdmans Publishing Co, 2008), 55.

110 Johnson, Practicing Theology on a Sunday Morning, 33.

enables a kind of spiritual strength that helps the believer to carry the burdens and fight the battles of life.[111] For example, Israelites listen to God and affirm their faith. So, Christians ought to listen and reinforce their distinctiveness in Yahweh. This helps the worshipping community to grow.[112] Inviting people to worship and admonishing them to listen and obey the Lord are essential for proper Christian worship today. Worship is not just a feeling; it is listening to God and declaring the worthiness of God. As we enter into worship, we need to learn to anticipate and attend to the voice of God. Hence, Indian Christians today can be encouraged by the richness of the theological expression of the word 'listening' found in the enthronement psalms.

11.3.7. Thanksgiving in Worship

Thanksgiving is linked to the connotation of kingship metaphor because Yahweh deserves to be thanked for all his faithfulness towards humanity. As seen in the exegetical study, the Hebrew word תודה involves a thank offering. This thank offering is accompanied by an individual song of thanksgiving which has both a testimony of an individual and of the congregation besides giving thanks to God. It is an experience of God's benefits and the recipients have a reason to respond in praise to Yahweh.[113] The psalmist exhorts the community to praise and thank the creator (Ps 95:2).

Along with public thanksgiving, there is also personal or private thanksgiving. People individually thank God for healing them from sickness and for their prayers being answered.[114] People thank Yahweh directly as the king of Israel and the world. They have a genuine reason to thank and acknowledge because Yahweh saved the nation of Israel throughout her history and created the world as a secure place for them.[115] It is possible that some of Israel's expressions of thanksgiving used in worship were taken from prophetic oracles.[116] For instance, "Give thanks to the Lord of hosts, for the Lord is good, for his steadfast love endures forever" (Jer 33:11). Thanksgiving performs some important functions in worship. The congregation enters the sanctuary with jubilation and thanksgiving accompanied by the solemn act of worship. The thanksgiving liturgy in Israel's worship plays an essential role as

111 Warrant W. Wiersbe, *Real Worship* (Nashville: Thomas Nelson Publishers, 1990), 23.

112 Susan J. White, *Foundations of Christian Worship* (Louisville: Westminster John Knox Press, 2006), 5, 9.

113 Leslie, C. Allen, "ידה," in *New International Dictionary of Old Testament Theology & Exegesis,* vol. 2. edited by William VanGemeren (Carlisle: Paternoster Press, 1997), 406-407.

114 Mowinckel, *The Psalms in Israel's Worship*, 26-31.

115 Menezes, Rui de, *The Legacy of Israel: Collected Essays*, vol. 3 (Mumbai: St Pauls, 2012), 42.

116 Gunkel, *Introduction to Psalms: The Genres of the Religious Lyric of Israel*, 246-247.

the congregation is invited to come into the presence of God with thanksgiving (Pss 100:4, 107:1).[117]

Among the texts that I have considered in this study, Psalm 100 especially highlights worship with thanksgiving. The liturgical role of the psalm in Israel's worship is noticeable in a number of ways. It is a processional song by the people as they enter through the gates of the temple into its courts. The main purpose of the procession is to offer the Lord with thanksgiving and praise. תודה means both the sacrifice of thanksgiving and the act of giving thanks which is a vital part in Israel's worship.[118] In the worship of Israel, homage with thanksgiving, praise, and adoration are paid to Yahweh, the king.[119] Worship involves the entire attitude of one's life in relationship to Yahweh. True worshippers begin with a disposition of thanksgiving. Thanksgiving opens the gates and prepares the heart of worshippers to offer acceptable worship. Thanksgiving is an inward offering to God and plays an essential part in the life of the people and it causes the people to draw closer to God.[120] Praise and thanksgiving are part of a single whole, however, thanksgiving is more about recognizing what God has done and, therefore, is responsive and thankful.[121] To speak of God as good and thank him is to affirm that the Lord of Israel is the source of all that makes life possible and worthwhile. It is an all-encompassing attribute that human beings receive in life and often is experienced specifically in God's deliverance of people from distress and success.[122] Goldingay argues "Thanksgiving combines words and music, word and noise, the voice and the whole being." תודה is used for a thank offering and it draws together the idea that a thank offering is vocalised as well as expressed in action.[123] There are three common visible structures of thanksgiving: *First,* an opening introduction in which the psalmist praises God for deliverance from suffering and distress. *Secondly,* the body tells how the psalmist cried out for help and protection and had been answered. *Thirdly*, in conclusion, the psalmist promises to witness continually to the faithfulness of God by giving thanks to the faithful God.[124]

In the post-exilic period, it became the central liturgical utterance of the congregation. Why is God so deserving of our thankfulness? Yahweh is creator

---

117 Kraus, "Psalms 1-59," 69.

118 Mays, *Psalms: Interpretation a Bible Commentary for Teaching and Preaching*, 317.

119 Kraus, *Psalms 60-150*, 248.

120 Mays, *The Lord Reigns: A Theological Handbook to the Psalms*, 64.

121 Miller, *Enthroned on the Praises of Israel,* 10.

122 Miller, *Enthroned on the Praises of Israel,* 12.

123 Goldingay, *Old Testament Theology: Israel's Life*, 311-312.

124 Watts, John D.W, "Psalms of Trust, Thanksgiving, and Praise." *Review Expositor* 3, no. 81 (Summer, 1984): 399.

and owner of the land and calls upon the people to acknowledge the ownership of Yahweh with loyal devotion. Thanksgiving keeps the relationship with God alive and gives it expression. Worshippers express deep gratitude and thankfulness by proclaiming the greatness of God and also declaring how deserving God is.[125] The concrete nature of thanksgiving focuses on proclaiming all the things that Yahweh has done. It is also a testimony addressed to other people because lifting him up in worship becomes a great witness to people. Besides that, thanksgiving testifies to Yahweh's faithfulness.[126] The role which thanksgiving plays in the life of an individual and community includes thanking, receiving and acknowledging the faithfulness of Yahweh's actions and giving visible expression of that acknowledgement in the congregation.[127]

Thanksgiving is our recognition of the things God has done on our behalf and looks back to prayer and deliverance. It encourages worshippers to renew their commitment, open their hearts to his guidance and be thankful to God. In Israel's worship, whatever the form of liturgical activities may have been, the element of thanksgiving was included.[128] Gunkel rightly points out that the core of thanksgiving is "to announce the experience of Yahweh's help."[129] The psalmist emphasizes that Yahweh loves the righteous, delivers them from all wickedness and blesses them with all the provisions. It is the desire of Yahweh that the people rejoice and wholeheartedly give thanks to the creator God (Pss 95:2, 97:12).[130] Schaefer points out that the psalmist gives a double invitation to rejoice and be glad and ends with a double invitation addressed to the righteous to rejoice and be thankful to God (Ps 92:1, 8, 12).[131]

This is a rhetorical way of addressing the worshipping community about acknowledging the kingship of Yahweh.Thanksgiving gratifies God's heart and increases the faith of a believer in God. Arthur pointed out three principles of thanksgiving. *First,* thanksgiving reminds people constantly of Yahweh's goodness. *Secondly*, it acknowledges Yahweh as the giver. *Thirdly*, it helps people to depend upon Yahweh, the great king. *Finally,* it inculcates in the heart a true spirit of humility and gives glory to God.[132] Psalm 100 which talks about the thanksgiving offering, however, looking at the phrase "thanks to Yahweh for the Lord is good" shows that this phrase has an application as a

---

125 Arthur, *God Deserves Our Worship*, 15.

126 Goldingay, *Old Testament Theology: Israel's Life*, 314-316.

127 Brueggemann, *Theology of the Old Testament*, 473-474.

128 Miller, "Him Only Shall You Serve Reflections on the Meaning of Old Testament," 143.

129 Gunkel, *Introduction to Psalms: The Genres of the Religious Lyric of Israel*, 242.

130 Kizhakkeyil, *The Psalms: The Prayer Book of the Bible*, 362.

131 Schaefer, *Psalms*, 240.

132 Arthur, *God Deserves Our Worship*, 168.

hymn and was used for several occasions in Israel's worship (Ps 100:4-5).[133] This emphasizes the importance of thanksgiving in all occasions of Israel's worship.

I suggest all the thanksgiving practices in Israel's worship could be used as thanksgiving offerings or thanksgiving hymns for enhancing today's worship. Psalm 100 specifically mentions three motives for thanksgiving: *God is good, merciful* and *faithful* in all generations. Thus, God deserves an expression of thanksgiving. Thankfulness keeps our ears and mind open to God's voice. The people of God are to thank God for everything as thanksgiving is an act of worship. Thanksgiving is also a testimony of God's deliverance after witnessing how God intervenes in the situations of distress in the lives of individuals and communities at large. In Israel's worship, thanksgiving played a significant role as a declaration of thanks for specific divine acts. Therefore, even today, thanksgiving is an expression of faith and cannot be taken for granted in worship.

11.3.8. Making Music in Worship

Music is connected to the connotation of kingship metaphor because Yahweh deserves all our singing and praises for all his mighty works. The word music describes and covers both vocal and instrumental music. Music was a central element in Israelite worship as people celebrated Yahweh's victory over chaos with music (Ps 47:7). It is a divine gift from God and when it is utilized properly, it reveals God to all humanity.[134] The Hebrew word ידה is to praise or to confess. Praise can be any type of praise but the word ידה tends to be specific, that is, giving praise or making music to God. [135] The praise of God is the regular form of Israel's worship as worshippers exalt the name of the Lord above all names. They acknowledge God's perfection and mighty work through their music. True praise from the mouth is a clean vocal adoration focused on God (Pss 99:3, 100:4).

The enthronement psalms are joined by the common focus of the praise of the Lord's kingship. Praise represents the "response of a grateful Israel to the work and word of God in nature and history."[136] The worshippers sing praises to Yahweh because Yahweh is distinctively holy, powerful, trustworthy

133 Gunkel, *Introduction to Psalms: The Genres of the Religious Lyric of Israel*, 207.

134 Bartel, Dietrich,*Musica Poetica: Musical-Rhetorical Figures in German Baroque Music* (Lincoln, Nebraska: University of Nebraska Press, 2007), 4.

135 Allen, " ידה," 406.

136 Samuel L.Terrien, *The Psalms and Their Meaning for Today* (New York: The Bobbs-Merrill Company, Inc., 1952), 191.

and salvific.[137] McCann points out that "Praising God is the goal of every living thing, the goal of all creation."[138]

In Israel's worship, the psalmist leads worship by instructing the people to sing a joyful song to Yahweh with great joy (Pss 47:1, 98: 4-8). In my view, praise is the keynote to Yahweh's worthiness and kingship. The majesty of Yahweh is praised in Israel's worship and this is a common feature of all the enthronement psalms, Psalms 93, 97, 98 especially extend the praise of Yahweh.[139] My mouth will speak the praise of the Lord (Ps 145: 21). The truth applies not only to praise spoken privately, but also to congregational prayer, praise and worship. "I will greatly praise the Lord with my mouth; yes, I will praise Him among the nation multitude" (Pss 35:18, 111:1; 109:30).[140] In Israel's worship, Yahweh is "the sole and real subject of praise."[141] The role of music plays an essential part where the worshippers of Yahweh offer their praises and magnify Yahweh the king in an enthusiastic manner. When we praise God, we worship God and when we worship God, we praise God. This is a concurrent phenomenon. As seen in the previous chapter, Yahweh's victory over the nations demonstrated that Yahweh is praiseworthy because Yahweh is king over all the kings.[142] God desires people to use their voices in worship. The power of music magnifies Yahweh. Through music, Israel truly demonstrated that Yahweh is more prominent and visible than the other gods.[143]

The psalmist affirms that the praise of God is included for all the nations who accept the kingship of Yahweh. It is clear that an act of worship is taking place in which Israel and other nations are to praise the ultimate sovereignty and kingship of Yahweh (Ps 47:2-3).[144] Worship is making music to God for what he has done. Music moves people emotionally. Thus, emotion can be an indication that the spirit is at work at a deeper level in people's hearts. Music

---

137 Eaton, *The Psalms*, 29.

138 McCann, *A Theological Introduction to the Book of the Psalms,* 56. See Joncas, Jan Michael, "Music as Worship," in *The New Westminster Dictionary of Liturgy and Worship*, edited by Paul Bradshaw (Louisville: SCM Press, 2002), 326-327. James Luther Mays, *The Lord Reigns: A Theological Handbook to the Psalms* (Louisville: Westminster John Knox Press, 1994), 81.

139 Claus Westermann, *The Psalms Structure, Content & Message*, translated by Ralph D. Gehrke (Minneapolis: Augsburg Publishing House, 1980), 114.

140 Ernest B. Gentile, *Worship God: Exploring the Dynamics of Psalmic Worship* (Portland: City Bible Publishing, 1994), 142-143.

141 Gerstenberger, *Psalms, Part I, with An Introduction to Cultic Poetry,* 16.

142 Schäder, "Psalm 47-How Universal Is Its Universalism? 48.

143 Brueggemann, *Worship in Ancient Israel: An Essential Guide*, 45-46.

144 Peter C. Craigie, "Psalms 1-50," in *Word Biblical Commentary*, vol. 1, edited by David A. Hubbard and Glenn W. Barker (Waco: Word Books, 1983), 347-348.

engages our emotions and this is how it enriches our experience. In fact, music extols God's greatness. Psalms of exalting Yahweh, generally, begin with an imperative call to worship.[145]

Worshippers sing praises to God because it is the greatest delight which the worshippers experience in their relationship to God. When we pour our hearts into worship, we are filled with the spirit that changes and transforms us. God rightly deserves our praises and we ought to praise God whole heartedly.[146] In the Psalter, the praises of God's people resound more clearly than elsewhere. We have a great deal of OT evidence, especially in the Psalter, for the use of music in worship and the use of specific instruments for liturgical purposes. This indicates that the very essence of God is revealed in and through the musical proportion. Through music, the invisible becomes perceptible.[147]According to Ho and Lin, "The celebration of the Lord's victory is liturgically expressed as singing a new song with a variety of musical instruments such as lyre, trumpet, and horn. Where there is salvation, there is joy; where there is joy, there is singing; where there is singing, there are musical instrument."[148]

Adding musical instruments to corporate or individual worship enriches the worship experience because it impacts the entire atmosphere of worship and also the life of worshippers. At the same time, music serves as an aid in the training of souls for people of all ages. Christian worship music becomes life-giving to worshippers and can be a means to communicate the text and bring it to light afresh in the heart of true worshippers of God.[149] According to Sánchez, music comprises two forms. "As artifact, music has the capacity to represent a set of values or ideals. As art, music has the capacity to produce and communicate meaning creatively and persuasively, and to foster a certain way of doing things."[150]

In Christian worship, music, beginning from preludes and to postlude, is offered to God and produces a sound and melody that pleases God and serves the purpose of helping people meaningfully to worship God.[151] The essential role of music in worship is to help people to glorify God. The word of God is preached through music in Christian worship today. Music bears witness to

145 Anderson, *Understanding the Old Testament*, 505.

146 Byars, *Christian Worship: Glorifying and Enjoying God*, 4.

147 Bartel, *Musica Poetica: Musical-Rhetorical Figures in German Baroque Music*, 3.

148 Ho and Lin, *Psalms 73-150*, 96.

149 Leopoldo A. Sánchez M, "Theology in Context Music as a Test Case," *Concordia Journal,* vol. 38, no. 3 (Summer, 2012): 205-206.

150 Sanchez, Leopoldo A, "Theology in Context Music as a Test Case," *Concordia Journal,* vol. 38, no. 3 (Summer, 2012): 207.

151 Dawn, *Reaching Out Without Dumbing Down,* 82.

the beauty of God and helps people embrace the power of God in worship. Music helps the Church rejoice and grow in the word of God. Often, music can draw the attention of young people to participate in worship. However, in my opinion, music is not just for young people but equally important for every age group participating in worship. The chart below shows the function of music in Christian worship.

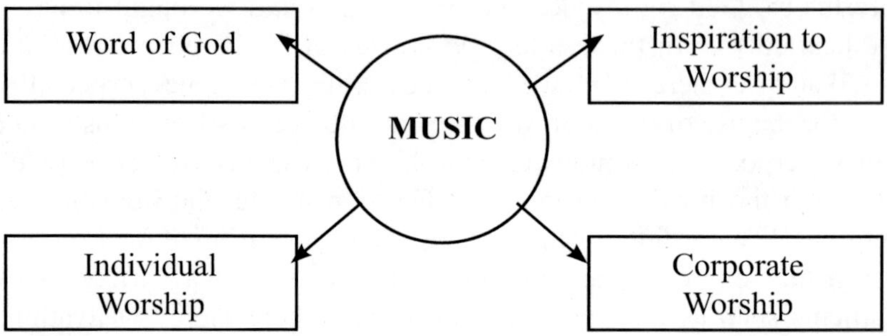

First, music contains the word of God and the word of God is in music. The joy of singing with musical instruments is a rich manifestation of the spirit for every human being. What is inside a person is expressed joyfully through music.[152] *Secondly*, music inspires the heart of worshippers. Johnson suggests that music is a vehicle whereby people enter into a cheerful celebration of God's kingship and express their feeling of gladness and joy to the Lord.[153] *Thirdly*, music is effective even in individual worship. In our private worship, the word through music is essential for the worshippers to hear from God. *Finally,* music plays a significant role in corporate worship. It unites the hearts of the people. Leslie stresses that music belongs in both individual and corporate worship. Besides that, music has power to kindle the hearts of whole congregations and elevate the experience into inspired moments.[154] Stirred on by music, words begin to flow from the worshipper's heart leading to a state of being enveloped by God's powerful transforming presence.

Therefore, in my opinion, singing praises expresses our worship to God. In this context, a connection of our spirit to the spirit of God is essential for worshipping. Worshippers can feel emotions for God and can express their feelings audibly in praising. Examples of this are: "Shout unto God with the voice of triumph" (Ps 47:1). "Let us make a joyful noise to the rock of our salvation" (Ps. 95:1-2). To praise God means to respond to the worthiness of God. It is the will of God to give praise to the Almighty (1 Thess 5:18).

152 Antonio Dongshi, *Words and Gestures in Liturgy* (Collegeville: Liturgical Press, 2009), 40.

153 Johnson, Practicing Theology on a Sunday Morning, 39.

154 Leslie, *The Psalms*, 26.

Therefore, musical instruments, congregational hymns and group singing are encouraged to be used in community worship.

When we look at music and its relevance, its cultural element has to be taken into consideration, since music has a close relationship with culture. A glimpse at the Indian context, the Hindu tradition of Varkari,[155] shows *mantras* and *bhajans* are the essential parts of its liturgy. Varkari is a religious sect within the Bhakti spiritual tradition of Hinduism. The Varkaris are well known for performing *bhajan* and singing songs of saints. The word "*bhajan* is derived from *bhaj* which means to serve in Sanskrit."[156] This is a popular type of devotional singing. It is sung in temples and usually sung in groups. A lead singer, usually, sings the first lines and is followed by the choral group. *Bhajan* singing is, usually, accompanied by musical instruments. *Bhajans* are meant for larger gatherings rather than for individual worship.[157]

The meaning of *bhajan* is connected with the word 'worship.' Worship is also defined as a service. Priests recite *mantras* and laity sings *bhajans* in the context of worship. Worshippers can express themselves better through the traditional patterns of music which are familiar to them.[158] Music and worship are intertwined. In Christian worship, music should appeal to the whole being of a person's will, emotions and intellect.[159] It has got the ability to bring out the innermost feelings of the heart of the worshipper and evokes a declaration of faith and devotion to God. It has the power to break down barriers which prevent true worship and acts as a catalyst for openness towards God.[160] Music has always been at the centre of the Israelite worshiping community. We can see that singing was accompanied by plucking strings, percussion and instruments, not less than the worship of neighbouring peoples who also used musical instruments in their songs.[161]

---

155 The term *Varkari* is made up from two words (Marathi) *Vari* means pilgrimage and a pilgrim is called a *Varkari*. The *Varkari* is a religious sect within the *Bhakti* spiritual tradition of Hinduism.

156 Raj Kumar, *History and Cultural Series: Essays on Indian Music*, edited by Raj Kumar (New Delhi: Discovery Publishing House, 2003), 12.

157 G. M. Pawar, "Marathi," in *Medieval Indian Literature: An Anthology Survey & Selections Assamese, Bengali, and Dogri*, vol. 1, edited by K. Ayyappa Paniker (New Delhi: Sahitya Akademi, 1997), 351.

158 John Prabhakar, A. "Christian Worship: A Dalit Perspective." *South Asia Theol. Research Institute,* vol. 2, no. 1, (May, 2008): 28.

159 Dawn, *Reaching Out Without Dumbing Down,* 175.

160 Watts, "Singing the Songs of Babylon in the Worship of the Church," *Encounter,* vol. 74, no. 2 (2013): 4-5.

161 Eaton, *The Psalms: A Historical and Spiritual Commentary with an Introduction and New Translation*, 10. The Psalter has occupied a distinctive role in both Israel and the Christian Church, as the prayer book and the hymnal of both their worshiping communities. See Waltke& Houston, *The Psalms as Christian Worship A Historical Commentary,* 10. Cf.

As shown in above discussions, music has been a powerful medium to carry the truth of God in worship. It has always been a rich and profound tool to engage the gathered Church in expressing corporate praise and worship to God. It engages worshippers' hearts, emotions and intellect in expressing the truth of the relationship with God. In my opinion, Church services today would be incomplete without music as it is a powerful tool for worship. Out of many essential elements in Christian worship in the Indian context, the element of music has been influential for worshippers. Like the people of Israel, today, we can make use of all bamboo instruments and our native music in praising God to make our worship relevant to the context.

11.3.9. Witnessing Yahweh in Worship

Witnessing is linked to the connotation of kingship metaphor because Yahweh is the King of kings and Lord of lords. In other words the message of Yahweh's love need to be proclaimed to all the nations. Worship is all about witnessing the kingship of Yahweh. Therefore, worshippers are called to be true witnesses of Yahweh to the ends of the world (Mt 20:19-20). In the psalms, 'witness' means 'to proclaim God,' the one enthroned. Israel, as a recipient of Yahweh's favour, has been given the responsibility to witness to the kingship of Yahweh for the sake of all life. Therefore, the election of Israel is for the task of God to reach the entire world.[162] The entire congregation is a witness to Yahweh's saving act (Ps 22:22).[163] Israel's worship is characterized by praises and joy. It seems that the enthronement psalms present praising as a function of witnessing. All peoples, the whole of creation, heaven and earth, unite in the praise of the divine king and creator in worshipping Yahweh.[164]

The chosen people witness that their God is the true God. They emphasizes on the mighty acts of God through words of praises. For instance, in Israel's worship, making noises and clapping hands are considered as witnessing the true God. The psalmist urges all people to witness to the kingship of Yahweh by shouting and giving homage because Yahweh alone is worthy to receive all our praises and adoration. The praise in psalms envisions a worldwide scope. The psalmist says, "Let everything that breathes praise the Lord" (Ps 150:6). For Mays, praise has an evangelistic role, which means witnessing Yahweh through words of praises. Thus, the praise of the people of God in Israel's worship has

---

Joseph S. Thong & Phanenmo Kath, *Glimpses of Naga Legacy and Culture* (Kottayam: Society for Naga Student's Welfare, 2011), 76-77.

162 Theodore Mascarenhas, *The Missionary Function of Israel in Psalms 67, 96, and 117* (New York: University Press of America, 2005), 31.

163 Kraus, *Psalms 1-59*, 79.

164 Hans-Joachim Kraus, *Theology of the Psalms*, translated by Keith Crim (Minneapolis: Augsburg Publishing House, 1986) (Cf. Pss 97:6-9, 98:7-9, 99:1-5, 100:1).

missional function.[165] Similarly, Miller comments that, theologically, praise is greater than any other human act because God is declared in all fullness and glory in praising him.[166]

The purpose of praise is to respond to the experience of God's grace and power, to exalt the one who is gracious and powerful, and to bear witness to all who hear that Yahweh is the King of kings. It is always a devotion that tells about God, the theology that seeks to draw others into the circle of those who worship God.[167] Besides that, the character of praise is a declarative act through which it propagates knowledge of God's great deeds. In this act, the Lord is praised and all the nations are summoned and encouraged to acknowledge and worship the Lord of Israel. The manner in which God is worshipped is a message and a witness about God and it also reveals the nature of God to others.[168] Mays suggests that the enthronement psalms articulate that praise and worship are a proclamation, they witness to the present and coming reign of the Lord. The motive for openness is to reach out to all the nations.[169]

The heart of worship contains the call to proclaim the gospel to all nations. As seen in the above discussions, the word witnessing of God is demanded in both the testaments. I suggest that all these theological understandings of who Yahweh is and what Yahweh does work together to prompt praise. Praise rhetorically aims to demonstrate that God alone is worthy of worship. Hence, praise has much significance for witnessing Yahweh to the people of other faiths. So, acknowledge today and take to heart that the Lord is God in heaven above and on the earth beneath; there is no other.[170] Thus, praise has great implications for Indian churches who have the responsibility of sharing the gospel in a multi-religious context.

---

165 Mays, *The Lord Reigns: A Theological Handbook to the Psalms*, 65.

166 Miller, *Enthroned on the Praises of Israel*, 8.

167 Miller, *Enthroned on the Praises of Israel*, 9, 13. This call to the nations and peoples to praise the Lord is no incidental or exceptional matter. It is pervasive in the Psalms, where 'all the earth' (Pss 33:8; 66:1; 96:1; 98:4; 100:1), 'the earth' (Ps 97:1), 'the coastlands' (Ps 97:1), 'all the inhabitants of the earth' (Ps 33:8), 'all flesh' (Ps 145:21), 'peoples' (Pss 47:2; 66:8; 67:4, 148:11; Deut. 32:43) are called to praise and bless the Lord. The scope of declaration and praise is not, confined to human. All the works of God, the whole creation, the heavenly beings praise God (Pss 29; 69:34; 97:6; 98:7-8; 148; Isa. 42:10f; 44:23; 49:13; Joel 2:21ff, etc.). All these text indicates that the Creator whose power and glory is reflected in the creation. 14.

168 Dawn, *Reaching Out Without Dumbing Down,* 96.

169 Mays, *The Lord Reigns: A Theological Handbook to the Psalms*, 68.

170 Deut 6:4-5, 32:39, 2 Sam 7:22, 2 Kgs 5:15, 19:15, Neh 9:6, Ps 86:10, 11:5, 10, 135:10, Jer 10: 3-5, 16:20, Isa 44:6,8, 46:9, Hos 13:4, Zech 14:9, Mk 12:29-34, Jn 17:3, Rom 3:30, 1 Cor 8:4-6, Gal 3:20, Ephe 4:6, 1 Tim 2:5, Jas 2:19.

Summary

The literary context of Yahweh's kingship expresses that the kingship metaphor is not only used in OT and NT worship but also in Church history. The kingship psalms have wide implications for worship. *First,* kingship metaphor of Yahweh has implications for both OT and NT worship. Kingship metaphor helps worshippers to develop godly character, equips them to glorify God and aids them in enjoying the presence of God. *Secondly,* the kingship of Yahweh played an essential role during the time of the Church fathers and for the reformers to hold unto the authority of God. *Thirdly,* the denotation and connotations of kingship metaphor bring vital implications for the Indian Christian in the multi-religious context as they reveal the particularity and universality of God. Yahweh demands an undivided, absolute and complete worship. The Bible clearly talks about Yahweh as the only God (Jn 5:44, 17:3) one God, the Father (1 Cor 8:6) who deserves our wholehearted worship. *Finally,* the kingship metaphor has implications for propagating gospel to all the nations. Thus, recognizing the essential principles of worship mentioned in the enthronement psalms and incorporating them into the life and worship of the Indian Churches today can have a major role in helping the believers.

Chapter 12

Findings and Conclusion

In chapter 11, I have dealt with the kingship metaphor of Yahweh and its implications for early Christian worship. I also have dealt with the denotation and connotations of kingship metaphor and its implications especially for worship in a pluralistic context of India today. The final chapter deals with the *conclusion* and *findings*. The *first* part of the final chapter deals with findings in relation to the kingship metaphor of God and the implications of these for worship in a pluralistic context for the church in India today. The *second* part of the final chapter gives the possible leads for further research and a summary of the present research.

In this thesis, *kingship* in the enthronement psalms has been discussed from a historical literary perspective. The kingship metaphor and its implications for Israel's worship have been analysed. In addition to this, I have considered the literary and historical context of enthronement psalms where Yahweh appears as מלך. The phrase יהוה מלך is the key which connects all the enthronement texts with a single theme. Gunkel, Mowinckel, Weiser and Eaton discussed the kingship metaphor of Yahweh in the Psalter, but they did not give much importance to the kingship metaphor in relation to worship. Thus, I have looked at the kingship metaphor from the perspective of worship.

The *King* is considered to be a root metaphor in the canonical texts in the Old Testament, and we have seen the kingship metaphor viewed through the lens of denotation and connotations. This idea of Yahweh's rulership is the central key which leads people to know God as the God who rules over every individual's life, and he is the one who deserves to be worshipped as the divine ruler.

12.1. Findings in Relation to the Kingship Metaphor of God for Worship in a Pluralistic Context

Here, I have listed out some of my findings from both the primary denotation and the primary connotations of the kingship metaphor of Yahweh in relation to worship. Also few connotations which have a direct reference to worship. This is the primary denotation which emerge out of my exegesis.

12.1.1. Primary Denotation in Relation to the Kingship Metaphor

Sovereignty is a primary denotation of the kingship metaphor of Yahweh. The texts point out the denotative meaning of the sovereignty of Yahweh as powerful, which includes the notions of dominion and royal authority. Being powerful, Yahweh is definitely the mightiest and most majestic king in the Hebrew Bible. His sovereign power as creator and King of kings is never-ending. This is exercised through his divine nature. The psalmist challenges us to trust that, despite the threat of evil forces, Yahweh is the sovereign God who continues to reign and subdues all chaos. As a result, he deserves our worship as sovereign king and is the sole subject and object of our worship.

Yahweh is portrayed as the ruler because he is the sovereign God. The enthronement psalms indicate that he rules over the whole universe which includes humans, the heavens, the earth, the seas, the fields and all the trees. He is the one who *rules* over all the kings and nations; no other king can be compared with him. Another aspect of his rule is that it is *eternal*. Since he rules eternally, sincere worship must be offered to Yahweh alone and to no other.

There is the aspect of the exclusive worship of Yahweh. The *sovereignty* of Yahweh points to the notion of exclusive worship of Yahweh. Other nations have their own gods, but Yahweh alone is the God to whom Israel must give due worship. The enthronement psalms regard other gods and idols as worthless. The concept of exclusive worship in the enthronement psalms is in line with other books like Exodus, Deuteronomy and Isaiah (Ex 20:3, Deut 6:4, Isa 46:9). This exclusive worship is reaffirmed in the NT especially with the 'I am saying' Jn 14:6-7 a also with the Pauline epistles (1 Cor 8: 6). Yahweh is the greatest king above all others claiming divinity. Thus, Yahweh deserves our devoted worship.

Today, in the context of Indian society, addressing Yahweh as the true God and the affirmation of God as absolute over other gods is a great challenge in the landscape of religious plurality. However, it is important to maintain the distinctiveness of the sovereign God of the Bible in a multi-religious and multi-cultural context without hurting the sentiments of those of other faiths.

12.1.2. Primary Connotations in Relation to the Kingship Metaphor

The primary connotations that emerge out of my exegesis are: *Firstly*, there is *universal worship* of Yahweh. The metaphor of Yahweh's kingship has dual aspects as the king over all *Israel*, and over the *universe*. The psalmist invites people to claim Yahweh as the king of all. The phrase 'Yahweh reigns' does not refer simply to Yahweh's reign over Israel but over the whole world. All nations must witness that Yahweh is the king of kings. God is forever the Lord of the whole world. The psalmist urges worshippers to rejoice in the presence of Yahweh who rules the universe. All the nations are called upon to come into the presence of Yahweh. This indicates that the kingship of Yahweh and salvation are not limited to the covenant people of God but they can be embraced by all who claim that Yahweh is the true God.

Along with the OT, the NT talks about universal worship: All nations will come and worship God and every tongue shall confess that Jesus Christ is Lord to the glory of God the Father (Rev 15:4; Phi 2:11).

Secondly, Yahweh is the *righteous judge*. The connotative meaning of kingship shows that Yahweh is the *righteous judge* who loves acts of righteousness and justice, and opposes injustice and iniquity. Evidently, Yahweh governs and judges the people with equity. As the texts mention, Yahweh's coming to deliver and give a right judgment brings justice not only to the people, but also the whole of creation. This gives a wider perspective on God's involvement in the life of people. Therefore, when we talk about Yahweh as king, it denotes divine kingship governing in justice as well as righteousness, faithfulness, compassion and stability. Thus, the righteous judge and his judgements are to be honoured and held with utmost reverence.

Thirdly, Yahweh is the *protector* of the people. One of the primary meanings of the connotations of kingship refers to Yahweh as the *protector* of the people. Therefore, Yahweh the king governs history, religious orders and the social life of his people. The metaphor of Yahweh's kingship has much to say regarding the dominion of Yahweh in all spheres of the lives of the people of Israel. The enthronement texts indicate that worship, which consists of homage, praises, thanksgiving and confession, arises out of a sense of thanksgiving to Yahweh who guards and defends their well-being. Looking at all these aspects, the people were encouraged to worship Yahweh the protector and refuge of the people.

12.1.3. Relevance of the Connotations of Kingship Metaphor to Worship

Additionally, the study has brought out some further connotations which have a direct relevance to worship. These connotations and their implications for worship are detailed below.

Firstly, humility in worship of Yahweh is emphasized. The enthronement texts address *humility in worship*. In relation to humility, the psalmist points out explicit postures and gestures which were significant in Israel's worship. Body language can express an individual's relationship to God, and it is not surprising that worship involves certain body movements. For instance, bowing and kneeling portray appropriate respect and honour. Prostrating oneself is the biblical word for worship and it is a sign of self-lowering before Yahweh. Kneeling and bowing are symbolic acts of worshippers which show humility and submission in the presence of Yahweh. Through these, worshippers express and present themselves to Yahweh. In my view, the acts of kneeling and bowing inspire and encourage worshippers to pour themselves before God.

A humble mind is an essential aspect of the worship of God. It encourages worshippers to thank Yahweh in humility and acknowledge the full authority of his kingship. Postures help worshippers express humility and communicate with God. These postures of humility have many possibilities and implications even for today's worship because true worshippers need to have a mind of humility in order to worship and serve God sincerely.

Secondly, music in the worship of Yahweh is significant. The enthronement psalms repeatedly mention זמר 'to make music or sing praises to God' (Pss 47:5, 98:5-6). Music was an essential element in Israel's worship. Music in enthronement psalms reflects th*e being of God*. Through music*, the being of Yahweh the king* is proclaimed in glory. All nature reveals the greatness of Yahweh. This is how humanity, and even nature, glorify the divine being of God. Music is one way in which worshippers fully express their worship to Yahweh. This idea is seen even in the NT where worshippers are encouraged to sing psalms and make melody to the Lord (Eph 5:19; Rev 4:8, 15:2-3).

Music in worship involves the mind, soul and body together to glorify God. Here, a *human's total being* is involved in the worship of Yahweh. Music is an important way of approaching the *mystery* of God and of expressing the joy of being in God's presence. Without a doubt, worshippers can express a wider intensity of feeling through music in worship. Singing with a musical instrument is an intrinsic part of religious expression. I fully support that the use of musical instruments along with vocals enhances today's worship of Yahweh as it has over the centuries. Thus, the use of music has immense implications for Christian worship.

Thirdly, rejoicing is an important aspect in the worship of Yahweh. The psalmist mentions יהוה מלך with its exhortation גיל to 'rejoice.' As I found in my exegesis, *rejoicing in the Lord* is important in worship. Rejoicing is an essential characteristic of the enthronement psalms. The psalmists clearly announce the kingship of Yahweh and persuade the earth to rejoice. For example, Zion has heard and rejoices, so as the daughters of Judah on account of the righteous judgment of God. The heavens and the earth declare the greatness of Yahweh and rejoice. The people rejoice because Yahweh is the king as well as the one who judges the people in uprightness. The psalms urge both Israel and the world as a whole to rejoice in Yahweh (Pss 96, 97, 98). Again, this idea is seen in the NT (Phil 4:4). Worship is not just about asking for blessings from God, it is all about rejoicing in the Lord because Yahweh is the king of kings and the one who gives us salvation through Jesus Christ. *Rejoicing is a sign of giving oneself to God faithfully* and it indicates a right relationship with God. To rejoice is to engage our whole being in exalting God in the highest. In today's worship, it is important to encourage people to rejoice in God, and the psalmist's reminder to the people to rejoice and give due worship to the Lord is relevant to us today.

12.1.4. Missional Concern of the Enthronement Psalms in a Pluralistic Context

The *particularity and universality has missional implications*. Yahweh has chosen the nation of Israel to be the light of the world. According to Christopher J. H. Wright, "the mission of God is to bless all nations on earth."[1] "The goal of God's plan was always to invite all human beings to salvation, because from the very beginning the plan of redemption was never concealed nor reserved only for one family, group, or nation. Through Abraham and his posterity, all the families of the earth were to be blessed."[2] Abraham is not chosen over against the rest of the peoples and nations, but for the sake of the rest of the whole nations. Abraham is presented in the enthronement psalms as a model of God's mission especially in Psalm 47.

Psalm 96 is a call for *global praise.* The God of Israel is a living God and the true King. It is a call for all the nations, all the peoples, all the earth to worship and praise and tremble before Yahweh the king. The enthronement psalms, and particularly into psalms 47 and 96, presents a sufficient mandate for the mission of God and the vision of mission which is inclusive in nature. In Psalm 96:2–9, the psalmist calls believers to proclaim and it appears in the imperative intensive form of the verb to 'declare' or recount God's salvation among the nations.

The call to worship in Psalm 96 echoes the *missional message* of all enthronement psalms when it calls for declaring God's glory among the nations. All people belong to Yahweh and so the psalmist summons the nations into the courts of Yahweh. The mission of Yahweh extends beyond Israel and is open for the nations to come in and worship (Pss 47, 96). The people of

---

1 Christopher J. H. Wright, *Knowing the Holy Spirit through the Old Testament* (Downers Grove: InterVarsity Press, 2006), 99.

2 Jiri Moskala, "The Mission of God's People in the Old Testament," *Journal of the Adventist Theological Society* 9, no. 1-2 (2008): 58.

Israel are called to be a representative to all the nations in order to extend the kingship of Yahweh. Nothing is more important than the commandment of God for the people to come and worship Yahweh.[3]

The people of God are to be an agent of Yahweh's kingship to the nations. When people of all colours and races of the world come under the kingship of Yahweh and sing praises to Yahweh, they acknowledge the true God apart from all other gods. The fact that worship invites all people implies that the grace of Yahweh is for all people. And in response to that, every nation is called to acknowledge Yahweh faithfully and sincerely (cf. Jer 10:7, 10; Mal 11). The God of Israel opens the doors of salvation for all those who choose to follow him. The mission of God flows from the roots of the faith in the OT, and it is the same God who entrusts his mission to the people in the NT as in the great commission (Mt 28:19-20). We see there is universality in particularity because mission is all about inviting all the peoples of the earth to hear God. Thus, the kingship metaphor of Yahweh in relation to worship has a *missional function* in a religious pluralistic context.

12.2. Possible Leads for Further Research

I would like to conclude by giving two significant leads or prospects for further study stemming from my work:

First, perspectives on the *singularity* of Yahweh within a religiously pluralistic society could be further explored. The implications in a religious pluralistic society, including hostile reactions to the singularity of God or synchronism, need to be explored. This area of research deals with the question of how Yahweh interacts with culture.

Secondly, another lead area is the *theology of praising Yahweh*. In various places, the psalmists declare the kingship of Yahweh and follow it with an exhortation to the people to give praise to God. Praise touches the whole range of the enthronement psalms, and, therefore, the researchers can bring out new insights into praise.

Summary

In *Chapter 1*, I have defined the terms and method of research adopted in this thesis. In *Chapter 2*, I have discussed the kingship metaphor of Yahweh in Ancient West Asian religions. I focused on how the kingship metaphor impacted all aspects of life of the people of AWA and of Israel and how Yahweh becomes the king of the entire world. I have shown the significance of the kingship of God and worship in the poetic traditions of the Hebrew Bible. I have also compared the ideology of kingship of God in West Asia, poetic traditions in Old Testament and enthronement psalms. It reflects the high point

3 Glasser, *Announcing the Kingdom: The Story of God's Mission in the Bible*, 29.

of Yahweh's exaltation as the king. *Chapters 3 to Chapter 10* dealt with the historical and literary analysis of all the enthronement psalms with exegetical tools by giving special consideration of form criticism. Each chapter discusses the significance of each individual enthronement psalm. All the enthronement psalms expressed the kingship metaphor of Yahweh in connection to worship and this is the unique point. Based on the exegetical studies in *Chapter 11*, I have focused on the kingship metaphor and its implication for worship in a pluralistic context. Thus, this chapter addresses the implications of denotation and connotations of Yahweh's kingship metaphor in relation to worship especially in the Indian context. Thus, in *Chapter 12*, I have mentioned some of my findings from both the primary denotation and the primary connotations of the kingship metaphor of Yahweh in relation to worship. Finally, the implications of these for worship and missional aspect in a pluralistic context for India today have been discussed.

The significance of my thesis is that it brings out how worship is embedded in the enthronement texts through the kingship metaphor. The enthronement texts prompt true worship of Yahweh, the high king, who is the centre of universal adoration. Denotation is linked to Yahweh's character as sovereign, powerful and transcendent. This particularity leads to universality. It is the connotations that are linked to the universality of Yahweh, who goes out to the nations in justice, righteousness and shepherd care. The fruit of such a literary analysis connectedness to particularity and universality gives us a tool by which to motivate a congregation of believers to give due worship to Yahweh. Thus, it shows how this kingship of Yahweh impacted Israel's worship and how it can continue to have an effect on worship today.

Appendix-I Musical Instruments

The musical instruments שופר 'horn,' כנור 'lyre' *and* חצצרה 'trumpet' are mentioned in the enthronement psalms. "Make music to the Lord with a lyre, with trumpets and the sound of the horn (Pss 47:6, 98:5-6). These instruments performed a special role in the worship of Yahweh.

שופר is used as a signaling instrument (Pss 47:6, 98:6). Unlike the other instruments, the horn was blown before and after solemn occasions and celebrations. ונכ is a stringed instrument and used to accompany vocals (Ps 98: 5). The lyre is a melodious instrument considered to be one of the widely used instruments in olden days חצצרה was mostly played by the priests rather than by the Levites. It is similar to horn and used for summoning people for worship (Ps 98:6).

שופר (HORN)

כנור (KINNOR)

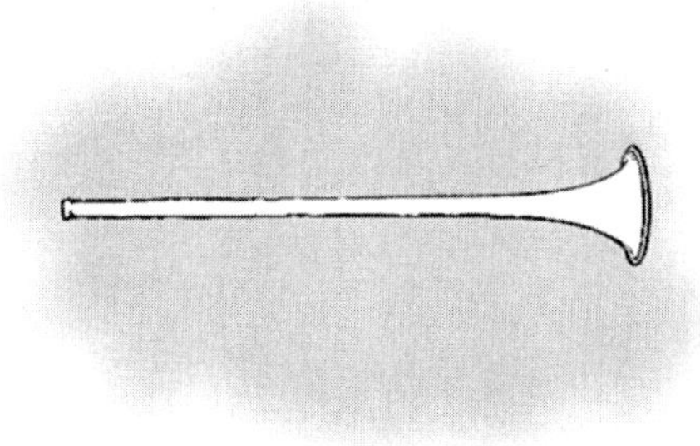

חצצרה (TRUMPET)

Appendix–II Postures and Gestures

The Hebrew Bible mentions various postures and gestures in connection with worship. In the enthronement psalms, however, only *clapping, bowing, kneeling and shouting* are mentioned. These postures and gestures play a vital role in Israel's worship and still in today's worship.

תקע clapping hands appears twice in the enthronement psalms (Pss 47:2, 98:8). Clapping of hands indicates joyous moments in the worship of Yahweh. כרע bowing is significant in Israel's worship. It is a sign of respect and humility in the presence of God (Ps 95:6). ברך kneeling is an essential part of Israel's worship (Ps 95:6). It is an act of submission and surrendering oneself before God. רוע is shouting and it is an expression of rejoicing at the highest level in the presence of God. It is also used in proclaiming the victory of God over his enemies (Pss 47:1, 95:1-2, 96:12, 98:4, 6).

תקע (CLAPPING)

כרע (BOWING)

ברך (KNEELING)

רוע (SHOUTING)

Bibliography

Aitken, K.T. "שמע." In *New International Dictionary of Old Testament Theology & Exegesis.* Vol. 4. Edited by William A. VanGemeren, Carlisle: Paternoster Press, 1996, 175-181.

Albertz, R. "פלא." In *Theological Lexicon of the Old Testament.* Vol. 2. Edited by Ernst Jenni and Claus Westermann. Translated by Mark E. Biddle. Peabody: Hendrickson Publishers, Inc., 1997, 981-986.

Allen, Leslie, C. "ידה." In *New International Dictionary of Old Testament Theology & Exegesis.* Vol. 2. Edited by William VanGemeren. Carlisle: Paternoster Press, 1997, 405-408.

Allen, Leslie C. "שִׁיר." In *New International Dictionary of Old Testament Theology & Exegesis.* Vol. 4. Edited by William A. VanGemeren. Grand Rapids: Zondervan, 1997, 90-100.

Alter, Robert. *The Art of Biblical Narrative.* New York: Basic Books, 1981.

———. *The Art of Biblical Poetry.* New York: Basic Books, 1985.

Anderson, A.A. "The Book of Psalms: Psalms 1-72." In *New Century Bible Commentary.* Vol. 1. London: William B. Eerdmans Publishing Company, 1985.

———. "The Book of Psalms: Psalms 73-150." In *New Century Bible Commentary.* Vol. 2. London: William B. Eerdmans Publishing Company, 1989.

Anderson, Bernhard W. *Out of the Depths: The Psalms Speak for Us Today.* Louisville: Westminster John Knox Press, 2000.

Arthur, James P. *God Deserves Our Worship.* Mustang, Oklahoma: Tate Publishing & Enterprises, 2010.

Averbeck, Richard E. "Worship God in Spirit." *Authentic Worship: Hearing Scripture's Voice, Applying Its Truths.* Edited by Herbert W. Bateman. Grand Rapids: Kregel Publications, 2002.

Avrahami, Yael. "בוש in the Psalms-Shame or Disappointment?" *JSOT,* Vol. 34, No. 3 (2010): 295–313.

Bainton, Roland H. *Here I Stand: A Life of Martin Luther*. New York: Abingdon Press, 1950.

Barber, Michael. *Singing in the Reign: The Psalms and Liturgy of God's Kingdom*. Steubenville: Emmaus Road Publishing, 2001.

Bartel, Dietrich. *Musica Poetica: Musical-Rhetorical Figures in German Baroque Music*. Lincoln, Nebraska: University of Nebraska Press, 2007.

Barton, John. *Understanding Old Testament Ethics: Approaches and Explorations*. Louisville: Westminster John Knox Press, 2003.

Beale, G. K. *The Temple and the Church's Mission: A Biblical Theology of the Dwelling Place of God, New Studies in Biblical Theology*. Edited by D. A. Carson. Downers Grove: InterVarsity Press, 2004.

Beeke, Joel R. "Calvin on Piety." In *The Cambridge Companion to John Calvin*. Edited by Donald K. McKim. Cambridge: Cambridge University, 2004.

Bellinger, W.H. *Psalms: Reading and Studying the Book of Praises*. Peabody: Hendrickson Publishers, Inc., 1990.

Bernhard, Anderson W. *Understanding the Old Testament*. New Jersey: Pearson Prentice Hall, 2007.

Best, Harold M. "Music in Israelite Worship." In *The Biblical Foundations of Christian Worship*. Vol. I. Edited by Robert E. Webber. Peabody: Hendrickson Publishers, Inc., 1993.

Block, Daniel I. *Beyond the River Chebar: Studies in Kingship and Eschatology in the Book of Ezekiel*. Cambridge: James Clarke & Co, 2014.

———. *The Gods of the Nations: A Study in Ancient Near Eastern National Theology*. Grand Rapids: Baker Books, 2000.

Braulik, George P. "Psalter and Messiah: Towards A Christological Understanding of the Psalms in the Old Testament and Church Fathers." *Psalms and Liturgy*. Edited by Dirk J. Human and Vos. London: T & T Clark International, 2004.

Breckbill, David. "Love, Music, and the Bible: In Praise of Interpretive Flexibility." *Union Biblical Seminary Journal,* Vol. 8. No. 2, Vol. 9. No. 1 (September, 2013, March, 2015): 129-136.

Brettler, Marc Zvi. *God is King: Understanding an Israelite Metaphor*. Sheffield: Academic Press, 1989.

Bridge, Edward J. "Loyalty, Dependency and Status with YHWH: The Use of עבד in Psalms." *Vetus Testamenttum* No. 59 (2009): 360–378.

Briggs, Charles A. "An Inductive Study of Selah." *Journal of Biblical Literature.* No. 18 (1899): 132–42.

Briggs, Charles Augustus, and Emilie Grace Briggs. "A Critcal and Exegetical Commentary on the Book of Psalms." In *The International Critical Commentary,* Vol. 1. Edinburgh: T & T Clark Ltd, 1906.

———. "A Critical and Exegetical Commentary on the Book of Psalms." In *The International Critical Commentary*.Vol. II. Edinburgh: T&T Clark Ltd, 1907.

Bromiley, G.W. "Zwingli and Bullinger." In *The Library of Christian Classics*. Vol. XXIV. London: SCM Press, 1958.

Brown, Francis, S.R. Driver, and Charles A. Briggs. *Hebrew and English Lexicon of the Old Testament*. Oxford: Oxford University Press, 1907.

Brown II, A. Philip, and Bryan.W Smith, eds. *A Reader's Hebrew Bible*. Zondervan, 2008.

Broyles, Craig C. "The Psalms and Cult Symbolism: The Case of the Cherubim-Ark." *Interpreting the Psalms: Issues and Approaches*. Edited by Philip S. Johnston and David G. Firth. England: InterVarsity Press, 2005.

Brueggemann, Walter. "First and Second Samuel." *Interpretation, A Bible Commentary for Teaching and Preaching*. Louisville: John Knox Press, 1990.

———. "Psalm 100." *Interpretation*. Vol. 1, No. 39 (1985): 65–69.

———. *The Message of the Psalms: A Theological Commentary*. Minneapolis: Augsburg Publishing House, 1984.

———. *Theology of the Old Testament*. Minneapolis: Fortress Press, 2005.

———. *Worship in Ancient Israel: An Essential Guide*. Nashville: Abingdon Press, 2005.

Brueggemann, Walter, and W.H. Bellinger. "Psalms." In *New Cambridge Bible Commentary*. Edited by Ben Witherington III. New York: Cambridge University Press, 2014.

Bruner, Frederick Dale. "The Churchbook Matthew 13-28." In *Matthew A Commentary*. Grand Rapids: William B. Eerdmans Publishing Company, 2004.

Burns, Marie. *The Poetic Books Part II: Psalms 73-150 & Proverbs*. Bloomington: Author House, 2005.

Byars, Roland R. *Christian Worship: Glorifying and Enjoying God*. Louisville: Westminster John Knox Press, 2000.

Childs, Brevard S. *Old Testament Theology in a Canonical Context*. London: SCM Press Ltd, 1985.

Chinitz, Jacob. "The Three Tenses in The Kingdom of God: God of Israel or of the World." *Jewish Bible Quarterly*. Vol. 38, No. 4 (2010): 255–60.

Chisholm, Robert B. "A Theology of the Psalms." *A Biblical Theology of the Old Testament*. Edited by Roy B. Zuck. Chicago: Moody Press, 1991.

Chuzho, Husazulu. "A Theological Appraisal of Worship of Yahweh Alone in Old Testament with Special Reference to the Book of Psalms." *BTC Journal*. No. V (2014): 1–18.

Clarke, Arthur G. *Analytical Studies in the Psalms*. Grand Rapids: Kregel Publications, 1979.

Clifford, Richard J. *Psalms 1-72: Abingdon Old Testament Commentaries*. Nashville: Abingdon Press, 2002.

Collins, C. John. "כבד." In *New International Dictionary of Old Testament Theology & Exegesis.* Vol. 2. Edited by Willem A. VanGemeren. Grand Rapids: Zondervan, 1997, 577-587.

———. "נשק." In *New International Dictionary of the Old Testament Theology & Exegesis.*Vol. 3. Edited by Willem A. VanGemeren.Grand Rapids, Michigan: Zondervan, 1997, 196-197.

Cook, Stephen L. *The Social Roots of Biblical Yahwism*. Atlanta: Society of Biblical Literature, 2004.

Cornelius, I. "הדם." In *New International Dictionary of Old Testament Theology & Exegesis.* Vol. I. Edited by Willem A. VanGemeren. Carlisle: Paternoster Press, 1997, 1011-1012.

Courvoisier, Jaques. *Zwingli: A Reformed Theologian*. Virginia: John Knox Press, 1963.

Craigie, Peter C. "Psalms 1-50." In *Word Biblical Commentary*. Vol. 1. Edited by David A. Hubbard and Glenn W. Barker. Waco: Word Books, 1983.

Croft, Steven J.L. *The Identity of Individual Psalms*. Sheffield: Sheffield Academic Press, 1987.

Cundall, A.E. "Baal." In *The Zondervan Pictorial Encylopedia.*Vol. I. Edited by Merrill C. Tenney. Grand Rapids: Zondervan, 1976.

Curtis, Edward M. "Ancient Psalms and Modern Worship." *Bibliotheca Sacra.* Vol. 154, No. 615 (July-September, 1997): 285–86.

Dahood, Mitchell. *Psalms 51-100: The Anchor Bible*. New York: Doubleday, 1968.

Davis, Ellen F. "Psalm 98 Rejoicing in Judgment." *Interpretation.* No. 46 (1992): 171–75.

Dawn, Marva J. *Reaching Out Without Dumbing Down: A Theology of Worship for the Turn-of-the-Century Culture*. Grand Rapids, Michigan: William B. Eerdmans Publishing Company, 1995.

Dawn, Marva J. "Worship to Form a Missional Community." *Direction.* Vol. 28, No. 2 (1999): 139–52.

Day, John. *God's Conflict with the Dragon and the Sea: Echoes of a Canaanite Myth in the Old Testament*. Cambridge: Cambridge University, 1985.

———. *Psalms*. New York: T&T Clark International, 2003.

deClaisse-Walford, Nancy, Rolf A. Jacobson, and Beth LaNeel Tanner. "The Book of Psalms." In *The New International Commentary on the Old*

Testament. Edited by Robert L. Hubbard. Grand Rapids, Michigan: Wm. B. Eerdmans Publishing Co, 2014.

Dongshi, Antonio. *Words and Gestures in Liturgy*. Collegeville: Liturgical Press, 2009.

Dudley, Martin. "Movement in Worship." In *The New Westminster Dictionary of Liturgy and Worship*. Edited by Paul Bradshaw. Louisville: SCM Press, 2002, 325.

Dunn, James D.G. *Unity and Diversity in the New Testament: An Inquiry into the Character of Earliest Christianity*. London: SCM Press, 1993.

Durlesser, James A. "Trishagion Und Gottesterrschaft: Psalm 99 Als Neuinterpretation von Tora Und Propheten." *Journal Biblical Literature* Vol. 3, No. 110 (1991): 519–20.

Dyrness, William. *Themes in the Old Testament Theology*. Illinois: InterVarsity Press, 1977.

Eaton, John. *Psalms of the Way and the Kingdom: A Conference with the Commentators*. Sheffield: Sheffield Academic Press, 1995.

———. *The Psalms: A Historical and Spiritual Commentary with an Introduction and New Translation*. London: Continuum International Publishing Group, 2005.

Eaton, John.H. *Kingship and the Psalms*. Sheffield: JSOT Press, 1986.

Eichrodt, Walter. "Ezekiel: A Commentary." In *The Old Testament Library*. Philadelphia: The Westminster Press, 1970.

Elliger, Karl, and Wilhelm Rudolph, eds. *Biblia Hebraica Stuttgartensia*. Stuttgart: Biblia Hebraica Stuttgartensia, 1997.

Endres, John C. "The Spiritual Vision of Chronicles: Wholehearted, Joy-Filled Worship of God." *Catholic Biblical Quarterly*. No. 69 (2007): 1–21.

Enns, Peter. E. "Creation and Re-Creation: Psalm 95 and Its Interpretation in Hebrew 3:1-4:13." *Westminster Theological Journal*. No. 55 (1993): 255–80.

Firth, David G. "The Teaching of the Psalms." In *Interpreting the Psalms: Issues and Approaches*. Edited by Philip S. Johnston and David G. Firth. England: InterVarsity Press, 2005.

Flynn, Shawn W. *YHWH is King: The Development of Divine Kingship in Ancient Israel*. Leiden: Koninklijke Brill NV, 2014.

Frankfort, Henri. *Kingship and the Gods: A Study of Ancient Near Eastern Religion as the Integration of Society & Nature*. Chicago: The University of Chicago Press, 1948.

Fretheim, Terence E. "חוה." In *New International Dictionary of the Old Testament Theology & Exegesis*. Vol. 2. Edited by William VanGemeren. Carlisle: Paternoster Press, 1996, 42-44.

Fretheim, Terrence E. "אל." In *New International Dictionary of Old Testament Theology & Exegesis*. Vol. I. Edited by Willem A. VanGemeren. Grand Rapids: Zondervan, 1997.

Friedmann, Jonathan L. *Music in Biblical Life: The Roles of Songs in Ancient Israel*. Jefferson, North Carolina: McFarland & Company, Inc., Publishers, 2013.

Futato, Mark D. *Interpreting the Psalms: An Exegetical Handbook*. Grand Rapids: Kregel Academic & Professional, 2007.

Gan, Jonathan. *The Metaphor of Shepherd in the Hebrew Bible: A Historical -Literary Reading*. Lanham: University Press of America, 2007.

———. "The Metaphor of the Shepherds in Zachariah 11: 4-17. M.Th Thesis." University of South Africa. 2010.

Gentile, Ernest B. *Worship God: Exploring the Dynamics of Psalmic Worship*. Portland: City Bible Publishing, 1994.

Gerstenberger, Erhard S. *Psalms, Part 2 and Lamentations: The Forms of the Old Testament Literature*. Vol. XV. Grand Rapids: William B. Eerdmans Publishing Company, 2001.

———. *Psalms, Part I, with an Introduction to Cultic Poetry:The Forms of the Old Testament Literature*. Vol. XIV. Grand Rapids: William B. Eerdmans Publishing Company, 1988.

———. "Singing a New Song: On Old Testament and Latin American Psalmody." *Word World*. Vol. 2, No. 5 (Spring, 1985): 155–67.

Giuliano, R. Mark. "Psalm 47: A Note on Clapping in Worship." *Encounter*. Vol. 72, No. 2 (2012): 83–84.

Glasser, Arthur F. *Announcing the Kingdom: The Story of God's Mission in the Bible*. Grand Rapids: Baker Academic, 2003.

Goldingay, John. *Key Questions about Christian Faith: Old Testament Answers*. Grand Rapids: Brazos Press, 2010.

———. *Old Testament Theology: Israel's Faith*. Vol. 2. Illinois: InterVarsity Press, 2006.

———. *Old Testament Theology: Israel's Life*. Vol. 3. Downers Grove: InterVarsity Press, 2009.

———. "Psalms 1-41." In *Baker Commentary on the Old Testament Wisdom and Psalms*. Vol. 1. Edited by Tremper Longman III. Grand Rapids: Baker Academic, 2006.

———. "Psalms 42-89." In *Baker Commentary on the Old Testament Wisdom and Psalms*. Vol. 2. Edited by Tremper Longman III. Grand Rapids: Baker Academic, 2007.

———. "Psalms 90-150." In *Baker Commentary on the Old Testament Wisdom and Psalms*. Vol. 3. Edited by Tremper Longman III. Grand Rapids: Academic Press, 2008.

———. *Songs from a Strange Land: Psalms 42-51*. Illinois: InterVarsity Press, 1978.

Gordon, Robert P. "טוב." In *New International Dictionary of Old Testament Theology & Exegesis.*Vol. 2. Edited by Willem A. VanGemeren. Carlisle: Paternoster Press, 1997, 353-356.

Gordon, R.P. *1 & 2 Samuel*. Sheffield: Sheffield Academic Press, 1993.

Greef, Wulfert de. "Calvin's Writings." In *The Cambridge Companion to John Calvin*. Edited by Donald K. McKim. Cambridge: Cambridge University, 2004.

Greifsward, H.J. Zobel. "חסד." In *Theological Dictionary of the Old Testament.* Vol. V. Edited by G. Johannes Botterweck and Ringgren, Helmer. Translated by Green, David E. Grand Rapids: William B. Eerdmans Publishing Company, 1986, 44-64.

———. "עליון." In *Theological Dictionary of the Old Testament.* Vol. XI. Edited by G. Johannes Botterweck., Grand Rapids: William B. Eerdmans Publishing Company, 2001, 121-139.

Grogan, Geoffrey W. *Psalms: The Two Horizons Old Testament Commentary Psalms*. Grand Rapids: Wm. B. Eerdmans Publishing Co, 2008.

Gunkel, Hermann. *Die Psalmen Ubersetzt Erklart*. Göttingen: Vandenhoeck & Ruprecht, 1925.

———. *Genesis*. Translated by Mark E. Biddle. Macon: Mercer University Press, 1997.

———. *Introduction to Psalms: The Genres of the Religious Lyric of Israel*. Macon, Georgia: Mercer University Press, 1998.

Guthrie, Harvey H. *Israel's Sacred Songs: A Study of Dominant Themes*. New York: The Seabury Press, 1978.

Hale, Thomas. *The Applied Old Testament Commentary:Applying God's Word to Your Life*. Eastbourne: David C. Cook, 2007.

Hanson, Howard Elvin. "The Canaanite God El: His Role in Ugaritic Literature." Master of Arts. Thesis, McMaster University, Ontario, 1970.

Hargreaves, John. *A Guide to Psalms*. Delhi: ISPCK, 1987.

Haroutunian, Joseph, ed. "Calvin: Commentaries." *The Library of Christian Classics*. Vol. XXIII. London: SCM Press Ltd, 1958.

Haselock, Jeremy. "Gestures." *The New Westminster Dictionary of Liturgy and Worship*. Louisville: SCM Press, 2002, 227-230.

———. "Posture." In *The New Westminster Dictionary of Liturgy and Worship*. Edited by Paul Bradshaw. Louisville: SCM Press, 2002, 377-379.

Heiser, Michael S. "The Baal Cycle as Backdrop to Daniel 7: A Paradigm for Jewish Binitarianism and the New Testament's High Christology." *ETS Atlanta* (2003).

Hilber, John W. "Psalms." In *Zondervan Illustrated Bible Backgrounds Commentary*. Vol. 5. Edited by John H. Walton. Grand Rapids: Zondervan, 2009.

Hill, Andrew E. "צור." In *Dictionary of Old Testament & Exegesis*. Vol. 3. Edited by Willem A. VanGemeren. Grand Rapids: Zondervan, 1997, 793-794.

Ho, Shirley, and Feng Yi Lin. "Psalms 73-150." In *Asia Bible Commentary Series*. Edited by Bruce J. Nicholls. Manila: Asia Theological Association, 2013.

House, Paul R. *Old Testament Theology*. Downers Grove: InterVarsity Press, 1998.

Howard, David M. *The Structure of Psalms 93-100*. Winona Lake: Eisenbrauns, 1997.

Hulst, A.R. "עמ." In *Theological Lexicon of the Old Testament*. Edited by Ernst Jenni and Claus Westermann. Peabody: Hendrickson Publishers, Inc., 1997, 896-919.

Hustad, Donald P. "The Psalms as Worship Expression: Personal and Congregational." *Review Expositor* Vol. 81, No. 3 (Summer, 1984): 407-424.

Jacobson, Delmar L. "The Royal Psalms and Jesus Messiah: Preparing to Preach on a Royal Psalm." *Word World* (1985): 192–98.

Jesurathnam, Kondasingu. *Dalit Liberative Hermeneutics: Indian Christian Dalit Interpretation of Psalm 22*. Delhi: ISPCK, 2010.

Johnson, Aubrey. *Sacral Kingship in Ancient Israel*. Cardiff: University of Wales Press, 1967.

———. *The Cultic Prophet and Israel's Psalmody*. Cardiff: Universality of Wales Press, 1979.

Johnson, B. "משפט." In *Theological Dictionary of the Old Testament.* Vol. IX. Edited by G. Johannes Botterweck. Translated by David E Green. Grand Rapids: William B. Eerdmans Publishing Company, 1998, 86-89.

———. "צדק." In *Theological Dictionary of the Old Testament.* Vol. XII. Edited by G. Johannes Botterweck. Grand Rapids: William B. Eerdmans Publishing Company, 2003, 243-264.

Johnson, Barry C. *A Change is Gonna Come: The Transformation of a Traditional to a Contemporary Worship Celebration*. Bloomington: Author House, 2008.

Johnson, H.Wayne. "Practicing Theology on a Sunday Morning: Corporate Worship as Spiritual Formation." *TRINJ* No. 31 (2010): 27–44.

Jones, Ivor H. "Musical Instruments." In *The Anchor Bible Dictionary.* Vol. 4. Edited by David Noel Freedman. New York: Doubleday, 1992.

Jonker, Louis. "רעה." *New International Dictionary of Old Testament Theology & Exegesis.*Vol. 3. Edited by William A. VanGemeren. Grand Rapids: Zondervan, 1997, 1138-1146.

Kaiser, Walter C. *Toward Old Testament Ethics*. Grand Rapids: Zondervan Publishing House, 1983.

Kaniarakath, George. "The Merciful God of the Prophets." *Bible Bhashyam* Vol. XXX1, No. 1 (March-December, 1981): 17–29.

Kayser, Phillip G. *Delighting in God's Kingship Over Worship*. Omaha: Biblicalblueprints. Org, 2009.

Kidd, Virginia Bates. *Stones of Grace*. Bloomington, Indiana: Virginia Bates Kidd, 2009.

Kiel, Heinrich Greeven. "Προσκυνεω." In *Theological Dictionary of the New Testament.* Edited by Gerhard Friedrich. Translated by Geoffrey W. Bromiley. Volume VI. Grand Rapids, Michigan: Wm. B. Eerdmans Publishing Co, 1968, 758-766.

Kizhakkeyil, Sebastian. *The Psalms : The Prayer Book of the Bible*. Ruhalaya, Ujjain: Ruhalaya Publications, 2005.

Knight, George, A.F. *Psalms: The Daily Study Bible Series*. Edited by John C.L. Gibson. Edinburgh: Saint Andrew Press, 1983.

Koehler, Ludwing, and Walter Baumgartner. *The Hebrew and Aramaic Lexicon of the Old Testamentt*. Vol. 1. Leiden: Koninklijke Brill NV, 2001.

Konkel, August. "The Exaltation of the Eternal King." *Διδασκαλία* (1990): 14–22.

Koopmans, William. "ברק." In *New International Dictionary of Old Testament Theology & Exegesis.*Vol. I. Edited by Willem A. VanGemeren. Carlisle, Cumbria: Paternoster Press, 1996, 769-770.

Korada, Manoja Kumar. "Idolatry: A Problem in the Old Testament." *Bible Bhashyam.* Vol. XXXX, No. 4 (2014): 195–214.

Kraus, Hans-Joachim. "Psalms 1-59." *A Continental Commentary*. Translated by Hilton C. Oswald. Minneapolis: Fortress Press, 1993.

———. "Psalms 60-150." *A Continental Commentary*. Translated by Hilton C. Oswald. Minneapolis: Fortress Press, 1993.

———. *Theology of the Psalms*. Translated by Keith Crim. Minneapolis: Augsburg Publishing House, 1986.

———. *Worship in Israel: A Cultic History of the Old Testament*. Translated by Geoffrey Buswell. Oxford: Basil Blackwell, 1966.

Kumar, Raj. *History and Cultural Series: Essays on Indian Music*. Edited by Raj Kumar. New Delhi: Discovery Publishing House, 2003.

Kumar, Rathna. "The Role of the Environment in the Worship of Israel." *ABS Journal* Vol. 3, No. 1 (April, 2011): 58–69.

Kurtz, Dean. *God's Word the Final Word on Worship and Music: A Biblical Study*. Waterton: Xulon Press, 2008.

Lama, Ajoy K. "The Placement of Psalm 145 in Book V: A Compositional Analysis." Doctor of Philosophy, Dissertation, Trinity International University, 2002.

Leslie, Elmer A. *The Psalms: Translated and Interpreted in the Light of Hebrew Life and Worship*. New York: Abingdon Press, 1949.

Leupold, H.C. *Exposition of Isaiah: Chapters 1-39.* Vol. I. England: Baker Book House Company, 1986.

Limburg, James. "Psalms." In *Word Biblical Commentary*. Edited by Patrick D. Miller and DavidL. Bartlett. Louisville: Westminster John Knox Press, 2000.

———. "The Book of Psalms." In *The Anchor Bible Dictionary*. Vol. 5. Edited by David Noel Freedman. London: Doubleday, 1992.

Lohse, Bernhard. *Marthin Luthers's Theology: Its Historical and Systematic Develpment*. Translated by Roy A. Harrisville. Minneapolis: Fortress Press, 2006.

Longman III, Tremper. "Literary Approaches to Old Testament Study." *The Face of Old Testament Studies: A Survey of Contemporary Approaches*. Edited by David W. Baker and Bill T. Arnold. Grand Rapids: Baker Books, 1999.

———. "Psalm 98: A Divine Warrior Victory." *JETS.* Vol. 27, No. 3 (September, 1984): 267–74.

Lucas, Ernest C. *Exploring the Old Testament: A Guide to the Psalms & Wisdom Literature*. Vol. 3. Downers Grove: InterVarsity Press, 2003.

Mascarenhas, Theodore. *The Missionary Function of Israel in Psalms 67, 96, and 117*. New York: University Press of America, 2005.

Massouh, Samir. "Exegetical Notes Psalm 95." *TrinJ.* No. 4 (1983): 84–88.

Mays, James L. "Worship, World and Power: An Interpretation of Psalm 100." *Interpretation.* Vol. 23, No. 3 (1969): 315–30.

Mays, James Luther. *Psalms: Interpretation a Bible Commentary for Teaching and Preaching*. Louisville: John Knox Press, 1994.

———. *The Lord Reigns: A Theological Handbook to the Psalms*. Louisville: Westminster John Knox Press, 1994.

McCann, J. Clinton. *A Theological Introduction to the Book of the Psalms: The Psalms as Torah*. Nashville: Abingdon Press, 1993.

———. "Righteousness, Justice and Peace: A Contemporary Theology of the Psalms." *Horizons Biblical Theology.* Vol. 23, No. 2 (December, 2001): 111–31.

———. "The Hope of the Poor: The Psalms in Worship and Our Search for Justice." *Touching the Alter: The Old Testament for Christian Worship.* Edited by Carol M Bechtel. Grand Rapids, Michigan: Wm. B. Eerdmans Publishing Co, 2008.

McGlone, Matthew, S. "What is the Explanatory Value of a Conceptual Metaphor?" *Language Communication.* No. 27 (2007): 109-126.

McGrath, Alister E. *Reformation Thought: An Introduction.* Oxford: Blackwell Publishing, 1999.

McKinnon, James. *Music in Early Christian Literature: Cambridge Reading in the Literature of Music.* Cambridge: Cambridge University Press, 1987.

Menezes, Rui de. *The Legacy of Israel: Collected Essays.* Vol. 3. Mumbai: St Pauls, 2012.

Merrill, Eugene H. *Everlasting Dominion: A Theology of Old Testament.* Nashville: Broadman & Holman Publishers, 2006.

Miller, Patrick D. "El the Warrior." *Harvest Theological Review.* No. 60 (1967): 411–31.

———. "Enthroned on the Praises of Israel: The Praise of God in Old Testament Theology." *Interpretation.* Vol. 39, No. 1 (January, 1985): 5–19.

Miller, Patrick D. "Him Only Shall You Serve Reflections on the Meaning of Old Testament." *Andover Newton Quarterly.* Vol. 11, No. 3 (January, 1971): 139–49.

Miller, Patrick D. *Interpreting the Psalms.* Philadelphia: Fortress Press, 1986.

———. *The Religion of Ancient Israel.* Louisville: Westminster John Knox Press, 2000.

———. *The Way of the Lord: Essays in Old Testament Theology.* Michigan: William B.Eerdmans Publishing Company, 2007.

Mills, Mary E. *Images of God in the Old Testament.* Collegeville: The Liturgical Press, 1998.

Moberly, R.W.L. "אמן." In *New International Dictionary of Old Testament & Exegesis.* Vol. 1. Edited by Willem A. VanGemeren. Carlisle: Paternoster Press, 1997, 427-433.

Mohol, Eliya. "Metaphors of Zion Traditions and their Relevance for Mission." *UBS Journal.* Vol. 5, No. 1 (March, 2007): 85–98.

———. "Prophetic and Popular Responses to Religious Pluralism in Jeremiah." *UBS Journal.* Vol. 6, No. 2 (2009): 31–55.

———. "The Confessional Community of Isaiah 56-66." *Missiology for the 21st Century: South Asia Perspectives*. Edited by Roger E. Hedlund and Paul Joshua. Bhakiaraj. Delhi: ISPCK, 2004.

———. "The Covenantal Rational for Membership in the Zion Community Envisaged in Isaiah 56-66." Unpublished PhD Thesis, Coventry University, 1998.

———. "Zion." In *Dictionary of Mission Theology*. Illinois: InterVarsity Press, 2007, 447-451.

Moore, Anne. *Moving Beyond Symbol and Myth: Understanding the Kingship of God of the Hebrew Bible through Metaphor*. New York: Peter Lang Publishing, 2009.

Moritz, Thorsten. *A Profound Mystery: The Use of the Old Testament in Ephesians*. Leiden: E.J. Brill, 1996.

Moskala, Jiri. "The Mission of God's People in the Old Testament." *Journal of the Adventist Theological Society.* Vol. 9. No. 1–2 (2008): 40–60.

Motyer, J.A. *The Prophecy of Isaiah*. Leicester: InterVarsity Press, 1993.

Mounce, Robert H. "The Book of Revelation." In *The New International Commentary on the New Testamnet.* Grand Rapids: William B. Eerdmans Publishing Company, 1998.

Mowinckel, Sigmund. *The Psalms in Israel's Worship*. Translated by D.R. Ap-Thomas. Oxford: Basil Blackwell, 1962.

———. *The Psalms in Israel's Worship, Two Volumes in One*. Translated by D.R. Ap-Thomas. Grand Rapids: William B. Eerdmans Publishing Company, 2004.

Moyise, Steve. "The Psalms in the Book of Revelation." *The Psalms in the New Testament*. Edited by Steve Moyise and Maarten J.J. Menken. London: T & T Clark International, 2004.

Muilenburg, James. "Abraham and the Nations: Blessing and World History." *Interpretation.* Vol. 19, No. 4 (1965): 387–98.

Muis, Jan. "God Our King." *HTS.* Vol. 64, No. 1 (2008): 269–88.

Munroe, Myles. *The Purpose and Power of Praise and Worship*. Shippensburg: Destiny Image, 2000.

Muthunayagom, Daniel Jones. "Kingship of God and Creation in the Old Testament." M.Th. Thesis, United Theological College, Bangalore, 1982.

———. "The Image of God as King and the Nature of His Power in the Old Testament." *Bangalore Theological Forum.* Vol. XLI, No. 2 (December, 2009): 24–48.

Nassis, Chrysostom. "The Use of Music in Christian Worship: Background and Early Evidence." *Phronema.* No. 22 (2007): 23–36.

Naude, Jackie A. "קדש." In *New International Dictionary of Old Testament & Exegesis.* Vol. 3. Edited by Willem A. VanGemeren. Grand Rapids: Zondervan, 1997, 877-887.

Nel, Philip J. "בוש." In *New International Dictionary of Old Testament Theology & Exegesis.* Vol. I. Edited by Willem A. VanGemeren. Carlisle: Paternoster Press, 1997, 621-627.

———. "מלך." In *New International Dictionary of Old Testament Theology & Exegesis.* Vol. 2. Edited by Willem A. VanGemeren. Grand Rapids: Zondervan, 1997.

Nolland, John. "Luke 1-9." In *Word Biblical Commentary.* Edited by David A. Hubbard and Glenn W. Barker. Dallas: Word Books, 1989.

Nützel, J.M. "Προσκυνεω." In *Exegetical Dictionary of the New Testament.* Vol. 3. Edited by Horst Balz and Gerhard Schneider. Grand Rapids, Michigan: William B. Eerdmans Publishing Company, 1982, reprinted 1994, 173-175.

Obenhaus, Stacy R. "The Creation Faith of the Psalmists." *Trinity Journal* (2000): 132–42.

Okoye, James Chukwuma. *Israel and the Nations: A Mission Theology of the Old Testament.* New York: Orbis Books, 2006.

Old, Hughes Oliphant. *Worship: Reformed According to Scripture.* Louisville: Westminster John Knox Press, 2002.

Olison, Kennon D. *Music in Worship: An Examination of the Contemporary Music in the Churches of Christ.* Bloomington: Kennon D. Olison, 2012.

Ollenburger, Ben C. *Zion the City of the Great King: A Theological Symbol of the Jerusalem Cult.* Sheffield: Sheffield Academic Press, 1987.

Olley, John W. "Forensic Connotation of Bos." *Vêtus Testamentum.* Vol. 26, No. 2 (April, 1976): 230–34.

———. "The God of Heaven: A Look at Attitudes to Other Religions in the Old Testament." *Colloquium.* Vol. 27, No. 2 (1995): 76–94.

Oswalt, John N. "The Book of Isaiah Chapters 40-66." In *The New International Commentary on the Old Testament.* Edited by R.K. Harrison. Grand Rapids: William B. Eerdmans Publishing Company, 1998.

———. "דמם." *New International Dictionary of Old Testament Theology & Exegesis.* Vol. I. Edited by William VanGemeren. Grand Rapids: Zondervan, 1997, 972-973.

Parrish, V. Steven. *A Story of the Psalms: Conversation, Canon, and Congregation.* Collegeville: Liturgical Press, 2003.

Patterson, Richard D. "Singing the New Song: An Examination of Psalms 33, 96, 98 and 149." *Bibliotheca Sacra.* Vol. 656, No. 164 (October-December, 2007): 416–34.

Paul, Mark Sagayam. "Enthronement Psalms/Psalms of Yahweh's Kingship." *Psalms for the People of God*. Edited by Mathew Thekkekara. Bangalore: Asian Trading Corporation, 2008.

Paul, N.J. *Effortless Prayers through Psalms*. Madurai: Word of Christ, 2003.

Paul, Pravan. "Being Light and Salt: Meaning and Mission of the Bible in Multi-Cultural and Multi-Religious Contexts of India." *UBS Journal* Vol. 8. No.2, Vol. 9, No.1. (September, 2013, March, 2015): 30–37.

———. *Power and Love in the Book of Hosea: A Postcolonial Reading*. Delhi: Living Insight Translators & Publisher Pvt. Ltd, 2015.

Pawar, G.M. "Marathi." *Medieval Indian Literature: An Anthology Survey & Selections Assamese, Bengali, And Dogri*. Vol. 1. Edited by K. Ayyappa Paniker. New Delhi: Sahitya Akademi, 1997.

Perdue, Leo G. "Yahweh Is King over All the Earth: An Exegesis of Psalm 47." *Restoration Quarterly.* Vol. 17, No. 2 (1974): 85–98.

Petersen, Allan, Rosengren. *The Royal God: Enthronement Festivals in Ancient Israel and Ugarit*. Sheffield: Sheffield Academic Press, 1998.

Pezhumkattil, Abraham. "Israel's Faith Reflected in the Psalms." *Bible Bhashyam.* Vol. XVI, No. 3 (September, 1990): 156–72.

Philips, John. *Exploring Psalms: An Expository Commentary*. Vol. 2. Grand Rapids: Kregel Publications., 2002.

Pleins, J. David. *The Psalms: Songs of Tragedy, Hope, and Justice*. Maryknoll: Orbis Books, 1993.

Porter, Daniel. "God among the God's: An Analysis of the Function of Yahweh in the Divine Council of Deuteronomy 32 and Psalm 82." Master of Arts. Thesis, School of Religion, Lynchburg, Virginia, 2010.

Potter, G. Richard. *Zwingli*. Cambridge: Cambridge University Press, 1976.

Prabhakar, A. John. "Christian Worship: A Dalit Perspective." *South Asia Theological Research Institute.* Vol. 2, No. 1 (May, 2008): 24–48.

Prasad, Jacob. "Psalms 47: A Case Study in Poetic Techniques in the Psalm." *Bible Bhashyam.* Vol. XXIX, No. 1 (March, 2003): 5–25.

Praven, Jerald. "A Search for a Theology of the Psalter." *ETJ.* Vol. 2, No. 2 (May, 2013): 7–18.

Preuss, H.D. "השתחוה חוה." In *Theological Dictionary of the Old Testament.* Vol. IV. Edited by G. Johannes Botterweck and Helmer Ringgren. Translated by David E. Green. Grand Rapids, Michigan: William B. Eerdmans Publishing Company, 1980, 248-256.

Pritchard, James B. ed. "Akkadian Myths and Epics," *Ancient Near Eastern Texts: Relating to the Old Testament*. Third Edition with Supplement. Translated by Grayson, A.K. Princeton: Princeton University Press, 1969.

——— ed. "Collections of Laws from Mesopotamia and Asia Minor." *Ancient Near Eastern Texts: Relating to the Old Testament*. Third Edition with Supplement. Translated by S.N. Kramer. Princeton: Princeton University Press, 1969.

——— ed. "Egyptian Hymns and Prayers." *Ancient Near Eastern Texts: Relating to the Old Testament*. Third Edition with Supplement. Translated by John A. Wilson. New Jersey: Princeton University Press, 1969.

——— ed. "Hittite, Myths, Epics, and Legends." *Ancient Near Eastern Texts: Relating to Old Testament.* Third Edition with Supplement. Translated by Goetze Albrechet. Princeton: Princeton University Press, 1969.

——— ed."Sumero-Akkadian Hymns and Prayers." Stephens. *Ancient Near Eastern Texts: Relating to the Old Testament*. Third Edition with Supplement.Translated by Ferris J. Princeton: Princeton University Press, 1969.

Rad, Gerhard von. *Old Testament Theology: The Theology of Israel's Historical Traditions*. Vol. 1. Louisville: Westminster John Knox Press, 2001.

Raj, John Samuel. "Cosmic Judge or Overseer of the Word-Order? The Role of Yahweh Portrayed in Psalm 7." *Bangalore Theological Forum*. Vol. XXXIV, No. 2 (2002): 1–15.

Renz, Christopher J. "Come, Let Us Listen to the Voice of the Lord." *Worship*. Vol. 70, No. 2, (March, 1996): 140–53.

Ringgren, Helmer. "Enthronement Festival or Covenant Renewal?" 7 (1962): 45–48.

Roberts, J.J.M. "The Enthronement of Yhwh and David: The Abiding Theological Significance of the Kingship Language of the Psalms." *Catholic Biblical Quarterly*. No. 64 (2002): 675–86.

Robertson, O. Palmer. "The Books of Nahum, Habakkuk, and Zephaniah." *The International Commentary on the Old Testament.* Edited by R.K. Harrison. Vol. 28. Grand Rapids: William B. Eerdmans Publishing Company, 1991.

Rogerson, J.W. *Psalm 1-50*. London: Cambridge University Press, 1977.

Rome, R. North. "חדש." In *Theological Dictionary of the Old Testament.* Vol. IV. Edited by G. Johannes Botterweck and Helmer Ringgren. Translated by David E. Green. Grand Rapids: William B. Eerdmans Publishing Company, 1980, 225-244.

Ross, Allen P. *Holiness to the Lord: A Guide to the Exposition of the Book of Leviticus*. Grand Rapids: Baker Academic, 2002.

Routledge, Robin. *Old Testament Theology: A Thematic Approach*. England: InterVarsity Press, 2008.

Rowley, H.H. *Worship in Ancient Israel: Its Forms and Meaning*. London: S.P.C.K, 1967.

Samartha, S.J. *One Christ Many Religions: Toward a Revised Christology*. Bangalore: SATHRI, 1992.

Sanchez, Leopoldo A. "Theology in Context Music as a Test Case." *Concordia Journal.* Vol. 38, No. 3 (Summer, 2012): 205–24.

Saucy, Robert L. "Doctrine of God." *Evangelical Dictionary of the Theology*. Edited by Walter A. Elwell. Grand Rapids: Baker Book House, 1984, 500-504.

Schäder, Jo-Marí. "Psalm 47- How Universal Is Its Universalism? An Intra-, Inter- and Extratextual Analysis of the Poem." Magister Artium in Ancient Languages and -Cultural Studies in the Faculty of Humanities, Thesis, University of Pretoria, 2008.

Schaefer, Konrad. "Psalms." *Studies in Hebrew Narrative & Poetry.* Edited by David W. Cotter. Collegeville: The Liturgical Press, 2001.

Schnabel, Eckhard J. "Israel, the People of God, and the Nations" Vol. 45, No. 1 (March, 2002): 35–57.

Schneider, C. "Καταφιλέω." In *Exegetical Dictionary of the New Testament.* Vol. *2*. Edited by Horst Balz and Gerhard Schneider. Grand Rapids, Michigan: William B. Eerdmans Publishing Company, 1991.

Schroeder, Christoph O. *History, Justice, & the Agency of God: A Hermeneutical and Exegetical Investigation on Isaiah and Psalms*. Leiden: Koninklijke Brill NV, 2001.

Selman, Martin J. "The Kingdom of God in the Old Testament." *Tyndale Bulletin.* Vol. 40, No. 2 (1989): 161–83.

———. "אור." In *New International Dictionary of Old Testament & Exegesis*. Vol.1. Edited by Willem A. VanGemeren. Carlisle: Paternoster Press, 1997, 324-328.

Seybold, Klaus. *Introducing the Psalms*. Edinburgh: T&T Clark, 1990.

Smith, Gary V. "The Concept of God /The Gods as King in the Ancient Near East and the Bible." *Trinity Journal.* No. 3 (1982): 18–38.

Smith, James E. *The Wisdom Literature and Psalms*. Joplin, Missouri: College Press, 2007.

Smith, Ralph L. "Micah-Malachi." In *Word Biblical Commentary*. Edited by David A. Hubbard and Glenn W. Barker. Vol. 32. Waco: Word Books, 1984.

Snaith, Norman H. "Selah." *Vetus Testamentum.* Vol. 2, No. I. (January, 1952): 43–56.

Soggin, J.A. "רעה." In *Theological Lexicon of the Old Testament.* Vol. 3. Edited by Ernst Jenni and Claus Westermann. Translated by Mark E. Biddle. Peabody: Hendrickson Publishers, Inc., 1997, 1246-1248.

Soskice, J.M. *Metaphor and Religious Language*. Oxford: Clarendon, 1985.

Spero, Shubert. "Biblical Metaphor and the Dynamics of Jewish Demography: A Modern Midrash." *Jewish Bible Quarterly.* Vol. 28. No. 4 (2000): 222-227.

Spickard, Paul R. and Kevin M. Cragg. *A Global History of Christians: How Everyday Believers Experienced their World.* Grand Rapids: Baker Academic, 1994.

Stähli, H.-P. "הוה." In *Theological Lexicon of the Old Testament.*Vol.1. Edited by Ernst Jenni and Claus Westermann. Translated by Mark E. Biddle. Peabody: Hendrickson Publishers, 1997, 398-400.

Stewart, Jeremy J. "King of Kings: The Enthronement of Yahweh." *Studia Antiqua.* Vol. 2. No. 1 (2002): 101–27.

Stoebe, H.J. "טוב." In *Theological Lexicon of the Old Testament.* Vol. 2. Edited by Ernst Jenni and Claus Westermann. Translated by Mark E. Biddle. Peabody: Hendrickson Publishers, Inc., 1997, 486-495.

Stolz, F. "ציון." In *Theological Lexicon of the Old Testament.* Vol. 2. Edited by Ernst Jenni and Claus Westermann. Peabody: Hendrickson Publishers, Inc., 1997, 1071-1076.

Stuhlmueller, Carroll. *Psalm: A Biblical Theological Commentary.* Wilmington: Michael Glazier, 1983.

Sylva, Dennis. "The Rising נהרות of Psalm 93: Chaotic Order." *Journal for the Studyof Old Testament.* Vol. 36, No. 4 (2012): 471–82.

Tate, Marvine E. "Psalms 51-150." In *Word Biblical Commentary*. Vol. 20. Edited by David A. Hubbard. Dallas: Word Books, 1990.

Taylor, William R. "The Book of Psalms." In *The Interpreter's Bible.*Vol. IV. Edited by George Arthur Buttrick. New York: Abingdon Press, 1955.

Terrien, Samuel L. *The Psalms and their Meaning for Today*. New York: The Bobbs-Merrill Company, Inc., 1952.

———. "The Psalms: Strophic Structure and Theological Commentary: Psalms 1-72." In *Eerdmans Critical Commentary.*Vol. 1. Edited by David Noel Freedman. Grand Rapids: Eerdmans Publishing Company, 2003.

———. "The Psalms: Strophic Structure and Theological Commentary: Psalms 73-150." In *Eerdmans Critical Commentary.*Vol. 2. Edited by David Noel Freedman. Grand Rapids: William B. Eerdmans Publishing Company, 2003.

Thong, Joseph S. *Glimpses of Naga Legacy and Culture*. Kottayam: Society for Naga Student's Welfare, 2011.

Tomasino, Anthony. "עולם." In *New International Dictionary of Old Testament Theology & Exegesis.* Vol. 3. Edited by Willem A. VanGemeren. Grand Rapids: Zondervan, 1997, 345-351.

Tucker, Gene. M. *Form Criticism of the Old Testament*. Philadelphia: Fortress Press, 1982.

Verhoef, Pieter A. "חדש." In *New International Dictionary of the Old Testament Theology & Exegesis.* Vol. 2. Edited by Willem A. VanGemeren. Grand Rapids: Zondervan, 1997, 30-37.

Vetter, D. "הוד." In *Theological Lexicon of the Old Testament.* Vol. I. Edited by Ernst Jenni and Claus Westermann. Translated by Mark E. Biddle. Peabody: Hendrickson Publishers, Inc., 1997, 355-356.

Vienna, W. Kornfeld. "קדש." In *Theological Dictionary of the Old Testament.* Vol. XII. Edited by G. Johannes Botterweck. Translated by Douglas W. Stott. Grand Rapids: William B. Eerdmans Publishing Company, 2003, 521-526.

Virkler, Henry A. *Hermeneutics: Principles and Processes of Biblical Interpretation*. Grand Rapids: Baker Book House, 1981.

Vollmer, J. "עשה." In *Theological Lexicon of the Old Testament.* Vol. 2. Edited by Ernst Jenni and Claus Westermann. Translated by Mark E. Biddle. Peabody: Hendrickson Publishers, 1997, 944-951.

Wallace, Robert E. *The Narrative Effect of Book IV of the Hebrew Psalter*. New York: Peter Lang Publishing, Inc., 2007.

Waltke, Bruce K. and James M. Houston. *The Psalms as Chritian Worship: A Historical Commentary*. Grand Rapids: William B. Eerdmans Publishing Company, 2010.

Walton, John H, Victor H. Matthews, and Mark W. Chavalas. *Old Testament: The IVP Bible Background Commentary.* Downers Grove: IVP Academic, 2000.

Watt, Jan G. Van Der. *Family of the King: Dynamics of Metaphors in the Gospel According to John*. Leiden: Koninklijke Brill NV, 2000.

Watts. "Singing the Songs of Babylon in the Worship of the Church." *Encounter.* Vol. 74. No. 2 (2013): 1–17.

Watts, John D.W. "Psalms of Trust, Thanksgiving, and Praise." *Review Expositor.* Vol. 3, No. 81 (Summer, 1984): 395–406.

Watts, Rikk. "The Psalms in Mark's Gospel." *The Psalms in the New Testament*. London: T & T Clark International, 2004.

Wehmeier, G. "הדר." In *Theological Lexicon of the Old Testament.* Vol. I. Edited by Ernst Jenni and Claus Westermann. Translated by Mark E. Biddle. Peabody: Hendrickson Publishers, Inc., 1997, 353-355.

Weiser, Artur. "The Psalms: A Commentary," In *The Old Testament Library.* Edited by Peter Ackroyd. Philadelphia: Westminster John Knox Press, 1962.

———. "The Psalms: A Commentary." *The Old Testament Library*. Edited by Peter Ackroyd. Philadelphia: Westminster John Knox Press, 1962.

Werner, E. "Music." In *The Interpreter's Dictionary of the Bible: An Illustrated Encyclopedia.* Vol. 4. Edited by George Arthur Buttrick. Philadelphia: Westminster John Knox Press, 1962, 457-469.

Westermann, Claus. *Isaiah 40-55: A Commentary*. Philadelphia: The Westminster John Knox Press, 1969.

———. *The Praise of God in the Psalms*. Translated by Keith R. Crim. Virginia: John Knox Press, 1965.

———. *The Psalms Structure, Content & Message*. Translated by Ralph D. Gehrke. Minneapolis: Augsburg Publishing House, 1980.

Whitelam, Keith W. "King and Kingship." In *The Anchor Bible Dictionary*. Vol. 4. K-N. Edited by David Noel Freedman. New York: Doubleday, 1992, 40-48.

White, Susan J. *Foundations of Christian Worship*. Louisville: Westminster John Knox Press, 2006.

Wiersbe, Warrant W. *Real Worship*. Nashville: Thomas Nelson Publishers, 1990.

Wilcock, Michael. "The Message of Psalms 1-72." In *The Bible Speaks Today*. Edited by Alec Motyer. England: InterVarsity Press, 2009.

———. "The Message of Psalms 73-150: Songs for the People of God." In *The Bible Speaks Today*. Edited by Alec Motyer. 2. Nottingham: InterVarsity Press, 2001.

Williams, J.R. "Holiness." In *Evangelical Dictionary of the Theology*. Edited by Walter A. Elwell. Grand Rapids: Baker Book House, 1984, 514-516.

Wilson, Gerald H. "Shaping the Psalter: A Consideration of Editorial Linkage in the Book of Psalms." In *The Shape and Shaping of the Psalter*. Edited by J. Clinton McCann. Sheffield: Sheffield Academic Press, 1993.

Wilson, Gerald Henry. *The Editing of the Hebrew Psalter*. Chico: Society of Biblical Literature, 1985.

Wright, Christopher J.H. *God's People in God's Land: Family, Land, and Property in the Old Testament*. Grand Rapids: William B. Eerdmans Publishing Company, 1990.

———. *Knowing Jesus through the Old Testament*. Chennai: UESI Publication Trust, 2001.

———. *Knowing the Holy Spirit through the Old Testament.* Downers Grove: InterVarsity Press, 2006.

———. *The Mission of God: Unlocking the Bible's Grand Narrative*. Illinois: InterVarsity Press, 2006.

Wright, George, Ernest. "God the Warrior." In *The Flowering of the Old Testament Theology: A Reader in Twentieth-Century Old Testament Theology, 1930-1990*. Edited by David W. Baker. Winona Lake: Eisenbrauns, 1992.

Zorn, Walter D. "Psalms." In *The College Press NIV Commentary*. Vol. 2. Joplin: College Press Publishing Co, 2004.